where to weekend around OHIO

Fodor's

WITHDRAWN

Fodor's Travel Publications   New York Toronto London Sydney Auckland

Fodor's Where to Weekend Around Ohio

Editor: Mary Beth Bohman
Editorial Production: Linda K. Schmidt
Editorial Contributors: Nicki Chodnoff, Amy S. Eckert, Ann Fazzini, Joe Frey, Todd Fritz, Clark Henderson, Gil Kaufman, Susan Reigler, Julie Tomasz, Rich Warren, Geoff Williams
Maps: David Lindroth, *cartographer;* Bob Blake and Rebecca Baer, *map editors*
Design: Fabrizio La Rocca, *creative director;* Guido Caroti, *art director;* Sophie Ye Chin, *designer*
Cover Art: Jessie Hartland
Production/Manufacturing: Robert B. Shields

Copyright

First Edition

ISBN 1–4000–1304–6
ISSN 1547–6766

Special Sales

Fodor's Travel Publications are available at special discounts for bulk purchases for sales promotions or premiums. Special editions, including personalized covers, excerpts of existing guides, and corporate imprints, can be created in large quantities for special needs. For more information, contact your local bookseller or write to Special Markets, Fodor's Travel Publications, 1745 Broadway, New York, New York 10019. Inquiries from Canada should be directed to your local Canadian bookseller or sent to Random House of Canada, Ltd., Marketing Department, 2775 Matheson Boulevard East, Mississauga, Ontario L4W 4P7. Inquiries from the United Kingdom should be sent to Fodor's Travel Publications, 20 Vauxhall Bridge Road, London SW1V 2SA, England.

PRINTED IN THE UNITED STATES OF AMERICA

10 9 8 7 6 5 4 3 2 1

Where to Weekend Around Ohio

What are you doing this weekend? Just the word *weekend* implies such promise—a break from the workaday rhythm, a bit of downtime, a chance to see friends and family, a good time to be had by all. Two things are certain: there aren't enough weekends, and they're always too short. You can make them feel longer, however, by going away, seeing someplace different, and really leaving the concerns of home life behind. And, surprise, planning a weekend getaway doesn't have to be stressful, regardless of whether you're deciding where to go next month or next weekend. That's where this book comes in.

Where to Weekend Around Ohio helps you plan trips to 25 destinations in and around the state. In the dozens of towns and parks we describe, you'll find hundreds of places to explore. Some may be places you know; others may be new to you. This book makes sure you know your options so that you don't miss something that's right around the next bend—even practically in your backyard—just because you didn't know it was there. Maybe you usually spend your summer weekends on Kelleys Island. Why not consider the eastern coast of Lake Erie for a change? Are the trails in Clifton Gorge starting to look a little too familiar? Why not strike out on a new path in the Hocking Hills? Perhaps your favorite inn is booked solid and you can't wait to get away, or you're tired of eating at the same three restaurants in Columbus. With the practical information in this book, you can easily call to confirm the details that matter and study up on what you'll want to see and do and where you'll want to eat and sleep. Then toss *Where to Weekend Around Ohio* in your bag for the journey.

There's no substitute for travel advice from a good friend who knows your style and taste, but our contributors are the next best thing—the kind of people you would poll for weekend ideas if you could.

Award-winning travel writer **Nicki Chodnoff** has covered and discovered her home state of Ohio for more than 15 years. Her articles have appeared in *Better Homes & Gardens, Home & Away, Travel Agent,* and the *Chicago Tribune.* Nicki is always on the lookout for the unusual and keeps uncovering new ways to experience the tried-and-true as the editor for the "Travel Savings Alerts Newsletter" and as travel reporter for WOSU's *Open Line Travel Show.*

Amy Eckert has never lived more than an hour's drive from the Great Lakes. A Michigan native, she writes about the American Midwest for *Ohio Magazine, Long Weekends Magazine, Booth Newspapers,* and the *Chicago Daily Herald.* Amy is a member of the Midwest Travel Writer's Association.

Although she was born and raised a Buckeye, **Ann Fazzini**'s career as a writer and editor has taken her everywhere from New York's Fashion Week to the mountain villages of Taiwan and, of course, all over Ohio. Ann's work has appeared in *Jane, Ohio Magazine, Country Living,* and the *Columbus Dispatch.*

Born in, raised in, driven out of, and welcomed back to Ohio, **Joseph Frey** has enjoyed every corner of the state, and everything in between. He has experienced the Buckeye State from the back of a metallic green 1973 Dodge station wagon, the relative comfort of a chartered bus, the cramped seating of a rented van, and the driver's seat of a Volkswagen Passat. His travel pieces have appeared in *Cleveland Magazine, Ohio Magazine,* and *Long Weekends Magazine.*

Born and raised in Cleveland and educated in Athens, **Todd L. Fritz** considers the road between these two Ohio cities his third home, spending seemingly equal amounts of time among the three. Since re-relocating to Cleveland, he has contributed travel pieces to *Southeast Ohio Magazine* and *Cleveland Magazine.*

Clark Henderson has traced the Allegheny and Monongahela rivers to their sources from his home in Pittsburgh, exploring all the way the natural and social history of western Pennsylvania. He covers the Pittsburgh area for Fodor's, has written for the *Pittsburgh Post-Gazette,* and teaches American literature at the University of Pittsburgh.

Gil Kaufman is a Cincinnati-based freelance writer and editor whose work regularly appears in *Rolling Stone,* MTV.com, VH1.com, *iD, HOW, Wired,* and the *Cincinnati Enquirer.* Favorite Ohio memories include driving 20 miles one way on muggy summer nights for a soft pretzel and a ride on the Beast at Kings Island, and being ejected from the USAF museum on Wright-Patterson Air Force Base when he was nine for trying to climb into the cockpit of a Mercury rocket.

Ohio Valley native **Susan Reigler** is the author of *Kentucky,* published in the Compass American Guide series from Fodor's. She has been the restaurant critic and regional travel writer (covering Kentucky, southern Indiana, and southern Ohio) for the *Louisville Courier-Journal* since 1992.

Rich Warren's travels have taken him to South American jungles and Himalayan peaks, but he finds plenty of adventure at home in the Buckeye State driving cattle at dude ranches, participating in séances in haunted homes, or riding in wagon trains and tall ships. His work has appeared in *Ohio Magazine,* the *Cincinnati Enquirer,* the *Columbus Dispatch,* and *Country Living,* a statewide publication in Ohio.

Geoff Williams, a freelance journalist based in Loveland, has written for *Parenting* and *National Geographic Kids.* Geoff has traveled roads and byways throughout the Queen City, as a frequent contributor to *Ohio Magazine* and a former *Cincinnati Post* features reporter.

Contents

How to Use This Book

Our goal is to cover the best sights, activities, lodgings, and restaurants in their categories within each weekend-getaway destination. Alphabetical organization makes it easy to navigate through these pages. Still, we've made certain decisions and used certain terms that you need to know about. For starters you can go on the assumption that everything you read about in this book is recommended by our writers and editors. It goes without saying that no property mentioned in the book has paid to be included.

ORGANIZATION

Bullets on the map, which follows How to Use This Book, correspond to the chapter numbers. Each chapter focuses on one getaway destination; the directional line at the start of each chapter tells you how far it is from Cincinnati, Columbus, and Cleveland. The information in each chapter's What to See & Do section is arranged in alphabetical order, broken up by town in many cases. Parks and forests are sometimes listed under the main access point. Where to Stay and Where to Eat follow, with suggestions for places for all budgets, also arranged alphabetically and usually by town as well. The Essentials section provides information about how to get there and other logistical details.

Pit Stops, which follow the map, are places to pull off the highway and grab a snack, as well as local spots perfect for filling your picnic basket or for fueling up for the next adventure. For ideas about the best places for kids, the best museums, the best views, as well as the best places for racing, driving, and hiking, flip to the Fodor's Choice listings.

WHAT TO SEE & DO

This book is loaded with sights and activities for all seasons, budgets, lifestyles, and interests, which means that whether you want to escape to a lakeside retreat or wander along Main Street in a sleepy small town, you'll find plenty of places to explore. Admission prices given apply to adults; substantially reduced fees are almost always available for children, students, and senior citizens.

Where they're available, sightseeing tours are listed in their own section. Sports are limited to area highlights. Biking is an option most everywhere, so we give details only when facilities are extensive or otherwise notable. The same can be said of shopping, but we tell you about shopping standouts such as farmers' markets, antiques centers, and city shopping districts. Use Save the Date as a timing tool, for events you wish to attend (and perhaps crowds you'd prefer to avoid).

WHERE TO STAY

The places we list—including homey B&Bs, mom-and-pop motels, grand inns, chain hotels, and luxury retreats—are the cream of the crop in each price and lodging category.

Baths: You'll find private bathrooms unless noted otherwise.

Credit cards: AE, D, DC, MC, and V following lodging listings indicate that American Express, Discover, Diner's Club, MasterCard, and Visa, respectively, are accepted.

Facilities: We list what's available but we don't specify what costs extra. When pricing accommodations, always ask what's included. The term *hot tub* denotes hot tubs, whirlpools, and Jacuzzis. Assume that lodgings have phones, TVs, and air-conditioning and that smoking is permitted, unless we note otherwise.

Closings: Assume that hostelries are open all year unless otherwise noted.

Meal plans: Hostelries operate on the European Plan (EP, with no meals) unless we specify that they use the Continental Plan (CP, with a Continental breakfast) or Breakfast Plan (BP, with a full breakfast).

Prices: Price categories are based on the price range for a standard double room during high season, excluding service charges and tax. Price categories for all-suites properties are based on prices for standard suites.

WHAT IT COSTS

$$$$	. . . . .over $180
$$$	. . . .$141–$180
$$	. . . .$101–$140
$	. . . .$70–$100
¢	. . . . .under $70

WHERE TO EAT

We make a point of including local food-lovers' hot spots as well as neighborhood choices, with options for all budgets.
Credit cards: AE, D, DC, MC, and V following restaurant listings indicate that American Express, Discover, Diner's Club, MasterCard, and Visa, respectively, are accepted.
Dress: Assume that no jackets or ties are required for men unless otherwise noted.
Meals and hours: Assume that restaurants are open for lunch and dinner unless otherwise noted. We always specify days closed and meals not available. When traveling in the off season, be sure to call ahead.
Reservations: They're always a good idea, but we don't mention them unless they're essential or are not accepted.
Prices: The price categories listed are based on the cost per person for a main course at dinner or, when dinner isn't available, the next most expensive meal.

WHAT IT COSTS

$$$$	. . . . .over $25
$$$	. . . .$19–$25
$$	. . . .$13–$18
$	. . . .$8–$12
¢	. . . . .under $8

ESSENTIALS

Details about transportation and other logistical information end each chapter. Be sure to check Web sites or call for particulars.

AN IMPORTANT TIP

Although all prices, opening times, and other details in this book are based on information supplied to us at press time, changes occur all the time in the travel world, especially in seasonal destinations, and Fodor's cannot accept responsibility for facts that become outdated or for inadvertent errors or omissions. So always confirm information when it matters, especially if you're making a detour to visit a specific place.

Let Us Hear from You

Keeping a travel guide fresh and up to date is a big job, and we welcome any and all comments. We'd love to have your thoughts on places we've listed, and we're interested in hearing about your own special finds. Our guides are thoroughly updated for each new edition, and we're always adding new information, so your feedback is vital. Contact us via e-mail in care of editors@fodors.com (specifying *Where to Weekend Around Ohio* on the subject line) or via snail mail in care of *Where to Weekend Around Ohio*, at Fodor's, 1745 Broadway, New York, NY 10019. We look forward to hearing from you. And in the meantime, have a great weekend.

—*The Editors*

Pit Stops

When you're on the go, either speeding along the interstate or in the midst of the day's adventure, these are the places to rest and refuel or to stock up on provisions.

NORTH WEST

Mayhew's
One block from Jet Express dock, three blocks from Island Rocket dock.
Missed your ferry to Put-In-Bay by a minute? Rather than fuming on the dock for half an hour, why not head over to Mayhew's? A homemade donut and a cup of joe will soothe your frazzled nerves and remind you that you are on vacation after all. > 128 W. Perry, Port Clinton, tel. 419/732–3259. MC, V. No dinner. ¢

NORTH CENTRAL

Dutch Heritage
I–71 Exit 165, south of Mansfield
Midway between Cleveland and Columbus, this is a good stop for drivers on I–71. Dutch Heritage is an easy jaunt from the interstate. Even road construction looks better after a lunch of comfort foods like fried chicken and mashed potatoes. > 720 Rte. 97 W, off I–71 Bellville, tel. 419/886–7070. DC, MC, V. Closed Sun. $

NORTH EAST

Swenson's
You're bound to run into a Swenson's during your trip to Cuyahoga Valley National Park—there are six of the drive-in spots around the valley. Cruise on in for a cheeseburger that has found favor with the locals since 1934. > 7635 Broadview Rd., Seven Hills, tel. 216/986–1934. No credit cards. ¢

CENTRAL

City Barbecue
I–270 Exit 41, south of the airport
City Barbecue is a handy name to remember in the Columbus area. The Reynoldsburg location is ideal for those flying into town, as well as for drivers circling Columbus en route to other Ohio destinations. The "Pig Up 'n Go Packs" of pulled pork, chicken, and ribs with all the fixings make airport food but a distant bad memory. > 5979 E. Main St., Reynoldsburg, tel. 614/755–8890, www.citybbq.com. AE, D, MC, V. ¢–$

SOUTH

Miguel's Pizza and Rock Climbing Shop
KY 11, 1½ mi south of Slade
Before you head out to conquer the cliffs in Red River Gorge, duck into this local climbers' hangout for a slice, a map, and some advice. > 1890 Natural Bridge Rd., Slade, tel. 606/663–1975.

SOUTHWEST

Toot's
5 mi northwest of Paramount's Kings Island
Got a carful of kids in Mason on the eve of a Kings Island visit? Shuttle them over to Toot's for burgers, dill-pickle chips, and games. Tuck into the breaded catfish or ribs yourself—you're going to need a lot of energy tomorrow. > 12191 Montgomery Rd., Mason, tel. 513/697–9100. AE, D, DC, MC, V. $

WEST

Palmer Farms
Off U.S. 33 at Rte. 540
Whatever the activity you've planned for your day in Logan County—be it shopping, skiing, or spelunking—your first stop should be Palmer Farms for supplies. The Cornish hens will add a touch of elegance to your picnic basket. > 936 E. Sandusky Ave., Bellefontaine, tel. 937/599–1400. No credit cards. ¢

Fodor's Choice

The towns, sights, activities, restaurants, hotels, and other travel experiences listed on this page are Fodor's editors' and writers' top picks for each category.

DRIVES

Ashtabula Covered Bridges, Eastern Coast of Lake Erie > Chapter 7
Lake Erie Circle Tour, Cedar Point & the Sandusky Area > Chapter 3
Paris Pike (U.S. 27) Horse Farms, Bluegrass Country > Chapter 18
Wines & Vines Trail, Six Flags & the Western Reserve > Chapter 6

GARDENS & PARKS

Eden Park, Cincinnati > Chapter 20
Holden Arboretum, Eastern Coast of Lake Erie > Chapter 7
Malabar Farm State Park, Mansfield > Chapter 11

GOLF

Maumee Bay Golf Course, Maumee Bay & Crane Creek > Chapter 1
Quail Hollow Country Club, Six Flags & the Western Reserve > Chapter 6
Sleepy Hollow Golf Course, Cuyahoga Valley National Park > Chapter 5

HIKING

Grandma Gatewood Trail, Hocking Hills > Chapter 15
John L. Rich Trail in Clifton Gorge, Dayton & Yellow Springs > Chapter 23
Wildcat Hollow Trail, Athens & the Wayne National Forest > Chapter 14

HISTORIC PLACES

Ohio State Reformatory, Mansfield > Chapter 11
Portsmouth Floodwall Murals, Ohio River Scenic Byway > Chapter 17
Serpent Mound prehistoric effigy mound, Ross County Area > Chapter 16
Waynesville Main Street, Waynesville & Wilmington > Chapter 22

MUSEUMS

Behalt at the Mennonite Information Center, Amish Country > Chapter 10
Contemporary Arts Center, Cincinnati > Chapter 20
Rock and Roll Hall of Fame, Cleveland > Chapter 4

THE NATURAL WORLD

Cave Pearl Formations in Zane Shawnee Caverns, Logan County > Chapter 24
Migratory Birds in the Ottawa National Wildlife Refuge, Maumee Bay & Crane Creek > Chapter 1
Old-Growth Forest in the Heart's Content National Scenic Area, Allegheny National Forest > Chapter 9

RACING

Keeneland Race Track, Bluegrass Country > Chapter 18
Mid-Ohio Sports Car Course, Mansfield > Chapter 11
The Racer, Roller coaster in Paramount's Kings Island > Chapter 21

STERNWHEELERS, STEAM ENGINES, & TOWPATHS

BB Riverboats, Cincinnati > Chapter 20
Dennison Railroad Tours, Amish Country > Chapter 10
Miami and Erie Canal, Grand Lake St. Mary's > Chapter 25

VIEWS

Ferris Wheel, Cedar Point > Chapter 3
Marblehead Lighthouse, Lake Erie Islands > Chapter 2
Natural Bridge, Natural Bridge & Red River Gorge > Chapter 19

WINTER SPORTS

Downhill Skiing at Boston Mills Brandywine Ski Resort, Cuyahoga Valley National Park > Chapter 5

Downhill Skiing at Mad River Mountain Ski Resort, Logan County > Chapter 24

Tobogganing at the Chalet at Mill Stream Run, Cleveland > Chapter 4

WITH KIDS

Boonshoft Museum of Discovery, Dayton & Yellow Springs > Chapter 23

COSI Columbus, Columbus > Chapter 13

Little Sky Riding Trails, Cambridge & Zanesville > Chapter 12

TECUMSEH! outdoor drama in Ross County > Chapter 16

Maumee Bay & Crane Creek

Maumee Bay is 125 mi west of Cleveland, 150 mi north of Columbus, and 215 mi northeast of Cincinnati.

By Amy S. Eckert

THE PRISTINE NATURAL OASIS bounded by Maumee Bay and Crane Creek is a surprise, near as it is to Toledo, one of Ohio's largest cities. Thousands head to this northwest region of Ohio every year, attracted not by nightlife, sporting events, shopping, or culture. Rather, they are looking to escape.

Ten thousand years ago this area of Ohio was entirely under water. Lake Erie was much larger than it is today, ranging from western New York to Fort Wayne, Indiana. Over centuries the lake waters receded to their present bank and a great flat plain was left behind; 120 mi long and 35 mi wide, the plain became known as the Great Black Swamp due to the color of the soil and the dark shade trees. Native Americans of the Ottawa tribe settled near the well-drained lands along the Maumee River and its tributaries.

For many years the swamp posed an insurmountable barrier to western settlement. Most settlers traveled by boat on Lake Erie to reach southern Michigan and beyond. Major cities of the area circled the perimeter of the swamp; none lay within it except Bowling Green. In 1859 a law was passed providing for a system of public ditches to drain the land. By 1870 the swamp was about half its original size and eventually, after a period of intense lumbering and draining, the swamp nearly vanished. The rich, dark soil left behind made the area an important agricultural region, and off to the west Toledo became a transportation hub, exporting goods into the Great Lakes.

Remains of the Great Black Swamp can be seen in the wetlands in and around Maumee Bay and Crane Creek. The southern Lake Erie shoreline location, the rich food supply, and the concentration of several protected habitats combine to make northwestern Ohio one of the nation's top birding spots. After having flown north from Latin America, the Caribbean, and the southern United States, thousands of migratory birds make northern Ohio their temporary home, resting, eating, and gaining strength before making the final difficult journey over Lake Erie and on to points north.

Bird-watching is an important tourist draw in and around Maumee Bay, but it isn't the only outdoor activity to enjoy. Lake Erie and its shores provide the stage for swimming, boating, sailing, parasailing, fishing, sunbathing, and simple walks along the beach. Hiking and bicycling are also favorite pastimes in the wild areas around Maumee Bay.

Maumee Bay State Park is about 10 mi east of Toledo, and about 8 mi east of Oregon. If you're focusing on a weekend of outdoor pursuits, you will probably not want to spend much time in either Toledo or Oregon, but both are good options for inexpensive lodging and dining, as well as chain restaurants. Crane Creek is about 10 mi east of Maumee Bay, north of the small town of Oak Harbor.

WHAT TO SEE & DO

Maumee Bay State Park Nearly 1,500 acres of prime Lake Erie shoreline comprise this gem of a park 8 mi east of Toledo. The park's proximity to the lake and its varied geography would attract plenty of wildlife on their own, but Maumee Bay State Park is the westernmost link in a chain of protected natural areas, including the Cedar Point Wildlife Refuge, the Magee Marsh Wildlife Area, Crane Creek State Park, and the Ottawa National Wildlife Refuge. Taken together, the wetlands, meadows, and forests surrounding Maumee Bay form an ideal sanctuary for migratory birds and mammals.

A network of hiking trails crisscrosses the lush **Maumee Bay Campground,** which also has two fishing ponds for use by park visitors. **Erie Beach** skirts the park's northern boundary. The beach attracts swimmers and sunbathers when the summer sun has warmed the waters of Lake Erie. Rest rooms, showers, a snack bar, and beachside personal-watercraft rentals are available. **Inland Lake** warms up more quickly, inviting swimmers who find Lake Erie's water a bit too frigid or choppy in late spring and early summer. Facilities include rest rooms, showers, and a snack bar. Recreational activities like boating, canoeing, and fishing are popular, as are the free outdoor concerts staged in the amphitheater on the lake's northern shore during the summer months. Farther inland nearly 10 mi of paved hiking and biking trails traverse acres of meadows and woodlands. Big Hill is especially appealing to children who like to walk up its steep sides and enjoy views of the surrounding countryside from the park bench at its summit.

The **Wetlands Area** is in the park's easternmost region. A pleasant 2-mi boardwalk winds through swamp and marsh wetlands. Wildflowers and 12-foot-tall stands of a feathery reed called Phragmites fool visitors into believing they're much farther from civilization than they really are. A wheelchair-accessible loop, interpretive signs, and an observation blind and tower facilitate wildlife viewing. It's common to see whitetail deer at dawn and dusk, as well as songbirds, Canada geese, bald eagles, and ducks. **Trautman Nature Center** (tel. 419/836–9117, Sun.–Thurs. 10–5, Fri.–Sat. 10–7) adjacent to the Wetlands Area, is staffed year-round by a naturalist who can answer questions about local ecology, geography, and wildlife. The nature center is equipped with interactive displays, a programming auditorium, research laboratory, and wildlife viewing windows.

Maumee Bay Golf Course (tel. 419/836–9009, daily dawn–dusk, weather permitting) is also within the State Park. Unpredictable Lake Erie winds and the extra-long rough lend Scottish-links style to this par-72, 18-hole course. The twisting layout of the signature 14th hole is the course's most challenging, with two large water hazards off the tee, the fairway, and the green. **Quilter Lodge** (tel. 800/282–7275 lodge and cabin reservations), the hotel portion of the Maumee Bay Resort, makes it possible to escape to nature without roughing it. Its comfortable accommodations are a key draw, but there's more to the building, including indoor and outdoor pools, a fountain, free sports activities, restaurants, gift shops, and unsurpassed views of Lake Erie.
> Maumee Bay State Park, 3 mi north off Rte. 2, Oregon, tel. 419/836–7758 park administration, 419/836–1466, www.ohiostateparks.org. Free. Daily dawn–dusk.

Crane Creek State Park Most people think Crane Creek State Park is much larger than it is. Bordered on the west by the Ottawa National Wildlife Refuge and on the south and east by Magee Marsh Wildlife Area, the 80-acre track of Lake Erie shoreline is limited to 3,500 feet of swimming beach, picnicking facilities, and several large parking areas. In spring, focus shifts to bird-watching along the ½-mi boardwalk just

south of the parking lots. In summer, the beautiful sandy beach of Crane Creek provides the perfect way to cool off in Lake Erie. > 13531 W. Rte. 2, Oak Harbor, tel.
419/898–2495 or 419/836–7758, www.ohiostateparks.org. Free. Daily dawn–dusk.

NEAR THE PARKS

Magee Marsh Wildlife Area This 2,000-acre wildlife refuge is one of the nation's top
birding spots. Three hiking trails are within the park: one loops through prime bird
habitat near the beach; another stretches along the Lake Erie shoreline; and the third
circles around the **Sportsmen's Migratory Bird Center.** The Center displays exhibits
on animal life, Native American history, the fur trade, and duck hunting. You can pick
up maps and wildlife guides as well. Access to the trails is limited to Saturday afternoons and Sundays mid-October–November to open the area to duck hunting.
> 13229 W. Rte. 2, Oak Harbor, tel. 419/898–0960 Sportsmen's Center. Free. Wildlife
area daily dawn–dusk. Sportsmen's Center Mar.–Nov., weekdays 8–5, weekends 11–5;
Dec.–Feb., weekdays 8–5.

Ottawa National Wildlife Refuge More than 9 mi of pathways and an observation
deck give you a bird's-eye view of the spring and autumn flocks of migratory birds, especially waterfowl. A system of dikes maintains adequate water levels to attract large
quantities of ducks and geese. A staffed gift shop and information center provides
brochures and other information about the birds in the park. > 1400 W. Rte. 2, 1 mi
east of Rte. 590, Oak Harbor, tel. 419/898–0014 Information Center. Free. Refuge
daily dawn–dusk. Information Center weekdays 8–4.

Sports

BIRD-WATCHING

Ohio's northwestern lake coast comprises part of the Atlantic Flyway, a migration
route that extends from the Gulf of Mexico into Canada. In spring, thousands of
songbirds and waterfowl make their way north to their summer nesting grounds,
pausing to rest and feed near Maumee Bay and Crane Creek before making the final
leg over Lake Erie. The natural areas in this region of the state are considered one of
the nation's prime bird-watching spots for the sheer number of species that can be
observed. If you arrive between late April and mid-May, you'll see hundreds of avid
birders, most outfitted with binoculars, viewing scopes, cameras, and even high-
tech listening and recording devices. Pick up a copy of *Wing Watch,* an Ohio shoreline birding guide, from one of the state parks or the Magee Marsh Sportsmen's
Center. The free guide, published by the Ohio Division of Wildlife, includes a list of
more than 250 bird species seen in the area, viewing tips, and lists of other area
birding spots.

Magee Marsh Wildlife Area Start your visit at the Sportsmen's Migratory Bird Center near the entrance, where there are interpretive exhibits and local birding experts
on hand to offer viewing advice. The marsh is a favorite place to view more than
three-dozen varieties of warblers. > 13229 W. Rte. 2, Oak Harbor, tel. 419/898–0960.

Maumee Bay State Park The park's best birding is along its eastern boardwalk, where
wetlands provide perfect feeding and nesting grounds. Fragrant buttonbush blossoms
attract songbirds in summer, including the red-winged blackbird, yellow warbler,
killdeer, and swamp sparrow. In addition to the songbirds, waterfowl and bald eagles
inhabit the area. An observation tower allows for good viewing and a nature center
near the boardwalk provides interpretive exhibits and viewing guides. > 1400 State
Park Rd., off N. Curtice Rd., Oregon, tel. 419/836–7758, www.ohiostateparks.org.

Ottawa National Wildlife Refuge The footpaths through this national refuge might leave a bit to be desired in their layout for the casual hiker, but they are ideal for the avid bird-watcher. Rather than wending their way through the scenery, trails run for nearly 6 mi along the tops of dikes surrounding roughly rectangular tracks of land. These dikes promote wildlife diversity by controlling and maintaining optimum water levels, thereby protecting the habitats of nesting shorebirds, waterfowl, and bald eagles, many of which you'll see as you pass through the refuge. A viewing platform is near the center of the refuge. > 14000 W. Rte. 2, 1 mi east of Rte. 590, Oak Harbor, tel. 419/898–0014.

BOATING

It's no surprise that boating is a popular sport around Maumee Bay, part of one of the world's largest freshwater lakes. Sailing and powerboating, as well as waterskiing and jet skiing, are very popular in summer. Maumee Bay State Park has an attractive marina, close to all of the best land-based recreation in the area. You can overnight on your own boat or in the park—either way you'll have access to all of the park's amenities. But the park has little in the way of boating supplies, and no fuel. For those items, or for Lake Erie fishing charters, check out Meinke's Marina.
EQUIPMENT **Maumee Bay State Park Marina** > 1400 State Park Rd., Oregon, tel. 419/836–1466, www.maumeebayresort.com. **Meinke's Marina East** > 12805 Bono Rd., Curtis, tel. 419/836–8610. **Meinke's Marina West** > 10955 Corduroy Rd., Curtis, tel. 419/836–7107.

HIKING

The diverse ecology of northwestern Ohio's Lake Erie shoreline attracts avid hikers from throughout the Midwest. Within the span of a few miles you'll encounter marshlands, swamplands, woodlands, meadows, lakes, and streams. And the large quantity of trails crisscrossing the region means you'll never have difficulty finding access to the area's best natural areas.

Magee Marsh Wildlife Area The 2,000 acres of protected marsh are adjacent to Crane Creek State Park. Just under 3 mi of hiking trails loop through portions of the preserve, while the remaining land is reserved for wildlife habitat. The Sportsmen's Migratory Bird Center near the marsh's entrance has trail maps. > 13229 W. Rte. 2, Oak Harbor, tel. 419/898–0960.

Maumee Bay State Park A 2-mi boardwalk on the park's eastern end passes through colonies of 12-foot plume cane, past deep purple wild irises and, in summer, fragrant buttonbush. It's easy to spy songbirds and butterflies and, if you visit near dawn or dusk, you're likely to spot whitetail deer grazing in the more heavily forested areas. In the park's western and central sections 8 mi of paved hiking and biking trails follow the Lake Erie shoreline and make their way inland through wildflower meadows, woods, and past several small lakes. > 1400 State Park Rd., off N. Curtice Rd., Oregon, tel. 419/836–7758, www.ohiostateparks.org.

Save the Date

MAY

International Migratory Bird Day Spectacular bird-watching, bird banding (marking birds with metal identification tags for research purposes), wagon rides, an optics tent, and food tents help to celebrate the return of migratory birds to the Magee Marsh Wildlife Refuge. > 13229 W. Rte. 2, Oak Harbor, tel. 419/898–0960.

Oregon Spring Fest The annual Spring Fest includes festival foods, a chicken barbecue, amusement rides, classic cars, arts and crafts, and a flower sale. > Between St. Charles Hospital, Coy Rd. and Dustin Rd., Oregon, tel. 419/693–0328.

JULY
Bugfest! The amazing world of insects is the theme at this annual celebration at the Magee Marsh Wildlife Refuge. Hands-on experiences are designed to instruct all ages. > 13229 W. Rte. 2, Oak Harbor, tel. 419/898–0960.

AUGUST
Flea Market/Antique/Craft Show For 30 years locals have encouraged browsing and buying at this event held at the Ottawa County Fairgrounds. Food stands and more than 200 booths are open to the public. > Rte. 163 W, Oak Harbor, tel. 419/734–4386 or 800/441–1271.

OCTOBER
National Wildlife Refuge Week Ohio's only national wildlife refuge celebrates the refuge system with displays, hands-on wildlife events, and lots of family activities. > Ottawa National Wildlife Refuge, 1400 W. Rte. 2, Oak Harbor, tel. 419/898–0014.

WHERE TO STAY

Maumee Bay Resort If you stay at the Maumee Bay Resort, you may be tempted not to stir until your weekend is over. There's little reason to go anywhere else. The resort is surrounded by Lake Erie to the north and nearly 1,500 acres of beautiful Maumee Bay State Park in all other directions. All guest rooms in Quilter Lodge have balconies or patios, most overlooking the lake, others overlooking the fountain or golf course. The lobby invites you to get comfortable in thickly stuffed chairs in front of either a big stone fireplace or floor-to-ceiling plate-glass windows overlooking Lake Erie and the immaculate resort grounds. Although the resort is not all-inclusive, so many recreational activities are free that the room rates are nothing short of a bargain. You can also choose to rent two- or four-bedroom cottages, some sleeping as many as 11 people, with extra space for families and large gatherings. > 1750 Park Rd., #2, Oregon 43618, tel. 419/836–1466 or 800/282–7275, fax 419/836–2438, www.maumeebayresort. com. 120 rooms, 24 cottages. Restaurant, snack bar, room service, in-room data ports, in-room safes, some in-room hot tubs, some kitchens, some kitchenettes, some microwaves, refrigerators, cable TV with movies, in-room VCRs, 18-hole golf course, tennis court, pro shop, pool, indoor pool, lake, pond, gym, hot tub, beach, dock, boating, jet skiing, marina, fishing, bicycles, basketball, hiking, racquetball, volleyball, cross-country skiing, ice-skating, lounge, recreation room, video game room, shops, children's programs (ages 4–15), playground, laundry facilities, concierge, business services, convention center, meeting rooms, no-smoking rooms. AE, D, DC, MC, V. **$$**

NEAR THE PARKS
Comfort Inn–Oregon Simple, affordable and in the heart of Oregon, this Comfort Inn is within a few blocks of most of Navarre Avenue's dining and shopping establishments. Maumee Bay State Park is about a 10-minute drive away. > 2930 Navarre Ave. (Rte. 2), Oregon 43616, tel. 419/691–8911 or 877/424–6423, fax 419/691–2107, www.comfortinn.com. 80 rooms. Some in-room hot tubs, kitchenettes, microwaves, refrigerators, cable TV with movies, in-room VCRs, pool, business services, meeting rooms, some pets allowed, no-smoking rooms. AE, D, DC, MC, V. CP. **$**
Sleep Inn & Suites This pleasant, moderately priced hotel includes several unique amenities: two private tanning booths, free movie theater–style popcorn nightly, and an unusual beer- and wine-dispensing vending machine. The hotel is adjacent to a shopping center and a 10-minute drive from Maumee Bay State Park. > 1761 Meijer Circle,

off I–280, Oregon 43616, tel. 419/697–7800 or 877/424–6423, fax 419/697–7810, www.sleepinn.com. 90 rooms. In-room data ports, some in-room hot tubs, some in-room microwaves, some in-room refrigerators, cable TV with movies, indoor pool, gym, hot tub, sauna, steam room, laundry facilities, concierge floor, business services, some pets allowed (fee), no-smoking rooms. AE, D, DC, MC, V. CP. $

CAMPING

Maumee Bay State Park There are few Lake Erie campgrounds that can compete with the scenic beauty and recreational options at Maumee Bay. Right on the shoreline, campers can swim or fish in the big lake or in one of the smaller ponds and inland lakes on state park property. There are also golfing, hiking, biking, a marina, boat rentals, free outdoor amphitheater concerts, and a nature center. Thick grass, spacious sites, and hardwood trees make the sites suitable for all camping options, from tenting to RVing. > 1400 State Park Rd., off N. Curtice Rd., Oregon 43618, tel. 419/836–7758, fax 419/836–8711, www.ohiostateparks.org. 256 partial hook-ups; 3 cabins; 1 Rent-A-Yurt. Flush toilets, partial hook-ups (electric and water), dump station, drinking water, laundry facilities, showers, fire pits, picnic tables, restaurant, electricity, public telephone, general store, ranger station, playground, swimming (lake). Reservations not accepted. AE, D, DC, MC, V. ¢

WHERE TO EAT

Icebreaker Lounge A nautical theme permeates this lounge, with weathered boats and old life preservers adorning the walls. The deep blue ceiling is speckled with tiny lights, giving the appearance of a night sky if you arrive after dark. Typical bar food is the fare here, including fresh, thick deli sandwiches, burgers, nachos, and salads. Although the room has a full bar, the restaurant is very family-oriented during lunch hours and afternoons. > 1750 Park Rd. #2, inside Maumee Bay Resort, Oregon, tel. 419/836–1466. AE, D, DC, MC, V. $

Water's Edge Restaurant There's scarcely a reason to ask for a window table at this restaurant in Maumee Bay Resort. Nearly every seat in the house has a gorgeous view of Lake Erie through the large plate-glass windows. Crystal glassware and navy linens mirror the sparkling blue water outside. Entrées include Great Lakes walleye, steaks, and mushroom and spinach lasagne. > 1750 Park Rd. #2, inside Maumee Bay Resort, Oregon, tel. 419/836–1466. AE, D, DC, MC, V. $–$$$

NEAR THE PARKS

Cousino's Steakhouse Cousino's warm, dimly lit restaurant is divided into a number of smaller rooms, each cozy, some furnished with a fireplace, giving the sense that you're in someone's home for dinner—albeit a rather large home. Steaks have been the specialty here since the restaurant opened in 1945, but you'll also find smothered chicken, sandwiches, or orange roughy. > 1842 Woodville Rd., Oregon, tel. 419/693–0862. AE, D, DC, MC, V. $–$$$

DG's DG's makes a great stop for an afternoon treat after hiking through the area's wildlife preserves and state parks. Ice cream, slushes, sundaes, and an astonishing 50 flavors of shakes and malts are the primary draw. But you can also purchase sandwiches, hot dogs, chili dogs, and burgers. > 10609 Jerusalem Rd. (Rte. 2), at Teachout Rd., Curtice, tel. 419/836–7254. No credit cards. Closed Oct.–Apr. ¢

Golden Jade Euro Asian Bistro An extensive array of Cantonese and Szechwan Chinese food is the primary attraction at this restaurant, but you'll also find a selection of American favorites—steaks, ribs, and chicken—as well as pizza. All meals are available to take out as well as for dining in. > 3171 Navarre Ave., Oregon, tel. 419/693–0515. AE, D, MC, V. $

Ralphie's Family Sports Eatery This sports-theme restaurant about 10 minutes from Maumee Bay Resort has a dozen TVs suspended from strategic points on the ceiling, each tuned to a different sporting event. The menu includes fried chicken, ribs, pasta, and salad. > 3005 Navarre Ave., Oregon, tel. 419/693–2500. MC, V. No breakfast. $–$$

Tony Packo's Cafe Autographed hot dog buns from celebrities ranging from Tip O'Neill to Tracy Ullman adorn the walls at Tony Packo's, a Toledo institution made famous by Jamie Farr when his character Klinger mentioned the restaurant on TV's M*A*S*H. Chili is the most-repeated word on the menu. You can order it by the bowl or on hot dogs, chips, or fries. Hungarian specialties include sausages, stuffed cabbage, chicken paprikas, and strudel for dessert. Enjoy live jazz Friday and Saturday evenings. > 1902 Front St., Toledo, tel. 419/691–6054. AE, D, MC, V. $

ESSENTIALS

Getting Here

If you plan to spend your entire weekend at Maumee Bay State Park, you can approach the park via boat on Lake Erie and dock at the Maumee Bay Resort Marina. However, the only way to explore the mainland between Maumee Bay and Crane Creek is via automobile. Air, train, bus, and mass transportation are nonexistent.

BY CAR

From the Ohio Turnpike (I–80/90) follow I–280 north and exit onto Route 2. From I–75, follow I–280 south to Route 2.

All of the parks and refuges lie just off Route 2, a rural, fast-moving two-lane road. Parking throughout the area is readily available and free.

Visitor Information

CONTACTS **Audubon Society of Ohio** > 692 N. High St., Suite 208, Columbus 43215, tel. 614/224–3303, www.audubon.org/states/oh/. **Ohio State Parks** > 1952 Belcher Dr., C-3, Columbus 43224, tel. 614/265–6300, www.ohiostateparks.org. **Toledo Chamber of Commerce** > 401 Jefferson Ave., Toledo 43604, tel. 800/243–4667, www.dotoledo.org.

The Lake Erie Islands

Port Clinton is approximately 80 mi west of Cleveland, 130 mi north of Columbus, and 222 mi northeast of Cincinnati.

2

By Amy S. Eckert

THE LAKE ERIE ISLANDS COME ALIVE with the sun. Surrounded as they are by one of the world's largest bodies of water, their livelihoods—and liveliness—are dependent on good weather.

Ocean-size waves are common during violent thunderstorms, and gale-force winds can blow through in the winter. It's no great surprise, then, that many businesses close shop during the winter months—both those on the islands and those in Marblehead and Port Clinton, which lie on the long, narrow Marblehead Peninsula. Ask a waitress, a hotel clerk, or a museum curator what her spring or fall hours are and you'll get a reflective pause. "Well, it depends on the weather . . . " is the most common response. If spring arrives early, and summer's warmth hangs on until October, you can expect longer business hours and increased ferry crossings. If winter lingers, hours are reduced.

When the late spring sunshine finally warms Lake Erie, ferry boats begin plying the waters again, carrying tourists and island residents to Put-in-Bay and Kelleys Island. Serious fishing, boating, and sailing begin. Weary migratory birds arrive bringing scores of bird enthusiasts with them. With all of that warm-weather activity, hotels, restaurants, and attractions throughout the area spring to life, and there's no better place to enjoy some of the Great Lakes' best outdoor recreation.

There are actually four primary islands north of Marblehead Peninsula: North, Middle, and South Bass Islands and Kelleys Island. North and Middle Bass Islands are virtually undeveloped (although that may change given the Ohio Department of Natural Resources' plans to one day create state parks on the islands). South Bass Island and Kelleys Island are best suited for visitors. The former, often known by the name of its only town, Put-in-Bay, was first inhabited by Iroquois Indians. The island became a vacation destination for the wealthy in the early 1800s when the world's largest summer resort hotel, the Victory Hotel, was constructed where the state park is today. The island has long had a reputation for heavy partying. You'll still find lots of bars downtown, and plenty of day-tripping partygoers. But Put-in-Bay has cleaned up the island's image over the last decade, attracting all ages to their unique historical sites, shops, and family-friendly festivals.

Kelleys Island is noticeably quieter than South Bass Island. Only 4 mi north of Marblehead, the island was originally inhabited by Erie, Ottawa, and Huron tribes at least as early as the 17th century. Two hundred years later two brothers named Kelley owned most of the island's land, setting up industries like wine-making, quarrying, fishing, and fruit production.

Today Kelleys Island is inhabited by summer cottage owners and by a few die-hard year-rounders (many of whom are descendents of the original Kelley brothers). Vacationers are drawn to the island's natural attractions, enjoying hiking, birding, camping, and water sports like swimming, boating, and fishing. Walleye, perch, and bass are caught in quantity, and downtown you can browse in the gift and clothing shops. Accommodations consist exclusively of inns and bed-and-breakfast establishments.

The mainland town of Port Clinton is just south of South Bass Island. Although the town has some nice beaches and attractions, Port Clinton serves primarily as a transportation hub for visitors anxious to catch the ferry. Such has been the history of the town since its early days. Founded in 1827, Port Clinton built its status as a tourism and shipping hub, its proximity to the Great Lakes and the heartland allowing access to Midwest, East Coast, and Canadian markets.

On the easternmost shore of the Marblehead Peninsula, the town of Marblehead was originally settled because of the huge limestone quarry nearby. Today the community serves as a tourist base. Ferries depart from Marblehead to Kelleys Island. Visitors also come to see the lighthouse, take in views of Lake Erie, boat, fish, and relax.

WHAT TO SEE & DO

KELLEYS ISLAND
Glacial Grooves State Memorial Since the late 1800s, tourists have flocked to Kelleys Island to see the world's largest glacial grooves in existence. These huge gouges—the largest is 400 feet deep and 35 feet wide—were carved out of the native limestone about 25,000 years ago by the advancement of the Wisconsin glacier. Scientists visit the site to increase their understanding of prehistoric glacial activity and to study the 350-million-year-old fossil remains in the rock. > Division St. and Titus Rd., adjacent to the State Park, Kelleys Island, tel. 419/797–4025, www.ohiohistory.org/places/glacial/. Free. Daily dawn–dusk.

Inscription Rock Pictographs of men, birds, and animals can be seen etched into the flat top of Inscription Rock, which sits on the Lake Erie shore near the Kelleys Island ferry dock. Discovered partly buried in the shoreline in 1833, the 32-foot by 21-foot rock is now entirely exposed and protected from further erosion by a roof and viewing platform. Archaeologists believe the inscriptions were made by the Erie tribe and date from sometime between AD 1200 and 1600. > E. Lakeshore Dr. at Addison Rd., Kelleys Island, tel. 419/797–4530, www.ohiohistory.org/places/inscript/. Free. Daily dawn–dusk.

Kelleys Island State Park State park land is scattered throughout the natural areas of Kelleys Island, but the largest track is on the island's northern shore. Park facilities include hiking trails, picnic areas, a sandy beach along the North Bay, a fishing pier, public boat launches, and a scenic beachside campground. The park is open year-round, but the water is shut off in late October and the boat docks are pulled in the winter. > Division St. and Titus Rd., Kelleys Island, tel. 419/746–2546 or 419/797–4530, www.ohiostateparks.org. Free. Daily dawn–dusk.

***Prince* Shipwreck** The *Prince*, a 1911 shipwreck submerged 18 feet underwater, is visible from the water's surface but not from shore. The ship lies 100 feet off the eastern coast of Kelleys Island and can be reached by boat or by swimming. Snorkeling and scuba gear are available at North Coast Scuba in Marblehead. > Eastern shore, tel. 419/798–5557. Free. Daily.

SOUTH BASS ISLAND
Aquatic Visitors Center Lake Erie produces more food fish than the rest of the Great Lakes combined, so it's only fitting that the Ohio Department of Natural Resources

operates an aquatic education center on this Lake Erie island. Inside this former fish hatchery, hands-on displays, geared primarily to teaching children, offer instruction on Ohio's fishing industry. Outside, you can borrow rods and reels and try your hand at angling off the fishing pier. Anglers 16 years and over must have a valid Ohio license to fish off the pier. > 1 Peach Point Rd., Put-in-Bay, tel. 419/285–3701. Free. Memorial Day–Labor Day, Tues.–Sat. 10–5.

Beer Barrel Saloon Since 1989, the saloon's counter has held the record for "the world's longest permanent bar" in the *Guinness Book of World Records*. It measures in at 405 feet, 10 inches, with 160 bar stools, 20 bartenders, and 56 beer taps. To get another sense of this bar's size, consider this: If it were stood on end, the Beer Barrel's bar would be taller than the Perry Monument downtown. But "The Barrel," as it's known locally, is hot for more than its architectural appeal. It's one of the most popular spots in town for nightlife and live musical entertainment. > 1618 Delaware Ave., Put-in-Bay, tel. 419/285–2337, www.beerbarrelpib.com. May–Oct., daily 1 PM–12:30 AM.

Heineman's Winery & Crystal Cave The "free" wine appears to be the primary appeal to many at Heineman's. Your entrance fee will include a sample cup of one of 18 wine or grape juice varieties (your choice), as well as a tour of the wine-making facility and Crystal Cave below the building. Crystal Cave is not actually a cave but rather the world's largest geode. You can also purchase wine by the bottle or the glass to drink at the bar. > 978 Catawba Ave., Put-in-Bay, tel. 419/285–2811, www.ohiowine.com/mzwinery.htm. $6. Memorial Day–Labor Day, daily 9–5; Apr., May, Sept., and Oct., weekends 9–5.

Kimberly's Carousel Climb aboard a hand-carved horse, rooster, pig, or—if you're quick—the local favorite, Pete the Perch. This 1917 merry-go-round is one of few remaining all-wooden carousels in the country. Hand-painted panels adorn the carousel's crown, each depicting a favorite island scene. > Delaware Ave. and Hartford St., Put-in-Bay. $1.50 per ride. Memorial Day–1 wk after Labor Day, daily dawn–dusk.

Lake Erie Island Historical Museum South Bass Island memorabilia is housed in this small museum, including Great Lakes shipping items, early wine-making equipment, and an old Fresnel lighthouse lens from the South Bass Island Lighthouse. Many of the exhibits relate to the 19th-century Victory Hotel, which once operated where the state park is today. > 441 Catawba Ave., Put-in-Bay, tel. 419/285–2804, www.leihs.org. Free. Mid-June–Labor Day, daily 10–6; Apr.–mid-June, Sept., and Oct. 11–5.

Perry's Cave Family Entertainment Center General Perry hid his arsenal of ammunition in this cave during the Battle of Lake Erie in the War of 1812. You can see precisely where that site was on 25-minute tours of the cave, which also includes highlights such as an underground lake and colorful geological formations. You can look for treasure at the cave's Gemstone Mining Sluice. Sift bags of rough mix under water to reveal hidden gems like topaz, amethyst, moon stone, and garnet. > 979 Catawba Ave., Put-in-Bay, tel. 419/285–2405, www.perryscave.com. Cave $6, mining $4–$9. June–Aug., daily 9–5; Apr., May, Sept., and Oct., weekends 11–sunset.

Perry's Victory and International Peace Memorial The 352-foot memorial dominating South Bass Island commemorates the War of 1812's Battle of Lake Erie, when Commodore Oliver Hazard Perry and his American fleet defeated the British, who controlled the lake. Following the battle Perry uttered his famous message: "We have met the enemy and they are ours." The memorial also commemorates the ensuing peace that has lasted between the United States and Canada. An adjacent visitor cen-

ter includes exhibits about the Battle of Lake Erie, a movie theater, and a gift shop.
> 93 Delaware Ave., Put-in-Bay, tel. 419/285–2184, www.put-in-bay.com/perry.htm.
Free, $3 observation deck. Mid-June–Labor Day, daily 10–8; late Apr.–mid-June, Labor
Day–mid-Oct., daily 10–5.

The Round House "130 years of Hot Music and Cold Beer!" So reads the sign in
front of the Round House, which first opened for business in 1873 as the Columbia
Restaurant, serving beer, wine, and food accompanied by piano music. Rock-and-roll
music and beer draw modern customers, making this one of Put-in-Bay's favorite
spots for nightlife. The building's round shape accounts for its current name.
> Delaware Ave., Put-in-Bay, tel. 419/285–2323, www.theroundhousebar.com. Memor-
ial Day–Labor Day, daily 11 AM–1 AM; varying hrs Apr., May, Sept., and Oct., depending
on weather.

South Bass Island State Park In the late 19th century, the fashionable place to enjoy
the Lake Erie Isles was at the Victory Hotel, the largest summer resort in the world, on
the western coast of South Bass Island. The hotel was destroyed by fire in 1919, and
today the site on which the hotel stood is occupied by South Bass Island State Park.
Ruins of the hotel can still be seen throughout the park. You'll also enjoy unsurpassed
views of Lake Erie, boating, fishing, camping, and hiking. > Catawba Ave. and Meechen
Rd., Put-in-Bay, tel. 419/285–2112 or 419/797–4530, www.ohiostateparks.org. Free.
Apr.–Oct., daily dawn–dusk.

MARBLEHEAD

East Harbor State Park On the shores of Lake Erie, East Harbor State Park is a prime
location for boating, fishing, swimming, picnicking, and camping. Nature enthusiasts
enjoy the abundance of waterfowl, shorebirds, and other species of wildlife found in
the park's scenic wetlands. East Harbor also has a marina. > 1169 N. Buck Rd. (Rte.
269), Marblehead, tel. 419/734–4424 or 419/734–5857, www.ohiostateparks.org. Free.
Daily dawn–dusk.

Lakeside The self-described "Chautauqua on the lake" resort of Lakeside began as a
Methodist religious retreat in 1873. Since then, it has become an ecumenical resort
emphasizing cultural, educational, and spiritual growth. The community is only occupied in summer, and most of its buildings are family summer cottages that have
been passed down for generations. But Lakeside is open to the public. An entrance
fee gives you admittance to nearly all Lakeside activities, including music concerts,
educational lectures, theatrical performances, and classes for all ages. The community's downtown area is lined with quaint shops and eateries, and it also has family-
rated movies, two hotels, and cottages for rent. > 236 Walnut St., Marblehead,
tel. 419/798–4461 or 866/952–5374, www.lakesideohio.com. $11.75 per day, $70.50
per wk. Late May–Aug., varying daily schedule.

Marblehead Lighthouse Ohio's newest state park is home to its oldest lighthouse.
Dating from 1821, Marblehead Lighthouse is actually the oldest continuously operating
lighthouse on the Great Lakes, and is one of the most photographed scenes in the
state. You can climb 77 spiral steps to the top of the lighthouse during open hours;
when the interior is closed, the lighthouse is still worth seeing from the outside. The
park's picnic area has great views of Lake Erie and the islands. You can also tour the adjacent Keeper's House, which houses a nautical museum and a gift shop. > 110 Lighthouse Dr., off Bayshore Rd., Marblehead, tel. 419/797–4530, www.ohiostateparks.org.
Free. Memorial Day–Labor Day, weekdays 1–4:45; June–Oct., 2nd Sat. each month 10–3.

PORT CLINTON

African Safari Wildlife Park More than 400 exotic species, including zebras, giraffes, camels, and alpacas, roam through this 100-acre drive-through safari. The park
also has pony and camel rides, a gift shop, educational programs, and the Jungle
Junction Playground. > 267 Lightner Rd., Port Clinton, tel. 419/732–3606 or
800/521–2660, www.africansafariwildlifepark.com. $15.95 summer, $12.95 off-season.
Apr. and May, Sept. and Oct., daily 10–5; Memorial Day–Labor Day, daily 9–7.

Catawba Island State Park This small day-use park sits on the Lake Erie shore 6 mi
north of Port Clinton. Facilities include a fishing pier, boat launch, picnic areas, a bath
house, and a swimming beach. > 4049 E. Moores Dock Rd., off W. Catawba Rd., Port
Clinton, tel. 419/797–4530, www.ohiostateparks.org. Free. Daily dawn–dusk.

Ottawa County/Lake Erie Islands Regional Welcome Center A one-stop travel
center for the entire Lake Erie Islands region, this welcome center opened in 2003.
The building is a good place to find brochures and other travel information for the
region, but it also includes educational videos, a giant aquarium, and displays about
the area as well as a bird-watching station. > 770 S.E. Catawba Rd., Port Clinton,
tel. 419/734–4386 or 800/441–1271, www.lake-erie.com. Free. Sun.–Thurs. 8–7, Fri.
and Sat. 8–8.

Tours

Put-in-Bay Tour Train Trains depart every 30 minutes for an hour-long narrated tour
of South Bass Island. Regular stops include Perry's Cave, Perry's Victory and International Peace Memorial, and Heineman Winery & Crystal Cave, but stops are added
during times of heavy tourism (mid-summer) and removed during slower periods.
The day-long ticket allows you to get off and on the train at any stop. > Toledo Ave.
near Delaware Ave., Put-in-Bay, tel. 419/285–4855, www.put-in-bay-trans.com.

Sports

BOATING

Boating is a popular pastime on Lake Erie, both for those who want to island-hop
under their own power and for those who want to relax or fish. While marinas and
private boat launches are abundant, the area's state parks provide free launches,
often in pristine, scenic, natural areas.

Catawba Island State Park This small day-use park sits on the Lake Erie shore 6 mi
north of Port Clinton. Facilities include a fishing pier, boat launch, picnic areas, a
bath house, and a swimming beach. > 4049 E. Moores Dock Rd., Port Clinton, tel.
419/797–4530, www.ohiostateparks.org.

East Harbor State Park Catawba Island's marina provides seasonal and day-use
dock rentals, fuel, launch ramps, supplies, and a restaurant. Boats and campers can
be stored year-round at the marina in a fenced enclosure. > 1169 Buck Rd. (Rte. 269),
Marblehead, tel. 419/734–4424 or 419/734–5857, www.ohiostateparks.org.

Kelleys Island State Park State park land is scattered throughout the natural areas
of Kelleys Island, but the large track on the island's northern shore is the place to
head for boating activities. Park facilities include a fishing pier, boat launches, and
a scenic beachside campground. > Division St. and Titus Rd., Kelleys Island, tel.
419/746–2546 or 419/797–4530, www.ohiostateparks.org.

South Bass Island State Park You'll enjoy unsurpassed cliffside views of Lake Erie
from this state park. Overnight and day-use dock rentals, launch ramps, and a large

fishing pier are available. Other fishing, boating, and camping supplies are available at the little camp store adjacent to the park. > Catawba Ave. and Meechen Rd., Put-in-Bay, tel. 419/285–2112 or 419/797–4530, www.ohiostateparks.org.

HIKING

The Boardwalk The newest addition to Kelleys Island's trail system, the Boardwalk, was constructed in 2002 and leads to the North Pond Nature Preserve. The pleasant 1-mi walk takes you past the island's prehistoric shoreline, through hardwood forests, and on to the North Pond and its observation tower. > Ward Rd., near the 4-H Camp, Kelleys Island.

Kelleys Island State Park The North Shore Loop Trail begins behind the Glacial Grooves and continues past the old crusher and lime kiln used in quarrying days. From there the trail winds through hardwoods and cedars and along the north shoreline. > Division St. and Titus Rd., Kelleys Island, tel. 419/746–2546 or 419/797–4530, www.ohiostateparks.org.

Lilac Walk The Lilac Walk is short, more of a maze than a trail, and it's not worth visiting unless the lilacs are blooming. But if they are, don't miss the opportunity to wander through this huge, wild lilac grove. The scent is intoxicating. The walk wanders through private land, but visitors are common and welcome. > Ward Rd., just east of Estes School, Kelleys Island.

Save the Date

MAY

Nest with the Birds Week The Audubon Society hosts this popular weeklong event, which begins on Mother's Day. There are daily nature programs, guided bird and wildflower walks, and, on Saturday, a bird banding program. > St. Michael's Hall, 219 Chappel St., Kelleys Island, tel. 419/746–2258, www.kelleysislandnature.com.

JUNE

Founder's Day A celebration of the founding of the island village by Jose DeRivera, Founder's Day includes an ox roast, entertainment, children's games and prizes, vendors, summer food fare, clowns and magicians, and an antique car parade. > DeRivera Park, downtown Put-in-Bay, tel. 419/285–2832, www.put-in-bay.com.

Mayfly Days Millions of mayflies emerge from Lake Erie each June. Marblehead celebrates one of the area's most unique returning species annually at Mayfly Days. You can learn all about the bugs on 7 mi of nature trails and through educational insect activities. > East Harbor State Park, 1169 Buck Rd., Marblehead, tel. 419/734–4386 or 800/441–1271, www.lake-erie.com.

JULY

Christmas in July Downtown Put-in-Bay is decorated for Christmas each year in July. Highlights include the Bay Parade of Lights, Reindeer Golf Cart Races, Santa, and games for the kids. > Downtown, Put-in-Bay, tel. 419/285–2832, www.put-in-bay.com.

Christmas in July Holiday music, Christmas movies, and a holiday decorating contest at the campground are highlights of this festival at East Harbor State Park. > East Harbor State Park, 1169 Buck Rd., Marblehead, tel. 419/734–4386 or 800/441–1271, www.lake-erie.com.

Island Fest Island arts and crafts, food, parades, fireworks, and outdoor dances are part of the fun at this annual summer island festival. > Kelleys Island Memorial Park, Division St., Kelleys Island, tel. 419/746–2360, www.kelleysislandchamber.com.

WHERE TO STAY

KELLEYS ISLAND

Himmelblau This 100-year-old Queen Anne Victorian inn has its own panoramic view of Lake Erie. The large, enclosed porch faces east, making it the best place to watch the sunrise on the island. The rooms are eclectic, with antique furnishings. > 377 Shannon Way, Kelleys Island 43438, tel. 419/746–2200, www.kelleysisland.com/himmelblauhouse. 3 rooms. In-room VCRs, lake, laundry facilities, some pets allowed. DC, MC, V. Closed Dec.–Apr. CP. **$**

Inn on Kelleys Island Antiques, pastel quilts, and nautical memorabilia decorate The Inn, a restored 1876 Victorian home a few blocks from downtown. The owners, Pat and Lori Hayes, will quickly make you feel like one of the family. Ask them for suggestions of places to see wildlife—they're members of the Audubon Society. All rooms have shared baths. > 317 W. Lakeshore Dr., Kelleys Island 43438, tel. 419/746–2258 or 866/878–2135, www.aves.net/the-inn. 4 rooms with shared bath. Fans, lake, beach; no a/c, no room phones, no kids. D, MC, V. Closed Nov.–Mar. CP. **$–$$**

Water's Edge Retreat This beautiful, three-story B&B retreat is what getting away is all about. Relax in the rockers on the front veranda and watch the waves roll in, or watch them from your room—most have lake views. Rooms have private baths, paddle fans, and air-conditioning; they are adorned with antiques and lots of hardwood. The inn is a few blocks from downtown and the ferry dock. > 827 E. Lakeshore Dr., Kelleys Island 43438, tel. 419/746–2455 or 800/884–5143, www.watersedgeretreat. com. 6 rooms. Dining room, some in-room hot tubs, lake, beach; no kids, no smoking. D, MC, V. Closed Nov.–Mar. BP. **$$$$**

SOUTH BASS ISLAND

Ashley's Island House B&B Just a few blocks from downtown, this B&B is furnished with hardwood floors, ceiling fans, antiques, and pastel quilts. Quiet and well away from Put-in-Bay's evening nightlife, Ashley's Island House makes a nice romantic getaway. Choose room 00, 1, 2, or 5 if you want a private bath. Adult guests preferred. There's no parking fee. > 557 Catawba Ave., Put-in-Bay 43456, tel. 419/285–2844, www.ashleysislandhouse.com. 12 rooms. 4 with bath. Some room TVs; no smoking. MC, V. Closed Nov.–Mar.; open weekends only Apr. and Oct., weather permitting. CP. **$–$$$**

Grand Islander Hotel Bright, pleasant rooms two blocks from downtown Put-in-Bay make the Grand Islander a good choice. In addition to the pool on site, you can also enjoy the five pools at the hotel's sister facility, the Islander Inn, next door. And since those pools are next door, the Grand Islander is a bit quieter. Alcohol is not permitted in the hotel, and the building is some distance from the partying downtown, so you'll feel comfortable staying here with kids. A $7 per day parking fee is assessed June–August. > 432 Catawba Ave., Put-in-Bay 43456, tel. 419/285–5555, www.grandislanderpib.com. 50 rooms. Restaurant, some in-room hot tubs, some microwaves, some refrigerators, cable TV, meeting rooms, no-smoking rooms. MC, V. Closed mid-Sept.–mid-May. **$$$–$$$$**

Islander Inn The pools—there are five of them, including a waterfall pool, a lazy river pool, a swim-up bar with underwater bar stools, and a 30-person Jacuzzi—are the best reason to stay at this pleasant hotel. A Caribbean theme permeates the property, which is 2 blocks from downtown Put-in-Bay. With the exception of the bar area, alcohol is not permitted in the hotel, making it a great choice for those who want to get away from the crowds downtown. You can rent golf carts from the front desk. A $7 per day parking fee is assessed from June through August. > 225 Erie St., Put-in-Bay 43456, tel. 419/285–7829, www.islanderinnpib.com. 50 rooms. Some in-room hot tubs, some microwaves, some refrigerators, cable TV, 5 pools, outdoor hot tub, 2 bars, playground, meeting rooms, no-smoking rooms. MC, V. Closed mid-Sept.–mid-May. **$$$–$$$$**

Park Hotel A restored Victorian hotel with individually decorated rooms, the Park Hotel has been operational since the 1870s. It's right next door to the Round House, Put-in-Bay's hottest nightlife spot—convenient if you plan to spend the evening partying. If you want peace and quiet, look elsewhere. There are no private baths; communal bathrooms are on each floor. There's no parking fee. > 234 Delaware, Put-in-Bay 43456, tel. 419/285–3581, www.islandresorts.put-in-bay.com/parkhotel. 25 rooms without bath. No room phones, no room TVs, no smoking. AE, D, MC, V. Closed Nov.–Mar.; open Apr. and Oct., weekends only. **$–$$$**

MARBLEHEAD

Lake Point Motel Most of the rooms in this reasonably priced hotel, literally steps from the shore, have lake views. You can stroll on the beach, go boating, or enjoy the facility's picnic area. The two-story hotel has one- and two-bedroom suites and caters to anglers—there are fish-cleaning facilities and a freezer on-site—and it's a five-minute drive from Kelleys Island ferry. > 908 E. Main St., Marblehead 43440, tel. 419/798–4684, www.lakepointmotel.com. 14 rooms. Some kitchenettes, some in-room hot tubs, cable TV with movies. MC, V. **¢–$**

Marblehead Inn Just down the road from the Marblehead Lighthouse, the inn faces a rocky shoreline and a view of such local attractions as Cedar Point Amusement park and Kelleys Island, as well as a parade of passing boats. Rooms are large and bright, decorated with floral themes, and some have kitchenettes and in-room hot tubs. The hotel is just a five-minute drive from Kelleys Island ferry. > 614 E. Main St., Marblehead 43440, tel. 419/798–8184 or 877/426–8439. 68 rooms. Some in-room hot tubs, some kitchenettes, some microwaves, some refrigerators, cable TV, some in-room VCRs, no-smoking rooms. AE, D, DC, MC, V. **$$–$$$$**

Old Stonehouse Bed & Breakfast Sunsets are beautiful from this unique inn, the largest B&B in Marblehead. The building was constructed in 1861 by Alexander Clemons using stone from his own quarry. Rooms are decorated with pastels and antiques as well as claw-foot bathtubs and pot-belly stoves, and most have lake views. > 133 Clemons St., Marblehead 43440, tel. 419/798–5922. 11 rooms. Dining room, some in-room hot tubs, lake, fishing; no kids under 10. D, MC, V. CP. **$$–$$$**

South Beach Resort Right on the Lake Erie shore and a 15-minute drive to Kelleys Island ferries, this resort on the southern coast of the Marblehead peninsula is a fun family getaway. You can choose among standard hotel rooms or reserve a cottage (some sleep 10–12 people). The pale blue tones in the rooms mirror the lake and sky outdoors, and most have views of Lake Erie from their private balconies. If you have a boat, you can dock it at the marina or take advantage of numerous outdoor recreational facilities on-site. Frontwaters is the attached restaurant. > 8620 E. Bayshore Rd., Marblehead 43440, tel. 419/798–4900 or 800/814–4396, www.sbresort.com. 55 rooms, 21 cottages. Restaurant, room service, in-room hot tubs, some kitchens, some kitchenettes, some microwaves, some refrigerators, cable TV, 3 tennis courts, 2 pools, wading pool, lake, outdoor hot tub, beach, dock, boating, marina, fishing, badminton, basketball, boccie, croquet, horseshoes, shuffleboard, volleyball, bar, playground, laundry facilities, no-smoking rooms. AE, MC, V. Closed Oct.–Apr. **$$$–$$$$**

PORT CLINTON

Comfort Inn Many of the rooms in this lakefront hotel enjoy views of Lake Erie; some have lakefront balconies. An outdoor pool and sundeck are also right on Lake Erie. The hotel is a five-minute drive to the ferry docks in Port Clinton. > 1723 E. Perry St., Port Clinton 43452, tel. 419/732–2929 or 800/221–2222, www.comfortinn.com. 50 rooms. In-room data ports, some in-room hot tubs, some refrigerators, cable TV with movies, pool, lake, laundry service, business services, meeting rooms, no-smoking rooms. AE, D, DC, MC, V. CP. $$$–$$$$

Country Hearth Inn This modern, regional chain hotel on the shores of Lake Erie is off State Route 2, 10 minutes from ferry service in Port Clinton. A country theme is evident in pastel colors, floral prints, and folk art. Also in the country mode, breakfasts, including waffles and oatmeal, are heartier than the typical Continental fare of muffins and Danish. > 1815 Perry St., Port Clinton 43452, tel. 419/732–2111 or 800/282–5711, fax 419/732–0206, www.countryhearth.com. 66 rooms. In-room data ports, cable TV with movies, pool, lake, business services, meeting rooms, no-smoking rooms. AE, D, DC, MC, V. CP. $$–$$$

Our Guest Inn & Suites Two 100-year-old Victorian-era homes were renovated and modernized to create a unique hotel in the heart of Port Clinton, across the street from the Put-in-Bay ferry docks. The old buildings are decorated with period furniture originals and reproductions, lace, and stained-glass windows; the hotel lobby is warmed by a large fireplace on chilly days. Our Guest Inn also has a modern 52-room hotel at the rear of the property. Rooms are modest, clean, and reasonably priced, but for a special stay, ask for a vintage room. > 220 E. Perry St., Port Clinton 43452, tel. 419/734–7111, www.ourguestinn.com. 52 rooms, 8 suites. Rooms service, some in-room hot tubs, some in-room kitchenettes, some microwaves, some refrigerators, cable TV, pool, meeting rooms, no-smoking rooms. MC, V. $–$$$

CAMPING

East Harbor State Park Ohio's largest state park campground, East Harbor is 7 mi west of Marblehead and sits on the eastern shore of the Catawba Island peninsula. In addition to standard campsites, campers can choose to overnight in rustic Camper Cabins or in a Rent-A-RV. There's also a marina, a boat launch, and a 1,500-foot beach. > 1169 N. Buck Rd. (Rte. 269), Marblehead 43440, tel. 419/734–4424 or 419/734–5857, www.ohiostateparks.org. 365 partial hook-ups; 205 tent sites; 2 cabins; 2 RVs. Flush toilets, partial hook-ups (electric and water), dump station, drinking water, showers, fire pits, picnic tables, restaurant, electricity, general store, ranger station, playground, swimming (lake). Reservations not accepted. AE, D, DC, MC, V. ¢–$

Kelleys Island State Park Right on the Lake Erie shoreline, Kelleys Island State Park provides superb views of the lake, great swimming, and clean, modern bath houses. All sites have thick grass, so tenters will be as happy here as RV campers. Sites 77–104 are closest to the lake and have the best views. You can also spend the night in a Camper Cabin (furnished with cots) or a Rent-A-Yurt (furnished with bunks, a sofa, table and chairs, refrigerator, and microwave). Right across the street from the campground is Uncle Dik's Island Outfitters, selling camping supplies, firewood, sandwiches, and ice cream. > Division St. and Titus Rd., Kelleys Island 43438, tel. 419/746–2546 or 419/797–4530, www.ohiostateparks.org. 84 partial hook-ups; 45 rustic; 2 cabins; 2 yurts. Flush toilets, partial hook-ups (electric and water), dump station, drinking water, showers, fire grates, fire pits, picnic tables, electricity, ranger station, swimming (lake). Reservations not accepted. MC, V. ¢–$

South Bass Island State Park Quiet, heavily wooded and overlooking lovely views of Lake Erie, this park is an ideal site to enjoy the quiet side of South Bass Island. If you're staying in a tent, ask for a cliff site. They're flatter, grassier, and they have unobstructed views of the lake. They're also off-limits to camping trailers or RVs. The park also rents "cabents," a combination cabin and tent, by the week. Cabents include efficiency kitchens, beds, a sofa, cookware, and a TV. You'll need to supply your own linens. > Catawba Ave. at Meechen Rd., Put-in-Bay 43456, tel. 419/285–2112, www.ohiostateparks.org. 10 full hook-ups; 125 tent sites; 4 cabents. Flush toilets, full hook-ups, dump station, drinking water, showers, fire grates, fire pits, picnic tables, electricity, public telephone, general store, ranger station. Reservations not accepted. MC, V. Nov.–Mar. ¢

WHERE TO EAT

KELLEYS ISLAND

Island Cafe and Brew Pub The island's only brew pub is a 10-minute drive from downtown and has indoor and outdoor dining with views of Lake Erie. The relaxed family restaurant serves burgers, sandwiches, and salads as well as full dinners, including Lake Erie walleye and perch, cinnamon-apple pork loins, and pasta. But the best reason to visit is for its hand-crafted brews. Kelleys Gold is a local favorite; Island Devil is a Belgian-style brew. If you can't make up your mind, order a tasting tray of samples. > Lakeshore Dr. and Cameron Rd., tel. 419/746–2314. Closed mid-Nov.–mid-Apr. Closed Mon.–Wed. AE, MC, V. $–$$

Village Pump Right in the heart of downtown, the Pump is where the locals go to eat. You can sit in the main part of the restaurant, but it's nicer on the sunny patio—which is really a giant screen porch—where you can enjoy views of Lake Erie. The menu includes lots of Great Lakes fish (you can buy it by the pound to go if you like), as well as pizza, chicken, and steak. > 103 E. Lakeshore Dr., Kelleys Island, tel. 419/746–2281. AE, MC, V. $–$$

Winking Lizard This fun bar and grill has tin ceilings, ceiling fans, and lots of dark wood. You can listen to the Beatles and the Doors while you eat. The creative menu includes "Lizard Lips" (chicken tenders), "Creek and Road Kill" (surf-and-turf selections), wraps, and pizza. You can't go wrong with Oreo Oblivion for dessert. > 101 W. Lakeshore Dr., Kelleys Island, tel. 419/746–2112. MC, V. $–$$

SOUTH BASS ISLAND

The Boardwalk This restaurant specializes in seafood, from fresh Maine lobster to Lake Erie perch. Every table has a good view of the marina, where you can enjoy the sunset. The restaurant also has live entertainment and free boat dockage. > Bay View Ave., tel. 419/285–3695, www.the-boardwalk.com. Closed Oct.–Apr. MC, V. $–$$$$

Boathouse Bar & Grill Keeping with the boathouse theme, this restaurant's walls are adorned with old, weathered life preservers, fishing boats, and other fishing paraphernalia. The interior bar resembles the inside of a boat, complete with portholes. Dinner options include walleye and steak dinners, as well as sandwiches and salads. > 218 Hartford Ave., Put-in-Bay, tel. 419/285–5665. MC, V. Closed Nov.–Mar.; open weekends only Apr. and Oct. $–$$

Pasquale's Cafe Cheerfully designed, with red-and-white-checked tablecloths, a shiny tin ceiling with fans, and Italian opera music in the background, Pasquale's is a fun place to enjoy any meal. Dinners include such Italian favorites as spaghetti and meatballs, pizza made with fresh bread dough, and *Aglio e Olio* (sauteed garlic, olive oil, and butter tossed with spaghetti and garnished with tomatoes and Parmesan). Breakfasts are hearty and large. > 66 Delaware Ave., Put-in-Bay, tel. 419/285–8600. AE, D, MC, V. Closed Nov.–Mar.; open weekends only Apr. and Oct. $–$$

Put-in-Bay Brewing Company A bit smoky, a bit dark, a bit noisy—this microbrewery has all of the elements of a neighborhood bar, but they brew their own suds on-site, and the food is better. Enjoy pizza, ribs, and sandwiches during the summer months; pizza only in spring and fall. > 441 Catawba Ave., Put-in-Bay, tel. 419/285–4677. AE, D, MC, V. Closed Nov.–Mar; open weekends only Apr. and Oct. ¢–$$$

Tipper's Restaurant The popular lunch and dinner buffet dominates the dining room in this downtown Put-in-Bay restaurant. Fill up on all-you-can-eat meats, vegetables, salads and soups. There's also an extensive menu including selections like walleye, steak, ribs, and pizza in the more formal dining room. Or order a sandwich in Tipper's casual lounge. > 324 Delaware Ave., Put-in-Bay, tel. 419/285–8477. AE, D, MC, V. Closed Nov.–Mar.; open weekends only Apr. and Oct. $–$$$

MARBLEHEAD

Big Boppers Just a few minutes' drive from Kelleys Island ferry, Big Boppers is famous locally for its Island Heat Chili. The owner must know what he's doing—he's a member of the International Chili Society. If you arrive too early in the day for chili, try an Island Heat Omelet. Bar food, such as barbecue chicken, hot wings, and sandwiches, fills out the rest of the menu. > 7581 E. Harbor Rd., Marblehead, tel. 419/734–4458. AE, D, MC, V. $–$$

Marblehead Galley You'll see all sorts in the Galley, from businesspeople in suits, to well-heeled cottage owners, to employees of the local Coast Guard station. The restaurant isn't fancy by any stretch of the imagination, but the simple, clean interior, friendly waitstaff, and proximity to Lakeside and Kelleys Ferry keep this place humming. Fried chicken, Lake Erie walleye and perch, burgers, and salads are on the menu. > 718 W. Main St., Marblehead, tel. 419/798–5356. D, DC, MC, V. No lunch or dinner Sun. $

Mariner's Retreat Restaurant & Mopey Dick's Lounge Have a fancy dinner or just grab a salad at this marina restaurant. Mariner's Retreat is more formal, with pastel table linens and crystal glassware. The wood-paneled dining room is broken up by large picture windows looking out over the marina. Daily specials include steaks, ribs, and fresh seafood. You can dock for free if you arrive by water. Mopey Dick's is more laid-back, with a full-service bar featuring sandwiches and lighter fare. > 6801 E. Harbor Rd., at Marina del Isle Marblehead, tel. 419/732–2587. Reservations not accepted. MC, V. Closed mid-Oct.–mid-Apr. and Tues. No breakfast. $–$$$

PORT CLINTON

Garden at the Lighthouse Once the site of Port Clinton's first lighthouse, The Garden's main dining room has floor-to-ceiling windows and a view of Lake Erie. Seafood dishes dominate the menu, accompanied by locally grown organic produce in season. Try the *poulet d'elegance* (a chicken breast stuffed with lobster tail and Swiss cheese and baked in a puff-pastry shell). Open-air dining is available from Memorial Day to Labor Day. > 226 E. Perry St., at Adams St., Port Clinton, tel. 419/732–2151. AE, D, DC, MC, V. Closed Sun. and Sept.–May. $$–$$$$

Mayhew's This simple home-town eatery is a favorite among locals. Since it's only a block away from the ferry docks, travelers like to stop in for a breakfast of homemade donuts on their way to a day on the islands. Lunchtime favorites include the char-grilled chicken salad, taco salad, and Little Sister Sandwich Plate—a cheeseburger with bacon, lettuce and tomato. > 128 W. Perry, Port Clinton, tel. 419/732–3259. MC, V. No dinner. ¢

Mon Ami Restaurant and Winery You'll get three restaurant choices in one at Mon Ami. Antique chandeliers and dark wood detailing dress up the restaurant's formal dining room, with a menu of seafood, steaks, and chops. The more casual (and slightly cheaper) chalet has a round fireplace in the center of the room and live jazz on weekends; its menu includes pastas, steaks, and seafood. Tucked between those two dining rooms is Jimmie's Back Bar, with a menu of sandwiches and salads. But all three dining rooms allow customers to order off any of the menus—the perfect solution if you want elegant dining in a casual dining room. Take time to visit the winery's tasting room and gift shop. Mon Ami produces some of the most highly regarded varieties in Ohio. > 3845 E. Wine Cellar Rd., Port Clinton, tel. 419/797–4445 or 800/777–4266. AE, D, MC, V. No breakfast. $–$$$$

ESSENTIALS

Getting Here

Whether you'll need a car in the Lake Erie Islands depends upon which area you visit. A weekend in Put-in-Bay is best spent without a car. Nearly all of the island's attractions are within easy walking distance of the ferry docks and parking and car ferry service is limited. Instead, drive to the Port Clinton ferry docks and leave your auto in the free parking lots. If you must have transportation other than your feet on South Bass Island, consider renting a bicycle or golf cart at the ferry dock.

If your weekend plans include a visit to Kelleys Island, a car is preferable, but not necessary. A drive around the perimeter of the island is relaxing and scenic, and you will need some means of transportation if you plan to visit Glacial Grooves, the state park, or the island's hiking trails. However, bicycle and golf cart rentals are available at the ferry dock and the island's downtown area and accommodations are largely within a few blocks of the dock.

You will need a car to get to the port cities of Port Clinton or Marblehead and to explore the mainland coastal areas. Bus, train, air, and public transportation are nonexistent.

BY CAR
From the Ohio Turnpike (I–80/90), follow Route 53 north to Port Clinton. From there, Route 163 runs from downtown Port Clinton east to Marblehead. Most ferry service to Put-in-Bay and Kelleys Island is on Route 163, a scenic road with frequent views of Lake Erie. Parking on the mainland and on Kelleys Island is readily available and free. Parking in Put-in-Bay is limited in the downtown area—try parking a few blocks away. Some Put-in-Bay hotels charge parking fees.

BY FERRY
Ferry service to Kelleys Island and Put-in-Bay varies widely depending on the weather. During the summer months most ferries run daily every half hour beginning around 8 AM; service ends around midnight in Put-in-Bay, 10 PM in Kel-

leys Island. Frequency slows down in spring and autumn months, with service to Put-in-Bay limited to weekends in May and October. Service halts entirely to both islands when storms blow in or when Lake Erie freezes over, usually November–April in Put-in-Bay and December–March on Kelleys Island. Schedules are available on-line and at all mainland hotels and tourist attractions in Port Clinton and Marblehead. Purchase tickets in person at the dock. All major credit cards and cash are accepted.

Island Rocket has several ferry routes from which to choose: a circular route between Put-in-Bay, Kelleys Island, and Sandusky; a direct passage to Put-in-Bay from Port Clinton; or direct routes between Cedar Point in Sandusky and either Kelleys Island or Put-in-Bay. Round-trip rates run between $17 and $32 per passenger, $5 per bicycle. There's no vehicle transport. The Rocket dock in Port Clinton is at Perry (Route 163) and Jefferson streets. Parking costs $5 per day.

Jett Express, the fastest ferry to South Bass Island, takes passengers to its dock in downtown Put-in-Bay. Round-trip fares are $20 per passenger, $5 per bicycle. There's no vehicle transport. The Jet Express Dock is in Port Clinton at Perry (Route 163) and Monroe streets. Parking at the adjacent Jet Express lot costs $6 a day, or park two blocks away at Harrison and Perry streets at the free Jet Express lot.

Kelleys Island Ferry Boat Line drops passengers and their vehicles in the heart of the downtown. Round-trip fares are $20 a vehicle, $10 per passenger, and $3 a bicycle. The Kelleys Island Ferry mainland dock is in Marblehead at the eastern end of Route 163. Parking is free.

Miller Ferry transports passengers and vehicles to Put-in-Bay from Catawba Island, 8 mi northeast of Port Clinton. Round-trip fares cost $24 per vehicle, $10 per passenger, and $4 a bicycle. The Miller Dock is on Water Street, at the northern end of Route 53. Parking is free.

FERRY LINES **Island Rocket** > Tel. 419/627–1500 or 800/854–8121, www.islandrocket.com. **Jet Express** > Tel. 800/245–1538, www.jet-express.com. **Kelleys Island Ferry Boat Line** > Tel. 419/798–9763, www.kelleysislandferry.com. **Miller Ferry** > Tel. 800/500–2421, www.millerferry.com.

Visitor Information

CONTACTS **Kelleys Island Chamber of Commerce** > 130 Division St., Kelleys Island 43438, tel. 419/746–2360, www.kelleysislandchamber.com. **Ottawa County Visitors Bureau** > 770 S.E. Catawba Rd. (Rte. 53), Port Clinton 43440, tel. 419/798–9777 or 800/441–1271, www.lake-erie.com. **Put-in-Bay Chamber of Commerce** > Box 250, Put-in-Bay 43456, tel. 419/285–2832, www.put-in-bay.com. **Sandusky/Erie County Visitors and Convention Bureau** > 4424 Milan Rd., Suite A, Sandusky 44870, tel. 419/625–2984 or 800/255–3743, www.VisitOhio.com.

Cedar Point & the Sandusky Area

Cedar Point is 65 mi west of Cleveland, 115 mi north of Columbus,
and 245 mi northeast of Cincinnati.

3

By Amy S. Eckert

CEDAR POINT CLAIMS to be the granddaddy of all amusement parks. It's a tough point to argue. The park has more roller coasters and thrill rides than any other park in the world. Perennial favorites like Ferris wheels, carousels, bumper cars, log rides, and various scrambling-and-twirling machines pack the Midway. Visitors of all ages enjoy a sandy beach and boardwalk, live theatrical performances, and shopping. Camp Snoopy and Peanuts Playground entertain the littlest thrill seekers.

But roller coasters have made Cedar Point famous. With 16 coasters on site, the park has something for every taste. The Woodstock Express gets the youngsters hooked on roller coasters early, and by the time they're teenagers they've worked their way up to the park's most recent addition: Top Thrill Dragster, the tallest and fastest coaster in the world. But it's a safe bet that title won't last for long. Year after year the park breaks its own records for fastest, highest, steepest, and roughest roller coasters. Coming years will likely produce more of the same.

Cedar Point traces its beginnings to 1870, when tourists flocked to the scenic Lake Erie peninsula for swimming, dancing, picnicking, and camping. Its first "thrill ride" was a water trapeze, from which adventurous bathers would leap into the lake water. In 1892 the park unveiled its first roller coaster, and Sandusky has never been the same.

But Sandusky's history doesn't begin with an amusement park. The Wyandot tribe settled the banks of the Sandusky River at Lake Erie, calling the site "Sandusky" or "at the cold water." The first white settlers arrived in 1775, paving a trade route from the eastern states to Detroit and opening a steady flow of migration, industry, and commerce. In the 19th century, Sandusky became an important stop on the Underground Railroad. The city's proximity to Lake Erie, a wide network of railroad lines, the Huron and Vermilion rivers, and the Milan Canal resulted in its establishment as a major Railroad terminal, code-named "Hope." And not long after, Thomas Edison was born in nearby Milan, changing the American landscape with his inventions, including the telephone, the phonograph, the motion picture camera, and the incandescent lightbulb.

The natural beauty of the Great Lakes region is on display in the Sandusky area as well. Enjoy great sunsets, as well as the natural flora and fauna while taking a boat tour or hiking along footpaths that wend their way through an estuarine reserve. Or venture a few miles southwest of Sandusky's city limits to visit area wineries for a tour, a taste, and a bottle to take home.

If white-knuckle thrills are what you seek, you won't be disappointed with Cedar Point. But if that's all you see of this Great Lakes region you'll be missing a lot.

WHAT TO SEE & DO

Cedar Point Perched at the tip of a peninsula, surrounded on three sides by Lake Erie, Cedar Point enjoys one of the loveliest settings of any of the nation's theme parks. Lake Erie's whitecaps lap the shores of Cedar Point Beach and colorful sailboats ply the water. All in all, the scene is stunning, albeit pierced by the spires and hills of brightly colored thrill rides. If you're not afraid of heights, take a ride on the 150-foot Ferris wheel or the Space Spiral just to enjoy the fabulous views.

Cedar Point is one of the world's largest and most complete amusement parks, with more roller coasters (16) and thrill rides (68) than any other park in the world. The park also claims the world's fastest and tallest coaster. Top Thrill Dragster is the first to break the 400-foot milestone, whipping screaming passengers down a 42-story hill at 120 mph. As you stroll through the park, whooshing cars and dangling legs pass overhead; screaming coaster enthusiasts are strapped into such rides as Mantis, the Raptor, Wicked Twister, and Iron Dragon. Calmer entertainment includes Midway rides (like bumper cars, a life-size carousel, and the Scrambler), water rides, and live entertainment (including Peanuts musicals, karaoke, and honky-tonk country and ice-skating shows). Sandy Cedar Point beach and the boardwalk are other quieter options.

Two children's parks provide entertainment and thrills for the youngest visitors—and help to cultivate Cedar Point's future thrill-seekers. Camp Snoopy is home to 11 rides and attractions, including a family roller coaster, Lolli Swings, and a WWI Flying Ace adventure. The Gemini Children's Area features more rides for youngsters, including bumper boats, miniature water rides, playground equipment, and Frog Hopper, a tame version of the popular adult ride, Power Tower.

Challenge Park (tel. 419/626–0830 RipCord reservations, $5–$30 per activity, Cedar Point admission not required, May–Labor Day, open 10 AM, closing hours vary. Generally closed 1 hr after Cedar Point. Labor Day–late Oct., weekends only), adjacent to Cedar Point, is most famous for the RipCord Skycoaster. The 15-story launch tower shoots riders around from the end of a steel tether in something of a cross between skydiving and bungee jumping. The park also has miniature golf and go-karts.

Soak City ($12–$24, Cedar Point admission not required, combination tickets available, Late May–Labor Day, daily 10 AM, closing hrs vary. Labor Day–mid-Sept., weekends only) is an 18-acre water park separate from but adjacent to Cedar Point. Activities include unlimited use of body and inner tube slides, a 500,000-gallon wave pool, and a lazy river float.
> 1 Cedar Point Rd., tel. 419/627–2350, www.cedarpoint.com. $44. Mid May–Labor Day, daily 10 AM, closing hrs vary; Labor Day–Oct., weekends only.

AROUND SANDUSKY

Battery Park Sunrise and sunset are popular times to visit Battery Park, which has a breathtaking view of Sandusky Bay and Cedar Point. The park is in the heart of downtown Sandusky, right on the water. Facilities include picnic tables and grills, a playground and tennis courts. > 701 E. Water St., at Meigs St., Sandusky, tel. 419/625–6142. Free. Daily.
Edison Birthplace Thomas Edison, inventor of the lightbulb, the phonograph, and the motion picture camera, was born in Milan in 1847. You can tour Edison's boyhood home and see displays related to his accomplishments. > 9 Edison Dr., off Rte.

Coaster Crazy

THE "ROLLER COASTER CAPITAL of the World" has a world-record 16 coasters. You can choose from 68 additional rides, many of them as thrilling as the wildest coasters. But there's no denying: Cedar Point is a roller-coaster lover's dream.

To make the most of your day, prepurchase tickets via phone and pick them up at the will-call window rather than waiting in line. And arrive 30 minutes before park opening hours so you can get started right away.

The park's newest coasters are its most exciting. **Top Thrill Dragster** whisks riders to a height of 420 feet and speeds of 120 mph, making it the tallest and fastest coaster on Earth. **Wicked Twister's** 215-foot-high, U-shape track has spiraling 450-degree corkscrews at each end and is known for shooting riders out of the gate at 72 mph—no long, drawn-out, clicking climbs into the clouds. When **Millennium Force** debuted in 2000 it was the world's fastest and highest coaster, reaching a height of 310 feet and speeds of 93 mph.

These three coasters are Cedar Point's stars. Hundreds of people wait between two and five hours for the privilege of riding them. Those visiting during the peak summer months may spend most of their day in line. If you can't wait until the hype dies down, ride as soon as the park opens or right before closing when wait times are shortest. But be aware that you're unlikely ever to wait less than 2 hours.

Coaster fans find lots to love outside of these rides; in fact, many of Cedar Point's most enjoyable coasters are not among its newest ones. The **Blue Streak,** the park's oldest, and **Gemini,** with twin tracks, are popular with wooden coaster enthusiasts and offer lots of hands-in-the-air fun. **Mean Streak,** a lurching wooden mammoth with a track that weaves in and out of its own supports, is as marvelous to look at as it is wild to ride.

Cedar Point's suspended steel coasters include the **Iron Dragon,** which swings its passengers over a misty lagoon, and **Raptor,** which leaves its riders' feet dangling free and flips them through corkscrew rolls and inverted loops. **Disaster Transport** whips passengers along in complete darkness, and **Corkscrew** twists through the center of the park, flipping screaming riders upside down over the heads of ogling pedestrians. **Mantis** passengers travel at 60 mph over hairpin turns, through loops and upside down, all while strapped in a standing position. And the massive 205-foot-tall **Magnum XL-200** offers unsurpassed views of Lake Erie before plunging riders into the abyss.

You can easily plan an exciting day around just these second-tier coasters, where wait times range from 10 minutes to 2 hours. If you plan to combine them with the park's biggies, cluster your visit to the less popular coasters during the busiest times of day. In any case, check out the estimated wait times posted at the entrance of each ride to make planning easier. And while you're standing in line decide where you'll go next so you don't waste time wandering around.

— Amy S. Eckert

13, Milan, tel. 419/499–2135, www.tomedison.org. $5. June–Aug., Tues.–Sat. 10–5, Sun. 1–5; Feb., Mar., Sept. and Oct., Tues.–Sun. 1–5; Nov. and Dec., Wed.–Sun. 1–4.

Firelands Winery Firelands Winery and tasting room pour samples of both whites and reds, all grown in Firelands vineyards on Isle St. George in western Lake Erie. > 917 Bardshar Rd., Sandusky, tel. 800/548–9463 or 419/625–5474, www.firelandswinery.com. Free. June–Sept., Mon.–Sat. 9–5, Sun. 1–5; Oct.–Dec., Mon.–Sat. 9–5; Jan.–May, weekdays 9–5, Sat. 10–4.

Follett House Museum At this research center in the home of Oran Follett, one of the founders of the Republican Party, you can view artifacts and drawings from Johnson's Island Prison, which housed captured Confederate officers during the Civil War. The 1830s Greek Revival house also displays period housewares, toys, clothing and furnishings. > 404 Wayne St., off Rte. 6, Sandusky, tel. 419/627–9608, www.sandusky.lib.oh.us. Free. June–Aug., Tues.–Sat. noon–4; Apr., May, and Sept.–Dec., Sat. noon–4, Sun. 1–4.

Milan Historical Museum Take a trip to the 19th century in this cluster of seven restored buildings, a full city block's worth of history that might best be described as a museum complex. The 1846 home of Dr. Leman Galpin, the physician who attended Thomas Edison's birth, houses three floors of 19th-century artifacts. The Doll and Toy House has 350 dolls of china, wax and papier-mâché. The Lockwood, Smith & Company General Store is a replica 1800s town market, where prescriptions, fabric, tools, and dry goods are on display. And the Blacksmith's Shop and Carriage Shop house smithy's tools, buggies, and farm implements. > 10 Edison Dr., Milan, tel. 419/499–2968, www.milanhist.org. $5. June–Aug., Tues.–Sat. 10–5, Sun. 1–5; Apr., May, Sept., and Oct., Tues.–Sun. 1–5.

Museum of Carousel Art & History Riding an antique carousel is just the beginning of the fun at this unique museum; you can also talk with wood carvers as they create new horses and restore old ones. A guided tour and changing carousel exhibits round out the experience. > Corner of Rte. 6 and Jackson St., Sandusky, tel. 419/626–6111, www.merrygoroundmuseum.org. $4. Memorial Day–Labor Day, Mon.–Sat. 11–5, Sun. noon–5; Labor Day–Dec., Wed.–Sat. 11–5, Sun. noon–5; Jan. and Feb., Sat. 11–5, Sun. noon–5.

Old Woman Creek National Estuarine Research Reserve and State Nature Preserve Northwestern Ohio was known as the Great Black Swamp until the mid-19th century, when a massive drainage system nearly eliminated the natural wetlands. Old Woman Creek at its junction with Lake Erie remains as a rare example of a Great Lakes freshwater estuary. The reserve and nature preserve serves as a scientific research center and a public indoor nature center. You can also hike the trails that run through the reserve's forest. > 2514 Cleveland Rd., off Rte. 6, Huron, tel. 419/433–4601, www.ohiodnr.com. Free. Visitor center: Wed.–Sun. 1–5; Preserve: Daily 8–5.

Sand Hill Vineyard The vineyards and the tasting facility are part of a farm property dating back to the early 1800s. You can sample wines and tour the old threshing barn. > 6413 Hayes Ave. (Rte. 4), 1 mi south of Rte. 2, Sandusky, tel. 419/626–8500. Free. Mon.–Thurs. 11–6, Fri. and Sat. 11–8.

Tours

Goodtime I Goodtime Island Cruises depart from downtown Sandusky Memorial Day through Labor Day. Day-long, island-hopping tours leave daily, exploring Sandusky Bay and making brief stops at Kelleys Island and Put-in-Bay. Shorter,

5-hour dance cruises head out Friday evenings and are limited to those age 21 and older. Day-long cruises cost $23; dance cruises cost $14. > Jackson St. Pier, tel. 800/446–3140 or 419/625–9692, www.goodtimeboat.com.

Lake Erie Circle Tour This 200-mi driving tour around the Lake Erie shore, which stretches along the entire length of Ohio's coast, follows Scenic Routes 2 and 6 in Sandusky and the surrounding area. You'll see views of Lake Erie, and the drive will take you through or near several nature preserves, including the DuPont Marsh, Erie Sand Barrens, and Old Woman Creek sanctuaries. To get the tour map, call or visit the Web site, and then plot your route. > Tel. 419/625–2984 or 800/255–3743, www.circle-erie.com.

Underground Railroad Tour Sandusky's proximity to Lake Erie, two rivers, and several railroad lines made the city an important destination on the Underground Railroad for fugitive slaves hoping to escape to Canada. You can visit many of the safe houses within Sandusky on a walking tour, or take a car and include the sites in nearby Huron. Write or call the Sandusky–Erie County Visitor & Convention Bureau for a brochure, map, and more information. > 4424 Milan Rd., Suite A, Sandusky, tel. 800/255–3743 or 419/625–2984, www.sanduskyohiocedarpoint.com.

Sports

BOATING

Fishing, sailing, and powerboating are very popular pastimes around Cedar Point in summer. It's no surprise, given the city is surrounded on three sides by Lake Erie, one of the world's largest freshwater lakes. If you have the time to explore, consider heading northwest to one of Ohio's Lake Erie islands.

Cedar Point Marina This large marina, connected by a boardwalk to the amusement park, has everything a boater might need—fuel, equipment, groceries, a restaurant, and short-term boat dockage. > 1 Cedar Point Rd., Sandusky, tel. 419/627–2334 or 888/273–6257, www.cedarpoint.com.

Cranberry Creek Marina In addition to offering complete marine services, Cranberry Creek has boat rentals. > 4319 Cleveland Rd. E, Huron, tel. 419/433–3932, www.cranberrycreekmarina.com.

Save the Date

JUNE–OCTOBER

Sandusky Farmer's Market and Bazaar From mid-June through the end of October you can find locally grown produce, crafts, and specialty items, like honey and black walnuts, at the Farmer's Market downtown. The market is held every Saturday 8–noon. > E. Market and Hancock Sts., tel. 419/625–1825.

JULY

July 4th Stars and Stripes Celebration Sandusky's annual celebration incorporates food and craft booths and an Independence Day parade in the heart of the city's downtown. > Tel. 419/625–3961.

Pioneers of Sawcreek Mill A deluxe convention center and vacation resort in nearby Huron, Sawcreek Mill steps back in time to the late 1700s at its annual pioneer days reenactment. Costumed actors display 18th-century clothing and demonstrate the cooking and daily living of the Native Americans, mountainmen, buckskinners, and other settlers of that era. Admission is free. > Sawmill Creek Resort, 400 Sawmill Creek Rd., Huron, tel. 800/729–6455, www.sawmillcreek.com.

WHERE TO STAY

Breakers Express Staying at one of Cedar Point's resorts has its advantages—you'll be less than a 5-minute drive from the park. There are few fancy amenities at Breakers Express, the least expensive of the Cedar Point resorts, but the hotel's location, access to Cedar Point Beach, and a Snoopy-shape pool make this a popular choice with families. Ask about ticket packages. > 1201 Cedar Point Dr., Sandusky 44870, tel. 419/627–2106, www.cedarpoint.com. 350 rooms. Cable TV, pool, hot tub, video game room, laundry facilities. D, MC, V. Closed mid-Oct.–Apr. $–$$$

Hotel Breakers When this hotel opened its doors in 1905, it claimed to be "the largest and greatest hotel on the Great Lakes." It's still impressive, with its Tiffany stained-glass windows and four-story rotunda with waterfall. Every room has a balcony—most have a view of Lake Erie. Kids like the Peanuts floor, where there are rooms with Peanuts characters on the walls, and a 1950s-style ice cream parlor called Beaches and Cream. The hotel is the most convenient of the Cedar Point resorts—a 2-minute walk takes you to the park entrance. Ask about ticket packages. > 1 Cedar Point Dr., Sandusky 44870, tel. 419/627–2106, www.cedarpoint.com. 650 rooms. 2 restaurants, café, coffee shop, grocery, ice cream parlor, pizzeria, some in-room hot tubs, microwaves, refrigerators, cable TV, 3 pools (1 indoor), lake, outdoor hot tub, spa, beach, marina, video game room, shops, laundry facilities, concierge, meeting rooms. D, MC, V. Closed mid-Oct.–Apr. $$$–$$$$

Sandcastle Suites Hotel At this lakefront Cedar Point hotel, every room is a suite, each with a screened-in balcony or patio, and a sofa bed. You can easily walk to the Cedar Point entrance gate, or to the Cedar Point beach adjacent to Hotel Breakers. Ask about ticket packages. > 1 Cedar Point Dr., Sandusky 44870, tel. 419/627–2109, www.cedarpoint.com. 187 suites. Café, some in-room hot tubs, some microwaves, refrigerators, cable TV, tennis courts, pool, outdoor hot tub, spa, beach, bar, shops. D, MC, V. Closed mid-Oct.–Apr. $$$$

AROUND SANDUSKY

Clarion Inn The Clarion Inn is near enough to Cedar Point to be convenient (10 minutes by car), but its proximity to shopping and dining make it a popular alternative to the amusement park mecca. The adjacent Sandusky Mall and eight-screen movie theater are popular additions for families with teenagers. A garden area with fountains provides a relaxing end to a busy day. > 1119 Sandusky Mall Blvd., tel. 419/625–6280 or 800/252–7466, fax 419/625–9080, www.clarionsandusky.com. 143 rooms. Restaurant, some in-room data ports, some microwaves, some refrigerators, cable TV with movies, indoor pool, exercise equipment, hot tub, dance club, video game room, laundry service, convention center, meeting rooms, some pets allowed. AE, D, DC, MC, V. $$–$$$

Great Bear Lodge Ohio's only indoor water park might well be a destination in itself, especially if you're traveling with kids. Seven multistory water slides, five pools, and more than 50 guest-activated water effects (like squirting water guns) provide hours of entertainment, rain or shine. A Northern lodge theme permeates the all-suites hotel, from its log furniture to its stone fireplaces and totem poles. Room rates include unlimited access to the water park. > 4600 Milan Rd. (Rte. 250), Sandusky 44870, tel. 888/779–2327 or 419/609–6000, www.greatbearlodge.com. 271 suites. 2 restaurants, in-room data ports, some in-room hot tubs, microwaves, refrigerators, cable TV with movies and video games, 5 pools (1 outdoor), exercise equipment,

2 hot tubs, lounge, video game room, shops, laundry facilities, Internet, meeting rooms; no smoking. AE, D, DC, MC, V. **$$$$**

Holiday Inn Holidome If you still have some energy left after your day at Cedar Point, the Holiday Inn Holidome is the hotel for you. The Holidome appeals to families with its sports facilities and its Kidsuites, including separate children's sleeping quarters designed to look like castles. > 5513 Milan Rd. (Rte. 250), Sandusky 44870, tel. 419/626–6671 or 800/465–4329, fax 419/626–9780, www.holidayinn-sandusky.com. 175 rooms, 15 suites. Restaurant, room service, in-room data ports, some in-room hot tubs, microwaves, refrigerators, cable TV, miniature golf, 2 pools (1 indoor), gym, hot tub, badminton, billiards, Ping-Pong, bar, video game room, laundry facilities, laundry service, business services, meeting rooms. AE, D, DC, MC, V. **$$–$$$**

Radisson Harbour Inn Each of the guest rooms at the Harbour Inn has a private deck or balcony, most of which look out over Sandusky Bay. The hotel is a 10-minute drive from Cedar Point, but it also appeals to business travelers with amenities such as writing desks and extra work space. Ask about Cedar Point ticket packages. > 2001 Cleveland Rd. (Rte. 6), Sandusky 44870, tel. 419/627–2500 or 800/333–3333, fax 419/627–0745, www.radisson.com/sanduskyoh. 237 rooms, 49 suites. Restaurant, café, room service, in-room data ports, some in-room hot tubs, cable TV with movies and video games, indoor pool, lake, gym, hot tub, dock, marina, lounge, sports bar, video game room, shops, laundry facilities, business services, convention center, meeting rooms. AE, D, DC, MC, V. **$$–$$$**

Sawmill Creek Resort A sprawling resort hotel, Sawmill Creek is about 20 minutes east of Sandusky on the shores of Lake Erie. Interiors are decorated in Native American and wildlife motifs. Sawmill Creek provides a relaxing contrast to the busy area around Cedar Point. Relax at the lodge's outdoor pool, play a round of golf, or check out the marina. > 400 Saw Mill Creek, off Rte. 6, Huron 44839, tel. 419/433–3800 or 800/729–6455, www.sawmillcreek.com. 192 rooms, 48 suites. 3 restaurants, some in-room data ports, some in-room hot tubs, some refrigerators, cable TV, 18-hole golf course, 2 pools (1 indoor), lake, gym, beach, dock, marina, bar, pub, sports bar, video game room, shops, laundry facilities, business services, convention center, meeting rooms. AE, D, DC, MC, V. **$$$–$$$$**

CAMPING

Camper Village Part of the Cedar Point resort system, Camper Village makes for ideal RV camping—easy back-in and pull-through sites, and a number of paved sites—but there are few good tent sites. The campground is within easy walking distance of Cedar Point's entrance. Ask about ticket packages. > 1 Cedar Point Dr., Sandusky 44870, tel. 419/627–2106 or 419/627–2109, www.cedarpoint.com. 59 full hook-ups, 224 partial hook-ups. Flush toilets, full hook-ups, partial hook-ups (electric), dump station, drinking water, laundry facilities, showers, grills, picnic tables, electricity, public telephone, general store, swimming (lake). Reservations essential. AE, D, MC, V. Closed late Oct.–Apr. ¢

Lighthouse Point Adjacent to Camper Village, Lighthouse Point is best described as a luxury campground. The resort is at the tip of Cedar Point peninsula and near its 1862 lighthouse. New England nautical is the theme, from weathered-looking lakeside cottages to the smaller, rustic cabins. Cottages and cabins come equipped with microwaves, refrigerators, and sleep up to six. The campground, with its boat dock, hot tub, and video game room, is within easy walking distance of the Cedar Point amusement parks. Ask about ticket packages. > 1 Cedar Point Dr., Sandusky 44870, tel. 419/627–2106, www.cedarpoint.com. 59 full hook-ups, 50 cottages, 10 cabins. Flush toilets, full hook-ups, drinking water, laundry facilities, showers, grills, picnic tables, electricity, public telephone, general store, playground, pool, swimming (lake). Reservations essential. AE, D, MC, V. Closed late Oct.–Apr. ¢

WHERE TO EAT

Bay Harbor Inn The bayside restaurant just outside Cedar Point amusement park is a favorite of park visitors: its elegance is welcome after a hard day's play, and the views of Sandusky Harbor and the marina can't be beat. Seafood dominates the menu, but there are also pasta, filet mignon, and New York strip steak. Cedar Point admission is not required. There's a kids' menu and no smoking. > Cedar Point Marina, 1 Cedar Point Dr., Sandusky, tel. 419/625–6373. AE, D, MC, V. No lunch. $$$$

Damon's Grill at Battery Park This sports bar chain has wall-size big-screen televisions, local sports team memorabilia, and electronic trivia games. Try the onion loaf appetizer, a tasty tangle of thin onion straws that are breaded and deep fried. Dock space. > 701 E. Water St., Sandusky, tel. 419/627–2424. AE, D, MC, V. $–$$$

DeMore's Fish Den Known for Great Lakes fish and clam chowder, DeMore's catch comes fresh from its own wholesale distributorship, the largest for yellow perch in the Midwest. Fresh perch and walleye are specialties, as is the Giant Perch Sandwich. Dine casually indoors, or enjoy lakeshore breezes on the outdoor patio. There's a kids' menu. > 302 W. Perkins Ave., Sandusky, tel. 419/626–8861. MC, V. ¢–$

Salmon Run Restaurant It won't surprise you to learn that Salmon Run considers salmon their specialty—chargrilled Nova Scotia salmon to be precise. Other favorites from the restaurant's lengthy menu include Lake Erie walleye, perch, and New York Strip glazed with Jamaican rum. The great food is complemented by fabulous views of Wilderness Creek and live weekend entertainment. > 400 Sawmill Creek, in the Lodge at Sawmill Creek Resort, Huron, tel. 419/433–3800. AE, D, DC, MC, V. $$–$$$$

ESSENTIALS

Getting Here

In the rural Midwest, the car is still king, and so it is in northern Ohio. The easiest and most convenient way to get to Cedar Point and to explore the area around Sandusky is via personal automobile. Mass transit is unavailable; public transportation, such as air, train, and bus service, is limited and inconvenient. And without a car, it's virtually impossible to explore the historic sites in Milan, the natural areas in Huron, or the wineries south of Sandusky.

If traveling by personal auto isn't possible, however, your best option is to select a hotel on Cedar Point property or immediately adjacent to it (such as the Radisson Harbour Inn). Rely on taxis and hotel or airport shuttles to take you to your hotel, and travel by foot or via hotel shuttle to the park.

BY BUS

Traveling into Sandusky via bus is not recommended. Although Greyhound does travel into Sandusky, its terminal is some distance from Cedar Point. There's no ticketing or baggage services at the Sandusky Greyhound station, and you will need to rely on taxi service to the park.

Greyhound travels from Toledo or Cleveland to Sandusky nearly every day. The trip takes about 90 minutes and costs $28 round-trip.

BUS DEPOT **Sandusky Greyhound Terminal** > 6513 Milan Rd. (Rte. 250), Sandusky, tel. 419/625–6907.

BUS LINES **Greyhound Lines** > Tel. 800/229–9424, www.greyhound.com.

BY CAR

To get to Cedar Point, take the Ohio Turnpike (I–80/90) to Exit 118(7) and follow U.S. 250 north; or take I–80/90 to Exit 110(6A) and follow Route 4 north. From either direction, simply follow the signs.

Try to arrive in Sandusky well before or after amusement park opening times, especially in July and August. Driving can be a nightmare along the major routes into the park, including Routes 2 and 6, but especially along Route 4 and Route 250. Stop-and-go traffic is the rule for miles before you reach the park's entrance if you arrive within an hour of opening time (a frustration only compounded by the kids in the back seat complaining, "I thought you said we were there!"). Instead, arrive the afternoon prior to your park visit. Check into your room, relax by the pool, have dinner—and avoid the traffic. Similarly, traffic along the same routes will be backed up at Cedar Point's closing time.

Parking within Cedar Point costs $8 per day for automobiles, and $13 per day for campers or cars with trailers, with fees waived for guests of any Cedar Point resorts or campgrounds except Breakers Express. Outside of park grounds, parking is generally free and easy to find.

If your weekend plans are limited exclusively to Cedar Point, you might not need transportation once you've arrived. Instead, choose a Cedar Point resort hotel. Entrance to the park is within walking distance.

Traffic moves quickly along the Ohio Turnpike. But if you're not in a hurry, you might consider the more scenic east–west Routes 2 and 6 instead, a scenic drive taking in broad views of Lake Erie and its islands.

BY TRAIN

Traveling into Sandusky via train is not recommended. Although Amtrak travels into Sandusky, its terminal is some distance from Cedar Point. There's no ticketing or baggage service at the station, and you will need to rely on taxi service to the park.

Sandusky and Erie County are serviced by four daily Amtrak trains. Amtrak's Lake Shore Limited stops twice daily with service to and from Chicago, Toledo, Cleveland, and points farther afield. Round-trip train fare costs about $30 from Cleveland, $75 from Columbus, $100 from Cincinnati.

TRAIN LINES **Amtrak** > Tel. 800/872–7245, www.amtrak.com.

TRAIN STATIONS **Sandusky Depot** > Depot St. at Hayes Ave., Sandusky.

Visitor Information

Sandusky/Erie County Visitors and Convention Bureau > 4424 Milan Rd., Suite A, 44870, tel. 419/625–2984 or 800/255–3743, www.sanduskyohiocedarpoint.com.

Cleveland

Cleveland is 128 mi northeast of Columbus and 249 mi northeast of Cincinnati.

4

By Joe Frey

FORGET THE JOKES about the Cuyahoga River catching fire and the city's default. Forget the scores of derisive monikers. Cleveland provides an affordable and diverse getaway in any season.

It's a year-round destination—although walking around the city is much easier without several inches of snow and a biting wind coming off Lake Erie—with the banks of the Cuyahoga and the lake shore providing seasonal land- and water-based activities, while the city's cultural institutions are open throughout the year.

Lake Erie borders the city to the north, while the Cuyahoga River roughly divides the city's east and west sides. Getting around town is relatively easy, thanks to the three interstates and multiple broad boulevards that connect east, west, and south neighborhoods. The farthest point west is no more than a 25-minute car ride from the farthest point east within the city limits.

Cleveland's diverse neighborhood pockets host renowned destinations, and within those neighborhoods shops and eateries reflect the community's residents.

Downtown Cleveland is a study in economic, cultural, and architectural revitalization and staying power, with the Rock and Roll Hall of Fame and Museum, Jacobs Field, and Gund Arena (known as the Gateway complex), and the resurgence of the Terminal Tower as a shopping destination acting as catalysts during the mid-1990s. Swanky hotels, numerous restaurants, and popular night spots sprouted next to those three institutions, and that trend continues to expand from the city's center.

Playhouse Square Center, a 10-minute walk east of the Terminal Tower, is the nation's second-largest theater district and hosts bound-for-Broadway shows and the New York hits alike. Four grand old theaters, which have been restored to their former glory, make up the complex. Although the theater district buzzes year-round, traffic really picks up just as winter settles into the city. The Broadway Series generally starts in September and runs through April, with the occasional musical performing in summer.

The Warehouse District and the Flats are the city's best known nightlife areas, but University Circle (a 15-minute drive east of downtown) and Ohio City (just west of the Flats) host their share of lively establishments, too. All are distinct in flavor and clientele, with young people gravitating to the Flats, young professionals hitting the Warehouse District and Ohio City, and a creative class venturing to University Circle. The Flats is a particular hot spot in summer because of its city and lake views, riverfront boardwalk, and superb people-watching venues.

Jacobs Field, the home of the Cleveland Indians, is one of the finest examples of the retro ball park design that major-league baseball clubs began craving in the mid-'90s. Most of the 43,000-plus seats provide excellent viewing; the modern concessions, family-oriented activities areas, and the park's inviting brick-and-steel facade solidify it as a highly popular destination from April through October.

University Circle—so called because of Case Western Reserve University's presence there—is the city's arts hub. Numerous museums, gardens, and cultural stops reside there, including the incomparable Cleveland Museum of Art.

Cleveland's parks and green spaces complement the city's neighborhoods, while providing excellent access to Lake Erie. Cleveland Lakefront State Park stretches from West Boulevard on the city's mid-west side to Euclid Beach on the city's far east end. Several satellite parks operate within the main state park. The parks are packed late spring through early autumn.

WHAT TO SEE & DO

Children's Museum of Cleveland Geared for kids ages one to eight, the museum's hands-on exhibits introduce children to science, technology, and cultural diversity. > 10730 Euclid Ave., University Circle, tel. 216/791–7114, www.museum4kids.com. $5. Daily 10–5.

Cleveland Botanical Garden The tranquillity, vibrancy, and soothing power of six permanent outdoor beds, including a Japanese "dry rock" garden and rose garden, are the mainstays of this sprawling urban horticultural oasis. Two rare ecosystems— a Madagascarian spiny desert and a Costa Rican cloud forest—await you within the confines of the Eleanor Armstrong Smith Glasshouse. The staff also reinvents six "living gardens" every other year as part of the outdoor flower showcase, held in late spring. > 11030 East Blvd., University Circle, tel. 216/721–1600, www.cbgarden.org. $7. Daily 10–5.

Cleveland Metroparks Zoo This zoo comprises 3,300 animals living in naturalistic habitats—giraffes and zebras roam in the African Plains Savanna, kangaroos hop around in the Australian children's area, and gray wolves and beavers occupy the Wolf Wilderness. Rain drenches two indoor acres of tropical Asia, Africa, and South America every 12 minutes in the Rain Forest. More than 300 reptiles and 10,000 plants live and are on display in the simulated environments, which are spread among three levels. An impressive waterfall spills from 25 feet above the "jungle's" floor. > 3900 Wildlife Way, Cleveland, tel. 216/661–6500, www.clemetzoo.com. $9. Daily 10–5.

Cleveland Museum of Art Cleveland's crown jewel is at the center of its cultural hub, University Circle. In its 70 galleries, the museum presents art chronologically, from the Mediterranean antiquity to the present. The museum is known for its medieval Asian, European, and pre-Columbian collections. Its holdings include works by Picasso, Michelangelo, Monet, and Van Gogh. Other popular exhibits are mummies, African masks, and medieval armor and weapons. > 11150 East Blvd., University Circle, tel. 216/421–7340, www.clevelandart.org. Free. Tues.–Sun. 10–5, Wed. and Fri. until 9 PM.

Cleveland Museum of Natural History A 70-foot-long dinosaur skeleton and a model of the world's oldest human fossil—"Lucy"—are among the treasures housed here. The collection contains artifacts and environmental samples from nearly 1,700 sites and documents more than 10,000 years of prehistoric life in Ohio. The largest specimen is the 3,600-year-old Ringler dugout, one of the oldest watercraft found in

North America. The museum is also known for its 1,500-piece collection of rare gems, and the Shafran Planetarium & Astronomy Exhibit Hall. Planetarium shows cost an additional $3 with your museum admission. > 1 Wade Oval, University Circle, tel. 216/231–4600, www.cmnh.org. $6.50. Mon.–Sat. 10–5, Sun. noon–5.

Cleveland Play House The oldest regional theater in America, founded in 1915, is an architectural landmark. A 1983 addition, designed by architect Phillip Johnson, incorporates four performance spaces under one roof. Throughout the year, there are productions of musicals, comedies, and classic and contemporary dramas. > 8500 Euclid Ave., Fairfax, tel. 216/795–7000, www.clevelandplayhouse.com.

Dunham Tavern Museum Now a curious structure among the modern buildings and warehouses in Cleveland's Midtown District, the museum is filled with artifacts from the Dunham family, the original residents. Walk the Cleveland Botanical Garden–manicured grounds for vignettes of early-19th-century life. > 6709 Euclid Ave., University Circle, tel. 216/431–1060, www.dunhamtavern.org. $2. Tours, Wed. and Sun. 1–4.

Edgewater Park Catch the best west-side, land-based view of Cleveland's skyline from upper Edgewater on the bluffs above Lake Erie's shore. Lower Edgewater is where you will find the park's swimming beach and summer sun–bathed playgrounds. A tree-lined path that buzzes with walkers, runners, and rollerbladers in summer connects the upper and lower parks. The lower park has a fishing pier, bait shop, and fitness course. The stiff wind off Lake Erie attracts kite flyers, boomerang enthusiasts, windsurfers, and the occasional hang glider. Picnic facilities are also available. > 8000 W. Memorial Shoreway, west of downtown Cleveland, accessible via the Shoreway's Edgewater Park and Edgewater Dr. exits, Cudell/Edgewater, tel. 216/881–8141, www.ohiostateparks.org. Free. Daily dawn–dusk.

Great Lakes Brewery The six buildings that make up the brewing complex were stables and a warehouse for the Schlather Brewing Company at the turn of the 20th century. The buildings have been restored to expose the grandeur of the gabled roofs and cork walls. The two-story brew house has full glass walls so you can see the brewmasters at work. The brewery's tap room houses artifacts excavated from the old Schlather Brewing Company site, including the building's hallmark keystones, beer bottles, and brass serving plates. The restaurant and bar attached to the brewery is smoke-free, a testament to the owners' renowned environmentally friendly practices. Tours leave every half hour. > 2516 Market Ave., Ohio City, tel. 216/771–4404, www.greatlakesbrewing.com. Free. Fri. 5–9, Sat. 2–8.

Great Lakes Science Center More than 300 interactive exhibits and daily demonstrations await you at this indoor-outdoor educational center. Science and technology displays include a bridge of fire, an indoor tornado, and an especially good area that focuses on the environment of the Great Lakes region. A 320-seat OMNIMAX theater is also on the premises. > 601 Erieside Ave., North Coast District, tel. 216/694–2000, www.glsc.org. $7.95. Daily 9:30–5:30.

HealthSpace Cleveland Formerly the Health Museum of Cleveland, HealthSpace has exhibits on wellness and nutrition, as well as an interactive theater, Head First!, named for its cranial shape. > 8911 Euclid Ave., Fairfax, tel. 216/231–5010, www.healthspacecleveland.org. $7.50. Weekdays 10–5, weekends noon–5.

International Women's Air & Space Museum The exhibits in Burke Airport's lobby and concourse chronicle centuries of female flight, from Napoleonic balloon captains to Space Age fliers. The museum is particularly rich in the recent history of female astronauts. > Burke Lakefront Airport, 1501 N. Marginal Rd., Room 165, North Coast District, tel. 216/623–1111, www.iwasm.org. Free. Exhibits, daily during Burke hrs; office and research, weekdays 10–4.

Karamu House Serving Cleveland for more than 75 years, Karamu House is the nation's oldest African-American cultural institution. Its theater program performs a plays by Amiri Baraka, Ossie Davis, and Langston Hughes. > 2355 E. 89th St., Fairfax, tel. 216/795–7070, www.karamu.com.

Lake View Cemetery A monument to Ohio native and former President James A. Garfield stands at his tomb in Lake View Cemetery. Some of Cleveland's most renowned citizens, including oil tycoon John D. Rockefeller and John Hay, President William McKinley's Secretary of State, are buried here. The Wade Chapel's interior was designed by Louis Comfort Tiffany. Tours of the grounds, cemetery, and architecture are available, weather permitting. > 12316 Euclid Ave., University Circle, tel. 216/421–2665, www.lakeviewcemetery.com. Daily 7:30–5:30, until dusk in summer.

NASA Glenn Visitor Center Space suits worn by astronauts who orbited the Earth and a moon rock are displayed at this out-of-this-world attraction. It also has a microgravity science laboratory and spacecraft replicas. Named after Ohio astronaut John Glenn, the center is west of the airport. > 21000 Brookpark Rd., North Coast District, tel. 216/433–2000, www.grc.nasa.gov. Free. Weekdays 9–4, Sat. 10–3, Sun. 1–5.

Peter B. Lewis Building Hidden from busy Euclid Avenue and East Boulevard, and insulated within Case Western Reserve University's campus, this Frank Gehry–designed structure is as much a work of art as it is a functional headquarters for the Weatherhead School of Management. A twisted and flowing stainless-steel roof caps the undulating brick and glass edifice, creating architectural movement and a centerpiece for Case Western's campus. The building is named for the chairman of Progressive Corporation, Peter Lewis, a renowned philanthropist and supporter of arts and cultural institutions. > Intersection of Ford Dr. and Bellflower Rd. University Circle, tel. 216/368–4771, weatherhead.cwru.edu. Free. Tours weekends 1–3.

Playhouse Square Center The second-largest theater district in the United States, Playhouse Square houses four beautifully restored, landmark theaters: large Broadway musicals play the **Palace Theatre** and **State Theatre**; the **Allen Theatre** and **Hanna Theatre** stage more intimate shows. The center hosts the Cleveland Opera, dance companies, pop performers, first-run and touring Broadway shows, and several theater companies, including the Great Lakes Theater Festival.

Reduced-price tickets for many of the Playhouse Square Center stages are available at **Ctix Booth** (Star Plaza, 1302 Euclid Ave., tel. 216/771–9118)

Free tours of the theaters are available the first Saturday and Sunday of every month, departing every 15 minutes beginning at 10 AM. > 1501 Euclid Ave., Downtown, tel. 216/771–4444, www.playhousesquare.com. Tours free, show prices vary. Weekends 10–11:30 AM.

Rock and Roll Hall of Fame and Museum The I. M. Pei–designed building has everything from the ridiculous (Jim Morrison's Cub Scout uniform) to the sublime (John Lennon's hand-written lyrics for "Lucy in the Sky with Diamonds"). Stage costumes that once belonged to Chuck Berry and Iggy Pop, handwritten lyrics by Jimi Hendrix, Janis Joplin's Porsche, and the Sun recording studio, where Elvis Presley, Carl Perkins, and Roy Orbison made their first records are among the museum's holdings. Interactive kiosks provide video and sound explorations of performers' contributions to the rock genre. > 1 Key Plaza, 751 Erieside Ave., North Coast District, tel. 216/781–7625, www.rockhall.com. $18. Daily 10–5:30, Wed. until 9 PM.

Second City Improvisational- and sketch-comedy fans sit cabaret-style at Cleveland's Second City outpost for performances on Wednesday–Sunday nights. > 2037 E. 14th St., Downtown, tel. 216/466–2208, www.secondcity.com/theatre/cleveland.

Severance Hall A great orchestra deserves a great concert hall, and that's what Severance is to the Cleveland Orchestra. Renovations melded the hall's interior with the art deco style of its exterior, making the performance center as pleasing to look at as it is to listen in. Beginning in mid-September, the Orchestra performs works by contemporary and classical composers. > 11001 Euclid Ave., University Circle, tel. 216/231–1111 or 800/686–1141, www.clevelandorch.com.

Steamship *William G. Mather* Museum The former steel-and-coal–carrying behemoth churned through the Great Lakes for 55 years before retiring in 1980. State of the art when she put to sea in 1925, the ship is now a museum displaying how ships were once built and is replete with a brass and oak pilothouse, and an extravagant dining room. The *William G. Mather* is within walking distance of the Great Lakes Science Center and Rock and Roll Hall of Fame. > 1001 E. 9th St. Pier, North Coast District, tel. 216/574–6262, wgmather.nhlink.net. $5.50. May, Sept., and Oct., Fri. and Sat. 10–5:30, Sun. noon–5:30; June–Aug., Mon.–Sat. 10–5:30, Sun. noon–5:30.

Terminal Tower Cleveland's oldest skyscraper provides a noble view from its 42nd-floor observatory. Peer over Lake Erie or to the boundaries of the Western Reserve territory to the east. The tower was completed in 1930 and rises 52 stories. Pick up tickets at the Tower City Center visitor center in Public Square. > 50 Public Sq., Downtown, tel. 216/621–7981, www.towercitycenter.com. $1. May–Sept., weekends 11–4:30; Oct.–Apr., weekends 11–3:30.

USS *COD* Unaltered from its battle-ready state—bunks, guns, and all—this World War II submarine is docked on the banks of Lake Erie. Tours are available. Shore exhibits include the original torpedoes and a periscope with a view. > West of Burke Lakefront Airport, accessible via N. Marginal Rd., North Coast District, tel. 216/566–8770, www.usscod.org. $6. May 1–Sept. 30, daily 10–5.

Western Reserve Historical Society Museum This museum, which resides in two Italian Renaissance–style mansions, is considered Cleveland's oldest cultural institution. It chronicles the history of the Western Reserve, a tract of land on the south shore of Lake Erie in Northeast Ohio, and houses a library and a top-notch auto and aviation collection.

You can see how the rich—and their servants—lived at the **History Museum**. The museum includes the Chisholm Halle Costume Wing, one of the nation's top-ranked collections, with garments from the late 1700s to the present. Guided tours of the Hay-McKinney Mansion are given every day between noon and 5.

Car Collectors magazine has called the **Crawford Auto-Aviation Museum** one of the top 10 collections in the nation. Nearly 200 antique, vintage, and classic automobiles, from Model T's and the first enclosed automobile to late-model Jaguars, are on display. There are models dating to 1895, when Cleveland was a center of car manufacturing. The aviation collection includes a 1912 Curtiss Hydroaeroplane.

The **Library of the Western Reserve Historical Society** (Tues.–Sat. 9–5, Wed. until 9 PM, Sun. noon–5) has more than 6 million items, including prints and photographs, manuscripts and newspapers, focusing primarily on Ohio's history. The library's vast collection of genealogical materials has made it one of the largest family-history research centers in the country.

One admission ticket covers all three museums at the complex. > 10825 East Blvd., University Circle, tel. 216/721–5722, www.wrhs.org. $7.50. Mon.–Sat. 10–5, Sun. noon–5.

Tours

Goodtime III Lake Erie and the Cuyahoga River are two of Cleveland's greatest assets, and the *Goodtime III* shows them off in style. The largest leisure cruise ship on the Great Lakes winds its way along the "crooked river" and the Erie shore for 2-hour cruises, providing the best skyline views of the city. Regularly scheduled tours begin at noon and 3 PM, running June–September. Cost is $15. > 825 E. 9th St. Pier, North Coast District, tel. 216/861–5110, www.goodtimeiii.com.

Jacob's Field Tours Get an insider's view of a magnificent modern, old-style ball park and its state-of-the-art facilities while on this tour. Stops include the visitor's clubhouse, indoor batting cages, and the Indians' dugout. The cost is $6.50, and tours are available May–September. > 2401 Ontario St., Gateway District, tel. 216/420–4385, www.indians.com.

Lolly the Trolley Tours of Cleveland Cleveland is a sprawling city, stretching some 400 blocks east to west, and Lolly the Trolley covers it all. Take a narrated 1- or 2-hour jaunt through the city's streets, catching some of the biggest attractions—the Rock and Roll Hall of Fame, Jacob's Field, the Terminal Tower, and University Circle—along the way. Lolly the Trolley is handicap accessible. Tickets for the daily tours cost $9–$15. > The Powerhouse, Elm St. and Winslow Ave., the Flats, tel. 216/771–4484 or 800/848–0173, www.lollytrolley.com.

Nautica Queen You can eat—and then eat some more—while cruising Lake Erie on this boat with two buffet dining decks and an open-air observation deck. The boat is docked at the west bank of the Flats. Tours are two hours at lunch, three hours during dinner. The ship cruises April–December, and the cost is $34.95–$44.95. > 1153 Main St., the Flats, tel. 216/696–8888 or 800/837–0604, www.nauticaqueen.com.

Walking Tours of Cleveland Get up close and personal with the city's avenues, architecture, neighborhoods, and history on one of these 2-hour strolls through downtown or Ohio City. These walks give you a chance to drink in Cleveland's many works of public art, including the ironic backwards "FREE" stamp at City Hall. Tours begin at 10 AM on Tuesday, Thursday, and Saturday. Cost is $10. > Public Sq., under the clock in front of Tower City, Downtown, tel. 216/575–1189, www.clevelandwalkingtours.com.

Nightlife

Beachland Ballroom This far-east–side intimate ex-ballroom, with its creaky hardwood floor and cathedral ceiling, hosts up-and-coming national and regional music acts of all kinds. It's not uncommon to hear jazz, Afro-beat, punk, and folk all in one weekend. Bands that draw smaller crowds play the **Beachland Tavern** next to the ballroom. A small parking lot adjacent to the ballroom and tavern fills up fast, but there are plenty of spaces along Waterloo and neighboring side streets. > 15711 Waterloo Rd., Cleveland, tel. 216/383–1124, www.beachlandballroom.com.

Nautica Entertainment Complex The 11 venues that comprise this complex dominate the West Bank of the Flats. The concert stage at **Nautica Pavilion** (tel. 216/241–5555) hosts national rock and pop acts throughout the spring, summer, and early autumn. **Shooters on the Water** (tel. 216/861–6900), an indoor-outdoor restaurant and night club, has easily the West Bank's best view of downtown, Lake Erie, the busy Cuyahoga River inlet, and native Clevelanders. Summer is the best time to visit Shooters, enabling you to enjoy the summer lake breeze and din of a bustling entertainment district. Seating is cabaret-style at the comfortable **Improv Comedy Club** (tel. 216/696–4677, www.symfonee.com/Improv/Cleveland/home/Index.aspx). Attentive servers bustle throughout the club, arriving with drinks, but cause little distraction. The Improv's familiar brick wall on stage and white-hot spotlight emphasizes the entertainment, but also reminds the audience that the comedy business can be lonely at times. Dinner is served before the first show every night. For nationally known comedians, buy tickets in advance via the Web site. Even for regional acts, arrive early or be prepared to sit extreme stage right or stage left. > The Powerhouse in the Flats, 2000 Sycamore St., www.nauticaflats.com.

Ohio City New construction melds with old to create this vibrant, revitalized—yet urbanely charming—neighborhood a 2-minute drive across the Cuyahoga River and west of downtown. The centerpiece of this neighborhood's night spots is Market Avenue, which houses the **Great Lakes Brewing Company** (2516 Market Ave., tel. 216/771–4404), a smoke-free restaurant and brewery nationally known as much for its environmentally friendly practices as it is for its ales. Across Market Avenue to the south is the **Flying Fig** (2523 Market Ave., tel. 216/241–4243), where martinis are king and appetizers are irresistible. Arguably the best-stocked wine bar in Cleveland, the **Market Avenue Wine Bar** (2526 Market Ave., tel. 216/696–9463) has a warm, snug interior, and seasonal alfresco seating is ideal for sipping Riesling, Pinot Noir, or Malbec. The city's jazz scene thrives at the **Cleveland Bop Stop** (2920 Detroit Ave., tel. 216/771–6551, www.clevelandbopstop.com). In a unique building that faces Lake Erie, the two-level cabaret seating mixes excellent acoustics with an intimate atmosphere. There's no smoking on the lower level, plenty of free parking in the lot and on Detroit Avenue, a well-stocked bar, and a house vibrato player. > Between Detroit Ave. and Lorain Ave., north to south; between W. 25th St. and W. 30th St., east to west, www.ohiocity.org.

Pickwick & Frolic Restaurant & Club Unique in presentation and scope, this cabaret, martini bar, restaurant, and comedy club brings magic, flair, and entertainment with style to the Gateway neighborhood. Dinner-show packages are available, which provide an intimate magic show, fine cuisine, and preferred seating at Hilarities 4th Street Theatre, located within the establishment. Kevin's Martini Bar, in the basement of Pickwick & Frolic, hosts happy hours 4–7 PM nightly, and houses an impressive selection of fine liquors. Velvety soft decor hushes the bar, despite large crowds. Valet parking ($4) is available and recommended. > 2035 E. 4th St., Gateway District, tel. 216/241–7425, www.pickwickandfrolic.com.

Tremont Professor, Literary, and University are the street-name remnants of an ill-fated plan to put a college in this near-west-side neighborhood. On those streets, however, are fine dining establishments and nightclubs. **Lava Lounge** (1307 Auburn Ave., tel. 216/589–9112), true to its name, sports 1960s-style molten-wax lamps throughout the two-level cozy environment. This trendy establishment hosts a diverse crowd, and is comfortable for a quiet drink. **The Treehouse**'s (820 College Ave., tel. 216/696–2505) signature spectacle is its hand-crafted tree sprouting from the root of the bar. Like most spots in Tremont, expect a house packed with young professionals every Friday and Saturday night. Not to be outdone by its night spot neighbors, Tremont has its own wine bar, too, **806 Wine and Martini Bar** (806 Literary Rd., tel. 216/696–4806). > Between Fairfield and Starkweather, north to south; between W. 7th and W. 14th Sts., east to west.

Warehouse District Cleveland's trendiest night-spot neighborhood has dance clubs, restaurants, outdoor patios, and rock venues living side-by-side newly renovated l uxury loft apartments, all within a 3-minute walk of the heart of downtown. The unassuming redbrick exterior of the **Funky Buddha** (1360 W. 9th St., tel. 216/776–7777, www.funkybuddhabar.com, $10) belies the thumping-bass electronica interior. The upper and lower levels of this disco throb weekend nights with masses of diverse revelers. The club opens at 10 PM but doesn't hop until midnight. Another venue with a view, the **Velvet Dog** (1280 W. 6th St., tel. 216/664–1116, www.velvetdogcleveland.com) has three options for your entertainment pleasure. The martini bar in the Third Level Lounge is comfortably low-key, DJ-driven house music thumps on the main floor, and the top-floor outdoor patio provides a unique (and seasonal) look at downtown and an excellent dance floor. > Between W. 9th St. and W. 6th St. running east–west; between Lakeside Ave. and Superior Ave. running north–south, www.warehousedistrict.org.

Sports

BASEBALL
Cleveland Indians The Indians, Cleveland's boys of summer, meet their American League opponents at Jacobs Field, a downtown ball park, every April through October. If available, grab tickets in the angled seats down the right- or left-field lines. The bleachers offer excellent viewing of the action, too. Expect to pay $12–$30 for the aforementioned seats. > 2401 Ontario St., Gateway District, tel. 216/420–4487, www.indians.com.

BASKETBALL
Cleveland Cavaliers Cleveland's pro basketball team battles its NBA Eastern Conference rivals at Gund Arena. Tickets cost $10–$75. > 100 Gateway Plaza, Gateway District, tel. 216/420–2000, www.nba.com/cavs/.

FOOTBALL
Cleveland Browns Cleveland's NFL team plays football from September to December at Cleveland Browns Stadium, a modern facility in every sense of the word. Tickets are scarce, but any remaining ones are put on sale on Wednesday the week of the game. Seats in the Dawg Pound, a lively area behind the northeast end zone, are highly desirable. > 1085 W. 3rd St., North Coast District, tel. 440/891–5050 or 888/891–1999, www.clevelandbrowns.com.

HORSE RACING
Thistledown Watch the ponies between March and December, with the Ohio Derby running in June. > 21501 Emery Rd., tel. 216/662–8600, www.thistledown.com.

ROCK CLIMBING
Cleveland Rock Gym So Cleveland's terrain isn't exactly alpine, but the guides here take all comers to rocky outcrops in the Cleveland Metroparks. Outdoor dates are limited to the summer, but the indoor facility, with its indoor climbing wall, is open year-round. The cost of a day pass is $10, and rental equipment and classes are available. The gym is a 10-minute drive from downtown Cleveland. > 21200 St. Clair Ave., Bldg. B3, Euclid, tel. 216/692–3300, www.clevelandrockgym.com.

TOBOGGANING
The Chalet at Mill Stream Run Reservation Zooming down a 1,000-foot sheet of ice is one of the most popular attractions in the Cleveland Metroparks in the middle of winter. The traditional wood toboggans reach speeds of 35 mph–40 mph. The chutes are open between the end of November and February, and the Chalet is 15

minutes south of downtown Cleveland. The cost is $8. > 16200 Valley Pkwy., Strongsville, tel. 440/572–9990, www.clemetparks.com.

Shopping

The Avenue at Tower City Center This renovated train terminal houses an upscale, indoor shopping mall with more than 120 shops and restaurants and an 11-screen movie theater. It's a beautiful space, with a glass-dome ceiling, marble staircases, and brass storefronts. The Terminal Tower building, which was the tallest building in the Midwest in 1930, is attached. > 50 Public Sq., Downtown, tel. 216/771–0033, www.towercitycenter.com/.

Lorain Avenue Antiques District Between West 35th Street and West 85th Street, antiques shops—from statues to furniture—are cropping up as part of the Lorain Avenue renaissance. **The Antiques Arcade** (4125 Lorain Ave., tel. 216/281–6040) and **Century Antiques** (7410 Lorain Ave., tel. 216/281–9145) are stand-outs. > Lorain Ave., between W. 35th St. and W. 85th St., Ohio City.

West Side Market Sample local fare and get in some excellent people-watching, perhaps the best in the city, at this indoor-outdoor market. More than 68 vendors sell everything from lamb chops to cigars in two buildings and an outdoor arcade, which is covered with tarps for the winter. The Grand Market Hall is over 241 feet long, with vaulted ceilings 44 feet high. > 1979 W. 25th St., Gateway District, tel. 216/664–3387, www.westsidemarket.com. Closed Tues., Thurs., Sun.

Save the Date

MARCH

Cleveland International Film Festival Cleveland's celluloid appeal is apparent in big Hollywood films, such as the 2003 release *American Splendor,* and the 1978 classic *Deerhunter,* and its film appreciation is equally robust, as 40,000 film-festival attendees prove every year. The cinemas at the Avenue at Tower City Center serve as the festival's headquarters. Feature films, as well as short programs, which showcase local and international directors, play throughout the 2-week event. > Tower City Center, 50 Public Sq., Downtown, tel. 216/623–3456, www.clevelandfilm.org.

APRIL

Tri-C Jazzfest Thousands of people line the streets of downtown Cleveland to listen to some of jazz's top musicians perform in concert. The 10-day series, sponsored by Cuyahoga County Community College, is held at various locations throughout the city. > Tel. 216/987–4400, www.cleveland.com/jazzfest.

JUNE

Parade the Circle Street performers, live bands, a parade, and festival atmosphere dominate University Circle during the waning days of spring. The Cleveland Museum of Art, Natural History Museum, Botanical Garden, and pretty much every other facility in University Circle stage special attractions and activities during the day's events. And don't worry about going hungry: A fine sampling of Cleveland's ethnic cuisine is available. > Wade Oval, between East Blvd. and Martin Luther King Jr. Dr., University Circle, tel. 216/791–3900, www.universitycircle.org.

JULY

Blossom Music Festival The Cleveland Orchestra's summer series runs from July 4th through Labor Day at the open-air Blossom Music Center in Cuyahoga Falls, a half-hour drive south of Cleveland. > 1145 W. Steels Corners Rd., Cuyahoga Falls, tel. 216/231–1111 or 800/686–1141, www.clevelandorch.com.

Cleveland Grand Prix CART racing's best snake around the tricky road course at Burke Lakefront Airport. > 1501 N. Marginal Rd., North Coast District, tel. 800/498–7223, www.clevelandgrandprix.com.

Walk and Dine Take a tour of the heart of downtown, Cleveland's Gateway neighborhood. In the spirit of the "progressive dinner," this event showcases the city's historic urban architecture and fine cuisine. > Between E. 4th and E. 14th Sts., Gateway District, tel. 216/771–1994, www.historicgateway.org.

AUGUST

Cuyahoga County Fair This agriculture-oriented event, one of the largest in Ohio, has all the usual fair fare—games, rides, exhibits, and more. It's held in Berea, southwest of downtown Cleveland. > 164 Eastland Rd., Berea, tel. 440/243–0090, www.cuyfair.com.

Slavic Village Harvest Festival Slavic Village, a historic Polish neighborhood on the Cleveland's near southeast side, holds a 10-block street fair on the last weekend in August. > E. 55th Fleet St.–E. 65th Fleet St., Slavic Village, tel. 216/429–1182, www.slavicvillage.org.

Vintage Ohio The state's largest wine festival takes place 30 minutes east of Cleveland, at Lake FarmPark in Kirtland. Count on live jazz and blues entertainment, fine finger and festival foods, arts and crafts, and sampling some of the nation's best boutique wines—made in Ohio. It's a 2-day event, and there's a carry-out store where you can purchase what you try. Downtown Cleveland hotels offer special rates and shuttle service. > 8800 Chardon Rd. (U.S. Rte. 6), Kirtland, tel. 800/227–6972, www.ohiowines.org.

SEPTEMBER

Cleveland National Air Show It began in 1923 with the Cleveland Air Races, and is still one of the premier air shows in the country, drawing more than 40 military and civilian aircraft to the Burke Lakefront Airport in downtown Cleveland for the 3-day Labor Day weekend. > 1501 N. Marginal Rd., North Coast District, tel. 216/781–0747, www.clevelandairshow.com.

NOVEMBER–DECEMBER

Cleveland Winterfest The lighting of the Christmas tree on Public Square kicks off this 2-week celebration of the holidays, snow, and the city's rich cultural heritage. Concerts, ice skating on Public Square, and special programs at the facilities in University Circle are festival highlights. > Tel. 216/791–3900, www.universitycircle.org.

WHERE TO STAY

Cleveland's hotels provide excellent weekend packages, and are adjacent to, if not located in, the city's activities hubs—Gateway, the Theater District, and the Warehouse District. There are several urban bed-and-breakfasts available, as well, proving charm can be quite urbane.

Baricelli Inn This B&B is in a three-story brownstone mansion, dating from 1896. Each of the spacious guest rooms has antique furnishings and modern amenities. It's in the University Circle neighborhood, 15 minutes from downtown. You can get passes to a local fitness center. > 2203 Cornell Rd., University Circle 44106, tel. 216/791–6500, fax 216/791–9131, www.baricelli.com. 7 suites. Restaurant, cable TV, business services, shop; no kids, no smoking. AE, MC, V. CP. $$$–$$$$

Brownstone Inn–Downtown You can't miss the peacock-blue double-entrance doors atop a short set of stone steps at this four-story guest house. Built in 1874, the building is on the National Register of Historic Places. Inside are numerous period details, such as pocket doors, a marble fireplace, and French wallpaper. The bridal suite has a four-poster bed. Cap off your day with a complimentary glass of sherry or port. Weather permitting, breakfast is served on the back deck. The inn is downtown between Playhouse Square and University Circle. > 3649 Prospect Ave., Downtown 44115, tel. 216/426–1753, fax 216/431–0648, www.brownstoneinndowntown.com. 5 rooms. Some kitchenettes, cable TV, in-room VCRs; no kids, no smoking. AE, MC, V. CP. $–$$

Cleveland Marriott Key Center Attached to Key Tower, the tallest building in Cleveland, this hotel faces the historic Mall "C" and abuts Public Square. Plush accommodations have fantastic views of Lake Erie and the downtown skyline. The rooms are neat and spacious, but the real star is the Key Tower where the hotel is located. The Key Tower is the tallest building between New York and Chicago. > 127 Public Sq., Downtown 44114, tel. 216/696–9200, fax 216/696–0966, www.marriott.com. 400 rooms, 15 suites. Restaurant, in-room data ports, refrigerators, cable TV with movies, indoor pool, gym, hot tub, sauna, lounge, concierge, business services, laundry service, laundry facilities, no-smoking rooms. AE, D, DC, MC, V. $$$–$$$$

Clifford House Bed and Breakfast This two-story, Tuscan-style brick home, built in 1868, is in the Ohio City neighborhood. The uncluttered, cozy rooms are painted in warm tones, have restored pine-plank, cherry, dark walnut, or maple floors, and quilt-cover beds. Most of the upstairs rooms have vaulted ceilings. Some rooms share a bath. > 1810 W. 28th St., Ohio City 44113, tel. 216/589–0121, www.cliffordhouse.com. 2 rooms with shared bath, 2 suites. Refrigerators, cable TV, some in-room VCRs, business services; no kids, no smoking. AE, D, MC, V. BP. $–$$$

Edgewater Estates I and II Directly across the street from Edgewater State Park, this 1920s English Tudor is a 3-minute drive from downtown. Rooms, furnished with period antiques, look out on either the gardens of the estate or Lake Erie. There are two kitchens (one for you to share with the rest of the guests) and two dining rooms. > 9803–5 Lake Ave., Cudell/Edgewater 44102, tel. 216/961–1764, fax 216/961–7043, www.edgewaterestatesbedandbreakfast.com. 5 rooms. Some microwaves, some refrigerators, hiking, beach, dock, boating, fishing, laundry facilities, airport shuttle, some pets allowed (fee), no-smoking rooms. AE, D, MC, V. BP. $–$$$

Embassy Suites Hotel Cleveland–Downtown This all-suites hotel in a 13-story, brick-and-stone, early-1900s building is in downtown's Reserve Square. The two-room suites have a bedroom with two double beds or a king-size bed, and a living room with a sofa bed. Connecting units are available. > 1701 E. 12th St., Downtown 44114, tel. 216/523–8000, fax 216/523–1698. 268 suites. Restaurant, microwaves, refrigerators, pool, gym, lounge, concierge, shops, laundry facilities, business services, meeting rooms, Internet, no-smoking rooms. AE, D, DC, MC, V. BP. $$–$$$$

Hampton Inn Cleveland–Downtown In the heart of the city is this hotel suited for the business traveler and tourist alike. Rooms are bright and not too cramped, with cream-color walls and green carpeting. The business center has audiovisual equipment. All guests have complimentary access to the swimming pool and exercise equipment across the street. > 1460 E. 9th St., Downtown 44114, tel. 216/241–6600, fax 216/621–4274, www.hampton-inn.com. 194 rooms. Shop, laundry service, Internet, business services. AE, D, DC, MC, V. BP. $$

Holiday Inn–Lakeshore Across from Burke Lakefront Airport and convenient to the train station, the Rock and Roll Hall of Fame and Museum, and the Great Lakes Science Center, this hotel has lake views and an unbeatable location. > 1111 Lakeside Ave., North Coast District 44114, tel. 216/241–5100, fax 216/241–1831, www.holiday-inn.com. 381 rooms, 2 suites. Restaurant, pool, gym, lounge, business services, Internet. AE, D, DC, MC, V. $–$$$

Renaissance Cleveland Hotel This grand 14-story hotel built in 1851 is within walking distance of the Cleveland Convention Center, the Flats, the Theater District, and the Rock and Roll Hall of Fame and Museum. Each tastefully furnished room has one or two queen-size beds or a king-size bed, a dark-wood entertainment center, plush sitting chair with ottoman, and a work desk. Jacuzzi suites are available. The lobby area has a towering atrium and the Sans Souci restaurant. > 24 Public Sq., Downtown 44113, tel. 216/696–5600, fax 216/696–0432, www.renaissancehotels.com. 491 rooms, 50 suites. 2 restaurants, shops, business services. AE, D, DC, MC, V. **$$$**

Ritz-Carlton Cleveland Antiques and original 18th-century art fill Cleveland's Ritz. Guest rooms have work desks and marble baths. The Century restaurant has a railroad theme and serves American fare with a flair. > 1515 W. 3rd St., Downtown 44113, tel. 216/623–1300, fax 216/623–0515, www.ritzcarlton.com. 208 rooms, 27 suites. Restaurant, pool, gym, lounge. AE, D, DC, MC, V. **$$$$**

Sheraton Cleveland City Centre Hotel Most of the rooms in this 22-story brick hotel opposite the Cleveland Convention Center have a view of Lake Erie and the Cleveland lakefront. Its proximity to the business district and convention center is appealing. > 777 St. Clair Ave., Downtown 44114, tel. 216/771–7600, fax 216/566–0736. 470 rooms, 32 suites. 2 restaurants, health club, lounge, lounge, shop. AE, D, DC, MC, V. **$$–$$$**

Wyndham Cleveland at Playhouse Square The 14 stories of the Wyndham overlook the bright lights of the vibrant theater district. The hotel's airy, modern lobby is flanked by Winsor's restaurant. The hotel is adjacent to the Halle Building, which also houses a food court for lunch. Each room is fitted with a luxurious Herman Miller chair, shower massage, and some provide views of Playhouse Square. > 1260 Euclid Ave., Downtown 44106, tel. 216/615–7500, fax 216/615–3355, www.wyndham.com. 205 rooms. Restaurant, pool, gym, lounge, shops, business services. AE, D, DC, MC, V. BP. **$$$–$$$$**

WHERE TO EAT

A smorgasbord of ethnic food stretches through Cleveland's neighborhoods. There are restaurant rows in the Flats, the Warehouse District, the area around Gund Arena and Jacobs Field, Little Italy, and on Coventry Road in Cleveland Heights. The buffet is complete; everything from Wiener schnitzel to chicken and waffles, filet mignon to bean-stuffed burritos is served.

Baricelli Inn Housed in a 19th-century mansion that's now a seven-room B&B inn, this restaurant in University Circle presents boneless rack of lamb as its house specialty. Other dishes include salmon with rosemary pesto, scallops with couscous, and veal tenderloin with a muscat reduction sauce and golden chanterelle mushrooms. Herbs used to season these dishes come from the inn's garden, and there's an extensive wine list. Open-air dining is available on the front patio. > 2203 Cornell Rd., University Circle, tel. 216/791–6500. AE, MC, V. Closed Sun. **$$$$**

Century A railroad theme prevails in this traditionally furnished dining room in the Ritz-Carlton Hotel. Shrimp, scallops, roast pork chops, and pastas fill the menu. On Friday evenings international fare is the highlight; a different country or region is showcased each month. There are also a sushi bar and a Sunday brunch. Breakfast, lunch, and dinner are served daily. > The Ritz-Carlton, 1515 W. 3rd St., Downtown, tel. 216/623–1300. Reservations essential. AE, D, DC, MC, V. **$$$–$$$$**

Don's Lighthouse Grille In a 1929 building with a steeple, the dining room has large windows, a high ceiling, chandeliers, and nautical murals. The catch of the day may be scrod, tuna, or salmon; you'll always find jumbo sea scallops, halibut, and sea scallop ravioli. > 8905 Lake Ave., West Side, tel. 216/961–6700. AE, D, DC, MC, V. No lunch weekends. $$–$$$$

Empress Taytu Ethiopian Restaurant Vegetarian meals, chicken, lamb, and beef are married with northern African music and culture in a dining experience you won't soon forget. One note of caution: meals are served without silverware—scooping food with bread is the preferred method of eating. Reservations are essential on the weekends. > 6125 St. Clair Ave., tel. 216/391–9400. AE, D, MC, V. Closed Sun.–Mon. No lunch. $$–$$$$

Frank Sterle's Slovenian Country House Meat loaf, Wiener schnitzel, from-scratch gravies, and a hint of grandma's tender loving care are staples at this Central European cafeteria–style restaurant on the near east side. > 1401 E. 55th St., Slavic Village, tel. 216/881–4181. AE, MC, V. Closed Mon. $$

Great Lakes Brewing Co The traditional grub at this pub southwest of downtown in Ohio City includes calamari, a sausage sampler, chili, black-bean ravioli, and ribs. A specialty is the brewmaster's pie—hot and mild Italian sausage, spinach, and mozzarella and ricotta cheeses, baked in a flaky pie crust and served on a bed of marinara sauce. Wash it down with one of the varieties of beer brewed here. Open-air dining is available in a courtyard with 25 tables. There's no smoking here. > 2516 Market St., Ohio City, tel. 216/771–4404. AE, DC, MC, V. $–$$$

Heck's Cafe Publike and in historic Ohio City, this eatery has an open kitchen and a glass garden atrium filled with plants. It's known for its bouillabaisse and grills arguably the best burger in town. > 2927 Bridge Ave., Ohio City, tel. 216/861–5464. AE, D, MC, V. $–$$$

Hyde Park Chop House Its fine wood, linen, and wine list make it elegant, and the service puts you at ease. The best steak house in Cleveland is adjacent to the Ritz-Carlton and Cleveland Renaissance Hotel. Valet parking is available. > 123 Prospect Ave., Downtown, tel. 216/344–2444. AE, D, DC, MC, V. Closed Sun. $$$–$$$$

Indigo Indian Bistro The intoxicating aroma of curry hits as you walk in from Prospect Avenue. The smart cherry-wood bar, high ceilings, and ample booths and tables create the casual and comfortable dining experience. Traditional Indian fare is served, and spicy mint chutney for your nan bread is worth a go. Reservations are essential on the weekends. > 503 Prospect Ave., tel. 216/357–3308. AE, D, MC, V. Closed Sun. $$$–$$$$

John Q's Steakhouse The hardwood floors, cherrywood, brass, and sports memorabilia complement the prime cuts of beef at this downtown chain restaurant known for its pepper strip steak and fresh vegetable sides. It's across the street from the Renaissance Cleveland Hotel. Open-air dining is available on the front patio. > 55 Public Sq., Downtown, tel. 216/861–0900. AE, D, DC, MC, V. No lunch weekends. $$$–$$$$

Johnny Mango Burritos, wraps, coleslaw with a kick, and fried bananas never tasted so good. The chips and salsa before dinner are notable, and the guacamole is outstanding. Make sure to get a booth toward the back of the restaurant to avoid incoming patrons. > 2130 Bridge Ave., tel. 216/575–1919. AE, MC, V. $–$$

Johnny's Bar on Fulton Mammoth portions of veal, pasta, and seafood draw diners to this small art deco hot spot in a 1917 building in Ohio City. A specialty is the red bell pepper pasta tossed with shrimp and a cayenne-spiked cream sauce. You can eat inside on white linen or, in good weather, have a meal outside on the backyard patio. The place fills up quickly on weekends. > 3164 Fulton Rd., Ohio City, tel. 216/281–0055. Reservations essential. AE, DC, MC, V. Closed Sun. $$$–$$$$

Lemon Grass Dine in the casual sunroom or the more formal front room at this restaurant in a suburb east of Cleveland. The menu includes lemongrass soup, a Thai hot-and-sour shrimp soup, steamed shellfish with chili powder, curry duck, and pad Thai. The seafood *choo chee* is a medley of shrimp, squid, and scallops with curry and vegetables. Open-air dining is available on a patio surrounded by a brick fence. > 2179 Lee Rd., Cleveland Heights, tel. 216/321–0210. AE, DC, MC, V. Closed Sun. No lunch Sat. $–$$$

Lola Bistro & Wine Bar Chef-owner Michael Symon has received national attention from food and wine critics for creations he describes as "urban comfort food." Best-sellers on the winter menu are seafood pierogi, and macaroni-and-cheese dish that features fresh rosemary, goat cheese, and roasted chicken. Fish and game are first-rate; desserts are out of this world. > 900 Literary Rd., Tremont, tel. 216/771–5652. Reservations essential. AE, D, DC,.MC, V. Closed Mon. $$$$

Luchita's With authentic Mexican food, generous portions, good margaritas, and friendly service, it's no wonder this restaurant with two locations is jammed on the weekends. The menu changes every three months. > 3456 W. 117th St., tel. 216/252–1169. AE, MC, V. Closed Mon. $–$$

Metropolitan Cafe Floor-to-ceiling windows provide a great view of the Cleveland skyline from this restaurant in a 100-year-old building in the Warehouse District. The café specializes in seafood cooked on a wood-enhanced grill. Pasta, steak, and chicken dishes are also available. > 1352 W. 6th St., Warehouse District, tel. 216/241–1300. AE, D, DC, MC, V. $$–$$$$

Morton's of Chicago The downtown Cleveland branch of the well-known chain in the Tower City Center has its trademark formal mahogany interior with white table-cloths. Large portions of choice cuts of beef and seafood are accompanied by baked or mashed potatoes, salad, and fresh vegetables. > 1600 W. 2nd St., Downtown, tel. 216/621–6200. AE, DC, MC, V. No lunch weekends. $$$$

Nate's Deli and Restaurant Deli fare, as well as Middle Eastern and vegetarian spe-cialties, is served at this breakfast and lunch spot on the West Side. The creamy hum-mus may be the best in town. > 1923 W. 25th St., West Side, tel. 216/696–7529. No credit cards. Closed Sun. No dinner. ¢–$

The Palazzo The two granddaughters of the original owner prepare and serve north-ern Italian cuisine just three nights a week in this romantic hideaway just west of downtown in the Cudell-Edgewater neighborhood. Whether turning out updated ver-sions of her recipes or new dishes inspired by annual trips back to Italy, they do their grandma proud. > 10031 Detroit Ave., Cudell/Edgewater, tel. 216/651–3900. AE, MC, V. Closed Sun.–Wed. No lunch. $$–$$$

Parker's New American Bistro White tablecloths and a warm fireplace dominate this bistro in Ohio City. Local ingredients are used extensively, so the menu changes with the harvest and the season. Whenever possible, organically grown vegetables are selected. Popular dishes include the signature rack of lamb and various pastas. > 2801 Bridge Ave., Ohio City, tel. 216/771–7130. AE, MC, V. Closed Mon. No lunch Sat.–Thurs. $$–$$$

Phil the Fire Chicken and waffles? You bet. Mac and cheese, collard greens, banana pudding, and catfish make the restaurant's self-proclaimed moniker "comfort food for the soul" right on. Phil the Fire is always packed, so arrive early for dinner. It's open for breakfast daily, too. > 2775 Moreland Blvd., Shaker Heights, tel. 216/458–3473. AE, MC, V. $$–$$$

Pier W Shaped like a ship, this restaurant in Lakewood, about 5 mi east of downtown Cleveland, juts out over Lake Erie, offering a good view of the city skyline and the water. The menu includes seafood dishes, fresh catch from Lake Erie, and beef and chicken entrées. There's entertainment on Friday and Saturday nights and a Sunday brunch. > 12700 Lake Ave., Lakewood, tel. 216/228–2250. AE, D, DC, MC, V. No lunch Sat. $$–$$$$

Sans Souci This French countryside–style restaurant in the Renaissance Cleveland Hotel has bright murals on the walls and a massive stone hearth. Hearty foods—especially seafood—from the coasts of Spain, Morocco, Italy, and France are highlights. Entrées include sautéed snapper, grilled salmon, grilled tuna steak, Black Angus strip steak, and veal saltimbocca. Lobster dishes are featured in October and November. The carrot soup with leeks and apples is a specialty. > 24 Public Sq., Downtown, tel. 216/696–5600. Reservations essential. AE, D, DC, MC, V. No lunch weekends. $$–$$$$

Sushi Rock This lively pink-and-purple hot spot is in the downtown Warehouse District. The illuminated pictures of New York may add to your general confusion as you try to categorize the cuisine: crab–lobster tater tots keep company with the dragon roll (a tumble of shrimp tempura, surimi, cucumber, avocado, and eel) as appetizers; entrées range from spice-rubbed pork to roasted sea scallops, served with tomato, cucumber, onion, and ginger salad. > 1276 W. 6th St., Warehouse District, tel. 216/623–1212. AE, MC, V. Closed Sun. No lunch Sat. $$$–$$$$

Tommy's A vegetarian institution on Coventry Road, Tommy's serves hefty salads and sandwiches and embarrassingly large but delicious milk shakes made with Cleveland's own Pierre's ice cream. > 1824 Coventry Rd., Cleveland Heights, tel. 216/321–7757. MC, V. ¢–$$

Watermark A waterside location in a restored warehouse in the Flats provides a view of river traffic. The menu changes daily and emphasizes exotic seafood such as ahi and sailfish. Steak, chicken, and pasta dishes are also available. Desserts include fresh strawberry zabaglione. Open-air dining is available on the riverfront patio. > 1250 Old River Rd., the Flats, tel. 216/241–1600. AE, D, DC, MC, V. $$–$$$$

ESSENTIALS

Getting Here

Travelers can fly, drive, bus, and train into Cleveland. Cleveland Hopkins International Airport and the business-traveler–oriented Burke Lakefront Airport have multiple-airline schedules, and both Amtrak and Greyhound provide service to the city.

While in the city, a rapid-transit and bus system is a good way to zip from stop to stop from downtown to the east and near-west sides; however, driving a car in the city is efficient, too.

BY BUS

Buses are inbound to Cleveland from all points. Greyhound is the major service, and the buses are timely, though they often arrive in Cleveland early in the morning or late at night, especially if travelers arrive from the East Coast or points west of Chicago. Weekenders coming in from cities within Ohio will find more flexible and convenient schedules.

The downtown bus terminal is large, with more than 20 gates. Frequent stops from departure to destination lengthen the trip relative to a car ride, but the service is dependable and safe.

Round-trip fares for two people inbound from Columbus, Ohio, cost about $80; from Cincinnati, around $140.

BUS DEPOTS **Greyhound Bus Terminal** > 1465 Chester Ave., Downtown 44113, tel. 216/781–0520, www.greyhound.com.

BUS LINES **Greyhound** > Tel. 800/229–9424 or 216/781–0520, www.greyhound.com.

BY CAR

I–90 runs east–west through downtown Cleveland. I–71 and I–77 come up from the south. Driving from the east on the Ohio Turnpike (I–80), take Exit 10 to I–71 N.

BY PLANE

Cleveland-Hopkins International Airport and Burke Lakefront Airport are the city's air traffic terminals. Hopkins receives most passengers, while Burke is known as a charter- and freight-service hub. Hopkins is located 12 mi southwest of downtown; Burke is downtown, adjacent to the lake.

The busiest times for Hopkins are between 7:30 and 9 AM and 5 and 6:30 PM. Continental Airlines maintains a hub at Hopkins and lands the majority of traffic here.

A light-rail line runs from Hopkins to downtown. It's about a 40-minute ride on the RTA, which costs $1.50. Several rental-car companies operate just north of the airport, and travelers must shuttle to the parking lots to arrange and pick up their autos. Driving from Hopkins to downtown is easy, thanks to the airport's convenient location next to I–71, which runs north–south, and I–480, the outer loop that connects the southwestern and southeastern suburbs.

AIRPORTS **Cleveland Hopkins International Airport** > 5300 Riverside Dr., Cleveland 44135, tel. 216/265–6000, www.clevelandairport.com.

CARRIERS **American Airlines** > Tel. 800/433–7300, www.aa.com. **Continental Airlines** > Tel. 800/525–0280, www.continental.com. **Delta Airlines** > Tel. 800/221–1212, www.delta.com. **Northwest Airlines** > Tel. 800/225–2525, www.nwa.com. **Southwest Airlines** > Tel. 800/435–9792, www.southwest.com. **United Airlines** > Tel. 800/241–6522, www.united.com. **U.S. Airways** > Tel. 800/428–4322, www.usair.com.

BY TRAIN

Amtrak's Lakeshore Limited service—connecting Cleveland with Boston, Chicago, New York, and points in between—debarks passengers between 2 and 3 AM, depending on the direction from which travelers are inbound. Service on the Capitol Limited—connecting Cleveland with points between Chicago and Pittsburgh via bus because Amtrak does not offer rail service—is much the same.

Both trains offer a number of services, including sleeping cabins, a lounge car, and dining accoutrements. Smoking is allowed in designated areas—usually the lounge car—but on overnight trips only. Walking the train end-to-end can ease the length of the trip in from the East Coast.

Two round-trip tickets from Boston to Cleveland cost around $480. Inbound from Chicago, the trip will cost approximately $340. Amtrak runs continuous specials, so check the Web site for availability.

TRAIN LINES **Amtrak** > Tel. 216/696–5115, www.amtrak.com.

TRAIN STATIONS **Amtrak** > 200 Memorial Shoreway NE, Cleveland, tel. 800/872–7245, www.amtrak.com.

Getting Around

BY CAR

I–71, I–77, I–90, and Route 2 are the major thoroughfares into downtown.
I–77 can be quite busy throughout the day, and traffic is heavy during morning
and evening rush hours. All roads and highways are well signed and there are
not too many narrow or one-way streets. Downtown, streets are consecutively
numbered; in the University Circle area, the other main tourist center, roads
are curvy and it can be challenging to stay on track.

A good option is to park downtown and ride the Rapid Transit Authority's red
line to University Circle. Metered parking is available in University Circle but
it's often difficult to find a spot. Parking garages are plentiful downtown. Depending on how early you arrive, you can pay between $2 and $10 for a full
day. If you do find parking on the street, be sure to put sufficient money in the
meter; meter maids are efficient.

BY PUBLIC TRANSIT

The Greater Cleveland Regional Transit Authority (RTA) operates buses and
three light-rail lines throughout the metro area. The system bridges east and
west, with the Terminal Tower as its hub. RTA buses travel from Public Square
on five downtown loop routes. A light-rail system, the Waterfront Line, links
the Terminal Tower with the Flats entertainment district, Cleveland Browns
Stadium, the Rock and Roll Hall of Fame and Museum, the Great Lakes Science Center, downtown shopping, and municipal parking lots.
Greater Cleveland Regional Transit Authority (RTA) > 1240 W. 6th St., Cleveland 44113, tel. 216/566–5100, www.gcrta.org.

Visitor Information

CONTACTS **Convention and Visitors Bureau of Greater Cleveland** > 50 Public
Sq., Suite 3100, Cleveland 44113, tel. 216/621–4110 or 800/321–1001,
www.travelcleveland.com.

Cuyahoga Valley National Park

The park is 26 mi south of Cleveland, 127 mi northeast of Columbus, and 228 mi northeast of Cincinnati.

5

By Joe Frey

THE CUYAHOGA IS A CROOKED BACKBONE of a river that flows from south of Akron to the Great Lake Erie, and, for part-time outdoor adventurers in northeast Ohio, the Cuyahoga Valley National Park is the nerve center.

The scenic Cuyahoga Valley spans 20 mi from just south of Cleveland to 10 mi north of Akron. Some of the views from the Brecksville area alone get the ganglions firing.

Hundreds of miles of trails—hiking, biking, bridle, and skiing among them—maneuver into and out of the valley. Likely the most-used portion of the park is the Towpath Trail, which essentially bisects the park as it winds along the banks of the Cuyahoga. The Towpath follows roughly the old Ohio & Erie Canal route, and it's a multipurpose track, serving hikers and joggers in summer and cross-country skiers in winter.

The park as a whole is a year-round destination that certainly is not undiscovered by locals. More than 3 million people (many of them northeast Ohioans) visit some part of the sprawling 33,000-acre site every year, and with two ski areas, ponds a plenty, and a raftload of golf courses, it's little wonder. Boston Mills/Brandywine Ski Resort is northeast Ohio's most popular winter-sports destination, and Sleepy Hollow Golf Course is a local favorite, too.

With such an expansive park, it will be difficult to see and do everything in one weekend—a double-edged sword, to be sure. The best way is to visit the park in thirds: northern, middle, and southern. The northern portion offers golf, hiking, horseback riding—if you own your own equines—and the Cuyahoga Valley Scenic Railroad, which is a must-do activity. The central part of the park has Brandywine Falls and Dover Lake Park, which promises good times for water-slide lovers. Boston Mills/Brandywine Ski Resort resides in the central portion, as well. Blossom Music Center, scores of miles of cross-country ski trails, Hale Farm & Village, and the Quarry—a great throwback swimming hole—highlight the southern edge of the park.

One of the interesting quirks of Cuyahoga Valley National Park is that there are no official camp sites within its boundaries, making it essentially a dawn-to-dusk park. The closest overnight campsites are about 20 mi to the east, so if you're looking to rough it, be prepared to drive; however, there's a cozy hostel smack in the middle of the park, as well as several lodging options within 10 mi. Hotels in Akron, Bath, and Peninsula serve visitors well thanks to their proximity to the park.

For your reward after a hard day's worth of play, the Cuyahoga Valley's surrounding area offers an exceptional array of relaxed, though sophisticated, dining establishments. Wine cellars are more big-city than big-country; menus challenge the palate while soothing the soul; and plush surroundings melt the strain from your muscles. Northeast Ohio's restaurants specialize in comfort food, so be prepared to sleep well after your fine dining experiences.

WHAT TO SEE & DO

Cuyahoga Valley National Park Ohio's only national park has been a haven for outdoor lovers for 30 years. Cuyahoga Valley National Park started as a designated "National Recreation Area" in 1974, then moved up to national-park status in October 2000. The park—and the crooked-running waters of the Cuyahoga—provide an escape from the two nearby growling metro areas of Cleveland and Akron.

Long ago the river carved steep walls out of the surrounding plateau, and old-growth forests cropped up along the banks, providing a habitat for several species of bats, coyotes, deer, and salamanders. Year-round outdoor activities abound: canoeing, fishing, hiking, horseback riding, skiing and snowboarding, and tobogganing, just to name a few. Remnants of the Ohio & Erie Canal also dot the Cuyahoga river along the Towpath Trail—a fine bike and running path that hugs the river bank. Heritage stops, such as the **Cuyahoga Valley Scenic Railroad** tours (Tours) provide low-impact diversions.

Within the borders of Cuyahoga Valley National Park, **Boston Mills/Brandywine Ski Resort** (7100 Riverview Rd., Peninsula, tel. 800/875–4241, www.bmbw.com) combines two resorts in one—much like the park combines two geologic formations in one. The terrain is undulating without being mountainous and borders the Cuyahoga River on the west. The resort is accessible from a number of interstates and state routes, and routinely hosts thousands of visitors during its summertime art festival.

The buildings of **Hale Farm & Village** (2686 Oak Hill Rd., Bath, tel. 330/666–3711, www.wrhs.org/halefarm, $12, Memorial Day–Oct., Wed.–Sat. 11–5, Sun. noon–5) are original structures, more than 170 years old. They've been moved here from various other locations over the past century and a half. The original farm was founded by pioneer Jonathan Hale during the canal years in Ohio. Craftspeople, such as a glass blower, candle maker, potter, and blacksmith, demonstrate the industries of the mid-1800s. On spring weekends, there are maple sugar festivities.

The **Happy Days Visitors Center** (Rte. 303, 2 mi east of Peninsula and ½ mi west of St. Rte. 8, Peninsula, tel. 330/650–4636 or 800/257–9477) serves as the Cuyahoga Valley National Park's information and nightly entertainment hub, hosting lectures, concerts, poetry readings, and myriad other activities year-round.
> Cuyahoga Valley National Park, Bolanz Rd. between Riverview and Akron-Peninsula Rds., Peninsula, tel. 216/524–1497, 330/650–4636, or 440/546–5991, www.nps.gov/cuva/. Free. Daily dawn–dusk.

The Quarry More an old swimming hole than a pool—but just as clean as a modern facility—The Quarry is a charming and practical spot for taking a dip in the Cuyahoga Valley National Park, especially since the Cuyahoga River is generally regarded as unsafe for swimming. The national park and the remains of several 19th- and 20th-century stone quarries act as this popular pool's boundaries. Concessions are available, and the bathhouse provides lockers. > Rte. 303, ½ mi west of Riverview Rd., Peninsula, tel. 330/644–2220, www.thequarry.org. $5. June–Aug., Mon., Wed., Thurs., and Sat., 12:30–7:30, Tues. and Fri. 12:30–8.

AKRON

Akron Zoo Favorite attractions at this zoo in Perkins Woods include Monkey Island, River Otters, and the Ohio Farmyard. There are Sumatran tigers, sun bears, and a tree house and train in the Tiger Valley exhibit. The zoo has a number of endangered species, including red pandas, bald eagles, and Chinese alligators. > 500 Edgewood Ave., Akron, tel. 330/375–2525 or 330/375–2550, www.akronzoo.com. $7.50. May–Oct., daily 10–5; Nov.–Apr., daily 11–4.

Dover Lake Waterpark Get soaked at this water park in Sagamore Hills just outside the Cuyahoga Valley National Park. Seven water slides, three inner-tube rides, a wave pool, a water whirl ride, and two speed slides are among the wet attractions that await. > 1150 W. Highland Rd., Sagamore Hills, tel. 330/467–7946, www.doverlake.com. $13.95 weekdays, $17.95 weekends, parking $3. June–Aug., daily 11–7.

F. A. Seiberling Naturealm Visitors Center The 100-acre Metro Parks nature center and arboretum is named in honor of F. A. Seiberling, founder of Goodyear Tire and Rubber Company. Seiberling donated more than 400 acres to help establish Sand Run Metro Park, of which the Naturealm is a part. There are a 16-acre arboretum, the Rock & Herb Garden, observation decks, three ponds, and hiking trails with a suspension bridge, and a tall-grass prairie demonstration area. > 1828 Smith Rd., Akron, tel. 330/865–8065, www.summitmetroparks.org. Free. Mon.–Sat. 10–5.

Portage Lakes State Park Swim, camp, hike, fish, boat, and enjoy the great outdoors at this 4,963-acre lake area, with 900 feet of beach-front property to boot. Its wetlands attract waterfowl and shorebirds, and the seven lakes and reservoirs provide ample space for canoeists, power boaters, and water-skiers. Nimisilla Reservoir—the southern most body of water in the park—is reserved for electric motors only. > 5031 Manchester Rd., Akron, tel. 330/644–2220, www.ohiostateparks.org. Free. Daily 6 AM–11 PM.

The Winery at Wolf Creek Andy and Deanna Troutman continue producing excellent, medal-winning wines from grapes grown in nearby Summit County vineyards. The tasting room, which seats 50, frames astounding views of the Akron skyline and the Barberton Reservoir. There's outdoor seating for 300. The 2002 Cabernet Franc is an excellent example of Ohio's cool-climate vintages. > 2637 S. Cleveland-Massillon Rd., Norton, tel. 330/666–9285. Free. Jan.–Mar., Thurs. noon–9, Fri. and Sat. noon–11, Sun. 1–9; Apr.–Dec., Mon.–Thurs. noon–9, Fri. and Sat. noon–11, Sun. 1–9.

Tours

Brandywine Falls Tours If you don't have a horse, the only way to see the Cuyahoga Valley National Park by horse power is through the carriage tours at Carriage Trade Farms. Discover Brandywine Falls, a 65-foot sandstone-and-shale sluice, on sleigh rides in winter, as well as on hay rides and narrated and romantic tours from May through October. Reservations are required, and expect to pay between $35 and $85 per couple, depending on the type of tour. > 8050 Brandywine Rd., Northfield, tel. 330/467–9000, www.brandywinefalls.com.

Cuyahoga Valley Scenic Railroad From February through December, this line offers a smorgasbord of tours—wine-tasting, train-and-hike, foliage, murder-mystery, and plain old see-the-countryside. It's the only operating touring railroad in northeast Ohio, and as one of the mid-20th-century locomotives pulls you through the Cuyahoga River's scenic bottoms, you wonder why more railroads like this don't sprout up. The wine-tasting train is particularly popular, selling out weeks, sometimes months, in advance. There are several boarding areas for the train, and tour lengths vary between 2½ and 7 hours, and tour costs range from $8 to $20. > Peninsula Depot, intersection of Akron-Peninsula Rd. and Rte. 303, Peninsula, tel. 800/468–4070 or 330/657–2000, www.cvsr.com.

St. Helena III **Ohio & Erie Canal Tours** Ease down the northern edge of Ohio's old waterway connection as a team of horses pulls the *St. Helena III* and its passengers through history. Tours last about an hour and depart between 1 and 3 PM daily June–August. In May, September, and October, the boat slides through the canal waters on weekends only. Admission is $6.50. > 103 Tuscarawas Street W, Canal Fulton, tel. 800/435–3623 or 330/854–3808, www.canalwayohio.com.

Sports

Cuyahoga Valley National Park and the surrounding area offer an extensive list of summer and winter sport and leisure activities. In addition to the 125 mi of hiking trails throughout the park, biking, fishing, golfing, skiing, and swimming draw large numbers of visitors.

A couple of words of caution, however: Cuyahoga River water quality is poor, due to the amount of industry up river in Akron, so stick to the ponds for fishing and swimming. In addition, several excellent bridle trails snake through the park, but because of the high cost of liability insurance, there are no stables in the area that rent equipment.

BASEBALL

Akron Aeros Smack in the middle of Akron, Canal Park is a beautiful venue for baseball, and the Aeros—the Cleveland Indians' Double-AA affiliate—are perennial contenders in the Eastern League. > 300 S. Main St., Akron, tel. 330/253–5153, www.akronaeros.com.

CROSS-COUNTRY SKIING & SNOWSHOEING

Kendall Lake Winter Sports Center The Cuyahoga Valley National Park's main site for winter sports serves as a lodge and equipment-rental site for cross-country skiers, ice skaters, and snowshoers. There are more than 125 mi of trails, with the Towpath—a 20-mi stretch along the Cuyahoga River—as the central artery. You can rent cross-country skis for $15 a day and snowshoes for $5 a day. The center is open December–February. > Truxell Rd., between Akron-Cleveland and Akron-Peninsula Rds., Boston Twp., tel. 216/524–1497 or 800/445–9667, www.nps.gov/cuva.

DOWNHILL SKIING

Boston Mills/Brandywine Ski Resort Northeast Ohio's winters provide plenty of coverage for the slopes at this 18-trail resort. The terrain is definitely not Colorado, but a 240-foot elevation change along with multiple mogul runs challenge seasoned skiers. The courses are open as soon as the snow starts flying—which can be as early as mid-October—through mid-March. Daily lift tickets cost $29–$39. Rental equipment costs $5–$25, depending on what you need. Lessons are available. The resort is 25 minutes south of downtown Cleveland. > 7100 Riverview Rd., Peninsula, tel. 330/467–2242 or 800/875–4241, www.bmbw.com.

GOLF

Boulder Creek Golf Club As this course matures, it's sure to become one of the toughest, most challenging 18 in Ohio, if not the United States. The island green on No. 17, which is surrounded by three sand bunkers, represents exactly what course-designer Joe Salemi imagined: a beautifully difficult golf course. Boulder Creek is a 15-minute drive from Six Flags World of Adventure. Expect to pay $48–$68.75 for your round. > 9700 Page Rd., Streetsboro, tel. 330/626–2828, www.bouldercreek.cc.

Sleepy Hollow Golf Course One of the most challenging sets of public links in northeast Ohio, Sleepy Hollow abuts the Cuyahoga River and frames a view of the valley's layered hillocks you can't see on any other course in the area. The rolling and narrow back nine features more intimate views. The first and second holes on the front nine are memorable, if not infuriating, because of their beauty and difficulty. If you escape No. 1 without losing a ball to the woods, you've won. What's more, escaping No. 2 with par means you can cruise through the next 16 holes and enjoy the view. Expect to pay $24–$39 for a round. > 9445 Brecksville Rd., Brecksville, tel. 440/526–4285, www.clemetparks.com.

Save the Date

JUNE–JULY

Boston Mills ArtFest The 30-plus-year-old event has everything an outdoor art festival should—music, food, artisans, fine arts and crafts, and the hill-and-hollow setting of Boston Mills Ski Resort. > 7100 Riverview Rd., Peninsula, tel. 330/467–2242, www.bmbw.com.

JULY

All-American Soap Box Derby Held since 1934, this race attracts more than 100 teams of kids from throughout the region. > Soap Box Derby International Race Track, 789 Derby Downs Dr., Akron, tel. 330/733–8723, www.allamericansoapboxderby.com.

OCTOBER

Harvest Festival During this annual fall festival at Hale Farm and Village you can take part in cider pressing, apple-butter making, grain threshing, and more. > 2686 Oak Hill Rd., Bath, tel. 330/666–3711 or 800/589–9703, www.wrhs.org.

WHERE TO STAY

Cuyahoga Valley Hi-Stanford Hostel This low-cost accommodation option is a 19th-century home in the Cuyahoga Valley National Park. Men and women sleep in separate quarters, and you must bring your own linen—no sleeping bags allowed—although you can rent sheets for $2 per night. The hostel is closed during the day, and bicycle and motorcycle storage is available. > 6093 Stanford Rd., Peninsula 44264, tel. 330/467–8711, hi-stanfordhostel@juno.com. 30 rooms. No a/c, no room phones, no room TVs, no smoking. No credit cards. ¢

AKRON

Comfort Inn Boston Heights Occupying a hill in the Montrose suburb 7 mi east of Akron, this two-story motel caters primarily to business travelers. There are plenty of fast-food and sit-down dining options within a mile or so of the motel. > 6731 Industrial Pkwy., St. Rte. 8 at Hines Mill Rd., Boston Heights 44236, tel. 330/650–2040, fax 330/650–6925, www.comfortinn.com. 51 rooms, 7 suites. Some in-room hot tubs, some microwaves, some refrigerators, cable TV, indoor pool, exercise equipment, business services, no-smoking rooms. AE, D, MC, V. CP. **$$**

Hilton Akron/Fairlawn With two swimming pools, a shopping mall across the street, and downtown Akron just 5 mi away, this hotel is a good option if you're traveling with the family. Guest rooms are spare and furnished with unassuming wood-veneer pieces. > 3180 W. Market St., Akron 44333, tel. 330/867–5000, fax 330/867–1648, www.hilton.com. 204 rooms. Restaurant, room service, in-room data ports, some refrigerators, cable TV, indoor pool, gym, sauna, bar, laundry facilities, business services, airport shuttle, some pets allowed, no-smoking rooms. AE, D, DC, MC, V. **$$**

PENINSULA

Holiday Inn Richfield Well-appointed, modern rooms—some poolside with Looney Tunes–theme decor—highlight this Holidome facility, not more than 5 minutes off Interstates 80 and 77. > 4742 Brecksville Rd., Richfield 44286, tel. 800/465–4329 or 330/659–6151, fax 330/659–3819, www.holiday-inn.com. 216 rooms. Restaurant, room service, in-room data ports, cable TV, miniature golf, 2 pools (1 indoor), wading pool, gym, outdoor hot tub, billiards, Ping-Pong, laundry facilities, business services, some pets allowed (fee), no-smoking rooms. AE, D, DC, MC, V. $$–$$$

Inn at Brandywine Falls Built in 1848, this inn offers proximity to charming Brandywine Falls, as well as a retreat from the daily grind. Plenty of strolling grounds surround the inn, and its porches and library offer pacific solitude. All rooms have private baths, and the dark-stained antique furniture and beds serve as focal points. Breakfast is included in the rates. > 8230 Brandywine Rd., Sagamore Hills 44067, tel. 330/467–1812 or 888/306–3381, fax 330/467–2162, www.innatbrandywinefalls.com. 6 rooms. Some in-room hot tubs, some refrigerators; no TV in some rooms, no smoking. AE, D, MC, V. BP. $$$–$$$$

Sheraton Suites Akron/Cuyahoga Falls Overlooking Cuyahoga Falls, the Sheraton Suites is an elegant facility with modern, airy, and spacious rooms. Ten penthouse suites are more condominium than hotel room, and multilevel suites provide views of the falls. The riverside balcony on the hotel's lower level also showcases the Cuyahoga's waters spilling over the falls. > 1989 Front St., Cuyahoga Falls 44221, tel. 800/325–5788 or 330/929–3000, fax 330/929–3031, www.sheratonakron.com. 214 suites. Restaurant, room service, in-room data ports, some kitchens, some kitchenettes, minibars, microwaves, refrigerators, cable TV, in-room VCRs, indoor pool, gym, lounge, laundry facilities, business services, meeting rooms, no-smoking rooms. AE, D, MC, V. $$–$$$$

CAMPING

Portage Lakes State Park Fishing and boating are particularly good at this park some 20 mi south of the Cuyahoga Valley National Park. The man-made lakes offer walleye, trout, and other native fish species, as well as fine canoeing and sailing. Turkeyfoot lake boasts 900 feet of beach, too. In winter, ice fishing and skating, and cross-country skiing are popular here. Camp sites are have no electricity and can be reserved by phone or on a first-come first-served basis; dump-stations are $8. Boat rental is not available at Portage Lakes. Some pets are allowed. > 5031 Manchester Rd., Akron 44319, tel. 330/644–2220, www.dnr.state.oh.us/parks. 74 sites. Portable toilets, dump station, picnic tables, public telephone, ranger station, playground, swimming (lake). AE, D, MC, V. ¢

West Branch State Park This is the closest campsite to the Cuyahoga Valley National Park, and it's loaded with amenities. Heated showers, indoor toilets, and boat rentals are available to campers, as well as 7 mi of dedicated mountain-biking trails. Twenty miles of bridle trails are also available, along with two campsites specifically designed for horses. However, there's no horse rental in the park. Boating is particularly good here, with boats of unlimited horsepower allowed on Kirwan Lake. Some pets are allowed. > 5708 Esworthy Rd., Ravenna 44266, tel. 330/296–3239, www.dnr.state.oh.us/parks. 53 partial hook-ups, 50 tent sites. Flush toilets, partial hook-ups (electric), laundry facilities, showers, picnic tables, snack bar, public telephone, ranger station, swimming (lake). AE, D, MC, V. ¢

WHERE TO EAT

BATH

Gasoline Alley You can get excellent cheap eats at this New York–influenced saloon. The Portobello mushroom sandwich is a favorite, and the bar is well stocked for an eclectic local crowd. Sunday brunch is served. > 870 N. Cleveland-Massillon Rd., Bath, tel. 330/666–2670. AE, D, MC, V. $–$$

Ken Stewart's Grille Filled with artwork and near-capacity crowds just about every night of the week, this restaurant has a sophisticated Southwestern theme. It's known for steaks, fresh lobster, and 10 or more imaginative daily specials, ranging from the latest trends to variations on old favorites. Chicken breast in phyllo with a light pepper-cream sauce; grilled pork tenderloin; potato-crusted halibut; and penne pasta with artichoke hearts, sun-dried tomatoes, and garlic are just a few examples. There's a kids' menu. > 1970 W. Market St., Akron, tel. 330/867–2555. Reservations essential. AE, D, DC, MC, V. Closed Sun. $$$–$$$$

Ken Stewart's Lodge The second Ken Stewart's to open is a rustic retreat on the outskirts of the sleepy village of Bath. Its bar is well stocked; its wine cellar impeccable; and its food is undeniably American, with Asian and Japanese accents. The seafood—particularly the lobster tail—and Kobe beef steaks are highly recommended, as are the extensive daily specials. > 1911 Cleveland-Massillon Rd., Bath, tel. 330/666–8881. Reservations essential. AE, D, DC, MC, V. Closed Sun. $$$–$$$$

Lockkeepers This contemporary American restaurant may house the best wine cellar—and coolest, because it resides on the second floor—in northeast Ohio. The cellar has been under the care of master sommeliers, and executive chef Morgan Jacobsen's creative menu matches as you would expect. Although the menu changes seasonally to take advantage of the area's offerings, sashimi tuna is offered year-round, twice a week as a house specialty. Dine alfresco and drink in the vistas of the Cuyahoga Valley National Park. > 8001 Rockside Rd., Valley View, tel. 216/524–9404. Reservations essential. AE, D, DC, MC, V. No lunch Sun. $$$$

Swensons For a taste of the 1950s and '60s—as well as a darn fine hamburger—Swensons drive-up restaurants can't be beat. It's a local chain that's been around since 1934, and with six spots in and around the Cuyahoga Valley, its popularity has certainly not waned. The Seven Hills location is convenient to the Cuyahoga Valley National Park, and after a long day of hiking, the so-named "America's best cheeseburger" is a fitting trophy. > 7635 Broadview Rd., Seven Hills, tel. 216/986–1934. No credit cards. ¢

Whitey's Booze 'N' Burgers The name says it all: A fully stocked bar and hearty portions of ground beef and fries await you at this hangout for local twenty- and thirtysomethings. The chili is also a good bet. On Monday nights in summer there's a mean game of volleyball, and Friday and Saturday live bands perform. > 3600 Brecksville Rd., Richfield, tel. 330/659–3600. AE, MC, V. ¢–$$

CUYAHOGA FALLS

Lanning's Dim lighting, windows with a view of a nearby wooded creek, and an open-flame grill in the intimate dining room make this a popular spot for special occasions. The delicious Lanning's Secret Sauce (the owner refuses to divulge the ingredients) is brushed onto all steaks prior to cooking. The restaurant also serves seafood dishes ranging from shrimp scampi to fillet of salmon. You can hear a pianist on Saturday. > 826 N. Cleveland-Massillon Rd., Bath, tel. 330/666–1159. AE, D, DC, MC, V. Closed Sun. No lunch. $$$–$$$$

Moe's An excellent martini selection, a menu of creative American fare that changes weekly, and a comfortable dining area make this spot on the banks of the Cuyahoga River a fine choice. The bar is open until 2:30 AM. > 2385 Front St., Cuyahoga Falls, tel. 330/928–6600. AE, D, DC, MC, V. Closed Sun. $$$$

ESSENTIALS

Getting Here

Travelers can fly, drive, bus, and train into the Cuyahoga Valley National Park area, but a car is essential to get around the 33,000-acre site—when you're not hiking and biking. The Interstate highway system provides several excellent entry and exit points, and both Amtrak and Greyhound provide service to Cleveland and Akron, north and south of the park, respectively. Cleveland Hopkins International Airport, as well as Canton-Akron Regional Airport, have multiple-airline schedules.

Flying, busing, and training into Cleveland will likely afford you more selections, while Akron's travel ports may provide cheaper options. You can't go wrong with either choice, however, because the park is between the two cities.

BY BUS

Buses are inbound to Cleveland from all points and at all times, and Akron is a secondary hub. Greyhound is the major service, and the buses are timely, though they often arrive in Cleveland early in the morning or late at night, especially if you arrive from the East Coast or points west of Chicago. Weekenders coming in from cities within Ohio will find more flexible and convenient schedules.

Cleveland's bus terminal is large, with more than 20 gates, and is in the heart of downtown. Frequent stops from departure to destination lengthen the trip relative to a car ride, but the service is dependable and safe.

Akron's bus terminal, which operates between 7 AM and 10 PM, is adjacent to the campus of the University of Akron.

Traveling to Akron will be cheaper—but also more time-consuming—than busing into Cleveland, and there are fewer buses running to Akron than Cleveland. For example, Greyhound runs two one-stop buses per day from Cincinnati to Akron, but it runs nine nonstop buses from Cincinnati to Cleveland daily.
DEPOTS **Greyhound Bus Terminal** > 1465 Chester Ave., Cleveland 44113, tel. 216/781–0520, www.greyhound.com. **Greyhound Bus Depot** > 781 Grant St., Akron 44311, tel. 330/434–9185, www.greyhound.com.
BUS LINES **Greyhound Lines Inc.** > Tel. 330/262–0341, www.greyhound.com.

BY CAR

Automobiles are the preferred method of getting around northeast Ohio. I–480 runs east–west, skirting north of Cuyahoga Valley National Park, while the Ohio Turnpike (I–80) is south of the park. I–77, Route 8, and Route 303 provide direct access to the park.

I–77 and Route 8 can be quite busy throughout the day, and traffic is heavy during morning and evening rush hours. The Turnpike is an excellent east–west highway, with light traffic throughout the day, and I–480 is a good access point for I–77. All roads and highways are well signed, and it's easy to find the park after exiting the highways.

Several local roads knife through the park, both east–west and north–south, but you'll be sharing the blacktop with bicyclists, hikers, joggers, and an occasional horseback rider, so be alert. Speed limits through the park, especially on the Towpath Trail along the Cuyahoga River are 25 mph or less.

There's ample parking within the park and at the park's visitors centers and destinations, such as Boston Mills/Brandywine Ski Resorts.

BY PLANE

Cleveland-Hopkins International Airport is a major air traffic terminal, while Akron-Canton Regional Airport is a secondary hub. Hopkins is located 29 mi northwest of Cuyahoga Valley National Park; Akron-Canton is approximately 25 mi south of the park.

The busiest times for Hopkins are between 7:30 and 9 AM and 5 and 6:30 PM. Continental Airlines maintains a hub at Hopkins, and lands the majority of traffic. Akron-Canton is a hassle-free airport, with AirTran, Delta, and U.S. Airways handling the majority of flights.

Several rental-car companies operate out of Hopkins and Akron-Canton airport, and travelers must shuttle to the parking lots to arrange and pick up their autos.

Driving from Hopkins to the park is easy, thanks to the airport's convenient location next to I–480, which connects to I–77, which you can then take to south to the park. Akron-Canton is equally convenient, with a 30-minute drive up I–77 to enter the park.

AIRPORTS **Akron-Canton Regional Airport** > 5400 Lauby Rd. NW, North Canton 44720, tel. 330/499–4059, www.akroncantonairport.com. **Cleveland Hopkins International Airport** > 5300 Riverside Dr., Cleveland 44135, tel. 216/265–6000, www.clevelandairport.com.

CARRIERS (AKRON) **AirTran** > Tel. 800/247–8726, www.airtran.com. **Comair (Delta Connection)** > Tel. 800/354–9822, www.delta.com. **Delta Airlines** > Tel. 800/221–1212, www.delta.com. **Northwest Airlines (Mesaba)** > Tel. 800/225–2525, www.nwa.com. **United Express** > Tel. 800/241–6522, www.united.com. **U.S. Airways** > Tel. 800/428–4322, www.usair.com.

CARRIERS (CLEVELAND) **American Airlines** > Tel. 800/433–7300, www.aa.com. **Continental Airlines** > Tel. 800/525–0280, www.continental.com. **Delta Airlines** > Tel. 800/221–1212, www.delta.com. **Northwest Airlines** > Tel. 800/225–2525, www.nwa.com. **Southwest Airlines** > Tel. 800/435–9792, www.southwest.com. **United Airlines** > Tel. 800/241–6522, www.united.com. **U.S. Airways** > Tel. 800/428–4322, www.usair.com.

BY TRAIN

If you're taking the train to the Cuyahoga Valley, set your destination for Cleveland, because Amtrak service to Akron is limited to two inbound trains per day.

Amtrak's Lakeshore Limited service connects Cleveland with Boston, Chicago, New York, and points in between. Service on the Capitol Limited—connecting Cleveland with points between Chicago and Pittsburgh via bus—is much the same. The Three Rivers train stops in Akron at 1 AM and 6 AM.

All three trains offer a number of services, including sleeping cabins, a lounge car, and dining accoutrements. Smoking is allowed in designated areas—usually the lounge car—but on overnight trips only. Walking the train end-to-end can ease the length of the trip in from the East Coast.

Amtrak runs continuous specials, so check the Web site for availability.
LINES **Amtrak** > Tel. 216/696–5115, www.amtrak.com.
STATIONS **Amtrak** > 200 Memorial Shoreway NE, Cleveland, tel.
800/872–7245, www.amtrak.com.

Visitor Information

CONTACTS **Akron/Summit Convention and Visitors Bureau** > 77 E. Mill St.,
44308, tel. 330/374–7560 or 800/245–4254, www.visitakron-summit.org. **Cuyahoga Valley National Park** > 15610 Vaughn Rd., Brecksville 44141, tel.
216/524–1497, 330/650–4636, 440/546–5991, www.nps.gov/cuva. **Ohio State
Parks** > 1952 Belcher Dr., C-3, Columbus 43224, tel. 614/265–6561 or
877/678–3337, www.ohiostateparks.org.

Six Flags & the Western Reserve

Aurora is 30 mi southeast of Cleveland, 142 mi northeast of Columbus, and 259 mi northeast of Cincinnati.

6

By Joe Frey

WEEKENDERS CAN RAISE THEIR BLOOD PRESSURE at Six Flags Worlds of Adventure—a clean and well-run amusement, water, and wildlife park. Sea World is gone, but the park still houses a killer whale for its crowd-pleasing marine mammal expo. Six Flags also purchased, cleaned up, and added more water slides to the erstwhile Geauga Lake to create their own water park.

After the break-neck pace of Six Flags, you can take a laconic trip down the upper Cuyahoga River—a session that resembles holistic therapy more than it does a canoe ride. If the Cuyahoga River ride proves too rustic, try the Sunday-drive speed of the getaway resorts in Aurora, in the heart of the Western Reserve. Pamper yourself at a spa or stroll the country grounds and learn the ways of the equine. There's premium outlet shopping in downtown Aurora, too.

The Western Reserve—a vast plot of land generally west and south of Cleveland, stretching east to the Pennsylvania border, and bordering the southern shore of Lake Erie—has contracted since the Connecticut Land Company first claimed and mapped it. What was once thought of as the edge of the frontier world is now a burgeoning suburban and tourist region, with ample highways crisscrossing the one-time sparsely populated plateau.

Much of the land is flat and was a 19th-century farming haven. Indeed, pockets of agriculture still exist, but they are squeezed out every year by residents and commercial enterprises. The northeast quadrant of the Reserve is more undulating than its southern and western counterparts—although it's hardly mountainous landscape. "Hilly" is the best description.

Key points of interest are situated in the northern and central tier of the Reserve, all within a 40-minute drive of one another. Cuyahoga, Geauga, Lake, and Summit counties encompass the majority of the properties and activities highlighted here.

Farther to the north—along and within a few miles of Lake Erie's shores—is a seemingly incongruous region with outsiders' perceptions of Ohio: wine country. Ohio has been making wine since the 19th century, when it was the nation's largest wine producer. The northeastern portion of the Reserve houses 17 wineries, many of which have garnered national and international fame for their locally grown and produced vintages.

Vintage Ohio, which celebrates the state's vintners and the fruits of their labor, is a must-do event. Twenty-odd wineries, dozens of artisans and caterers, as well as a few wine and food educators—not to mention approximately 25,000 wine enthusiasts from all over the country—pack Lake Farmpark the first weekend of August.

Matching the region's excellent wine are some exceptional and interesting eateries, open for both lunch and dinner, and accessible from nearly every point in the Reserve.

For golfers and outdoor folks, points north and east of Beachwood are the way to go. There are elevation changes thanks to ice-age glaciers, and river gorges have carved out some choice spots where challenging and visually interesting golf courses now lay. Hiking trails at Punderson State Park also showcase the region's slightly rocky terrain.

Shoppers and thrill-ride seekers: Go south young men and women! Beachwood, unmistakably suburban, is chock full of chic stores, while more gentrified Aurora hosts a premium outlet mall, and Six Flags will give the most enthusiastic roller-coaster seekers a high (and low and upside down) time.

WHAT TO SEE & DO

Six Flags Worlds of Adventure Modern mind-bending and face-stretching thrill rides like Superman Ultimate Escape and X-Flight are one reason to coast the day away at Six Flags. Classic coasters remaining from this park's previous incarnation as Geauga Lake are another: There are few experiences that match the bone-rattling minute-and-a-half ride on the primordial Big Dipper. Tamer midway-style rides, such as the Dodgems, Ferris Wheel, paddle boats, and a carousel, give your body a brief respite between roller-coaster jumps. For little tykes—and adults who need a rest from the break-neck rides—Looney Toons BoomTown provides low-speed entertainment, as well as jungle gym–type fun.

During summer's dog days—which are frequent between June and September—you can cool off at Six Flag's **Hurricane Harbor** (free with Six Flags admission, Memorial Day–Labor Day, daily 11–7; May, weekends, weather permitting), a water park with a 25,000-square-foot wave pool, a relaxing "lazy river," a tube slide complex, and high-speed, plummeting wet slides. Turtle Beach is a water playground for younger kids; Hook's Lagoon is a family attraction with a five-story tree house, special-effects lagoons, water gadgets, and water slides.

Sea World Ohio, once home to the famous Shamu the killer whale, is now a scaled-down but tidy **Wildlife Park** (free with Six Flags admission, Memorial Day–Labor Day, daily 11–7; May, weekends, weather permitting) at Six Flags. Although Shamu was shipped out, Six Flags brought in Shouka the killer whale for the longtime Sea World staple: the marine mammal show, featuring the killer whale in its water-defying glory. Several other noteworthy exhibits, such as Tiger Island, constitute the wildlife side of Six Flags, and there are kiddie coasters, too.
> 1060 N. Aurora Rd., Aurora, tel. 330/562–8303, www.sixflags.com. $39.99. Memorial Day–Labor Day, daily 10–10; May and Oct., weekends 10–6.

THE WESTERN RESERVE
Northfield Park Live harness racing year-round four nights a week, simulcast derbies, and an on-site microbrewery make this a popular night spot. The track is a half-mile, and racing begins at 7 every night, rain or shine. > 10705 Northfield Rd., Northfield, tel. 330/467–4101, www.northfieldpark.com. $1.75. Mon., Wed., Fri., and Sat., post time 7 PM.
Punderson State Park With 1,000 lush acres of forest, this park is a great place for boating, hiking, and camping. One of a handful of Ohio state parks that double as a resort, Punderson has a lodge, cabins, camp sites, and a golf course. One of the three lakes in the park has a beach, and 14 mi of hiking trails keep you busy in the

park's slightly elevated terrain. Nature programs in the amphitheater are also popu-lar. > 11577 Kinsman Rd., Newbury, tel. 440/564–2279, www.ohiostateparks.org. Daily dawn–dusk.

Tours

Wines & Vines Wine Trail Yes, there are wineries in northeast Ohio—and plenty of them. The area is generally regarded as Ohio's wine country, thanks to the weather-abating effects of Lake Erie: the lake keeps the land relatively cool in summer and, more importantly, warm in winter, which allows several varieties of grapes to grow. Sure there are the old standbys—Concord, Delaware, and Niagara—but Ohio's wineries, such as **Chalet Debonne** (7743 Doty Rd., Madison, tel. 440/466–3485, www.debonne.com), **Harpersfield Vineyard** (6387 St. Rte. 307, Geneva, tel. 440/466–4739, www.harpersfield.com), and **Ferrante Winery** (5585 St. Rte. 307, Geneva, tel. 440/466–8466, www.ferrante.com) are producing world-class wines that *Wine Spectator* can no longer ignore. There are 17 wineries on this trail—too many to hit in one trip. But block off a Saturday and Sunday afternoon, take a self-guided tour, smell the grapes, and take home a case (or two). > Various locations along St. Rte. 307, and points east and south, tel. 440/466–4417, www.ohiowines.org.

Sports

With several state parks and the Cuyahoga River within its borders, the Western Re-serve is a prime spot for all kinds of outdoor fun, year-round.

The Reserve's expanse and interesting terrain make it a prime location for golf, and many good courses are here for the playing. Plus, it doesn't hurt when the golf world–famous Pete Dye designs links in the area.

The Lake Erie snow machine, which kicks in every year in November when cold air moves over the warm lake waters, ensures nice snow packs at local ski areas. The ele-vation change is minimal, however, because the Reserve is a plateau, after all.

CANOEING

Camp Hi Canoe Livery Much of the Cuyahoga River is unsuitable for canoeing, but the 30-mi stretch near Hiram Falls more than makes up for what the rest of the crooked river lacks. The Upper Cuyahoga is the most scenic and tranquil section of the river, and Camp Hi Canoe is your best river-trekking bet. Trips last between two and six hours, depending on your preference. Expect to pay $14–$18 per person to rent a canoe, and a bit more for a kayak. > 12274 Abbott Rd., Hiram, tel. 330/569–7621, www.camphicanoe.com.

DOWNHILL SKIING & SNOWBOARDING

Alpine Valley About 5 mi southwest of Chardon, this ski resort is in the heart of northeast Ohio's snowbelt and never wants for the white stuff. There's downhill ski-ing, day and night, on 10 trails; snowboarding in Xtreme Park, which has a half pipe with its own lift; and a long snowtubing hill, also with its own lift. Expect to pay $36 for an all-day lift ticket, plus costs for renting equipment. > 10620 Mayfield Rd., Chesterland, tel. 440/285–2211, 440/729–9775 snow line, www.alpinevalleyohio.com.

GOLF

Fowler's Mill Golf Course More difficult than the Maple Nine, the Lake Nine and the River Nine have cunning design. The split fairway on No. 9 and the shallow green on No. 3 of the River Nine demand perfection. Never mind that the hole known as the "blue monster" in local golfing circles—No. 4 on the Lake Nine—can ruin the

Ohio's Wines

ALONG THE COUNTRY ROADS in Madison and Thompson, Ohio, in mid-September, the aroma of wine grapes hangs in the air. Harvest is no more than three weeks out, and bunches of Cabernet Franc, Chambourcin, Pinot Noir, and Riesling make their last push toward ripening in the late afternoon sun.

As you drive along these roads, the vineyards of 19 northeast Ohio wineries—which represent approximately one-third of the winemakers in the state—mature before your very senses, intimating the finished product they will yield in little more than a year.

The majority of these grapes do not grow in 50-year-old vineyards, producing classic vintages. Rather, they are new—hybrids and vinifera species (Cabernets, Chardonnays, Pinots) that Ohio's pioneering winemakers planted no more than 30 years ago (some even newer than that). These new grape fields are slowly replacing the native species of Catawba, Concord, and Niagara that dominated the landscape for so long.

During the 19th century, the Catawbas and Concords from Ohio were to wine in America what California's Cabernets and Chardonnays are today. The Buckeye State was the number one wine producer in the Union after the Civil War and held high status in the wine-making community of the States through the early 20th century.

Prohibition stomped America's wine-grape producers, and Ohio's growers turned to juice and jelly companies to sell their crops. Welch's snapped up Ohio's Concord crops and paid handsomely. Over the course of 50 years, however, juice companies cut the price they were willing to pay, consumer tastes changed, and power in America's winemaking industry shifted to California and New York. Ohio's grape industry was literally dying on the vine.

During the late 1960s, Arnie Esterer traveled to New York's Finger Lakes region to meet Konstantin Frank, a legendary winemaker who proved quality vinifera vineyards would thrive in cool climates. Esterer studied under Frank and brought back to Ohio what he learned. Esterer, who started Markko Vineyard in 1969, is regarded as Ohio's winemaking pioneer. He continues to produce high-quality wines from his Conneaut estate vineyard.

Growing vinifera grapes in cool climates is not easy, however. Northeast Ohio has a relatively short growing season, is not overly warm (and when it's warm, it's usually humid), receives a fair amount of rainfall, and experiences some brutally cold winters. Although Lake Erie acts as a blanket for vineyards 5 to 10 mi inland, grape growers battle deep freezes and excessive moisture year after year. It has taken a handful of hearty souls 30 years to begin returning Ohio to its 19th-century winemaking status.

Over the past five years, northeast Ohio's wineries have produced multiple international and national medal-winning vintages and are surprising critics and consumers alike. **Vintage Ohio** (800/227–6972), a 9-year-old event held the first weekend in August in Kirtland, is one of the most well-attended wine festivals east of the Mississippi River. Wine Spectator, the critical voice of wine consumption, has favorably reviewed more Ohio wines within the past 2 years than it had during the previous 10. Most importantly, new wineries run by enthusiastic, smart, and tireless growers pop up in Ohio's northeastern corner almost every year.

A groundswell is taking place, and the fragrance of ripening grapes heralds a return to excellence.

— Joe Frey

rest of your day with one wayward tee shot. Course architect Pete Dye certainly threw down the gauntlet when he built this 27-hole links. Greens fees range between $42 and $55, with a cart. > 13095 Rockhaven Rd., Chesterland, tel. 440/729–7569, www.golfersweb.com/fowlers.htm.

Quail Hollow Country Club Former PGA Pro Tom Weiskopf tucked his 18-hole course in and around northeast Ohio's gently undulating landscape. But don't let the charm fool you. This is a monster golf course, measuring nearly 7,000 yards. The other 18-hole course is no slouch, either. It's 6,700 yards and has played host to pro tour events. The golf courses are adjacent to the Renaissance Quail Hollow Resort. > 11080 Concord-Hambden Rd., Painesville, tel. 440/350–3563, www.quailhollowcc.com.

StoneWater Golf Club Well-placed trees, sand bunkers, and water hazards will challenge even the scratch golfer here. There are five sets of tees to allow players to set their own degree of difficulty. Holes 7, 8, and 18 are especially tricky, given their lengths and the strategically placed water. Greens fees range $39–$84, depending on the time of year, and caddies are available. > 1 Club Dr., Highland Heights, tel. 440/461–4653, www.stonewatergolf.com.

Shopping

Aurora Premium Outlets Shopping is a sport unto itself, and the enormous outlet mall in Aurora is like an Olympic Village for shoppers, with more than 70 stores featuring labels like Polo Ralph Lauren, Tommy Hilfiger, Saks Fifth Avenue, Gap, and Levis. It's 5 mi north of I–80 on Route 43, and a 10-minute drive from Six Flags. > 549 Chillicothe Rd., Aurora, tel. 330/562–2000, www.premiumoutlets.com.

Beachwood Place Nordstrom and Saks Fifth Avenue—two stores that locals can't get anywhere else—anchor this upscale mall. J. Crew and Mario's International Spa are also big draws, as is Mad 4 You Bistro, a local eatery that specializes in Mediterranean fare. It's approximately 15 mi north of Aurora and Six Flags. > 26300 Cedar Rd., Beachwood, tel. 216/464–9460, www.beachwoodplace.com.

Save the Date

APRIL

Geauga County Maple Festival This festival celebrates maple-sugar season and is held every year on the first weekend after Easter on the square in Chardon Village. There are rides, food, maple syrup displays, parades, bath tub races, quilts, and entertainment. > Between Main St. and E. Park St., Chardon, tel. 216/286–3007, www.maplefestival.com.

AUGUST

Twins Days The spectacle is almost like suffering vertigo. Twins and triplets are everywhere. You're seeing double. If you're not a twin, you're more than welcome, but there's an eerie aura—something Stephen King–esque—that surrounds you if you're not. Imagined doppelganger creepiness aside, this festival is two tons of fun because of the special bonds twins and their parents share—and it's something non-twins don't have. The Twins Days festival hosts a parade, twins games, a talent show, and more, and thousands of doubles flock to Twinsburg the first weekend of August to partake. > Glenn Chamberlain Park, west of Ravenna Rd. (St. Rte. 91), Twinsburg, tel. 330/425–3652, www.twinsdays.org.

Vintage Ohio The state's largest wine festival takes place 20 mi north of Aurora and Six Flags, at Lake Farmpark in Kirtland. Count on live jazz and blues entertainment, fine finger and festival foods, arts and crafts, and a sampling of some of the nation's best boutique wines—made in Ohio. It's a 2-day event, and there's a carry-out store where you can purchase what you try. > 8800 Chardon Rd. (U.S. 6), Kirtland, tel. 800/227–6972, www.ohiowines.org.

WHERE TO STAY

AURORA

Aurora Inn of Mario's International Words like "lavish," "indulgent," and "opulent" do not do Mario's justice. This is a place that will melt away your troubles and pamper you like no other. Its rooms are exquisitely appointed, all with whirlpool tubs, federal-period furniture, and plush carpet, and many with fireplaces. It's an excellent couples getaway, catering to both men and women with an array of spa treatments and golf and spa packages. > 30 Shawnee Trail, Aurora 44202, tel. 330/562–6121 or 800/444–6121, fax 330/562–5249, www.marios-spa.com. 69 rooms. Restaurant, room service, some in-room hot tubs, cable TV, health club, sauna, spa, business services, meeting rooms, airport shuttle, no-smoking rooms. AE, D, DC, MC, V. **$$$–$$$$**

Bertram Inn & Conference Center Finely decorated cozy rooms have modern furniture and matching Persian-pattern carpet and drapes. The staff is attentive, and the Leopard restaurant on-site is exceptional. The Inn is within five minutes of Six Flags and Aurora Premium Outlets. > 600 N. Aurora Rd. (Rte. 43), Aurora 44202, tel. 330/995–0200 or 877/995–0200, fax 330/561–9163, www.thebertraminn.com. 162 rooms. Restaurant, room service, in-room data ports, minibars, cable TV, outdoor pool, fitness center, lounge, Internet, business services, meeting rooms, airport shuttle, no-smoking rooms. AE, D, DC, MC, V. **$$$**

Inn at Six Flags Shouka the Whale and Hara the Tiger—costumed entertainers—greet kids at the all-you-can-eat breakfast buffet (included with the stay), and there's free shuttle service to the amusement parks. This two-story brick lodging was built in the early '70s; now it's under the wing of the Six Flags Ohio management. Downtown Aurora is about 2 mi away. > 800 N. Aurora Rd. (Rte. 43), Aurora 44202, tel. 330/562–9151 or 866/657–1877, fax 330/562–5701, www.sixflags.com. 145 rooms. Restaurant, room service, cable TV, miniature golf, indoor pool, hot tub, bar, video game room, laundry facilities, business services, no-smoking rooms. AE, D, DC, MC, V. **$$$$**

Walden Country Inn & Stables Set back from the highway on a pleasant country road, this getaway offers bucolic views, unsullied air, a challenging golf links, horseback rides, and fine dining. The golf club is private, but guests can procure tee times, subject to availability. The stables are also open to guests, and rides are $65 per hour. The inn's staff is well-trained and attentive, and the decor is a mix of old country and new art. Plus, don't pass up a chance for an in-room massage. Strolling the grounds, you'd never know you were so close to a big city (Cleveland is a mere 27 mi away). > 1119 Aurora Hudson Rd., Aurora 44202, tel. 330/562–5508, fax 330/562–8001, www.waldenco.com. 25 suites. 2 restaurants, café, room service, cable TV, in-room VCRs, 18-hole golf course, horseback riding, laundry service, concierge, Internet, business services, meeting rooms; no smoking. AE, D, DC, MC, V. **$$$$**

BEACHWOOD

Avalon Gardens This 1870s Victorian farmhouse with bay windows is on the grounds of a working nursery. Rooms filled with antiques look out on the gardens and nearby Alpine Valley Ski Resort. You can eat your hearty breakfast in the sunny parlor and drink your tea on the spacious patio, where there's an outdoor fireplace.

> 12511 Fowlers Mill Rd., Chardon 44024, tel. 440/286–2126, fax 440/729–3240, www.avalongardensinn.com. 2 rooms with shared bath. No room phones, no room TVs. MC, V. BP. **$$**

Embassy Suites This all-suites hotel occupies a section of a suburban commercial strip lined with other lodgings, independent and chain restaurants, and dozens of shops. Start the day off on a refreshing note—or wind down after dark—in the four-story atrium and garden. A cooked-to-order breakfast and waterfall views are complimentary. > 3775 Park E Dr., Beachwood 44122, tel. 216/765–8066 or 800/362–2779, fax 216/765–0930, www.embassysuites.com. 216 suites. Restaurant, in-room data ports, microwaves, refrigerators, cable TV with video games, indoor pool, hot tub, exercise equipment, bar, laundry facilities, business services, meeting rooms, no-smoking rooms. AE, D, DC, MC, V. BP. **$$$**

Holiday Inn–Beachwood This four-story hotel in a largely commercial area outside downtown Beachwood is surrounded by restaurants and other lodgings. Kids eat free here, and the hotel is close to several major interstate highways. > 3750 Orange Pl., Beachwood 44122, tel. 216/831–3300, fax 216/831–0486, www.holiday-inn.com. 172 rooms. Restaurant, in-room data ports, cable TV with movies, indoor-outdoor pool, sauna, exercise equipment, bar, laundry facilities, business services, no-smoking rooms. AE, D, DC, MC, V. **$–$$**

Residence Inn By Marriott–Cleveland-Beachwood This four-story brick hostelry in the Beachwood business district is comfortable for a longer stay; it's an all-suites property with studios and one- and two-bedroom units. > 3628 Park E Dr., Beachwood 44122, tel. 216/831–3030, fax 216/831–3232, www.marriott.com. 174 rooms. In-room data ports, kitchens, microwaves, refrigerators, cable TV with movies, tennis court, outdoor pool, gym, laundry service, laundry facilities, some pets allowed (fee), no-smoking rooms. AE, D, DC, MC, V. CP. **$$$–$$$$**

Super 8 Hotel A number of restaurants and retail stores are within walking distance of this two-story motel in Beachwood's business district. A sizeable shopping mall is 2 mi away, and Six Flags is a 20-minute drive to the south. Children under 12 stay free, and there's a complimentary Continental breakfast included. > 3795 Orange Pl., Beachwood 44122, tel. 216/831–7200, fax 216/831–0616, www.super8.com. 128 rooms. In-room data ports, some microwaves, some refrigerators, cable TV, outdoor pool, business services, airport shuttle, no-smoking rooms. AE, D, DC, MC, V. CP. **$**

WHERE TO EAT

AURORA

The Leopard A well-trained staff and an inventive menu—prepared with a bit of devil-may-care flair—await you at this establishment. Porcini-mushroom–encrusted rack of lamb is the signature dish. Huge display windows, pillars, and leopard-print rugs enliven the space. The prix-fixe, seven-course meals, on Friday nights for $90 per couple, are a steal. > 600 N. Aurora Rd., Aurora, tel. 330/562–2111. Reservations essential. Jacket required. AE, D, DC, MC, V. Closed Sun. and Mon. **$$$–$$$$**

BEACHWOOD

Bass Lake Taverne Beside a pastoral road, this tavern in the woods has hand-hewn beams and brickwork. The menu includes large cuts of meat, hearty burgers, and fresh catch from nearby Lake Erie. There's open-air dining in a courtyard that seats about 40 and entertainment on Friday and Saturday. > 426 South St., Chardon, tel. 440/285–3100. AE, D, DC, MC, V. **$$–$$$**

Benihana Japanese Steak House Delicate paper screens and austere black-lacquer tables set the scene in the dining room at Benihana. The menu presents a fairly standard selection of steak and seafood, which plays second fiddle to the show put on by the experienced chefs, who slice, dice, and cook your meal tableside. The chicken-and-shrimp combo is popular. Also try the flambéed shrimp, the teppanyaki filet mignon, or the sirloin steak. There's a kids' menu, too. > 23611 Chagrin Blvd., Beachwood, tel. 216/464–7575. AE, D, DC, MC, V. $$–$$$$

Blake's Seafood Grill The Chagrin River is known to overflow throughout the year, and here your plate will, too, if you're looking for seafood. It's fresh, it's creative, and the overlook of the Chagrin Falls is exceptional. Everything is prepared fresh daily over cherry, hickory, and oak wood–fired grills. The lobster mashed potatoes are out-of-this-world good. You can get steaks, too, at this outlet of the Hyde Park Restaurant Systems, known for its steak houses. > 17 River St., Chagrin Falls, tel. 440/893–9910. AE, D, DC, MC, V. No lunch Sun. $$–$$$

Charley's Crab Sea critters are the stars at this comfortable East Coast–style crab house with wall-size seascape murals, mahogany-frame windows, and white linen tablecloths. In addition to the seafood entrées, there are several pasta dishes (most include seafood in the sauce) and filet mignon, roast rack of lamb, and grilled chicken breast. There's a kids' menu. > 25765 Chagrin Blvd., Beachwood, tel. 216/831–8222. AE, D, DC, MC, V. No lunch Sun. $$–$$$$

Lion and Lamb Stained- and leaded-glass windows, large wooden booths, and dim lighting give this casually intimate spot an almost reverent feel. The chef prepares several different beef entrées, plus pasta and specialty veal entrées. There's entertainment Tuesday to Saturday. The dining room is nonsmoking. > 30519 Pine Tree Rd., Pepper Pike, tel. 216/831–1213. Reservations essential. AE, D, DC, MC, V. No lunch Sun. $$$–$$$$

Mad 4 You Bistro Presentations are innovative and artistic here; the off-white and yellow-brown of pan-roasted diver scallops resting on a thin, red bath of tomato puree is striking. You can choose from Mediterranean-influenced beef, seafood, pasta, and chicken selections, or stop by for daily happy-hour specials at the finely stocked bar during your shopping break. Stained-glass windows and warm, faux-finish walls belie this restaurant's mall location. > Beachwood Place, 26300 Cedar Rd., Beachwood, tel. 216/378–0344. AE, D, DC, MC, V. $$$–$$$$

Ristorante Giovanni Though jeans and sneakers are not allowed, the overall warm demeanor of this small Northern Italian restaurant makes you feel as though the owners have invited you into their home for dinner. A Cleveland-area institution since the late 1970s, Ristorante Giovanni can be counted on to serve dependably good pastas. The seafood dishes, including Maryland crab cakes and sweetwater prawns with asparagus, are noteworthy as well. > 25550 Chagrin Blvd., Beachwood, tel. 216/831–8625. Reservations essential. AE, D, MC, V. Closed Sun. No lunch Sat. $$–$$$$

Shuhei Dressed in traditional kimonos, the waitstaff sweep quietly from table to table in this spare, stylish dining room. Shuhei's artfully presented tempura and sushi are among the best in town; the house specialty—the somewhat dauntingly titled Spider Maki—is a whole soft-shell crab drizzled with spicy mayonnaise. You can also order traditional Japanese noodle and seafood dishes. > 23360 Chagrin Blvd., Beachwood, tel. 216/464–1720. AE, D, DC, MC, V. No lunch Sun. $$–$$$$

ESSENTIALS

Getting Here

As with most of northeast Ohio, travelers can fly or take a bus or train into the area, but a car is essential to get around, even if you're spending your days at Six Flags. The Interstate highway system provides excellent access to all points near and far within the Western Reserve, and you'll need it to jaunt from Aurora to Beachwood to Madison. Amtrak and Greyhound provide service to nearby metro Cleveland, and Cleveland Hopkins International Airport hosts multiple airlines.

BY CAR

I–90 runs northeast–southwest through the northern end of the Western Reserve. It connects with I–271, which slices right down the heart of the area, reaching Beachwood and Aurora. The Ohio Turnpike (I–80) is also an optional route, skirting south of Aurora and Six Flags. I–480 comes into play briefly when it merges with I–271 south of Beachwood.

I–271 is one of the busiest highways in Ohio, with express and local lanes serving thousands of cars per day. Take care when merging from the express to the local lanes, especially during rush hour. The speed limit may be 60 mph, but it's likely drivers will be zooming by. All roads and highways are well signed and there are not too many narrow or one-way streets.

Beachwood's main drag is U.S. 422, or Chagrin Boulevard—another extremely busy thoroughfare during the day. It's wide enough, but so many cars use it, you may feel cramped, and trying to make a left turn into any of the eating or shopping establishments there is difficult.

State Route 82 cuts through Aurora and connects with I–480. It's a bit of a country road with only one lane occasionally each way, and gets busy during rush times and when visitors are pouring into Six Flags.

The quickest way to get to Six Flags is via I–480, U.S. Route 422, and State Routes 91 and 43. Coming from the north and west, it's best to drive I–480 to U.S. 422, exiting at Route 91—a busy four-lane road. Take Route 91 south to Route 43 and follow the signs from there.

Visitor Information

CONTACTS **Ashtabula County Convention & Visitors Bureau** > 1850 Austinburg Rd., Austinburg 44010, tel. 440/275–3202 or 800/337–6746, www.accvb.org. **Beachwood Chamber of Commerce** > 24500 Chagrin Blvd., #110, Beachwood 44122, tel. 216/831–0003, www.beachwood.org. **Ohio State Parks** > 1952 Belcher Dr., C-3, Columbus 43224, tel. 614/265–6561 or 877/678–3337, www.ohiostateparks.org. **Ohio Wine Producers Association** > Box 157, Austinburg 44010, tel. 440/466–4417 or 800/227–6972, www.ohiowines.org. **Western Reserve Historical Society** > 10825 East Blvd., Cleveland 44106, tel. 216/721–5722, www.wrhs.org.

The Eastern Lake Erie Coast

Ashtabula is 65 mi east of Cleveland, 205 mi northeast of Columbus, and 312 mi northeast of Cincinnati.

7

By Rich Warren

TOO MANY LAKE ERIE VACATIONERS SUCCUMB to the flashy allure of the islands and the Sandusky area with the famed roller coasters and rowdy nightlife found there. But for those in the know, the Buckeye State's North Coast has an equally beautiful, albeit more sedate, side to it—the counties east of Cleveland have gems of their own to offer those seeking a sojourn on the Inland Seas. Beaches, including Ohio's longest, are plentiful, not to mention lagoons, river estuaries, and ample opportunities for fishing or boating. If you should grow weary of the water, a few miles from the coast is a land of covered bridges and wineries, of woodlands and farmlands, all in a landscape of gentle hills crisscrossed by rivers snaking through picturesque valleys and dramatic gorges.

Lake and Ashtabula counties, respectively Ohio's smallest and largest counties, offer a melange of attractions and activities enough to fill several weekends' itineraries. Ranging in character from suburban to truly isolated, these two counties offer astonishing diversity. You can sample some of Ohio's finest wines, see one of the largest concentrations of covered bridges in the state, visit the country's largest arboretum, or frolic in Ohio's first lakeside resort community. Or you can take in an "agricultural theme park," relax on the banks of two of the state's designated scenic rivers, the Grand and the Chagrin, or visit offbeat little museums like one filled with Victorian baby buggies. Historical sites also abound, including the home of President Garfield, the first Mormon temple, and numerous sites related to the Underground Railroad.

The first-time visitor might be surprised that this is Ohio. The region's plentiful vineyards are reminiscent of the California wine country, for example. And the many saltbox houses and white, high-steepled churches suggest another locale—New England. There's good reason for the distinctively Yankee flavor. This whole area of northeastern Ohio was first settled by pioneers from Connecticut-granted western lands in exchange for their service in the Revolution. Called the "Western Reserve" to this day, this part of Ohio is pervaded by its New England heritage, not only in town names but also in the architecture of homes and public buildings built around town squares or commons. The towns close to the water also take on a nautical flavor with a good measure of the Midwest thrown in to boot.

Long an important east–west corridor, even for the Native Americans, the area's major highways still follow paths established by those long-gone travelers. Though these roads can still whisk you quickly from one attraction to another, be advised these highways with their lines of strip malls and chain restaurants are best abandoned to sample the region's rural charms. Even in western Lake County, still part of metropolitan Cleveland, you'll be surprised how quickly the meadows and woodlands start appearing when you've left the main roads behind.

But even in places you can't see it, the Lake's influence is everywhere. The shoreline's lighthouses and once bustling ports at Ashtabula and Conneaut show how the area has long looked to the Lake as a source of commerce, attracting ethnic groups like the Finns and the Hungarians, just as Cleveland did. The much-touted "Lake effect" carries its influence far inland with cooling breezes in summer and savage snowstorms in winter, although the benign climate makes for a prolonged growing season, thus fostering a substantial nursery and fruit-growing industry. The landscape was carved by the same glaciers that scraped out the Great Lakes, but rather than leaving flat-as-a-pancake terrain, the region's topography is rolling and, in places, quite hilly. Travel to "Little Mountain," south of Painesville, for example, for views of the Lake and vistas of the varied countryside.

Though compact, Lake and Ashtabula counties are best enjoyed with itineraries that focus on one of several clusters of attractions. In western Lake county, the charming towns of Willoughby, Kirtland, Painesville, and Fairport Harbor radiate around the typically suburban town of Mentor, making it a good focal point for that area. Farther east, the resort town of Geneva-on-the-Lake can easily be a destination in its own right, but from there it's an easy shot to the historic towns of Unionville and Madison as well as the northernmost of Ashtabula County's fabled covered bridges, including the longest of them. Likewise, as you move closer to the state border, the city of Ashtabula offers plenty of its own diversions but is also within easy reach of Conneaut and the 19th-century gem of a small town, Jefferson, the county seat. From any of these places you're never far from the water if a lakeside visit is your main goal. Likewise, I–90 will take you quickly into Cleveland, and back out again. It's just a short jaunt nearly anywhere for attractions both nautical or non-nautical.

You'll be delighted by the contrasts here. Deep ravines are steps away from quaint downtowns. A scant mile or so off I–90 are sleepy crossroads towns that seem untouched by time. With so many sights in so small an area, why not be brave? Point your car down a county road or quiet highway, and be assured you'll find panoramas unmatched by any in rural America. In this tourist-friendly country, abundant signs point the way to the next covered bridge or other attractions. So go ahead, get lost, and take the road less traveled.

WHAT TO SEE & DO

ASHTABULA & NEARBY TOWNS

Ashtabula has everything a water-lover could wish for, from sailing and fishing to jet skiing and windsurfing. Easy access to Lake Erie is available from four public beaches and a number of area marinas. Once you've dried off, head for the Bridge Street area, where 19th-century storefronts house a hodgepodge of restaurants, antique shops, and other boutiques. Nearby, the famed Bascule lift bridge has a unique see-saw effect—it goes up every half hour to let pleasure craft pass. From there, it's an easy walk up the hill to Point Park for views of the Lake, the lighthouse, and the remains of the once-mighty industrial port.

From Ashtabula, drive east to the city of Conneaut, which also celebrates its lakefront with a string of green parks and sandy beaches and a cluster of shops and eateries near the harbor area. Or drive south to Jefferson, where the well-preserved old homes and churches and the annual Covered Bridge Festival take you back in time.

Ashtabula Arts Center This busy arts venue hosts many music, dance, theater, and visual arts events throughout the year, including performances of *The Nutcracker* in December. In the summer months, productions move outdoors to a covered, open-air theater; most of these shows are musicals. > 2928 W. 13th St., Ashtabula, tel. 440/964–3396.

Conneaut Historical Railroad Museum Housed in the town's old railroad depot, which was built in 1900, this tribute to the locomotive includes a steam engine and railroad cars. > 342 Depot St., Conneaut, tel. 440/599–7878. Free. Memorial Day–Labor Day, daily noon–5.

Great Lakes Marine and U.S. Coast Guard Memorial Museum First a lighthouse-keeper's home, then a Coast Guard station, this building is now a museum of nautical memorabilia showing what a sailor's life is like on the Great Lakes. Especially impressive is the pilothouse from a Great Lakes ore boat and the working model of a hulett, a giant ore-unloading machine. > 1071–73 Walnut Blvd., Ashtabula, tel. 440/964–6847. $4. Memorial Day–Labor Day, Thurs.–Sun. and holidays noon–5; Sept., weekends noon–5.

Hubbard House Underground Railroad Museum This 1841 house-turned-museum on Lake Erie once served as the endpoint of the Underground Railroad. Runaway slaves would wait in the barn until a ship could come to take them to Canada. Period furnishings and Civil War artifacts specific to Ashtabula are on display. > Walnut Blvd. and Lake Ave., Ashtabula, tel. 440/964–8168. $5. Memorial Day–end of Sept., Fri.–Sun. 1–5. By appointment year-round.

Victorian Perambulator Museum Step into the world of children of the 19th century in this offbeat museum with dozens of ornate, beautifully crafted Victorian baby buggies, many of them in such fanciful forms as swans, gondolas, even a model-T. In addition to the buggies, you'll see antique toys, dolls, sleds, and games. The twin sisters who have amassed this collection, and who lead tours, are characters in their own right. > 26 E. Cedar St., Jefferson, tel. 440/576–9588. $4. Sept.–May, Sat. 11–5 and by appointment.

GENEVA-ON-THE-LAKE & SURROUNDING AREA

Billed as Ohio's first summer resort, Geneva-on-the-Lake hasn't changed much since its heyday in the 1950s and '60s. Perhaps it's that frozen-in-time quality that keeps luring families back year after year, sometimes to the third and fourth generations. The mile-long "Strip" is a perpetual carnival, with its string of arcades, fun houses, open-air restaurants, dance halls, and the oldest miniature golf course in continuous use in the United States. Though the town's beach has eroded substantially, you'll still find a sandy stretch at nearby Geneva State Park. Just a short drive away from the shoreline takes you to the more sedate town of Geneva with its interesting shops, and still farther south takes you to the edge of covered-bridge country and some of the region's finest wineries, not to mention the historical sites in Unionville and the antique shops and teahouses in Madison, just over the border with Lake County.

Debonné Vineyard Perched on the edge of Ohio's "Grand Canyon" (the deep valley of the Grand River) is a patchwork of vineyards thriving in a unique microclimate created by the river's gorge. Debonné Vineyard cultivates nearly 80,000 vines and 21 grape varieties. Take a free tour of the winery, then, for a modest charge, enjoy a wine tasting in the Chalet or on one of the canopied porches or under the grape arbor. Gourmet dining is offered by reservation from early June through the end of August on Friday and Saturday evening. > 7743 Doty Rd., Madison, tel. 440/466–3485, www.debonne.com. Tour free; tastings $2.50–$4.50. Tues.–Sat. 1:30–5.

Erieview Park On Geneva-on-the-Lake's "Strip," this park's attractions rival that of a county fair's, with class rides like bumper cars, a Tilt-a-Whirl, a merry-go-round, a Ferris Wheel, and an Octopus. The park's water slides can be enjoyed separately or as part of a package with the rides. > 5483 Lake Rd., Geneva-on-the-Lake, tel. 440/466–8650. Ride and slide packages $7–$15.50. Rides: May–Sept., daily 2–10. Slides: May–Sept., daily noon–9.

Ferrante Winery & Ristorante The full range of Ohio wines, both dry and sweet, can be sampled at Ferrante, now in Harpersfield Township south of Geneva. The Ferrante family originally established their winery in 1937 in Cleveland's ethnic Collinwood neighborhood. The wine cellar is open for tours on weekends only, but the restaurant serves wine year-round. The ample windows look onto vistas of vines stretching to the horizon. In the summer months you can sit outdoors or in the gazebo. > 5585 Rte. 307, Geneva, tel. 440/466–8466, www.ferrantewinery.com. Free. Weekend afternoons.

Geneva State Park Stretching along 2 mi of Lake Erie, this park offers a natural 300-foot beach, several areas of freshwater marsh, and beautiful mature woods. The east break wall at the marina is capped with a sidewalk providing a scenic panorama of the shoreline. Boaters can use a six-lane boat ramp or dock at the marina, which also rents bicycles and wave runners. Here there are a full-service campground, cottages with kitchens and cable TV, and an 18-hole public golf course. At this writing, a sizeable new state lodge is slated to open in May 2004 with 109 guest rooms, and a conference center. > 429 Padanarum Rd., tel. 440/466–8400, www.ohiostateparks.org. Free. Apr.–Nov., daily dawn–dusk.

Old Firehouse Winery This unique Ohio winery, host to a restaurant and a slew of annual events, overlooks Lake Erie. Tours of the winery can be arranged for groups; otherwise, one of the amiable staff members will show you the production room and let you look around the facilities. Each of the 22 wines is available for sale by the bottle. If it's a nice day, you can order the sample tray and sit under the gazebo, enjoying the view and the wine. > 5499 Lake Rd., Geneva-on-the-Lake, tel. 440/466–9300, fax 440/466–8011, www.oldfirehousewinery.com. Free. June–Aug., daily noon–1 AM; Sept.–Dec., Mon.–Thurs. noon–7, Fri. and Sat. noon–midnight, Sun. 1–6; Jan.–Apr., Fri. and Sat. noon–11, Sun. 1–5.

Shandy Hall Several generations of the locally influential Harper family resided in this home, built in 1815 and still packed with many of the family's original furnishings and artifacts. The house's 17 rooms include the formal parlor with American Empire furniture and a splendid banquet room with a coved ceiling and French wallpaper hand-painted with colorful scenes. > 6333 South Ridge Rd. W, Geneva, tel. 440/466–3680, www.wrhs.org/sites/shandy.htm. $4. May–Oct., weekends noon–5.

WESTERN LAKE COUNTY

Don't think of this suburban area as suburban in character. From Mentor, the site of Lawnfield, President Garfield's home, the charming and interesting towns of Willoughby, Kirtland, Painesville, and Fairport Harbor radiate outward like spokes on a wheel. To the west, Willoughby offers a historic downtown shopping district extending from a town square with a gazebo and tree-lined streets with stately homes. To the south, Kirtland is the home of the Holden Arboretum's vast collection of botanical treasures and historic sites associated with the founding of the Mormon Church. To the east, Painesville has a town square with a magnificent courthouse and typically New England architecture in many of the 19th-century homes in its historic core. And of course to the north are the Lake itself with the long sandy beach at Headlands State Park and the Mentor Lagoons and the nautical community of Fairport Harbor.

Fairport Marine Museum The real treat here is to climb the spiral staircase of the classic conical lighthouse for a panoramic view of the Lake and the town below. The adjoining lighthouse-keeper's home is now a museum of maritime artifacts, including the lighthouse's original beacon, navigation instruments, marine charts, and a fully equipped pilot house from a Great Lakes ship. > 129 2nd St., Fairport Harbor, tel. 440/354–4825, www.fairportlighthouse.com. $3. Memorial Day–Labor Day, Wed. and weekends 1–6.

Headlands Beach State Park This mile-long natural sand beach is the longest in Ohio. Though a magnet for swimmers and picnickers from Cleveland and beyond, the beach's sheer size ensures ample space for everyone. There are sand dunes at the park's eastern edge in a state nature preserve protecting many plant species not found elsewhere in Ohio. A long break wall extending out to the lighthouse is a popular spot for fishing. Park facilities include rest rooms (no showers), concessions, picnic area, playground, and trails. > 9601 Headlands Rd., Mentor, tel. 216/881–8141, www.dnr.state.oh.us/parks. Free. June–Sept., daily dawn–dusk.

Historic Kirtland A general store, an inn, a schoolhouse, a sawmill, and other structures re-create the 1830s village of Kirtland, depicting the time when Joseph Smith and his followers were working out the tenets of a new faith they called the Church of Jesus Christ of Latter-Day Saints. Today the Mormon Church offers guided tours in this place integral to their beginnings before they moved westward. > 7800 Kirtland-Chardon Rd., Kirtland, tel. 449/256–9805, www.lds.org/placestovisit/alphabetical. Free. Mon.–Sat. 9 AM–dusk, Sun. 11:30–dusk.

Holden Arboretum The largest arboretum in the United States and one of the largest in the world, this 3,400-acre "plant museum" is a preserve of horticultural collections and display gardens interspersed with ponds, open fields, deep ravines, and woodlands with trees dating back as much as 200 years. With magnolias, crab apples, lilacs, rhododendrons, and viburnums, something's always blooming at Holden during the summer months. In fall, the many maple trees offer spectacular foliage. With 20 mi of trails to choose from, you can take a short walk, a rugged hike, or a guided tour. Another option is to select from a slate of activities that includes birding or wildflower walks. > 9500 Sperry Rd., Kirtland, tel. 440/946–4400, www.holdenarb.org. $4. Tues.–Sun. 10–5.

Kirtland Temple From its hilltop vantage point, this gleaming white structure commands attention with its imposing blend of Greek, Georgian, Gothic, and federal architecture. The first Mormon temple in the United States, it was dedicated in 1836 when as many as 2,000 of Joseph Smith's followers resided in Kirtland and surrounding areas. Take the worthwhile tour of the interior, with its curious arrangement of facing altars and boxed pews with benches that could be moved to face either direction. > 9020 Chillicothe Rd., Kirtland, tel. 440/256–3318, www.kirtlandtemple.org. Free. Mon.–Sat. 9–5, Sun. 1–5.

Lake Farmpark Think of it as an agricultural theme park, a place where kids and adults alike can learn where their food comes from. Milk a cow, watch border collies herd sheep, ride in a horse-drawn wagon, or pet a lamb or an alpaca. You can even help with the chores here, if you'd like, or just watch as the fields are plowed or harvested. The farm buildings have interactive displays, including one of a giant tomato with vines as big as your waist. > 8809 Chardon Rd., Kirtland, tel. 440/256–2122 or 800/366–3276, www.lakemetroparks.com. $6. Daily 9–5.

Lawnfield (James A. Garfield National Historic Site) James A. Garfield, 20th president of the United States, made his home in this rambling Victorian mansion, the site of the first "front porch" presidential campaign. Following her husband's assassination, Garfield's widow constructed the first presidential library on the site. Though Garfield's presidency lasted less than a year, you can expect a thorough introduction to his life and political career from enthusiastic guides who make use of the many family items in the home as they relate anecdotes from Garfield's rise to power. Of note are a funeral wreath sent by Queen Victoria and the president's bronze death mask in the adjacent museum. > 8095 Mentor Ave., U.S. 20, tel. 440/255–8722, www.nps.gov/jaga. $7. May 1–Nov. 1, Mon.–Sat. 10–5, Sun. noon–5.

Tours

Ashtabula County Covered Bridge Tour This drive-yourself tour starts at any point in Ashtabula County with a sign bearing a covered bridge emblem. From that point you can wend your way through picturesque farmlands and villages to all of the 16 bridges in the county. There are two segments, one covering 69 mi, the other 66. One convenient starting point is Harpersfield Bridge. The longest of the bridges at 228 feet, it's close to Exit 218 of I–90. Contact the Ashtabula County Covered Bridge Association to get a brochure or map. > Ashtabula Covered Bridge Association, 25 W. Jefferson St., Jefferson, tel. 440/576–3769.

Sports

BASEBALL

Lake County Captains You needn't go to downtown Cleveland to watch professional baseball while vacationing on Ohio's northeast coast. In 2003, the Cleveland Indians' Class A affiliate, the Lake County Captains, relocated to Ohio from Georgia. The Captains plan to play 70 games annually in a new 6,500-seat ballpark. > Eastlake Ballpark, on Rte. 91, just north of St. Rte. 2, Willoughby, tel. 440/954–9467, www.captainsbaseball.com.

BIRD-WATCHING

The Lake Erie coastline is a major stopover point for migrating birds before and after they cross Lake Erie.

Mentor Lagoons A mile and a half of coastline containing a great diversity of wetland communities, this is a resting spot not only for birds but also for butterflies. > 8365 Harbor Dr., Mentor, tel. 440/205–3625.
Mentor Marsh The nature center here is open to the public on weekends from noon to 5 and guided walks are offered on Sundays. > 5185 Corduroy Rd., Mentor, tel. 440/257–0777.

BOATING

Geneva State Park Marina At this location, you'll find charter fishing, jet ski rentals, a marine shop and repair, bait, seasonal and transient docking, and a six-boat launch ramp. > 4499 Padanarum Rd., Geneva, tel. 440/466–7565.

CHARTER FISHING

Fishing for Lake Erie's prized walleye and perch can be tricky since the schools tend to migrate to favorable "thermoclines," which is to say they move to where the water is cool when it's hot outside and vice versa. These fish are also surprisingly mercurial about lures. Knowledgeable charter-fishing captains can help you sort out where the fish are biting and what you'll need to reel them in. Deep offshore fishing where you can troll 30 to 40 feet works best, so you'll want to hire not only the captains but their boats as well.

Burns Charters Besides fishing for trophy walleye from June through August, this charter also fishes smallmouth bass from April to June and perch in June and September. > Geneva State Park Marina, 4499 Padanarum Rd., Geneva-on-the-Lake, tel. 330/747-1797 or 440/415-1391.

Schoney Charters Captain Jim Schonauer has been taking charters into Lake Erie's Central Basin waters since 1985. Charters focus on small-mouth bass and perch in the spring, switching over to walleye and steelhead trout in the summer. > 6227 Thunderbird Dr., Mentor, tel. 440/951-4012.

Thumper Charters A fleet of 12 boats fishes Lake Erie's western basin near Sandusky in the spring and the Central Basin from June through September. Tackle and bait are provided. > 585 Nelmar, Painesville, tel. 440/639-0185 or 216/317-8092.

FISHING

The streams of this region are high-ranked in the up-and-coming sport of steelhead trout fishing. Public access areas for the Chagrin River include Woodland Park and Lake Shore Boulevard in Eastlake, as well as Gilson Park and Daniel Park in Willoughby. The west break wall at Headlands Beach State Park and the end of Water Street in Fairport Harbor give access to the Grand River. You can reach Arcola Creek in Madison Township from the end of Lake Road. The tackle shops listed here are good places for guidance and information on stream conditions.

OUTFITTERS **D & W Sports** > 786 Richmond Rd., Painesville, tel. 440/354-8473. **North Coast Salmon & Steelhead** > Tel. 440/779-5270, www.northcoastsalmonsteelheadguide.com.

Save the Date

JUNE

Northeast Ohio Polka Festival For an oom-pah-pah weekend, head for the Old Firehouse Winery in Geneva-on-the-Lake on the second weekend of June. Bands specializing in Slovenian, Chicago-style, and Polish polkas perform, and there are lots of pierogies and sausage. > 5499 Lake Rd., Geneva-on-the-Lake, tel. 440/466-9300.

JULY–AUGUST

Great Lakes Medieval Faire Knights in shining armor joust and minstrels perform while you savor food and ale and sample the wares of 120 juried artisans. Each weekend has a different theme. > St. Rte. 534, 7 mi south of Exit 218 on I–90, tel. 888/633-4382, www.medievalfaire.com.

AUGUST

Vintage Ohio Meet the winemakers from more than 20 wineries, browse among fine arts and crafts, and listen to the best regional bands on the grounds of Lake Farmpark. > 8800 Chardon Rd., Kirtland, tel. 800/227-6962.

SEPTEMBER

Geneva Grape Jamboree The streets of Geneva are alive with games, food, and parades during this annual celebration the last full weekend of September. > Main St. and Broadway, Geneva, tel. 440/466-5262.

Village Peddler Festival Billed as "a quaint outdoor American marketplace," this festival offers the wares, ranging from country to Victorian to primitive, of 150 craftspeople. > Buccaneer Lake, on St. Rte. 307 between Jefferson and Austinburg, tel. 440/466-8414.

OCTOBER
Ashtabula County Covered Bridge Festival A tour of 16 covered bridges is the high-light of this festival, which celebrates Ashtabula County's claim to fame as the covered bridge capital of the world. > Tel. 440/998–6998.

WHERE TO STAY

ASHTABULA & NEARBY TOWNS
Cedars Motel Parking spaces right outside of the rooms and knotty pine paneling lend a 1950s flavor to this single-story wood motel. Downtown Ashtabula is only a mile and a half away. > 2015 W. Prospect Rd. (U.S. 20), Ashtabula, tel. 440/992–5406, fax 440/992–0626. 17 rooms. Microwaves, refrigerators, cable TV, business services, laundry facilities, no-smoking rooms. AE, D, DC, MC, V. ¢
Michael Cahill Bed & Breakfast This 1880 Stick-style, late Victorian home is on the National Register of Historic Places. It's in the harbor district, two blocks from Walnut Beach. Rooms have views of Lake Erie and Victorian furnishings, with accents like Jenny Lind beds. It's an easy walk to historic Bridge Street and nearby museums. > 1106 Walnut Blvd., Ashtabula, tel. 440/964–8449, www.cahillbb.com. 4 rooms. No room TVs, no smoking. No credit cards. BP. ¢–$
Peggy's Bed and Breakfast This B&B gives you more privacy than most. Accommodations are in a cottage in the woods 100 yards from the main house. The cottage has a gas fireplace and a kitchen; with its loft, it sleeps four. There's a full kitchen and you'll have a menu of 30 items to choose from for breakfast. Peggy's is 2 mi from I–90, off Exit 223. > 8721 Munson Hill Rd., Ashtabula 44004, tel. 440/969–1996, fax 440/964–5767, www.peggysbedandbreakfast.com. 1 cottage. In-room VCRs; no smoking. MC, V. BP. $

GENEVA-ON-THE-LAKE & SURROUNDING AREA
Anchor Motel A family-run operation, the Anchor has views of the Lake from its shady grove. A picnic ground and a play area take full advantage of these natural assets. The cottages have kitchens and sleeper sofas; each cottage can accommodate up to five adults. > 5196 Lake Rd. E., Geneva-on-the-Lake 44041, tel. 440/466–0726 or 800/642–2978, www.anchormotelandcottages.com. 6 rooms, 7 cottages. Microwaves, refrigerators, cable TV, picnic area. D, MC, V. Closed Dec.–Feb. ¢
Charlma Bed and Breakfast The white frame house sits right on the shore of Lake Erie, and Geneva State Park is a short drive away. There are a TV in the two-story great room, and a hot tub in the screen porch facing the Lake. Rooms have brass beds, skylights, and antique furnishings. > 6739 Lake Rd. W, Geneva-on-the-Lake 44041, tel. 440/466–3646, www.charlma.com. 3 rooms. Hot tub; no room TVs, no smoking. Closed Sept.–June. No credit cards. BP. $–$$
Eagle Cliff Inn/Beach Club Originally a boarding house dating back to the 1880s, the property, which reopened in 2003 as an inn, is listed on the National Register of Historic Places. A "wine and vine" motif is carried out at the bed-and-breakfast, which is for adults only. Couples and small families are welcome in the cottages, which have kitchens with microwaves. Breakfast is not included in the rates for the cottages. Outside there's a private beach on the Lake. > 5254 Lake Rd. E, Geneva-on-the-Lake 44041, tel. 440/466–1110, fax 440/466–0315, www.beachclubbandb.com. 6 rooms, 3 cottages. Some kitchens, some microwaves; no smoking. MC, V. $–$$

Lakehouse Inn Take your pick—this homey lakeside inn offers both a B&B and cottages. There's a private beach, lighted decks, game room, and the inn has its own winery on the premises. It's just a short walk to the "Strip." Breakfast is not included for the cottages. Guests furnish their own linens for the cottages. > 5643 Lake Rd., Geneva-on-the-Lake 44041, tel. 440/466–8668, fax 440/466–2556, www.thelakehouseinn.com. 9 rooms, 9 cottages. Some kitchens, some microwaves, beach; no TV in some rooms, no smoking. AE, D, MC, V. $–$$$

Lucille's Lakefront Cottage Just 25 feet from a beach, these cottages with their magnificent coastline views have everything provided, even china. The grill and picnic table are perfect for afternoon barbecues. There are two two-bedroom cottages: one sleeps eight, the other sleeps five. > 4935 N. Putnam, Geneva-on-the-Lake 44041 (117 Argali Pl., Cortland 44410), tel. 330/638–7652, www.lucilleslakefront.com. 2 cottages. Kitchens, microwaves, cable TV, in-room VCRs, no-smoking rooms. AE, D, MC, V. $$–$$$

WESTERN LAKE COUNTY

Best Western Lawnfield Inn Like President Garfield's home down the street, this inn has a Victorian character with white wicker rocking chairs on the front porch and antiques and marble inside. There are Garfield artifacts, including photos of the late President and his family and copies of his letters, on display here. > 8434 Mentor Ave., Mentor 44060, tel. 440/205–7378 or 866/205–7378, www.bestwestern.com. 50 rooms. Microwaves, refrigerators, cable TV, pool, gym, Internet, meeting rooms, no-smoking rooms. AE, D, DC, MC, V. CP. $–$$

Fitzgerald's Irish Bed & Breakfast Just steps away from the town square in Painesville's historic district is this renovated French Tudor mansion with its distinctive turret. Gaelic signs add to the Irish flavor in the castlelike public areas, which include an 11-foot fireplace, a great room with a massive beamed ceiling, and an ornate staircase. Each of the three guest rooms has a private bath; the room in the attic has a full kitchen and Jacuzzi. > 47 Mentor Ave., Painesville 44077, tel. 440/639–0845, www.fitzgeraldsbnb.com/. 3 rooms. No kids under 13, no smoking. AE, D, MC, V. BP. $–$$

Renaissance Quail Hollow Resort The lobby at this grand resort has four-story, cherrywood walls, a magnificent stone fireplace, and comfortable Mission-style furniture. With two wooded golf courses, tennis, two pools, a jogging court, and fine dining on site, you may be tempted never to leave the grounds. Large quiet rooms have wood furnishings. At this writing, the tennis courts were under renovation but scheduled to reopen in late 2004. > 11080 Concord-Hambden Rd., Exit 200 of I–90, Concord 44077, tel. 440/497–1100, fax 440/497–1111, www.renaissancehotels.com. 17 rooms, 6 suites. Restaurant, room service, in-room data ports, cable TV with movies, 2 18-hole golf courses, tennis courts, 2 pools, gym, hot tub, sauna, lounge, business services, meeting rooms, no-smoking rooms. AE, D, DC, MC, V. $$–$$$

WHERE TO EAT

ASHTABULA & NEARBY TOWNS

Casa Capelli Italian, American, and Mexican options—including seafood and steaks—fill the menu at this former bank, which has stained glass and a beautiful arched skylight. The bank vault is now a private dining room. There's a kids' menu, and no lunch Saturday until 2. > 4641 Main Ave., Ashtabula, tel. 440/992–3700. AE, D, MC, V. **$–$$$$**

El Grande Despite the guns and holsters on the walls, the black leather tablecloths, and the photos of old-time cowboys like Gene Autry and Roy Rogers, the menu here is more Midwestern than Western. The steaks are cowboy-size, and there are plenty of seafood, pasta, and chicken dishes and sandwiches to round out the menu. > 2145 W. Prospect St., Ashtabula, tel. 440/998–2228. Closed Sun.–Mon. No lunch Sat. AE, D, MC, V. **$–$$**

GENEVA-ON-THE-LAKE & SURROUNDING AREA

Ferrante Winery and Ristorante Ample windows in this spacious high-ceilinged Italian restaurant face the extensive vineyards. Many dishes are prepared with wine, such as the Pollo Portobello and Nick's Pesce Pasta. > 5585 St. Rte. 307, Geneva, tel. 440/466–8466, www.ferrantewinery.com. Reservations not accepted. AE, D, MC, V. **$–$$$**

Mary's Kitchen Mary's has been a Geneva-on-the-Lake tradition for 60 years. The restaurant, which is just off "the Strip" on a side street near the Lake, occupies the bottom floor of a renovated house—complete with a screen porch. You might feel as if you're eating in someone's living room, especially when simple homey dishes such as liver and onions, cabbage rolls, and stuffed peppers arrive. Cinnamon bread and rolls are popular breakfast choices. > 5023 New St., Geneva-on-the-Lake, tel. 440/466–8606. No credit cards. Closed Labor Day–Mother's Day. **$**

Old Firehouse Winery Each of the vineyard's 22 wines are available with dinner in this restaurant, which is in a former firehouse. The menu focuses on traditional American items such as ribs, chicken, steak, and shrimp. You can sit indoors and out, and there are nightly entertainment and a kids' menu. > 5499 Lake Rd., Geneva-on-the-Lake, tel. 440/466–9300, fax 440/466–8011, www.oldfirehousewinery.com. Closed Jan.–Apr., Mon.–Thurs. AE, D, MC, V. **$–$$**

Old Tavern This local institution began as a log cabin in 1798, and, in the course of several expansions, it has served as a stagecoach stop and a station on the Underground Railroad. Ask to see the tunnel in the basement where, legend has it, runaway slaves crossed under the road to a false tombstone exit in the cemetery across the street. Locals believe Harriet Beecher Stowe wove stories she'd heard about this Unionville tavern into *Uncle Tom's Cabin*. Nowadays, there are sandwiches in a pub and dining in several rooms overlooking a garden and gazebo. Try an order of the famous corn fritters. Especially popular are the Friday night buffets and Sunday brunches. > St. Rte. 84 at County Line Rd., Unionville, tel. 440/428–2091 or 800/782–8376. AE, D, DC, MC, V. Closed Mon. **$$–$$$$**

WESTERN LAKE COUNTY

Brennan's Fish House Directly across the street from the water, Brennan's looks like a New England dockside restaurant, complete with a weathered clapboard exterior. Enjoy Lake Erie perch or walleye, with other house specialties including crab legs, bouillabaisse, and steak and scampi. > 101 River St., Grand River, tel. 440/354–9785. AE, D, MC, V. Closed Sun. **$–$$$$**

Grandon Family Restaurant The large plate-glass windows at this restaurant overlook Fairport Harbor's lighthouse. Stop by Grandon's for lunchtime melt sandwiches and homemade soup; dinners are hearty, with such mains as meat loaf, beer-batter cod, and pork chops. Save room for dessert—Grandon's is known for its 26 flavors of ice cream. It's open for breakfast. > 203 High St., Fairport Harbor, tel. 440/352–1393. AE, D, MC, V. ¢–$$

Molinari's There's a California air to both the dining room and the menu, which in-cludes a wide range of entrées, among them crab cakes, filet mignon stuffed with Gorgonzola and walnut pesto, mushroom pasta, risotto with beef tips, pasta put-tanesca (here made with chicken, sausage, mushrooms, and Asiago), and veal four seasons (with roasted red peppers, prosciutto, Portobello mushrooms, and artichoke hearts in vodka cream sauce). There's jazz Friday and Saturday. > 8900 Mentor Ave., Mentor, tel. 440/974–2750. Closed Sun. AE, D, DC, MC, V. $$–$$$$

Pickle Bill's You can literally step off your boat and up to a bar at this local institu-tion. You'll be taking a seat on a swing rather than on a bar stool, but that's part of the fun at this quirky, carnival-like spot. Pickle Bill's is known for its raw bar, all-you-can-eat walleye, Alaskan king crab legs, and barbecue ribs. > 101 River St., Grand River, tel. 440/352–6343. AE, D, DC, MC, V. Closed Mon. No lunch Sept.–May. $$–$$$$

Potpourri Fondue Mood lighting and wine racks make this a romantic place for din-ner, although dress is casual and guests of all ages eat here. The extensive fondue menu includes cheese, beef, shrimp, chicken, and chocolate. Steaks and pasta are also served. > 8885 Mentor Ave., tel. 440/255–4334. No lunch. D, MC, V. $–$$

ESSENTIALS

Getting Here

Lake County is accessible by public transportation, with Cleveland's system reaching to the county's edges and then the local Laketran system (800/400–1300) picking up from there. With curtailed weekend schedules, however, and with routes that don't always extend to the attractions you might want to see, planning itineraries using the local buses offers logistical chal-lenges at best. In Ashtabula County, you're even more on your own. Route 2 and I–90 offer quick access to Cleveland or farther east to Erie and the New York Thruway, although construction and severe weather in winter offer their own challenges as well.

BY CAR

You can zip through this region in a car quite readily, with a network of signs making it child's play to find the attraction you're seeking. U.S. 20 is a major east–west corridor but is distinctly lacking in charm along much of its journey. Route 84 is more varied in its offerings as it passes from urban to rural areas, as are the north–south paths of Routes 306 and 44. Ashtabula County is more reliably picturesque with its highways, except for U.S. 20, passing through vis-tas of meadows and farmlands.

A rule of thumb here is to head for the water, and not just the lakefront, al-though Route 531 between Conneaut and Ashtabula is a picturesque and un-hurried byway on the lake. But don't forget the other waterways of the region—the twisting river and creek valleys offer amazing panoramas of forested hills and deep gorges at points. If you find a good map with high-ways paralleling some kind of stream, it's definitely worth the chance of find-ing a vista.

With its proximity to Cleveland, western Lake County can get congested during typical rush hour times but travelers off the major roads should find few delays, and even the major highways are quite manageable at non-peak times.

Visitor Information

CONTACTS **Ashtabula County Convention and Visitors Bureau** > 1850 Austinburg Rd., Austinburg 44010, tel. 440/275–3202 or 800/337–6746, www.accvb.org. **Lake County Visitors Bureau** > 35300 Vine St., Eastlake 44095, tel. 440/975–1234 or 800/368–5253, www.lakevisit.com.

Erie Triangle Vineyards

350 mi northeast of Cincinnati, 100 mi northeast of Cleveland, and 230 mi northeast of Columbus.

8

By Clark Henderson

THE ERIE TRIANGLE OF PENNSYLVANIA IS that odd angular protuberance that reaches up along Lake Erie in the northwestern corner of the state, seemingly appropriating land from New York. By the time the first European explorers arrived in the early 17th century, the area was inhabited by the Erie, a Native American people that were nearly decimated by the Iroquois Confederacy by 1656. The French and British then vied for control over the region in the 18th century—the French building a fort at Presque Isle in 1753 only to have it captured and rebuilt by the British in 1760, who then had their fort destroyed by Seneca Indians inspired by the rebellion at Detroit led by Ottawa chief Pontiac.

After the establishment of the United States, the Triangle was again contested, this time principally by New York, Pennsylvania, and Massachusetts. Seneca chief Cornplanter arranged a transfer of the land from the Seneca occupiers to Pennsylvania by way of the federal government. In 1792 the Commonwealth purchased the area, about 200,000 acres and highly valued because it offered Pennsylvania a much-needed port on Lake Erie, for about $150,000. Soon thereafter the area was again the site of conflict in the War of 1812. The fledgling American fleet that fought against the British for control over Lake Erie was built in the Triangle. Today you can find historical sites and names commemorating events of the French and Indian War and the War of 1812 in and around the city of Erie.

In addition to the shipping and industry now centered around the city of Erie—from railroad equipment manufacturing to plastic—the Triangle is also known for its grape production. Pennsylvania ranks fifth in the country in grape production and 95% of its output is from the Lake Erie Triangle. You'll encounter miles of vineyards along the sloping shore of the lake east of Erie. A lot of the grapes grown here, the native Concord and Niagara grapes in particular, are used to make juice, but about 10% of the crop is used to make wine.

In Pennsylvania, viticulture, or the cultivation of grapes for winemaking, goes back to the 1600s when William Penn planted some European, or vinifera, vines in Philadelphia's Fairmount Park. Penn never got the desired grapes as the harsh Philadelphia winter proved to be too much for the transplant vines. The Lake Erie Triangle turned out to be the part of the state most conducive to wine-grape production, including the more delicate European varietals. The first winery in the area appeared in 1863, but wine production was brought to a halt in the Prohibition years and had difficulty recovering until the 1960s, when a couple of wineries started up in the small town of North East. Now several more exist and have added to the native labrusca grapes and French-American hybrids the more familiar vinifera, such as Chardonnay, Riesling, and Cabernet Sauvignon.

Unlike Penn, the Triangle vineyards have had some success growing these temperamental vinifera. Lake Erie moderates the climate along its shore—summers aren't as hot as in the surrounding area and, more importantly, winters aren't as cold. The constant breeze near the lake prevents the pooling of frosty air and also reduces damaging fungal growth on the grapes. Winter kill still happens, and as the grape farmers will tell you, growing the most-prized wine grapes can be a frustrating endeavor. The hardier hybrids, which offer some of the taste characteristics of the vinifera, have been more successful. The Seyval Blanc, derived from a Zinfandel, and the Chambourcin, a red whose lineage goes back to France's Loire Valley, are two that turn out able wines. The Triangle wineries also still produce a number of wines from the native grapes, which tend to be quite sweet and fruity.

Not as prolific as some of their competitors to the northeast, the wineries of the Finger Lake region of New York State, and not as acclaimed as the winemakers of the famous California valleys, the wineries of Lake Erie provide free tastings and tours with a friendly, down-home attitude in beautiful natural surroundings.

So you probably won't find wines that rival the best of Napa or Sonoma, but some are quite drinkable, especially for winemakers that have to contend with a harsher climate than those of Europe and California and that are relatively new at the difficult art of winemaking.

A dose of history, an abundance of grapes and tastes of wine, unique terrain and natural beauty, including sunsets over the vast blue of Lake Erie that locals insist are unparalleled anywhere in the world—these are reasons enough to give the Erie Triangle a try for a weekend.

WHAT TO SEE & DO

ERIE

Founded in 1795, Erie is Pennsylvania's only port town on the Great Lakes and its northernmost city. A military outpost for the French, British, and then Americans and an important site for shipbuilding during the War of 1812, Erie drew few people in its early years, but with the advent of the steam engine, canals, railroads, and the rise of commercial traffic on Lake Erie the town's population exploded. The bayfront area of the city has been extensively redeveloped and offers a museum, a public library, restaurants, walking trails, and views of the lake and city from the 187-foot observation tower. Today, the city and waterfront area are a popular summer destination, the beaches at Presque Isle filled during the warmest summer months.

Erie Art Museum The two-story Greek Revival building houses a permanent collection of American ceramics, Japanese prints, and Chinese porcelain and features an annual exhibit of local artists' work and traveling shows. The museum's offerings also include classes, workshops, concerts, kids' programs, and lectures. > 411 State St., tel. 814/459–5477, www.erieartmuseum.org. $3. Tues.–Sat. 11–5, Sun. 1–5.
Erie Maritime Museum This is the home port for the reconstructed U.S. Brig *Niagara*, the warship that, led by Commodore Oliver Perry, won the Battle of Lake Erie in the War of 1812. The museum, right on Presque Isle Bay, has multimedia exhibits on area maritime life and an exhibit about the Great Lakes ecosystem. > 150 E. Front St., tel. 814/452–2744, www.brigniagara.org. $6. Mon.–Sat. 9–5, Sun. noon–5.
Erie Zoo The zoo has more than 100 species and 500 animals from all over the world, including a polar bear, giraffe, and rhinoceros. With the addition of botanical gardens, there are also more than 600 species of flora. > 423 W. 38th St., tel. 814/864–4091, www.eriezoo.org. $5.50. Daily 10–5.

Presque Isle State Park The name is French for "almost an island." This sandy spit juts into Lake Erie, creating Erie's natural harbor. Presque Isle is a National Natural Landmark and has more than 300 species of birds, many endangered and rare. **Stull Interpretive Center** (near Barracks Beach on Peninsula Dr., tel. 814/833–0351) has exhibits and displays about the park and its wildlife. The 1873 **Presque Isle Lighthouse** with its 57-foot tower, overlooks Pennsylvania's only surf beaches and more than 10 mi of trails. > Peninsula Dr., Rte. 832, tel. 814/833–7424 or 888/727–2757, www.dcnr.state.pa.us. Free. Daily 5 AM–sunset.

Waldameer Park and Water World More than 75 rides, slides, pools, and games are here at Waldameer, the 11th oldest continuously operating amusement park in the country. Free fall seven stories on Ali Baba, ride a classic wooden roller coaster, and look out over Lake Erie 100 feet in the air on the Giant Gondola Wheel. Waterworld has 11 slides, five kiddie slides, and several pool areas. > 220 Peninsula Dr., tel. 814/838–3591, www.waldameer.com. Waldameer $14.50, Waterworld $12.50, combination pass $17. May–Aug., days and hrs vary.

MEADVILLE

The seat of Crawford County, this town is in the western foothills of the Allegheny Mountains, about 35 mi south of Erie. In addition to having 19th-century neighborhoods, a village green with a gazebo, and an operating market house that dates to 1870, Meadville is close to the Erie National Wildlife Refuge and Pymatuning State Park. Conneaut Lake, Pennsylvania's largest natural lake and a haven for boating and fishing enthusiasts, is also just 7 mi away.

Allegheny College Founded in 1815 and the oldest institution of higher education in northwestern Pennsylvania, the college has 36 buildings on 72 acres of land overlooking downtown Meadville. It also owns a 283-acre nature preserve full of flora and fauna. > 520 N. Main St., tel. 814/332–3100 or 814/332–4365, www.allegheny.edu. Free. Daily.

Baldwin–Reynolds House Museum Built in 1834 by Supreme Court Justice Henry Baldwin, the museum is on 3 acres overlooking the French Creek Valley. The 19th-century house and country doctor's office are on the National Register of Historic Places. Guided tours begin every 30 minutes, the last at 3:30. > 639 Terrace St., tel. 814/724–6080. $3. May–Aug., Wed.–Sun. 1–5. Closed Mon. and Tues.

Conneaut Cellars Winery Not in the Erie Triangle but using mostly grapes from North East, this winery is in the heart of the Conneaut Lake resort area and has guided tours and tastings of the winery's 24 different wines. A good place to start on your tour of the wineries if arriving from the south via I-79, the family-run business produces some of the best wines of the region. > 12005 Conneaut Lake Rd., Conneaut, tel. 814/382–3999 or 877/229–9463, fax 814/382–6151, www.ccw-wine.com. Free. Daily 10–6.

Erie National Wildlife Refuge About 10 mi east of Meadville, the 8,777-acre refuge is a habitat for waterfowl with its beaver ponds, pools, marshlands, and grasslands. Here you can hike, bird-watch, take scenic drives, and fish. > 11296 Wood Duck La., Guy Mills, tel. 814/789–3585, www.fws.gov. Free. Daily 30 mins before sunrise–sunset.

Pymatuning State Park Occupying a large portion of the park and extending into Ohio, the Pymatuning Reservoir was once a huge swamp inhabited by the aboriginal Mound Builders, named so because they buried their dead in large mounds. Later, the Seneca Nation of the Iroquois Confederacy occupied the area, providing its present name, Pymatuning, which means "the crooked-mouthed man's dwelling place."

Cornplanter

IF YOU TRAVEL UP THE WESTERN shore of the Allegheny Reservoir near Warren, Pennsylvania, just a few miles from the border with New York State, you'll pass a portion of what was Cornplanter's Grant, about 700 acres now mostly underwater as a result of the completion of Kinzua Dam in 1964. The Commonwealth of Pennsylvania gave this land, along with two other tracts along the Allegheny, to Chief Cornplanter of the Seneca for the role he played in ceding the Seneca-controlled Erie Triangle in 1791.

At the time of the American Revolution, the Iroquois Confederacy, comprising five other nations in addition to the Seneca, was split over which side to support in the war. Cornplanter advocated neutrality but eventually submitted to pro-British Seneca and fought as a field commander against the American army in several battles, including some led by George Washington. After the war, Cornplanter consistently negotiated for peace with the U.S. government, and George Washington came to value him as a crucial figure in preventing the Iroquois from aligning themselves with insurgent Ohio tribes. Believing that a position of accommodation was the best means to preserve the Iroquois peoples, Cornplanter supported several treaties (in 1784, 1789, and 1797) that ceded large amounts of Confederacy land to the federal government and states.

His conciliatory strategy isolated him at times from the Seneca, including his political rival Red Jacket, who advocated a more antagonistic stance to maintain Indian autonomy. In 1790 Cornplanter traveled to Philadelphia, then the federal capital, as a representative of the six Iroquois nations in response to what he saw as continued American encroachment on Indian lands. George Washington, then president, avowed the sanctity of Seneca land. This pledge was reiterated in the Canandaigua Treaty of 1794 when Washington's emissary, Timothy Pickering, assured the Six Nations that their lands would never be violated by the United States.

In the 1950s, this commitment was invoked when the federal government desired the removal of Cornplanter's descendants from the upper Allegheny River in order to construct Kinzua Dam as part of a federal flood-control project. The Cornplanter Grant land was to be held by Cornplanter's descendants in perpetuity, so many viewed the removal of the inhabitants of this land as yet another broken promise by the U.S. government. The dam also flooded one third of Allegany Reservation, located just across the border in New York, displacing in total over 500 Seneca. At the time, Johnny Cash devoted a song, "As Long as the Grass Shall Grow," to the Seneca and the controversy, with a line asking Cornplanter if he could swim.

According to some accounts, toward the end of his life Cornplanter became increasingly dissatisfied with the U.S. government's treatment of the Seneca and renounced his association with the government by destroying various awards and a uniform he received from the government. He had retired to his tract along the Allegheny and worked with Quakers in constructing a school there, an association with the Society of Friends that had begun at the advice of George Washington during his 1790 trip to Philadelphia. Cornplanter died in 1836, allegedly more than 100 years old. In 1869 Pennsylvania dedicated a monument to Cornplanter at his burial site along the upper Allegheny, thought to be the first monument to a Native American in the country.

— Clark Henderson

The reservoir is an effect of the Pymatuning Dam, completed in 1934. You can swim at one of the four beaches, explore the perimeter of the reservoir on hiking trails, and pitch a tent at one of 657 campsites. There are also 25 cabins with kitchens and bathrooms to rent. The park is about 17 mi west of Meadville. > 2660 Williamsfield Rd., Jamestown, tel. 724/932–3141, www.dcnr.state.pa.us. Free. Daily dawn–sunset.

NORTH EAST

In the Erie Triangle, this town, as its name is meant to indicate, is northeast of Erie, 15 mi from downtown. One of only a handful of towns on the shore of Lake Erie in Pennsylvania, North East has five wineries and exceptional views of the lake over miles of sloping vineyards.

Arrowhead Wine Cellars Longtime area grape farmer Nicholas Mobilia decided in the late 1990s that he'd double as a vintner and started Arrowhead with a friend. Try whites and reds, from Chardonnay and the area blend known as "Reflections" to Merlot and Pinot Noir. You can also pick fruit on his nearby farm, cherries in July, and grapes in September. > 12073 E. Main Rd., North East, tel. 814/725–5509, www.arrowheadwine.com. Free. Mon.–Sat. 10–6, Sun. noon–5; hrs vary in winter.

Lake Shore Railway Museum At this restored 1899 train depot, you can see static locomotives, a dining car, a sleeper, and a caboose. Also on display are dishes from the dining car, maps, and tools. Out back, diehard train-watchers set up chairs for a front-row view of the active yard, with more than 80 daily trains. > 31 Wall St., at Robinson St., tel. 814/825–2724. Free. June–Aug., Wed.–Sun. 1–5; May, Sept., and Oct., weekends 1–5.

Mazza Vineyards The processing plant at Mazza, one of Pennsylvania's oldest and largest wineries, has a touch of Mediterranean architecture. You can take a free tour of the production facilities before enjoying complimentary tasting. Try their ice wine, a dessert wine made from Vidal Blanc grapes harvested in December after they have frozen on the vine. Mazza also owns Penn Shore Winery, just down Route 5 at 10225 E. Lake Road. > 11815 E. Lake Rd., tel. 814/725–8695 or 800/796–9463, www.mazzawines.com. Free. July–Aug., Mon.–Sat. 9–8, Sun. 11–4:30; Sept.–June, Mon.–Sat. 9–5:30, Sun. 11–4:30.

Presque Isle Wine Cellars Set back from Route 6 along a wooded stream, this winery, like the others in the area, has French hybrid as well as native red and white wines. Presque Isle also specializes in supplies for the lay winemaker. > 9440 W. Main Rd., tel. 814/725–1314, www.piwine.com. Free. Mon.–Sat. 8–5; mid-Sept.–Oct., Mon.–Sat. 8–6, Sun. 8–2:30.

Save the Date

APRIL–SEPTEMBER

Erie SeaWolves Watch the Seawolves, a double-A baseball team in the Detroit Tigers' minor-league system, play at the 5,000-seat Jerry Uht Park, opened in 1995. > 110 E. 10th St., Erie, tel. 814/456–1300 or 800/456–1304, www.seawolves.com.

JULY

Harborfest The U.S. Navy SEAL's skydiving team makes an appearance at this annual, 4-day midsummer celebration that also includes hot-air balloons, musical entertainment, crafts, and activities for children. Held in Harborcreek, about 7 mi northeast of Erie on Route 2. > Harborcreek Community Park, Harborcreek, tel. 814/899–9173, www.harborcreek.org.

North East Cherry Festival A celebration of the cherry at harvest time, this festival has rides, games, and food, including cherry pies. > Downtown, North East, tel. 814/725–4336, www.lakeside.net/ne.

AUGUST

Erie Art Museum Blues and Jazz Festival Just like the name says, blues and jazz music, performed by local, regional, and national musicians, is here, all on one stage. > Downtown, Erie, tel. 814/870–1593, www.erieartmuseum.org.

Erie County Fair The oldest and largest fair in the county, this fair has amusement rides, truck and tractor pulls, and entertainers. It's held in Wattsburg, southeast of Erie on Route 8. > Erie County Fairgrounds, Wattsburg, tel. 814/739–2232, www.paeriecofair.com.

SEPTEMBER

Wine Country Harvest Festival Crafts, food, and winery tours are the order of the day at this wine and grape celebration, held in Gravel Pit Park and Gibson Park. > Downtown, North East, tel. 814/725–4262.

WHERE TO STAY

ERIE

Clarion Hotel and Convention Center An upscale hotel with a mission-style exterior, the Clarion is near Presque Isle State Park, Waldameer Park, shopping in strip malls, and chain restaurants. Rooms are available alongside the skylight-illuminated indoor pool area. > 2800 W. 8th St., Erie 16505, tel. 814/833–1116 or 800/888–8781, fax 814/838–3242, www.clarionhotel-erie.com. 130 rooms, 1 suite. Restaurant, room service, in-room data ports, some microwaves, some refrigerators, cable TV, indoor pool, gym, hot tub, sauna, bar, laundry service, business services, convention center, airport shuttle, no-smoking floor. AE, D, DC, MC, V. CP. **$$$**

Glass House Inn Here's a classic '50s motel with a Colonial design and affordable rates. The third-generation owners continue the family tradition with this motel, southwest of downtown close to the Presque Isle approach. > 3202 W. 26th St., Erie 16506, tel. 814/833–7751 or 800/956–7222, fax 814/833–4222, www.glasshouseinn.com. 30 rooms. Dining room, in-room data ports, cable TV, pool, laundry service, some pets allowed, no-smoking rooms. AE, D, DC, MC, V. CP. **$**

Lakeview on the Lake On the shore of Lake Erie about 10 mi east of downtown, the inn sits on 8 acres of lakefront property within a 10–15 minute drive of all the North East wineries. You can stroll along Lake Erie, play badminton or horseshoes on the grounds, and view sunsets over Lake Erie. > 8696 E. Lake Rd., Erie 16511, tel. 814/899–6948 or 888/558–8439, www.lakeviewerie.com/. 6 rooms, 3 suites, 3 1-room cottages, 1 mobile home. Some kitchens, some kitchenettes, microwaves, refrigerators, cable TV, pool, lake, badminton, horseshoes; no smoking. AE, D, MC, V. **$**

Marriott Residence Inn Built in the 1990s, this all-suites, four-story hotel has rooms with hot tubs, fireplaces, and kitchenettes. Staying here, you'll have all the amenities and be close to downtown restaurants. Splash Lagoon, an indoor water amusement park, is attached to the hotel. > 8061 Peach St., Erie 16509, tel. 814/864–2500, fax 814/864–0688, www.residenceinn.com. 78 rooms. Room service, in-room data ports, kitchenettes, microwaves, refrigerators, cable TV, in-room VCRs, indoor pool, laundry facilities, laundry service, meeting rooms, airport shuttle, some pets allowed (fee), no-smoking floors. AE, D, DC, MC, V. CP. **$$$–$$$$**

Spencer House Bed & Breakfast On Erie's old millionaire row, this grand Victorian house has original oak woodwork and staircase, four hanging stained-glass lamps and chandeliers, and several original mantles. After having a full breakfast in the sunny, richly paneled dining room, you'll have easy access to the bayfront activities and Presque Isle. > 519 W. 6th St., Erie 16507, tel. 814/454–5984 or 800/890–7263, fax 814/456–5019, www.spencerhouse.net. 7 rooms. Dining room, 1 in-room hot tub, cable TV, in-room VCRs, Internet, business services, some pets allowed; no smoking. AE, D, MC, V. BP. $–$$$

MEADVILLE

Days Inn Built in 1986, this hotel is just off I–79 at Exit 147A. It's 15–20 minutes from Conneaut Lake and 5 minutes from downtown Meadville. Davenport's, the full-service restaurant, has a 10% discount for adult hotel guests (kids staying at the hotel eat free). > 18360 Conneaut Lake Rd., Meadville 16335, tel. 814/337–4264 or 800/329–7466, fax 814/337–7304, www.daysinn.com. 163 rooms. Restaurant, room service, some in-room data ports, cable TV, indoor pool, gym, hot tub, bar, laundry facilities, Internet, business services, meeting rooms, some pets allowed (fee), no-smoking rooms. AE, D, DC, MC, V. BP. $–$$

NORTH EAST

Grape Arbor Bed & Breakfast Staying in one of this B&B's two mid-19th-century buildings, you'll be close to all the Triangle vineyards and can stroll through the village of North East and tree-lined Gibson Park. The rooms, each named for a grape grown in the area, are comfortably furnished in a country style, some with four-poster beds, wideboard floors, and original mantles. You'll get a four-course breakfast, which you can enjoy in the screened-in porch looking out over a flower garden. Each suite has three full rooms; one suite has a full kitchen. > 51 E Main St., North East 16428, tel. 814/725–0048 or 866/725–0048, fax 814/725–5740, www.grapearborbandb.com. 4 rooms, 3 suites. Dining room, in-room data ports, 1 in-room hot tub, 1 kitchen, 1 microwave, some refrigerators, cable TV, in-room VCRs; no kids under 12, no smoking. D, MC, V. BP. $–$$

WHERE TO EAT

ERIE

Matthew's Trattoria Housed in part of a renovated factory building where wringer washers were once manufactured, this design-conscious restaurant has pasta dishes, veal, beef tenderloin, chicken, salads with your choice of grilled meat or seafood, and, perhaps surprisingly for a largely Italian-influenced menu, sushi as an appetizer. After 10 PM on Fridays and Saturdays you can also have sushi with drinks in their lounge. > 153 E. 13th St., Erie, tel. 814/459–6458. AE, D, DC, MC, V. Closed Sun. and Mon. No lunch. $–$$$

Molly Brannigan's Too big to be called a pub but with a bar and Guinness and Harp on tap, this Irish restaurant has high ceilings, wood and stained-glass partitions, a stone hearth, and a menu that just might produce more North Atlantic cuisine enthusiasts. There's the requisite fish and chips, shepherd's pie, and corned beef, but also herb-crusted salmon, a veggie melt, and burgers. Try Paddy's Pot Roast Melt, already a local favorite. > 504 State St., Erie, tel. 814/453–7800. AE, D, MC, V. ¢–$$

Pufferbelly Named for the steam pumpers and engines that were here when it was a fire station in the early 20th century, this downtown restaurant has original fire-fighting equipment and photographs of helmeted firemen on the walls. The menu has a stuffed Portobello mushroom appetizer, steak Madagascar cooked in a mushroom sauce, and salmon salad. You can eat outside on a streetside patio. There's a buffet brunch Sunday. > 414 French St., Erie 16507, tel. 814/454–1558. AE, D, MC, V. **$–$$**
Sara's Right near the entrance to Presque Isle State Park, this seasonal '50s-style hot dog and hamburger joint has outdoor seating and drive-through service. They serve locally made Smith's hot dogs, which have natural casings and are touted by many in the area as the best in the world. > 25 Peninsula Dr., Erie, tel. 814/833–1957. Reservations not accepted. No credit cards. Closed Oct.–Mar. ¢

MEADVILLE
Julian's Just around the corner from the village green, this relaxed one-room restaurant serves breakfast and lunch. You can choose from large selection of burgers, chicken sandwiches, croissant sandwiches, and salads; they also have vegetarian options, including veggie burgers. > 299 Chestnut St., Meadville, tel. 814/337–8513. Reservations not accepted. No credit cards. Closed Sun. No dinner. ¢

NORTH EAST
CrayZ Parrot Adjacent to a marina, this Caribbean-theme restaurant has indoor and outdoor seating overlooking Lake Erie. There's lots of seafood, from crab dip to plank salmon and Cajun mahimahi. Or for the landed critters, try the Calypso pork chops, Jamaican jerk chicken breast, or Caribbean sirloin—all prepared with Caribbean spices. > 1950 E. Lake Rd., North East, tel. 814/725–4627. MC, V. **$–$$**
Johnny B's On Friday and Saturday evenings a piano player tickles the ivories at a dark brown 1920s upright in this village restaurant, filled with beer-themed mirrors. Entrées range from a 24-ounce prime-grade prime rib, to seafood Alfredo with shrimp, crabmeat, and fettucine noodles, to veal or chicken parmigiana. You can get breakfast here, too, and there's a kids' menu. > 37 Vine St., North East 16428, tel. 814/725–1762. AE, D, MC, V. Closed Sun. **¢–$$**

ESSENTIALS

Getting Here
To fully enjoy the area and its sights, a car is necessary. There are regular flights to Erie International Airport if you prefer to get there by air and then rent a car.

BY CAR
From Cincinnati, follow I–71 north to 271 north; then take I–90 east into Pennsylvania to I–79 north to Erie. From Cleveland, take I–90 east to 79 north. From Columbus, take 71 north to 271 north to 90 east; then take 79 north to Erie once in Pennsylvania.

For an alternate route in Pennsylvania with glimpses of the lake, take Exit 6 from 90 to 215 north to SR 5 east into Erie.

When travelling to North East and the wineries from Erie, take Route 5 east for great views of the lake and vineyards.

Visitor Information

CONTACTS **Crawford County Convention and Visitors Bureau** > 211½ Chestnut St., Meadville 16335, tel. 814/333–1258 or 800/332–2338, www.visitcrawford.org. **Erie Area Convention and Visitors Bureau** > 208 E. Bayfront Pkwy., Erie 16507, tel. 814/454–9191 or 800/524–3743, www.visiteriepa.com. **Meadville–Western Crawford County Chamber of Commerce** > 211 Chestnut St., Meadville 16335, tel. 814/337–8030, www.meadvillechamber.com. **North East Chamber of Commerce** > 21 S. Lake St., North East 16428, tel. 814/725–4262, www.nechamber.org.

Allegheny National Forest

Oil City is approximately 140 mi east of Cleveland, 230 mi northeast of Columbus, and 335 mi northeast of Cincinnati.

9

By Clark Henderson

ALTHOUGH IT'S ONE OF THE LEAST-VISITED PARTS of the Commonwealth, the Allegheny National Forest region of Pennsylvania has no shortage of enticing features: stunning topography, abundant and unique natural resources and wildlife, and a significant, interesting history make the area a great retreat from the mundane, workaday world.

The forest and its environs occupy the Allegheny Plateau, an elevated land mass averaging nearly 2,000 feet above sea level that runs into the Lake Erie Plain to the west and extends to the steep Allegheny Escarpment to the east. Numerous rivers and streams cut through the sylvan, rugged landscape of the forest and meander among the undulating hills surrounding the nearby towns of Franklin, Tionesta, and Tidioute to the west. In addition to patches of virgin woods and the extensive hardwood stands within the forest, in and around it lives an impressive range of animal life—from black bears and white-tailed deer to great blue herons and American bald eagles. Add to the 513,000 acres of Allegheny National Forest the seven state parks that circle it, and the area is hard to match throughout Pennsylvania and beyond in its unspoiled nature and recreational possibilities. With hundreds of miles of trails and waterways, hiking, cycling, and canoeing are favored activities in the warmer months; cross-country skiing, snowshoeing, and snowmobiling reign in winter. Anglers can find beautiful and generous spots for fishing year-round, and campers can choose from hundreds of campsites throughout the parks and forest, from the remote and primitive to the relatively luxurious. And then there's a human-made enhancement, the 92-mi Allegheny Reservoir where many water activities are possible and where you can even rent houseboats.

When Allegheny National Forest was established in 1923, it was hardly the densely wooded area that now extends through four counties. Years of logging for building lumber, for fuel for coal production, and for hemlock bark for the leather tanning industry had left the area nearly bare; locals in the 1920s, in fact, referred to the newly created national forest as the "Allegheny Brush-Patch." Because of the U.S. Forest Service's careful custodianship, however, this history comes as a surprise when the forest is experienced today.

Part of a national trend that led to the formation of state and national parks, concern about the exhaustion of the natural resources in the area arose in the latter half of the 19th century, not just because of the forest clear-cutting but also due to the area's other defining industry: petroleum. Crude oil had been bubbling up naturally in the Oil Creek Valley, just west of the forest, for years, but it wasn't until demand for refined oil as an illuminant—fuel for lamps—increased that more productive methods of procurement were sought. After the first successful oil well was drilled just outside of Titusville in the late 1850s, the area was decisively affected by the ensuing oil boom. Although Pennsylvania's version of the Gold Rush lasted only a few years— the area was the world's leading oil producer between 1859 and 1873—this boom determined the shape and fate of nearly every town in the area. You can see the vestiges of that period, from the stately towns that benefited most from the tremendous wealth produced by the lucrative commodity to the meager remains of less fortunate boomtowns—Pithole, Petroleum Centre, and Oleopolis, all not far from the more re-silient Oil City.

Franklin and Warren, in particular, have aged well, each with well-preserved late-19th-century architecture and each picturesquely situated near the juncture of the Al-legheny River and one of its tributaries. They offer small-town charm, ready views of the Allegheny foothills and of the waterways that were crucial to their success over a hundred years ago, and easy access to the delights of the forest.

You won't be without things to do in these parts at any time of year, but in early to mid-October the fall foliage is captivating. And in mid-June the forest is accented with pink mountain-laurel blossoms.

So pack a good pair of hiking boots and head out to the heart of what used to be called Penn's Woods, after that Quaker founder of Pennsylvania, and tour an area of great natural beauty and, quite ironically, where the fateful oil industry all started.

WHAT TO SEE & DO

Allegheny National Forest Administered by the Forest Service of the U.S. Depart-ment of Agriculture, the forest is home to more than 300 species of mammals, 70 species of fish, and hundreds of species of birds. It contains two significant old-growth forest stands, which have 300-year-old hemlock and beech trees. But it isn't just a nature preserve; the forest fully lives up to the Forest Service's motto, "Land of Many Uses." For recreational purposes, it has more than 600 mi of trails, 700 mi of streams, 20 campgrounds, and six boat launches.

The best place to observe fauna in the forest, **Buzzard Swamp Wildlife Viewing and Hiking Area** has more than 11 mi of trails suitable for hiking, mountain biking, and cross-country skiing. Stay alert, for you might catch glimpses of beaver, bear, coyote, wild turkey, and, if you're lucky, a bald eagle. Be sure to pack binoculars for a closer look at the wildlife and, in the warmer months, bring along insect repellant. There are also 15 ponds for fishing where you can catch largemouth bass, perch, catfish, crap-pie, and bluegill. There are two trailheads: the southern is 1 mi south of Marienville on Forest Road 157; the northern is 2½ mi east of Marienville on Lamonaville Road.

The **Kinzua Dam and Allegheny Reservoir** (1205 Kinzua Rd. [Rte. 59], 16365, tel. 814/727–0661) were completed in 1965 by the U.S. Army Corps of Engineers at a cost of $108 million. The construction of the flood-control dam resulted in the formation of the Allegheny Reservoir, which covers 12,000 acres and has 91 mi of shoreline. Park in the Big Bend Access Area near the visitor-center lot and hike up to the over-look for a view of the dam and reservoir ringed by the forest. Boating, canoeing, fish-ing, and camping are available in and around the reservoir.

The **Heart's Content National Scenic Area** (15 mi southwest of Warren; take Rte. 6 to Pleasant Dr.) is one of only two sections of the forest that has an old-growth stand of trees. Take the 1-mi scenic interpretive trail through this primeval forest of 300- to 400-year-old hemlock, beech, and white pine. For a longer hike, try the 12-mi Hickory Creek Trail, which traverses a designated wilderness area where there are no trail improvements and where vehicles of any kind—even bicycles—are prohibited. Heart's Content also has a cross-country ski area in winter.

Cliffs, rocks, and streams make the 7-mi **Minister Creek Trail** (about 15 mi southwest of Sheffield on Rte. 666) one of the most popular and memorable in the forest. Take the trail along the creek, past many mossy sandstone boulders, through a cleft in the cliffs, and up to the overlook for an unobstructed view of Minister Valley. Brook Trout can be caught in Minister Creek.

Pick up brochures and maps for the forest's many trails and recreation sites at the **Allegheny National Forest Supervisor's Office** (222 Liberty St., tel. 814/726–1465, weekdays 7:30–4:30); convenient for access via Route 6. If approaching the Forest directly from the south via I–80, you can gather brochures and maps at the **Marienville Ranger District Office** (Star Rte. 2, tel. 814/927–2285, free, weekdays 7:30 AM–4 PM, weekends 8–4:30).

The main access points for the Allegheny National Forest are Route 6 from the north through Warren and Route 66 from the south via Marienville. > Warren, McKean, Forest, and Elk counties in northwest Pennsylvania, www.fs.fed.us/r9/allegheny. Free. Daily.

FRANKLIN

The seat of Venango County, Franklin is on the banks of the Allegheny River 8 mi southwest of Oil City. The site of successive French, British, and American forts and a key position in the French and Indian War, Franklin became a center of oil production during the oil boom of the 1860s. Many elegant 19th-century homes are in the heart of the town, a legacy of the town's oil money. Just a 25-minute drive from I–80, Franklin has several antiques stores and a 15-mi scenic trail along the Allegheny.

Barrow-Civic Theatre This old vaudeville theater was renovated in the early 1990s to provide 497 seats for regular stage productions, music, and other performances. > 1223 Liberty St., Franklin, tel. 814/437–3440, www.barrowtheatre.com.
DeBence Antique Music World You can take a guided tour of the collection of more than 100 antique automated music machines from the mid-19th century through the 1940s, including nickelodeons, Swiss and German music boxes, merry-go-round band organs, pipe organs, and player pianos. > 1261 Liberty St., Franklin, tel. 814/432–8350 or 888/547–2377, www.debencemusicworld.com. $8. Apr.–Oct., Tues.–Sat. 11–4, Sun. 12:30–4; Nov.–Dec., Fri.–Sat. 11–4, Sun. 12:30–4.
St. John's Church Colorfully illuminating the nave of this stone Episcopal church are eight sets of religious-theme stained-glass windows by Louis Comfort Tiffany, a master of the late-19th- and early-20th-century American arts-and-crafts movement. Opposite the altar is one of the largest favrile-glass rose windows Tiffany Studios ever produced. > 1141 Buffalo St., Franklin, tel. 814/432–5161. $4 suggested donation. Call for appointment.

KANE

Named after the first man in Pennsylvania to volunteer his service in the Civil War, Kane was established in 1887. Known as the Black Cherry Timber Capital of the World, Kane averages more than 107 inches of snow every year, earning it the additional nickname "Icebox of Pennsylvania." It's a great area for snowmobiling and cross-country skiing, and ice fishing at the nearby Allegheny Reservoir, 9 mi north of Kane.

The Allegheny National Forest surrounds Kane on three sides, with campsites and trails nearby.

Kane Railroad Depot & Museum This old Pennsylvania Railroad Depot, constructed in the late 1800s, has been transformed into a community museum and cultural center to preserve the town's transportation heritage. > S. Fraley St., Rte. 6 at Rte. 66, tel. 814/837–8752 or 814/837–6565. Free. By appointment.

Kinzua Bridge State Park The 316-acre park is the site of the 2,053-foot Kinzua Railroad Bridge, which has been designated a National Engineering Landmark. The highest railroad bridge in the world at the time of its construction in 1882, it rises 301 feet. The park has a scenic overlook, picnic facilities, fishing in Kinzua Creek, and organized group camping. > 4 mi north of U.S. 6 at Mt. Jewett on Rte. 3011, Johnsonburg, 15845, tel. 814/965–2646 or 888/727–2757, www.dcnr.state.pa.us. Free. Daily 8 AM to sunset.

Knox & Kane Excursion Train You can board these train cars dating to the 1920s in Kane for a 32-mi round-trip to the Kinzua Bridge. When operating from June through October, there's one train daily from Kane; the round trip, including a half-hour layover takes 3½ hours. > Take Rte. 321 south to Highland Rd., Kane, tel. 814/927–6621, www.knoxkanerr.com. $16. June, Fri.–Sun.; July and Aug., Tues.–Sun.; Sept., Fri.–Sun.; Oct., Wed.–Sun.; call for times.

OIL CITY

Its name says a lot: oil built this city. At one time, the town produced more than 1 million barrels of oil a year. Although the boom ended long ago, the buildings from the period remain. You can tour Oil City's south side and see late-19th-century homes in styles that range from Second Empire and Italianate to Gothic Revival and Queen Anne.

Drake Well Museum Edwin L. Drake drilled the world's first oil well here in 1859. You can see a replica of Drake's engine house and an oil derrick, which offers a glimpse of how the oil industry began. Reproductions of Drake's steam engine and wood-fired boiler operate year-round. > 202 Museum La., off Rte. 8, 14 mi north of Oil City, south of Titusville, 16354, tel. 814/827–2797, www.drakewell.org. $5. May–Oct., Mon.–Sat. 9–5, Sun. noon–5; Nov.–Apr., Tues.–Sat. 9–5, Sun. noon–5.

Oil Creek and Titusville Railroad Take a 2½-hour train ride through "the valley that changed the world" in passenger cars and open gondolas, weather permitting. There are fall-foliage rides, murder-mystery dinner rides, and a haunted train ride. Board at Titusville, 15 mi north of Oil City. > 409 S. Perry St., Titusville 16354, tel. 814/676–1733, www.octrr.clarion.edu. $12. Weekends mid-June–Oct.; additional days during peak months; times vary.

Oil Creek State Park The 7,096-acre park has more than 52 mi of hiking trails, canoeing and fishing on Oil Creek, two picnic areas, a 9½-mi paved bicycle trail through Oil Creek Gorge, and 10 mi of cross-country skiing trails. The visitor center has displays on Petroleum Centre, an important town of the oil boom. > 4 mi north of Oil City on Rte. 8, tel. 814/676–5915 or 888/727–2757, www.dcnr.state.pa.us. Free. Daily 8 AM–sunset; Visitor Center, mid-June–mid-Oct., weekends noon–5.

Venango Museum of Art, Science, and Industry Rotating exhibits show the history of the oil region with displays on the Allegheny River, artifacts from the Oil Well Supply Company, and examples of early Pennzoil and Quaker State product advertising. > 270 Seneca St., Oil City, tel. 814/676–2007. $4. Tues.–Fri. 10–4, Sat. 11–4, Sun. 2–5.

Pennsylvania Crude

BLACK GOLD *in Pennsylvania? Even though telling brand-names (such as Pennzoil and Quaker State) remain, few people associate the Commonwealth with America's oil industry.*

Seneca Indians used petroleum (literally, rock oil) as an ointment for centuries in northwestern Pennsylvania. It simply seeped up through springs and was particularly abundant along what European settlers named Oil Creek, which runs between Titusville and Oil City. By the late 18th century, petroleum, or Seneca Oil as it became known, was sold commercially as a natural remedy. Amazingly, consumers would actually ingest the oil for its dubious salutary effects, while travelers through Venango County would soak their joints in pools of oil for pain relief.

Samuel Kier of Pittsburgh began selling crude oil as a cure-all in 1847 but soon discovered a market for it in refined form as lamp fuel: kerosene, or what Kier marketed as "carbon oil," emerged just as the whale population hunted for oil along the eastern seaboard declined, so demand surged for the black oil as an illuminant. In 1857 speculators employed retired railroad conductor Edwin Drake to improve the production of an oil spring near Titusville. Perceived as something of a lunatic in the area for thinking that the oil could be gotten through drilling, Drake persisted in his idea and in 1859 successfully drilled 69 feet for oil. After Drake's technological success, land leases throughout the Oil Creek Valley were quickly snatched up. Wooden derricks sprouted like weeds and property values soared. Bustling towns appeared seemingly within days.

Pithole, the most notorious boomtown, went from zero to a population of 15,000 in about 8 months and had 54 hotels. It was here that the world's first successful oil pipelines were laid, as a way to avoid teamsters' exorbitant fees. The oil in Pithole soon stopped flowing and the town was ravaged by fires, so the population

dwindled to less than 300 in 1870. By 1877, Pithole didn't exist at all.

Pithole is an extreme but revealing version of many towns in the area. During its ascendant years—1859 to 1873—the Oil Creek Valley region produced 56 million barrels of crude, with gross receipts in the tens of millions. But wells went dry and it soon became clear that the oil reserves weren't limitless as initially thought. Abandoned wells and derricks soon became commonplace. Many had made their profit and moved on.

Among those whom Pennsylvania crude enriched was John D. Rockefeller, who started an oil-refining business in the 1860s in Cleveland and would come to control 90 percent of the U.S. refining capacity by 1879. The area also produced Rockefeller's great nemesis, Ida Tarbell, the famed investigative journalist whose 19-part exposé on Standard Oil's monopolistic business practices for McClure's magazine contributed to the company's court-ordered breakup in 1911. Raised in the raucous Oil Creek Valley at its peak, Tarbell chronicled the environmental degradation, the human casualties of speculation and greed, and the abuse of power that she witnessed first hand.

Although the region's peak oil days are long past, there is still oil drilling and refining and natural gas in the area. McClintock Well, north of Oil City in McClintockville, is the oldest continuously operating oil well in the country, pumping petroleum since 1861. So while driving around you still might spot—in addition to numerous historical markers noting events from the oil heyday—a refinery getting Pennsylvania crude ready for market.

— Clark Henderson

WARREN

At the northern edge of the Allegheny National Forest, Warren was first known as a lumbering town, then like many towns in the area became centered around oil. By the early 1900s, 13 oil refineries were within 6 mi of this town. The downtown area of Warren has more than 600 well-preserved 19th- and early-20th-century buildings in more than 20 styles spread over 28 blocks. Today the town is a popular gateway to the forest; Buckaloons Recreation Area, Heart's Content Scenic Area, and the Allegheny Reservoir are a quick drive away.

Warren County Historical Society Fittingly located in the heart of Warren's historic district, the Historical Society has a period Victorian parlor, exhibits covering Warren's history, and extensive material for genealogical research. You can pick up a free self-guided walking tour booklet for the downtown area. > 210 4th Ave., Warren, tel. 814/723–1795, www.kinzua.net/warrenhistory. $1 donation suggested. Weekdays 8:30–4:30; Apr.–Nov., also Sat. 9–noon.

Sports

CANOEING

Canoeing is popular on the Allegheny River south of the Allegheny Reservoir all the way to Franklin, on the reservoir itself, and on the Clarion River near Cook Forest and along the southern edge of the Allegheny National Forest. In summer you can rent canoes near each of these scenic locations. In addition to canoes, Kinzua Boat Rentals also rents houseboats for use on the Allegheny Reservoir.

RENTALS **Allegheny River Canoe Rental** > 250 Elk St., Franklin, tel. 814/432–7644 or 800/807–5596, www.bluecanoeinc.com. **Allegheny Outfitters** > 2101 Pennsylvania Ave. E, Warren, tel. 814/723–1203, www.alleghenyoutfitters.com. **Kinzua Boat Rentals and Marina** > Rte. 59, Box 825, Warren, tel. 814/726–1650, www.kinzuamarina.com.

CROSS-COUNTRY SKIING

With five trails dedicated to cross-country skiing in winter, the Allegheny National Forest offers pristine snow for Nordic-skiing enthusiasts. Only one trail is groomed, Laurel Mill Trail in the southeast corner of the forest, which might be desirable for the less adventurous during periods of heavy snowfall.

RENTALS **Bike World of Warren** > 2025 Pennsylvania Ave. E, Warren, tel. 814/723–1758. **Love's Canoe Rentals** > 3 Main St., Ridgway, tel. 814/776–6285, www.ncentral.com/~dlove/.

Save the Date

JULY

Oil Heritage Festival Held the last week of July, this Oil City fair is one of the largest in northwestern Pennsylvania. You can go to rock, jazz, blues, country, and oldies concerts or watch the 5K race and volleyball and tennis tournaments. Guided tours of the neighborhood's Victorian homes are given from an Erie trolley car. > Oil City, tel. 814/676–8521 or 814/676–6296, www.oilcitychamber.org.

AUGUST

Titusville Oil Festival This festival, held annually in late August at the Ed Myer Complex in Titusville, has a slow-pitch softball tournament, an oil barge race, an art festival, tug-a-war, town square carnival, gazebo concert, and nightly fireworks. > Titusville, tel. 814/827–2732 or 814/827–2941, www.titusvillechamber.com.

Warren County Fair At this annual event, held the third week in August at the Warren County Fair Grounds in Pittsfield, there's everything you'd expect at a county fair, from animal judging and tractor pulls to a midway and live country music. > Pittsfield, tel. 814/563–9386, www.warrencountyfair.net.

OCTOBER
Applefest The biggest annual event in Franklin, this 2-day festival has more than 350 vendors of arts, crafts, and food, as well as entertainment, a 5K race, theater, and an antique-auto show. Apple-related events are an apple pancake breakfast, and an apple pie baking contest. > Downtown, Franklin, tel. 814/432–5823, www.franklin-pa.org.

WHERE TO STAY

FRANKLIN

Quo Vadis Built in 1867, this Queen Anne–style, three-story bed-and-breakfast is in the historic district of Franklin, a quick walk from downtown businesses. The rooms, filled with antiques, are named after local historical figures, including Johnny Appleseed who stayed in the Allegheny River Valley in the early 1800s. A full hot breakfast is provided on weekends. > 1501 Liberty St., Franklin 16323, tel. 814/437–7699 or 800/360–6598, www.quovadisbandb.com. 6 rooms. Dining room, in-room data ports, cable TV, in-room VCRs, some pets allowed; no smoking. D, MC, V. CP, BP weekends only. $

KANE

Kane Manor Country Inn Set back from the road on 250 acres of wooded property, this yellow-brick country mansion was built in 1897 for the wife of Civil War general Thomas Kane. Portraits of Kane family members line the main staircase leading up from the yellow-and-red tiles of the entryway to the second-floor rooms, each identified with whimsical hand-painted figures. This B&B is near many Allegheny National Forest locations and is a mile from the Knox and Kane train stop to Kinzua Bridge. > 230 Clay St., Kane 16735, tel. 814/837–6522, fax 814/837–6664, www.kanemanor.com. 10 rooms, 6 with bath. Dining room, cable TV, hiking, cross-country skiing; no phones in some rooms, no smoking. AE, D, MC, V. CP, BP on weekends. $–$$$

OIL CITY

Arlington Hotel Overlooking the Allegheny River, this modern five-story hotel is in downtown Oil City. The Venango Museum of Art, Science, and Industry is a short walk away; other sites in the Oil Heritage Region are nearby, with a car. > 1 Seneca St., Oil City 16301, tel. 814/677–1221 or 800/537–8483, fax 814/677–0492, www.oilcityhotel.com. 101 rooms, 2 suites. In-room data ports, some in-room hot tubs, some microwaves, some refrigerators, cable TV, pool, lounge, business services, meeting rooms, some pets allowed (fee), no-smoking floor. AE, D, DC, MC, V. $
Turtle Bay Lodge Each guest room at this lodge has a king-size bed, and one has a cannonball bed (named for its cannonball-like post finials). You can use a completely furnished kitchen and a great room with a big-screen TV and stone fireplace, as well as the 55-foot front porch overlooking the Allegheny River. Turtle Bay is 12 mi northeast of Oil City. > 472 President Village Rd., near Rte. 62, Tionesta 16353, tel. 814/677–8785, fax 814/677–5727, www.turtlebaylodge.com. 5 rooms. Dining room, picnic area, in-room data ports, in-room hot tub, cable TV; no smoking. D, MC, V. CP. $$–$$$

WARREN

Holiday Inn Two miles from downtown Warren, this hotel has many rooms with views of the Allegheny Mountains. If you want to explore the forest without roughing it, the Holiday Inn offers many amenities without being far from the major attractions of Allegheny National Forest. > 210 Ludlow St., 16365, tel. 814/726–3000 or 800/446–6819, fax 814/726–3720, www.holiday-inn.com. 112 rooms. Restaurant, café, in-room data ports, cable TV, indoor pool, sauna, exercise room, lounge, nightclub, laundry service, business services, meeting rooms, some pets allowed, no-smoking rooms. AE, D, DC, MC, V. $

Horton House B&B This late-19th-century house is in Warren's downtown historic district and within walking distance to restaurants and shopping. The house retains many of its original architectural details, including a ballroom that doubles as a game room, yet has been updated with a roof deck hot tub. > 504 Market St., Warren 16365, tel. 814/723–7472 or 888/723–7472, fax 814/726–3633, hortonhousebb.com. 5 rooms. Dining room, in-room data ports, cable TV, in-room VCRs, recreation room. AE, D, MC, V. BP. $–$$

CAMPING

Buckaloons Recreation Area In the northwest corner of the forest on the former site of a Seneca Native American village, this campground has 51 campsites, a hiking path that travels around the Allegheny River, and a boat launch for travel to one of seven nearby islands. > Near the intersection of Rtes. 6 and 62, 6 mi west of Warren, tel. 877/444–6777, www.fs.fed.us/r9/allegheny/recreation/camping. 15 partial hook-ups, 36 tent sites. Flush toilets, partial hook-ups (electric), dump station, drinking water, showers, fire grates, fire pits, picnic tables, playground. D, MC, V. ¢

Twin Lakes Once the site of factories, stores, and row houses for a company making wood alcohol, Twin Lakes has 50 campsites. The Black Cherry National Recreation Trail runs past the lake. > 8 mi SE of Kane off Rte. 321 in the Allegheny National Forest, tel. 877/444–6777, www.fs.fed.us/r9/allegheny/recreation/camping. 20 partial hook-ups, 30 tent sites. Flush toilets, partial hook-ups (electric), dump station, drinking water, showers, fire grates, fire pits, picnic tables, public telephone, playground, swimming (lake). Reservations recommended. D, MC, V. ¢

WHERE TO EAT

FRANKLIN

Bella Cucina This downtown restaurant has an Italian name, but the menu is eclectic. The lunch selections change daily and usually include wraps, burgers, and home-made soups. For dinner, you can choose from a roster of meats and seafood—veal and lamb to salmon and scallops—in the airy, tin-ceilinged dining room. No smoking here. > 1234 Liberty St., Franklin, tel. 814/432–4955. AE, MC, V. Closed Sun. No dinner Mon. $–$$$

Boston Garden On the main thoroughfare in Franklin, this casual restaurant has outdoor seating on a patio with live music in summer. For dinner you can get salads, pasta dishes, chicken, and seafood, but they're known for their steaks. No smoking inside except at the bar. > 1211 Liberty St., Franklin, tel. 814/437–1211. AE, MC, V. $–$$$

Primo Barone's Balloons, props, and other flying gear are on display in this brewpub and restaurant at the Franklin County Airport. You can view small engine planes coming and going while you try house specialties like fillet Italian style or the Tour of Italy, veal and chicken parmigiano with fettuccine Alfredo. > 1564 Airport Rd., Franklin, tel. 814/432–2588, www.primobarones.com. AE, D, DC MC, V. $–$$$

KANE

Texas Hot Lunch Locals who travel can hardly wait to return home for a Texas Hot— a hot dog with onions, mustard, and the house special sauce—from this popular eatery, which also serves Greek dishes such as souvlaki. It's two blocks from the old railroad depot and has a non-smoking room and an ATM. You can get breakfast here, too. > 24 Field St., Kane, tel. 814/837–8122. Reservations not accepted. No credit cards. ¢

Westline Inn Taxidermy abounds at this quintessential mountain-inn restaurant. Enjoy steak au poivre or grilled salmon with a lemon caper sauce under the mounted head of a caribou or buck. The menu is meat and seafood heavy, but they do serve a vegetarian platter. The Inn, 15 mi north of Kane, is a great place to eat after a day on the trails; cross-country and snowmobile trailheads are nearby. > 1 E. L. Day Dr., Westline, tel. 814/778–5103, www.westlineinn.com. AE, D, DC, MC, V. No lunch before 3 Sun.–Thurs. $–$$$

OIL CITY

Yellow Dog Lantern Named for the old lanterns used in local oil fields, this restaurant is filled with antique lamps and more than 100 sharpening stones of various sizes. You can choose from Maryland snow crab cakes, lobster, chicken fettucine, veal marsala, and prime rib. > 218 Elm St., Oil City, tel. 814/676–1000. Closed Sun. No lunch. AE, MC, V. $$–$$$

WARREN

Dagwood's The steak subs are a local favorite at this sandwich shop named after the character of the Blondie cartoon strip. Hamburgers share the menu with the subs, and there's a bar and lounge area. > 242 Pennsylvania Ave. W, 16365, tel. 814/723–1313. Reservations not accepted. No credit cards. ¢

Liberty Street Cafe Sit in the long, soothingly lighted dining area along the exposed-brick wall, and choose appetizers and entrées from a diverse menu—from sushi and Thai red-curry vegetables to Portobello-mushroom ravioli with pesto cream and Asiago, to smoked pork-loin chop with a potato-Gouda gratin. The menu changes daily, but expect a selection of grilled meats and fish. There's also an extensive brunch menu on weekdays and Sunday. No smoking. > 211 Liberty St., Warren, tel. 814/726–3082, www.thelibertystreetcafe.com. AE, D, MC, V. No dinner Sun. and Mon. No lunch Sat. $$–$$$

ESSENTIALS

Getting Here

Travel by car is the best way to get to and around the area. For air travel via the region's major airports, fly to Bradford Regional Airport at the northeast end of the forest or to Erie International Airport, about 50 mi northwest of Titusville, and then rent a car from there.

BY CAR

The Allegheny National Forest region is largely a rural area without much regular public transportation, so a car is essential for getting around. From Cincinnati, take I–71 north to I–76 east. Next take I–80 east near Youngstown, Ohio, into Pennsylvania. From Cleveland, take 480 east to I–80 east. From Columbus, follow I–71 north to I–76 east; then take I–80 east.

Once in Pennsylvania, continue on I–80 east to Exit 29, following Route 8 north to Franklin. Route 8 continues on to Oil City, about 8 mi, and Titusville, another 15 mi. To get to Warren, take Route 62 from Oil City. Once at Tionesta, 62 follows the east bank of the Allegheny River along the edge of the Allegheny National Forest up to Warren—you'll have a view of the river and forest together for 30 mi. Warren is 55 mi from Oil City and 39 mi from Titusville. From Warren, follow Route 6 southeast to Kane, about 28 mi.

Car travel around the area can be slow. The roads have many curves and most routes go through small towns where the speed limit is reduced. Don't expect to average more than 40 mph once you are off the interstate.

Gasoline is hard to come by in the forest, so fill up at towns outside if you intend to explore the many isolated forest roads, which are well worth the drive, weather permitting. In the major towns—Franklin, Oil City, Warren, and Kane—downtown metered parking is usually easy to find.

Visitor Information

CONTACTS **Allegheny National Forest Vacation Bureau** > 80 E. Corydon St., Suite 114, Bradford 16701, tel. 800/473–9370, www.allegheny-vacation.com. **Cook Forest Area Vacation Bureau** > Box 50, Cooksburg 16217, tel. 814/849–9377, www.cookforest.org. **Franklin Area Chamber of Commerce** > 1259 Liberty St., Franklin 16323, tel. 814/432–5823 or 888/547–2377, www.franklin-pa.org. **Kane Chamber of Commerce** > 54 Fraley St., Kane 16735, tel. 814/837–6565, www.kanepa.com. **Oil City Chamber of Commerce** > 41 Main St., Oil City 16301, tel. 814/676–8521, www.oilcitychamber.org. **Oil Heritage Region Tourist Promotion Agency** > Box 128, Oil City 16301, tel. 800/483–6264, www.oilregiontourist.com. **Titusville Chamber of Commerce** > 202 W. Central Ave., Titusville 16354, tel. 814/827–2941, www.titusvillechamber.com. **Warren County Chamber of Commerce** > 308 Market St., Box 942, Warren 16365, tel. 814/723–3050, www.warrenpachamber.com.

Amish Country

Amish Country is 79 mi south of Cleveland, 128 mi east of Columbus, and 226 mi northeast of Cincinnati.

10

By Joe Frey

THERE IS A LONG-RUNNING JOKE AMONG OHIOANS that any company could sell any product as long as it put the word "Amish" in the product's name. Ohio's Amish Country, however, is no punch line at all; rather it's a tranquil region that Ohioans visit in increasing numbers in order to escape from the breakneck commerce of the work week.

Stretching from Geauga County in northeast Ohio to the Ohio River in southeast Ohio, Amish Country attracts hundreds of thousands of visitors per year who are looking to trade a tachometer-shattering lifestyle for one of ease; to forget their cell phones and pagers; to golf some of Ohio's best public links; to purchase products they can't find at their local megamarts; or to drink in vistas that Thomas Kinkade wishes he could duplicate.

Perhaps Amish Country's allure is its pastoral landscape. Ohio's relative flatness gives way to gentle rises in Geauga, Stark, and Holmes counties, eventually breaking into full-blown foothills toward the Ohio River. During autumn's peak color season, a drive down Route 39 proves why hills provide better views than plains. Few buildings interrupt the foliage, and shallow dales and short hilltops frame the surroundings expertly. Mother Nature knew what she was doing.

Then again, maybe weekenders are looking for a shopping experience that they can only get by visiting stores where "quality hand-crafted works" is truth in advertising, not countryside hokum used to lure shoppers. Amish carpentry, furniture-making, and quilt-making are peerless, which makes choosing from among the wares of myriad stores difficult but fun. Ohio produces the largest amount of Swiss cheese in the nation, too, so finding a cheese boutique is as easy as finding holes in that famous moldy mass.

Ohio's history is inextricably bonded to agrarian life, and pockets of it survive in Amish Country—no doubt a modern marvel on many levels. Working 19th-century farms and stables show how farmers earned their keep before indoor plumbing, electricity, and hot-water heaters—reminders of the amount of work our ancestors endured simply to maintain a residence or cook a meal.

The Amish are living links to that past, eschewing electricity and automobiles for manual and horse power, and respect for their lifestyle is due when visiting. The Amish are shy of outsiders and generally do not wish to be photographed.

Amish Country encompasses a large portion of eastern Ohio, but the heart is just south of Canton in Holmes and Tuscarawas counties, with other major hubs to the south in Coshocton County, and west of Akron in Wayne County.

WHAT TO SEE & DO

BERLIN

Behalt at the Mennonite Information Center A 265-foot mural painted on the walls of a circular room tells the story of the Anabaptist movement in 17th-century Europe and how it led to the Amish settlement in Ohio. You'll also find books, videos, and other resources about the Amish, Mennonite, and Hutterite faiths. There's no charge to visit the information center, but the guided mural tours require an admission fee. > 5798 County Rd. 77, Berlin, tel. 330/893–3192, pages.sssnet.com/behalt/index.shtml. Free, tour $5.50. Mon.–Sat. 9–5; extended hrs: June–Oct., Fri. and Sat. 9–8.

Helping Hands Quilt Museum and Shop Handmade Amish quilts (both antique and new) are on display and for sale. Amish women give quilting demonstrations, and videos describe the history and details of Amish quilt patterns. If you're a quilter or aspiring quilter, you can buy fabric, stencils, and other supplies. If you're an admirer, you can order a custom-made quilt. > 4826 Main St. (Rte. 39), Berlin, tel. 330/893–2233. Free. Mon.–Sat. 9–5.

Kidron-Sonnenberg Heritage Center Mennonite caretakers maintain one of the largest databases of Swiss Anabaptist ancestry here, along with a strong collection of Amish, Mennonite, and Anabaptist Ohio history, including samples of Fraktur (pronounced frac-toor), a rare but once common form of German handwriting. > 13153 Emerson Rd., Kidron, tel. 330/857–9111. Free. June–Sept., Thurs.–Sat. 11–3; Oct.–May, Thurs. and Sat. 11–3. Closed Jan. and Feb.

Schrock's Amish Farm and Home The guides here (many of whom are Amish) lead you through a typical Amish home and explain how they live without electricity or telephones. Afterward you can pet the farm animals and take a buggy ride. > 4363 Rte. 39, Berlin, tel. 330/893–3232 or 888/717–4732, www.amish-r-us.com/farm.html. $7. Apr.–Oct., weekdays 10–5, Sat. 10–6.

COSHOCTON

Dennison Railroad Museum Once a hub of railroad commerce due to its proximity to Columbus and Pittsburgh, Dennison attracts rail buffs with its museum and scenic tours. Vintage engines, box cars, and passenger cars, as well as tools of a bygone era await you in the museum. An elaborate working model train is also in the museum. Periodic tours between Dennison and various points east and south are available. > 400 Center St., Dennison, tel. 877/278–8020, www.dennisondepot.org. $3. Tues.–Sat. 11–5, Sun. 11–3.

Roscoe Village This restored early-19th-century canal town serves as a window on life on the old Ohio & Erie Canal, with shopkeepers, field hands, and artisans working to maintain the area. Slip along the restored canal in the village's old-style canal boat, *The Monticello III* ($6, May–Sept., daily 1–5; Oct., weekends 1–5, weather permitting). Horses draw the craft on the 45-minute, 1½-mi tours. The boat departs on the hour. The village also houses the **Johnson–Humrickhouse Museum** (300 N. Whitewoman St., tel. 740/622–8710, www.jhm.lib.oh.us, May–Oct., daily noon–5; Nov.–Apr., Tues.–Sun. 1–4:30), which features Native American art and artifacts, as well as pieces from Japan. > 5798 County Rd. 77, tel. 740/622–7528 or 800/877–1830, www.roscoevillage.com. $5.50. Year-round, with seasonal hrs for various shops and attractions.

NEW PHILADELPHIA

Breitenbach Wine Cellars Truly a destination winery, Breitenbach is in the hills of Ohio's Amish Country. It's known for "Frost Fire," an internationally acclaimed white wine, as well as its excellent hand-crafted reds (the merlot is a nice surprise). Tours are only during the winery's Dandelion Festival, held in May. Der Marketplatz, a shop on the premises, offers an assortment of Amish cheeses and German meats that match well with the wine. There's a bed-and-breakfast here, too. > 5934 Old State Rte. 39 NW, Dover, tel. 330/343–3603 or 800/843–9463, www.breitenbachwine.com. Free. Daily.

Clark Gable Museum Ohio's connections to Hollywood run deep: Bob Hope, Dean Martin, Michael Douglas, and the King himself, Clark Gable. Visit the home in which Gable was born, and peruse personal effects and memorabilia, including his 1954 Cadillac. A gift shop is attached to the museum. > 138 Charleston St., Cadiz, tel. 740/942–4989, www.clarkgablefoundation.com. $4.50. Oct.–Apr., Tues.–Fri. 10–4; May, Tues.–Sat. 10–4; June–Sept., Tues.–Sat. 10–4, Sun. 1:30–4.

Gnadenhutten Village Museum The oldest existing settlement in Ohio is infamous for the 1782 massacre of 90 Native Americans. A colonial militia group surrounded the Native Americans one night, accused them of pillaging Pennsylvania settlements, and killed them without trial the next morning. A monument constructed in 1872 commemorates the victims, and a museum houses artifacts that date to the Revolutionary War period and later. > 352 S. Cherry St., Gnadenhutten, tel. 740/254–4756, gnaden.tusco.net. Free. June–Aug., Mon.–Sat. 10–5, Sun. 1–5; Sept. and Oct., Sat. 10–5, Sun. 1–5.

Schoenbrunn Village State Memorial The first established village in Ohio, this town appears as it did more than 200 years ago. It consists of 17 reconstructed log buildings, the original cemetery, and more than 2 acres of planted fields. You can hear a recorded tour in English or German. The village also has a museum and picnic facilities. > 1984 E. High Ave. Rd., New Philadelphia, tel. 330/339–3636 or 800/752–2711, www.ohiohistory.org/places/schoenbr. $6. May–Aug., Mon.–Sat. 9:30–5, Sun. noon–5; Sept. and Oct., Sat. 9:30–5, Sun. noon–5.

WOOSTER

Ohio Agricultural Research and Development Center Considered the top agricultural research center in the country, this facility is credited with inventing crop dusting and vitamin D–enriched milk. You can take a tour of the center. Stroll the grounds of the **Secrest Arboretum**, (1680 Madison Ave., tel. 330/263–3761), where more than 2,000 plants grow, and the May-blooming crab apple trees will fill your nose with sweet aromas while taking your breath away. > 1 mi south of Wooster, on Madison Rd., Wooster, tel. 216/263–3779, www.oardc.ohio-state.edu. Free. Weekdays, tours by appointment.

Quailcrest Farm Herbs, perennials, and flowers grow on this farm's 100 acres, 7 mi north of downtown Wooster. You can also visit the restored 19th-century schoolhouse on the premises and purchase farm products from the gift store. > 2810 Armstrong Rd., Wooster, tel. 330/345–6722, www.quailcrest.com. Free. Mar.–Dec., Tues.–Sat. 9–5, Sun. 1–5. Extended spring and Christmas hrs.

Troutman Vineyards Andy Troutman's first efforts as winemaker at his patch south of Wooster are exceptional—he's won gold medals in Ohio's competitions—and easy to drink. In addition to holding wine tastings for up to 50 people, Troutman runs a petting zoo on the premises, with roosters, lambs, and other menagerie animals.

> 4243 Columbus Rd., Wooster, tel. 330/263–4345, www.troutmanvineyards.com.
Free. May–Sept., Tues.–Thurs. 4–8, weekends noon–8.

Wayne County Historical Society Museum Housed in the 1815 Beall House, the
museum shows furniture, porcelains, Native American artifacts, mounted animals,
firearms, and clothing. On the grounds are a late-1800s log cabin and schoolhouse
with period furnishings, an old general store, and a carpenter shop with pioneer
tools. > 546 E. Bowman St., Wooster, tel. 330/264–8856, www.waynehistorical.org. $3.
Wed.–Sun. 2–4:30 and by appointment.

ZOAR

Fort Laurens State Memorial and Museum The Fort Laurens Memorial, about 3 mi
north of Zoar, commemorates the only fort built by the American Continental Army in
what is now Ohio. The tomb of Ohio's unknown patriot, a memorial to the heroes of
the American Revolution, is here. The fort has been restored and is open for tours.
Revolutionary War re-enactments are held on weekends. The museum has displays
on the Revolutionary War. > 5 mi west of junction I–77 and Rte. 212, Bolivar, tel.
330/874–2728 or 800/283–8914. Memorial free, museum $3. Memorial: Apr.–Oct.,
daily 9:30–dusk. Museum: June–Aug., Wed.–Sat. 9:30–5, Sun. noon–5; Apr., May,
Sept., and Oct., Sat. 9:30–5, Sun. noon–5.

Zoar Village This 12-block district includes original 19th-century homes, shops, and
businesses from a utopian community that comprised 75 families. You can see how
the German Society of Separatists lived throughout the 10-building complex, which
includes a blacksmith, tin shop, magazine, dairy, and Bimeler Museum. Period-
dressed staffers relate the history and significance of each building. Though the historic buildings are closed from November to March, shops and restaurants are open
year-round. The Bimeler Museum is open March–December. > 198 Main St., Zoar,
tel. 330/874–3011 or 800/262–6195, www.ohiohistory.org/places/zoar/. $6. Memorial
Day–Labor Day, Wed.–Sat. 9:30–5, Sun. noon–5; Apr., May, Sept., and Oct., Sat.
9:30–5, Sun. noon–5.

Tours

Dennison Railroad Museum Ride in diesel- and steam-powered trains on the Dennison Railroad's excursions through Amish Country. These rides are the only railroad
tours available in east-central Ohio. Prices vary widely (between $8 and $100), and
reservations are recommended. Trains depart from the Dennison Depot at the Dennison Railroad Museum. > 400 Center St., Dennison, tel. 877/278–8020,
www.dennisondepot.org.

Lantern Tours of the Ghosts of Zoar Those who dare tread among the creepy shad-
ows of the past can learn about the spooks whose earthly stays ended years ago—but
whose souls linger today. Advanced reservations are a must for the tours, which take
place on Friday and Saturday nights April through October. The cost is $12. > 198
Main St., Zoar, tel. 330/874–2002, www.haunted-ohio.com.

Shopping

Amish Country is a hotbed for the Great American Pastime: shopping. Selling everything from hand-made furniture to chocolates to quilts, stores in east-central Ohio
teem with browsers and buyers, especially on Saturdays (most stores are closed Sundays). Every town in Amish Country contains a number of shops—some have more
than others—but there's no central hub. Expect a short drive on one of many scenic
byways to hop from zone to zone.

The Cat's Meow Village As collectible—and perhaps as recognizable—as "Precious Moments" figurines, the Cat's Meow Village pieces are a hand-crafted cornucopia of carefully painted miniatures that display seasonal scenes, quaint villages, sports memorabilia, and regional places of interest. Vintage Village seekers can browse the "mewseum" attached to the shop. It features out-of-stock and retired pieces that make collectors purr. > 2163 Great Trails Dr., Wooster, tel. 330/264–1377, www.catsmeow.com. Closed Sun.

Coblentz Chocolates Watch candy makers spin mouth-watering morsels in this turn-of-the-20th-century chocolate haven. Coblentz is a Holmes County hidden gem, with enough chocolaty charm to sweet talk you into buying a couple of gift baskets. > 4917 St. Rte. 515, at Rte. 39, Walnut Creek, tel. 330/893–2995 or 800/338–9341. Closed Sun.

Homestead Furniture It's one of many stores in Amish Country that showcase the fine craftsmanship of Dutch carpenters. The smell of wood fills the show room, and bureaus, hutches, tables, and chairs—some custom-made—display the care Amish workers take when creating a piece. > 8233 St. Rte. 241, Mt. Hope, tel. 800/893–3702. Closed Sun.

Lehman's You won't find any pink flamingos at this new-old-fashioned hardware store, but you will find liniments, ointments, and the occasional portable composting toilet. (Those little ecofriendly appliances alone are worth a go-round in the store.) Look for hard-to-find items such as foot-powered sewing machines and sock darners. > 1 Lehman Circle, Kidron, tel. 330/857–5757 or 888/438–5346, www.lehmans.com. Closed Sun.

Middlefield Cheese Ohio is famous for its Swiss cheese, and Middlefield spins an excellent wheel. This remarkable Swiss chalet–style store in Geauga County in the northern section of Amish Country is holey cheese heaven, and worth a trip north from Holmes County. > 15815 Nauvoo Rd., Middlefield, tel. 800/327–9477, www.middlefieldcheese.com. Closed Sun.

Save the Date

MAY

Dandelion Festival You can eat, drink, and smell the dandelions around Breitenbach Wine Cellars' property during the first weekend of May. Events include an *Iron Chef*–like dandelion cook-off, a 5K run, and a dandelion-picking contest. Be sure to sample Breitenbach's dandelion wine while there. > 5934 Old State Rte. 39 NW, Dover, tel. 330/343–3603, www.breitenbachwine.com.

AUGUST

Tuscarawas County Italian American Festival An annual celebration of Italian heritage enlivens the Tuscarawas Valley the second week in August. Highlights of this three-day fete include a mayor's breakfast, Italian dancers, a commemorative plate auction, rides, and a spate of contests. > On the Square, Downtown, New Philadelphia, tel. 330/339–6405, www.italian-festival.org.

Zoar Harvest Festival The year's harvest is celebrated at Zoar Village with food, games, parades, and live entertainment. The festival also includes a renowned art-and-antiques show and sale. > 198 Main St., Zoar, tel. 330/874–3011, www.zca.org.

SEPTEMBER

Ohio Swiss Festival On the fourth Friday and Saturday after Labor Day, the German-Swiss heritage of the area is celebrated with Swiss cheese exhibits, a parade, contests for the best Swiss costumes, yodeling, stone-tossing, and live polka bands. > Follow signs from Rte. 32, Sugarcreek, tel. 330/852–4113, www.sugarcreekohio.org/swissfestival.htm.

Yankee Peddler Festival Colonial times resurface in historical Canal Fulton during the first three weekends in September. You won't trip over power cords, and amplified music won't blow you away. There's no electricity at this celebration of the old days: cooks prepare food over wood and charcoal grills, and if you're lost or looking for something, a town crier booms announcements to the crowd. > Clay's Park Resort, 13190 Patterson Rd., North Lawrence, tel. 800/535–5634, www.yankeepeddlerfestival.com.

WHERE TO STAY

BERLIN

Donna's Premier Lodging Just off the shopping strip on Berlin's Main Street, Donna's has cottages, chalets, and bed-and-breakfast rooms, decorated with lace and ruffles. > 309 East St., Berlin 44610, tel. 330/893–3068 or 800/320–3338, fax 330/893–0037, www.donnasb-b.com. 13 rooms. Some in-room hot tubs, some kitchenettes, some minibars, microwaves, refrigerators, cable TV, in-room VCRs; no smoking. DC, MC, V. $$$–$$$$

Guggisberg Swiss Inn Bucolic country views and charming horse-drawn sleigh rides accentuate the appeal of the comfortable rooms found here. Between Millersburg and Berlin, the inn draws its namesake from the renowned baby Swiss cheese produced nearby. The dining room is open for breakfast only. > 5025 St. Rte. 557, Charm 44617, tel. 330/893–3600 or 877/467–9477, www.guggisbergswissinn.com. 24 rooms, 1 suite. Dining room, in-room hot tubs, cable TV, in-room VCRs, pond, horseback riding, sleigh rides. AE, D, DC, MC, V. BP. $

Inn at Honey Run Secluded in the woods, this inn's main building is a wooden lodge furnished with over-stuffed chairs and homemade quilts. The honeycomb building is on the side of a hill; it's practically underground and barely visible. > 6920 County Rd. 203, Millersburg 44654, tel. 330/674–0011 or 800/468–6639, fax 330/674–2623, www.innathoneyrun.com. 37 rooms, 3 cottages. Dining room, some in-room hot tubs, some kitchenettes, some minibars, some microwaves, some refrigerators, cable TV, some in-room VCRs, meeting rooms, laundry facilities, no-smoking rooms. AE, D, MC, V. CP. $$–$$$

NEW PHILADELPHIA

Schoenbrunn Inn Amish quilts decorate the beds and locally made pieces fill the rooms in this modern motel done in Amish country style. It's 1½ mi from downtown, off I–77 Exit 81. Suites with kitchenettes are across the street. > 1186 W. High Ave., New Philadelphia 44663, tel. 330/339–4334 or 800/929–7799, fax 330/339–5749, www.christopherhotels.com/schoenbrunn/index.html. 64 rooms. In-room data ports, some in-room hot tubs, some microwaves, some refrigerators, cable TV, indoor pool, exercise equipment, hot tub, sauna, bar, laundry facilities, business services, meeting rooms, some pets allowed (fee). AE, D, DC, MC, V. CP. $

SUGARCREEK

Bed and Breakfast Barn Originally a cheese house built in 1858, this inn was transformed into a B&B, retaining its 19th-century atmosphere with original beams and flooring, and some fine 100-year-old oak detailing. All rooms and cabins have private baths. > 560 E. Sugarcreek St., Sugarcreek 44681, tel. 330/852–2337 or 888/334–2436, web.tusco.net/bedbarn. 12 rooms, 9 cabins. Dining room, some kitchenettes, some microwaves, some refrigerators, cable TV, spa; no smoking. D, MC, V. BP. ¢–$$

Breitenbach Bed & Breakfast The Bear family house is just down the road from Breitenbach Wine Cellars, which is in nearby Dover. Dana Bear, the aunt of Breitenbach Wine Cellars proprietor Anita Davis, is the innkeeper; her father constructed the house in 1953. All rooms have private baths and are decorated with Bear family antiques. You can sample some of Breitenbach's award-winning wine during evening snack time. A hearty breakfast is included. > 307 Dover Rd., Sugarcreek 44681, tel. 330/343–3603 or 800/843–9463, fax 330/343–8290, www.breitenbachwine.com. 4 rooms. Dining room, cable TV. D, MC, V. BP. $

Swiss Village Inn Rooms here have floral curtains and bedspreads and Amish-style oak furnishings. In addition to the inn, Victoria Station, a refurbished railroad sleeper, has six guest rooms, each with a private bath. You're within walking distance of many shops and restaurants in the commercial district of Sugarcreek. Continental breakfast is included in the rates during the summer only. > 206 S. Factory St., Sugarcreek 44681, tel. 330/852–3121 or 800/792–6822, www.swissvillageinn.com. 10 inn rooms, 6 railroad sleeper rooms. Dining room, some refrigerators, cable TV; no smoking. D, MC, V. CP. $

WALNUT CREEK

Carlisle Village Inn Wicker chairs, oak furniture, and plush sitting rooms recall an earlier, easier-paced age in this genteel country inn. The ample rooms are tastefully decorated, comfortable, and private, and the bucolic views of Ohio's farmland refresh the eyes and the mind. You can take horse-and-buggy rides May–October. > 4949 Walnut St. (St. Rte. 515), Walnut Creek 44687, tel. 330/893–3636, fax 330/893–2056, www.dutchcorp.com. 52 rooms, 4 suites. Restaurant, in-room hot tubs, cable TV, shops, Internet, meeting rooms; no smoking. AE, MC, V. CP. $$

WOOSTER

Harbor Hill's Black Squirrel Inn Retired college professors run this college-town inn. Near the College of Wooster and local shops, the 19th-century home has an intricately painted exterior, and 10-foot ceilings recall Victorian comfort. All rooms have private baths; two have period furniture. > 636 College Ave., Wooster 44691, tel. 330/345–9596 or 800/760–1710, www.bbonline.com/oh/blacksquirrel. 4 rooms. In-room hot tubs, cable TV, in-room VCRs. AE, DC, MC, V. BP. ¢–$

Wooster Inn The College of Wooster owns this hotel on the far eastern edge of the school's campus. Antique-style bureaus and plush easy chairs fill the bright rooms. The bathrooms also feature antique-style vanities. > 801 E. Wayne Ave., Wooster 44691, tel. 330/263–2660, fax 330/263–2661, www.wooster.edu/wooster_inn. 13 rooms, 2 suites. Restaurant, picnic area, cable TV, driving range, 9-hole golf course, putting green, business services, Internet, some pets allowed, no-smoking rooms. Closed 1st wk of Jan. AE, D, DC, MC, V. $$–$$$

ZOAR

Cowger House #9 Rooms are in an 1817 log cabin, an 1833 post-and-beam building, and a modern Amish-style B&B building. The cabin is the most rustic and historic, built in 1817 and brimming with antiques and dressed in century-old wood. The dining tables are from 1850. Staying at any one of the Cowger inns provides walking access to historic Zoar Village, the majority of which lies to the south of Cowger House # 9.

> 197 4th St., Zoar 44667, tel. 330/874–3542 or 800/874–3542, www.zoarvillage.com. 10 rooms. Restaurant, some in-room hot tubs; no TV in some rooms. AE, D, MC, V. BP. ¢–$$$

Zoar Tavern and Inn The inn's four rooms and one suite are Tudor-revival in style, with exposed dark wood beams and off-white stone-and-brick walls. Antique furnishings recall the days when the village doctor lived in this building, which is right in the center of town. > 162 Main St., Zoar 44667, tel. 330/874–2170 or 888/874–2170, www.zoar-tavern-inn.com. 4 rooms, 1 suite. Restaurant, room service, cable TV, bar; no smoking. AE, D, MC, V. CP. $–$$$$

WHERE TO EAT

BERLIN

Der Dutchman Generous portions of tasty comfort food, reasonable prices, and a charming view keep patrons coming back to this Holmes County restaurant just east of Berlin. Der Dutchman, one of seven in a locally owned chain, has a salad bar, kids' menu, and family-style service. There's no smoking here. > 4967 Walnut St., Walnut Creek, tel. 330/893–2981. D, MC, V. Closed Sun. $

Dutch Harvest Restaurant Except for its large size, the dining room could easily double for one in an Amish home. Traditional Amish dishes such as roast beef, baked ham, and roast turkey are all served with sides like mashed potatoes or corn. Pie varieties change daily but usually include seasonal fruits. Breakfast is served; it's also one of the few area restaurants open on Sunday. > 5330 County Rd. 201, Berlin, tel. 330/893–3333. D, MC, V. ¢–$

NEW PHILADELPHIA

Alpine Alpa About 10 mi northwest of New Philadelphia in a Swiss village market, Alpine Alpa is worth a stop just to see the 23-foot-tall cuckoo clock, considered to be the world's tallest, and the three-dimensional murals in the dining room. Home-style Amish and Swiss meals are served family-style. A house specialty is the Der Deutscher, a spicy German wurst accompanied by warm potato salad. There's a buffet on Sunday, kids' menus, and no smoking. > 1504 U.S. 62, Wilmot, tel. 330/359–5454. AE, D, MC, V. $–$$

Amish Door This eatery in the Amish countryside 10 mi northwest of New Philadelphia serves hearty, home-style fare. Try the broasted chicken dinner and one of the 19 varieties of pie for dessert. Service is family style, and there are kids' menus. Smoking is not allowed. > 1210 Winesburg St. (U.S. 62), Wilmot, tel. 330/359–5464. D, MC, V. Closed Sun. ¢–$

SUGARCREEK

Beachy's Country Chalet This "all-you-care-to-eat" restaurant features roast beef, turkey, ham, mashed potatoes, vegetables, fresh bread, and, for dessert, a dozen or more varieties of pie. Wooden bench-style seats and Amish quilts are homey touches. There's family-style service and kids' menus, and smoking is not allowed. > 115 Andreas Dr., Sugarcreek, tel. 330/852–4644. MC, V. Closed Sun. ¢–$

Swiss Hat All-you-can-eat buffets, Swiss steak, Wiener schnitzel, and Friday fish fry, plus homemade pies and apple dumplings for dessert make this a popular spot. > 108 E. Main St., Sugarcreek, tel. 330/852–2821. D, MC, V. $

WOOSTER

Granary at the Pine Tree Barn This luncheonette overlooks a private lake and a Christmas tree farm. You can order homemade soups, specialty sandwiches, and salads. Top off your meal with a lemon-crumb muffin or a slice of sour-cream fruit pie. > 4374 Shreve Rd., off Rte. 350, Wooster, tel. 330/264–1014. D, MC, V. No dinner. ¢–$

TJ's/C.W. Burgerstein's Upstairs, TJ's has five dining rooms adorned with wood, marble, and antiques. In these dressy-yet-cozy rooms you can indulge in veal, steak, prime rib, and seafood. Downstairs, C.W. Burgerstein's is a sports bar where you can watch the game while you munch burgers, wings, and specialty sandwiches. There are kids' menus and early-bird dinners. > 359 W. Liberty St., Wooster, tel. 330/264–6263. AE, D, DC, MC, V. Closed Sun. $–$$$

ZOAR

Inn on the River This canal inn built circa 1830 is reputedly haunted by a man named Allan Wallace (although folks call him "George"), who died of cholera in the mid-19th century. "George" spooks guests with everything from rattling bottles on the bar to making noises in the kitchen. Despite the seeming paranormal activity, it's a good special-occasion spot, right on Tuscarawas River. The menu features chicken, fish, steak, and pasta dishes. Reservations are recommended. > 8806 Towpath Rd. NE, Bolivar, tel. 330/874–3770. MC, V. No dinner Sun. and Mon. $$–$$$$

Zoar Tavern and Inn In addition to sandwiches and entrées of chicken, pasta, steak, and seafood, you can get German fare such as spaetzle and cabbage, schnitzel and sausages, and bread pudding for dessert. > 162 Main St., tel. 330/874–2170 or 888/874–2170. AE, D, MC, V. $–$$$$

ESSENTIALS

Getting Here

Getting to Amish Country by any other way than car (or charter bus) is a hassle. Rail lines exist here for the purpose of scenic tours; bus routes are limited; and the nearest airport of consequence is in Akron, a 30- to 90-minute drive from any given Amish Country spot. What's more, Amish Country is largely rural, and stops are separated by several miles at least. You'll need a rental car to get around the region, even if you fly or take a bus to get here.

Interstate 77 cuts a swath through the middle of the region, and a host of Ohio state routes filter traffic to the area's destinations, which make for easy, bucolic drives through the rolling hills.

BY BUS

If you must take a bus to Amish Country, Greyhound serves Wooster on the northern edge of the region. Three buses per day per city depart for Wooster from Cincinnati, Cleveland, and Columbus, and two buses arrive in Wooster daily from Toledo.

Round-trip tickets vary widely in cost, with prices ranging from $54 from Cleveland to $184 from Cincinnati.

BUS DEPOTS **Greyhound Bus Depot** > 213 S. Market St., Wooster 44691, tel. 330/262–0341, www.greyhound.com.

BUS LINES **Greyhound Lines Inc.** > Tel. 330/262–0341, www.greyhound.com.

BY CAR

The most efficient way to reach and to tour Amish Country is via automobile. Interstates 77 and 70 provide jumping off points for travelers, and Ohio State Route 39, U.S. Routes 250 and 62, as well as a spate of county roads reach into the hollows of these hills.

The roads are mostly rural two-laners that are maddening when you feel the need for speed (although some parts of Route 39 and U.S. 250 are four lanes). Be prepared for leisurely, if not slow-paced, drives on the weekends, when the roads are packed with visitors. Autumn is the busiest time, as tour buses and foliage seekers amble along, some at African safari–like speeds. Be prepared to brake and yield to the occasional horse and buggy while on state routes and county roads. Driving at dusk and dawn can be especially tricky with the traditional Amish and Mennonite transportation sharing the asphalt.

Holmes County provides some of the best drive-by viewing in Amish Country, with Routes 643 and 515 as the principal roads. Route 39 in Tuscarawas County (just west of Dover) is a favorite, winding over Ohio's east–central hills. Many shops and museums are along these routes, in addition to the scenic countryside.

Visitor Information

CONTACTS **Holmes County Chamber of Commerce and Tourism Bureau** > 35 N. Monroe St., Millersburg 44654, tel. 330/674–3975, www.visitamishcountry.com. **Ohio Historical Society** > 1982 Velma Ave., Columbus 43211, tel. 614/297–2300, www.ohiohistory.org. **Tuscarawas County Chamber of Commerce** > 1323 4th St. NW, 44663, tel. 330/343–4474 or 800/527–3387, www.neohiotravel.com. **Tuscarawas County Convention and Visitors Bureau** > 125 McDonald Dr. SW, New Philadelphia 44663, tel. 330/339–5453, www.neohiotravel.com. **Wayne County Convention and Visitors Bureau** > 377 W. Liberty St., Wooster 44691, tel. 330/262–5735, www.wooster-wayne.com.

Mansfield

Mansfield is 70 mi south of Cleveland, 70 mi northeast of Columbus, and 170 mi northeast of Cincinnati.

11

By Amy S. Eckert

ALL-AMERICAN MANSFIELD IS IN AN AREA described as Ohio's rooftop, thanks to several 1,400-foot hills, which are the gateway to the Appalachians farther south. In the flat farmland of rural central Ohio, 1,400-foot hills are something to brag about. But Mansfield's residents like to brag about more than the foothills: There's the community's history as Johnny Appleseed's hometown, its well-preserved turn-of-the-20th-century Main Street, its carousel-carving school. If you're looking for the quintessential heartland getaway, Mansfield is the place for you.

Fertile soil and a large, dependable spring drew the first white settlers to what was, in 1813, the very edge of the American frontier. The land also happened to lie in the heart of Indian territory, so settlers erected two blockhouses for protection in what is today Mansfield's Central Park. During the War of 1812 those blockhouses were vital to the survival of area residents, subject to attacks from local tribes. When the war ended and the American frontier moved west, the city of Mansfield grew up around the blockhouses. A 1906 reproduction of one of those early structures can be seen in the city's South Park, just west of the downtown.

Today the chief industries in Mansfield and Richland County include steel production, manufacturing, telecommunications, and medical research. Still, locals treasure their historic associations with at least two agricultural innovators, John Chapman and Louis Bromfield. Chapman, better known as Johnny Appleseed, spent the majority of his life in Richland county, planting trees and pioneering advances in apple production. Mansfield native Louis Bromfield, best known as a Pulitzer Prize–winning author of the 1920s and '30s, devoted his later years to practicing and promoting land conservation and environmentally sound farming. Sites associated with both agricultural innovators can be seen throughout Mansfield.

Mansfield's rolling terrain, especially southeast of the city, makes the area an ideal destination for outdoor enthusiasts. In the winter months, skiers head to Clear Fork and Snow Trails ski areas. In the warmer weather, favorite activities include boating, fishing, and canoeing at Charles Mill Lake Park and Mohican State Park. Cycling, skating, jogging, and cross-country skiing are popular pastimes along the B&O Trail, which twists through the countryside from Mansfield to Butler. And Bromfield's Malabar Farm, today a state park, is popular for hiking, horseback riding, and picnicking.

If your idea of a weekend away involves more in the way of man-made pleasures, Mansfield's downtown beckons. The city was one of only five in the United States awarded the "Great American Main Street" designation in 2001 in recognition of its revitalized downtown area. The attractive Carrousel District, three blocks of renovated Victorian buildings, offers historical museums and factory tours, shopping and dining, theater and the arts.

A community of roughly 55,000 residents, Mansfield is the geographical and economic hub of the immediate area. Loudonville is 25 mi southeast of the city. Lucas is 8 mi southeast, Lexington is 7 mi southwest, and Bellville is 10 mi south.

WHAT TO SEE & DO

Carousel Magic! One of the nation's premier carousel restorers and manufacturers, Carousel Magic! sits right across the street from its first local project—the Richland Carrousel Park. A 45-minute tour of the downtown facility will walk you through the entire carousel-making process. You'll see skilled craftspeople engaged in the carving, finishing, painting, and restoring of new and antique prancing ponies while also learning about the history, styles, and mechanical construction of carousels. > 44 W. 4th St., Mansfield, tel. 419/526–4009, www.carouselmagic.com. $4. Tues.–Sat. 10–4.

Charles Mill Lake Park Created as a reservoir to help control flooding along the Muskingum River, Charles Mill Lake is a popular place to escape the city and enjoy nature. Although there are hiking trails, picnic facilities, and a large campground, the most popular activities revolve around the water: fishing for bass, bluegill, crappie, and catfish, swimming (beach and pool), and boating (canoes and pontoon boats). > 1271 Rte. 430, Mansfield, tel. 419/368–6885, www.mwcdlakes.com/charles.htm. Free. Daily dawn–dusk.

Charles Mill Marina On the shore of Charles Mill Lake, the marina is a popular destination for boating and camping. You can rent motor boats, pontoons, canoes, or kayaks, or embark on a cruise boat with a captain. > 1277 Rte. 430, Mansfield, tel. 419/884–0166, www.charlesmillmarina.com. Free. Winter hours: Mon.–Fri. 9–5, Sat. 9–3, Sun. noon–4; Summer hours: Mon.–Fri. 9–7, Sat. 9–8, Sun. 9–7.

Jones Potato Chip Company You'll smell the Jones factory well before you enter the doors of their plant. Since 1945 the family-owned business has been frying up one of the nation's favorite snack foods in Mansfield. You can get a close-up view on a guided half-hour tour of the plant, where 20,000 pounds of potatoes are scrubbed, sliced, fried, salted, and bagged daily. Each tour includes a free sampling of hot potato chips, fresh from the fryer. Confirm tour availability in advance by phone if possible. > 265 Bowman St., Mansfield, tel. 419/522–2988, www.joneschips.com. Free. Mon.–Thurs. 8–1, occasional Fri., depending on work load.

Kingwood Center Local businessman Charles King, who made his fortune at the Ohio Brass Company in Mansfield, left most of his estate as a public garden. Kingwood Center is home to Kingwood Hall. You can take a self-guided tour of the 1926 French Provincial mansion, which is exquisitely decorated with floral fabrics, crystal chandeliers, and period furnishings. But the chief attraction at Kingwood is the estate's grounds. Nearly 50 acres of beautiful gardens, statuary, woods, flowering trees, and ponds attract gardening enthusiasts as well as strolling visitors. Several greenhouses shelter seasonal displays of flowers and tropical plants. > 900 Park Ave. W, Mansfield, tel. 419/522–0211, www.kingwoodcenter.org. Free. Gardens: Apr.–Oct., daily 8–dusk; Nov.–Mar., daily 8–5. Greenhouses: Apr.–Oct., daily 8–dusk; Nov.–Mar., daily 8–4:30; Kingwood Hall: Tues.–Sat. 9–5. Also open Sun. 1–5, Apr.–Oct.

Malabar Farm State Park Mansfield native Louis Bromfield was a prolific Pulitzer Prize–winning novelist and screenplay writer for 30 years beginning in 1925. He built his 32-room dream home and farm, called Malabar, on 914 acres of rolling land in 1939. He invited dozens of famous friends to stay, always insisting that they help out with the chores. Frequent guests included Shirley Temple, George and Gracie Burns, and Humphrey Bogart and Lauren Bacall, who were married in the foyer and honeymooned in an upstairs bedroom. During his later years Bromfield devoted his attention to conservation and ecologically sustainable agricultural innovations. Although Malabar is now owned by the state, it's still a working farm and remains a favorite among lovers, probably due to Bogie and Bacall's history here. The grounds are crisscrossed by miles of bridle and hiking trails; a hike up the farm's Mount Jeez is said to provide the best lookout in Ohio. The park is in Lucas, about 10 mi west of Mansfield. > 4050 Bromfield Rd., Lucas, tel. 419/892–2784, www.malabarfarm.org. Grounds free, house tour $4. Grounds daily dawn–dusk. House Apr.–Oct., daily 10–5; Jan.–Mar., weekends 10–5; Nov. and Dec., daily 11–5.

Mansfield Art Center Exhibitions at the Mansfield Art Center include several juried and invitational shows, borrowed displays from larger national museums, and art sales. Many exhibits include the works of local and regional artists. The center's modern wood-and-glass structure, which was designed by Don M. I. Hisaka and built in 1971, has won architectural honors and sits on 8 acres of meadow. > 700 Marion Ave., Mansfield, tel. 419/756–1700, www.mansfieldartcenter.com. Varies by exhibit. Tues.–Sat. 11–5, Sun. noon–5.

Mohican State Park Twelve miles of trails traverse Mohican State Park, including one that runs through the 1,000-foot-wide by 300-foot-deep Clear Fork Gorge. Clear Fork River, which is responsible for carving the spectacular gorge, and numerous waterfalls are the park's biggest draws. In autumn the park's numerous hardwoods ensure vibrant foliage. Naturalists enjoy the abundance of fern species, including the rare walking fern, and more than 15 species of warblers that nest here in spring and summer. Clear Fork River, a prime fishing spot, is stocked with brown trout. The park is in Loudonville, southeast of Mansfield. > 3116 Rte. 3, at Rte. 97, Loudonville, tel. 419/994–5125, 419/994-4290 camping info, www.ohiostateparks.org. Free. Daily 6 AM–dusk.

Oak Hill Cottage Built in the 1840s and restored several times since, Oak Hill Cottage is an excellent example of Victorian Gothic architecture. Highlights include seven gables, five double chimneys, and seven marble fireplaces along with a collection of original furnishings. Pulitzer Prize–winning author and Mansfield native Louis Bromfield immortalized the home in his novel, *The Green Bay Tree*. > 310 Springmill St., Mansfield, tel. 419/524–1765, www.mansfieldtourism.org/pages/members/Oakhill.html. $3. Apr.–Dec., Sun. 2–5.

Ohio State Reformatory In 1886 architect Levi Scofield designed Mansfield's correctional facility in the manner of Europe's grand chateaux, castles, and cathedrals. He aimed to spiritually transform the lives of the facility's young residents while they served their time and learned a trade. The reformatory served as a prison until 1990, when it was abandoned by the state. Four motion pictures were filmed here, including *The Shawshank Redemption* and *Air Force One,* and some of the movie props remain. Although the facility is still in need of much restoration, the original cell blocks make for a fascinating and eerie visit. You can join one of four 1-hour themed tours or join a Ghost Hunt searching for signs of the paranormal activity that experts say is exceptionally strong in the Reformatory. > 100 Reformatory Rd., off Rte. 545 Mansfield, tel. 419/522–2644, www.mrps.org. Tours: $8 for 1st tour, $5 for subsequent tours. Ghost Hunt: $50. Tours May–Oct., Sun. 1–4; ghost hunts twice monthly, May–Sept. and Nov., 8 PM–dawn.

Renaissance Theatre A magnificent 1928 movie palace, the Renaissance has marble floors and staircases, crystal chandeliers, and all the grand baroque details popular when Hollywood first took the nation by storm. After decades of decline the theater has been fully restored to its original grandeur. The Mansfield Symphony Orchestra,

Spooky Stuff

FROM FRIENDLY TO FEARSOME, Ohio has its share of ghosts and ghouls. The state is filled with chilling stories centered around unexplained events. Turn a cold shoulder to these tales and visit for the history. Or feel the chills and goosebumps from things that go bump in the night.

During its 94 years in operation, the **Ohio State Reformatory** (800/642–8282 or 419/522–2644) in Mansfield had at least one inmate who hanged himself, another who set himself on fire, and one who stuffed his murdered cellmate beneath a bunk. Tragedies weren't reserved for the prisoners, however. A warden's wife dislodged a pistol which hit the floor and inflicted a fatal wound. The warden suffered a heart attack and died. Tour guides say they hear a man and woman talking— perhaps the warden and his wife in an endless conversation from beyond the grave. The imposing fortress closed in 1990 but the structure survives, thanks to preservationists who began tours in 1996.

James Thurber didn't believe in ghosts. While at college studying journalism, Thurber wrote about his other wordly experience in "The Night the Ghost Got In." It seems a man who lived in the house paced around the dining room table, ran upstairs, and shot himself on the second floor. He committed suicide, driven to death by his cheating wife. Today, the third floor of the **Thurber House** (614/464–1032) in Columbus is often home to a writer-in-residence. Over the years, some of these writers have encountered the ghost. One wrote "it was usually after dark when I, too, heard footsteps, treading one floor below. . . . Sooner or later, whoever lived there heard footsteps . . ."

Squire's Castle (440/473–3370), a stone building in the Cleveland metroparks, isn't a castle, but rather a caretaker's house. Feargus Squire, a founder of Standard Oil, bought 525 forested acres near Cleveland, planning a summer estate. First Squire built a three-story caretaker's cottage. Its basement became a trophy room for the skins and heads of animals Squire hunted in exotic locations. Mrs. Squire hated the country, the cottage, and the thought of spending summers in the house her husband was planning. She developed insomnia and walked around the house at night, carrying a red lantern to light her way. One night she wandered into the trophy room. She screamed in terror, tripped, fell and broke her neck. Squire blamed himself for her death and abandoned plans for the house. Legends say Mrs. Squire still roams the cottage where her life was tragically cut short. Some hear screams or catch a glimpse of her red lantern. Curious visitors can wander around the cottage from dawn to sunset.

The ghosts that call **Bobby Mackey's Nightclub** (859/431–5588) in Wilder, Kentucky, home have gained national attention on television shows such as "Sightings," "Hard Copy," and "Geraldo." What is now a nightclub served as a slaughterhouse in the 1800s. The building's grisly history includes a period when it was used by satanic worshipers for their sacrifices. The discovery of the headless body of Pearl Bryan in 1896 was the most sensational episode. Two followers of the occult confessed to her murder and became the last two people hanged in Campbell County. Employees say the nightclub is haunted by Johanna and several other spirits. In the rest rooms, faucets turn on after you turn them off and visions of people you know come out of either rest room. The smell of roses is the tip that something is about to happen.

— Nicki Chodnoff

the Renaissance Broadway Series, and the Summer at the Renaissance Series share the space, which also hosts children's theater and classic films. > 138 Park Ave. W, Mansfield, tel. 419/522–2726, www.rparts.org. Varies by performance. Box office: weekdays 10–5; theater varies by performance.

Richland B&O Trail Once the location of the B&O Railroad line, the B&O Trail provides an ideal path for cycling, in-line skating, walking, or jogging in Mansfield and beyond. The paved route begins at North Lake Park in Mansfield's downtown and meanders south to the towns of Lexington, Bellville, and Butler. For a trail map contact the Mansfield & Richland County Convention and Visitors Bureau. > Tel. 419/525–1300 or 800/642–8282, www.mansfieldtourism.org. Free. Daily.

Richland Carrousel Park This heated pavilion in downtown Mansfield houses a beautiful, all-wood carousel. Designed and hand-carved in Ohio, the carousel was the first to be built since the early 1930s. Visitors of all ages enjoy climbing aboard. Snacks and souvenirs are available in the adjoining gift shop. > 75 N. Main St., at 4th St., Mansfield, tel. 419/522–4223. Pavilion: Free. Carousel rides: 1 ride–60¢; 2 rides–$1. Memorial Day–Labor Day, daily 11–5, until 8 on Wed.; Labor Day–Memorial Day, daily 11–5.

Richland County Museum Memorabilia illustrating the county's history is displayed in an 1850 schoolhouse in Lexington, a few miles south of Mansfield. The collection includes tools, clothing, children's toys, furniture, and paintings. > 51 W. Church St., Lexington, tel. 419/884–0277 or 419/884–2230. Free. May–Oct., Sun. 1:30–4:30.

South Park Nestled in the heart of Mansfield's Boulevard District, where grand, turn-of-the-20th-century homes occupy lush, tree-lined streets, South Park provides plenty of picnicking space and grassy areas for youngsters to let off steam. On the park's southernmost boundary is the Mansfield Blockhouse, a replica of the original 1812 structure built to defend early settlers against Indian attacks. Next to the blockhouse is a memorial to John Chapman, best known as Johnny Appleseed. The pioneer apple nurseryman made Richmond County his home for most of his life. > Park Ave. W at Brinkerhoff Ave., Mansfield. Free. Daily.

Upstairs/Downstairs This auto repair and restoration shop in downtown Mansfield is also a showroom for restored British, European, and American classic cars. Can't afford a 40-year-old Jaguar, Rolls Royce, Mustang, or Chevelle? Step inside anyway. The owners of Upstairs/Downstairs welcome visitors and fellow enthusiasts. > 40 W. 4th St., Mansfield, tel. 419/524–9663, www.updownauto.com. Weekdays 7:30–5:30.

Sports

AUTO RACING

Mid-Ohio Sports Car Course In summer six national and international motor sports events are held at the 330-acre road track 5 mi southwest of Mansfield. A variety of two- and four-wheeled motor vehicles race on the track, including vintage and contemporary race cars, motorcycles, and CART Champ Cars. The 2.4-mi course has a 15-turn configuration, while the 2.25-mi course has a 13-turn configuration. When there are no special events planned, racing enthusiasts can learn how to become drivers by enrolling in the Mid-Ohio School, and local automakers put their new vehicles through their paces. Mid-Ohio is often cited as the most competitive in the United States. Facilities include permanent grandstands, spectator viewing mounds, concessions, and souvenir stands. > 7721 Steam Corners Rd., east of Rte. 314, Lexington, tel. 419/884–4000 or 800/643–6446, www.midohio.com.

BIKING

Richland B&O Trail Bicycling is the sport of choice along the B&O Trail, once the site of a B&O Railroad bed. The features that made this route ideal for train travel—relatively flat terrain with only the gentlest of inclines and curves—also make it perfect for cycling. In-line skaters, walkers, joggers, and, in winter, cross-country skiers share the trail, but there's not a single motorized vehicle in sight. The 18-mi path begins in Mansfield's North Lake Park and ends in Butler's Hitchman Park on Elm Street, with numerous parking areas and rest rooms along the way. For a trail map contact the Mansfield & Richland County Convention and Visitors Bureau. > Tel. 419/525–1300 or 800/642–8282, www.mansfieldtourism.org.

RENTALS **Webster's Mountain Sports** > 307 E. Main St., Lexwood Plaza, Lexington, tel. 419/884–9699; 225 Grant St., Butler, tel. 419/883–3433; 855 Comfort Plaza Dr., I–71 at Rte. 97, inside Comfort Inn South, Bellville, tel. 419/886–4000; 1000 Comfort Plaza Dr., I–71 at Rte. 97, inside Ramada Inn, Bellville, tel. 419/886–7000; 1291 Home Rd., at Deer Park, Mansfield, tel. 419/529–8745; 28 Main St., at Whiffletree Restaurant, Butler, tel. 419/883–3282.

DOWNHILL SKIING

Within an easy distance of the only hills of any significance in the region, Mansfield is a godsend to local ski enthusiasts in central rural Ohio.

Clear Fork Ski Area You can schuss all day and all night at this ski area 15 mi south of Mansfield. Nine slopes are serviced by six lifts, winding through elevations of 2,100 to 2,400 feet. The vertical drop is 300 feet. Clear Fork is a good place to ski with the whole family—there are more beginner slopes here than at Snow Trails, and wide ski surfaces allow a little more room for error. Full-day lift tickets cost $24–$32; complete ski and snowboard rentals are available on-site and cost $24. Three restaurants and a lounge provide après-ski fun. > 341 Resort Dr., Butler, tel. 419/883–2000 or 800/237–5673, www.skiclearfork.com.

Snow Trails Just 2 mi from town, Snow Trails is Mansfield's original ski area. With elevations between 1,175 and 1,475 feet, and a vertical drop of 300 feet, Snow Trails is a bit more challenging than Clear Fork, with more intermediate-level runs. Six lifts deliver skiers to 16 runs as well as two free-style areas. All-day lift tickets cost $25–$37; complete ski and snowboard rentals cost $25. Warm up at the restaurant or lounge on site. > 3100 O'Possum Run Rd., Mansfield, tel. 419/774–9818 or 800/644–6754, www.snowtrails.com.

Save the Date

FEBRUARY

Ohio Winter Ski Carnival Ski and snowboard races, kids' games, a costume contest, and a ski patrol cookout make up this annual event at the Snow Trails Ski Resort in Mansfield. Lift ticket prices and ski equipment rental rates are lowered on the last weekend in February for the occasion. > Snow Trails Ski Resort, 3100 O'Possum Run Rd., tel. 419/774–9818 or 800/644–6754, www.snowtrails.com.

MARCH

Maple Syrup Festival A horse-drawn wagon will transport you back into the woods and back in time at Malabar Farm's annual celebration of the sugar season. Demonstrations of sugar making and re-creations of pioneer life are among the festivities. > Malabar Farm State Park, 4050 Bromfield Rd., Lucas, tel. 419/892–2784, www.malabarfarm.org.

MAY–OCTOBER

Auto Racing at the Mid-Ohio Sports Car Course Thousands of racing enthusiasts flock to Lexington every summer to enjoy the Mid-Ohio, a few miles south of Mansfield. Both amateur and professional drivers compete in modified cars. Races are held on weekends. > 7721 Steam Corners Rd., just east of Rte. 314, Lexington, tel. 419/884–4000 or 800/643–6446, www.midohio.com.

JUNE

Juneteenth Celebration Commemorate the emancipation of slaves following the Civil War with good food, educational activities, and vendor booths selling such items as African artifacts, clothing, and artwork. > Mansfield Central Park, Park Ave., between Diamond and N. Main Sts. Mansfield, tel. 419/522–1875.

AUGUST

Farm Fun Days and Fishing Derby Old-fashioned games, tobacco spitting, and hay bale throwing contests, and cow chip tosses are all part of the fun at Malabar Farm every summer. The fishing competition is open to kids under 16, with prizes awarded for the largest and longest catches. > Malabar Farm State Park, 4050 Bromfield Rd., Lucas, tel. 419/892–2784, www.malabarfarm.org.

Richland County Fair Almost everyone knows everyone else at this hometown county fair, but out-of-towners are welcome with open arms. Take in some of the livestock shows, sample the food, and by all means hit a few of the thrill rides. > 750 N. Home Rd., tel. 419/747–3717, www.richlandcountyfair.com.

SEPTEMBER

Ohio Heritage Days Actors and actresses portray Native Americans and pioneer settlers during this annual celebration of Ohio's history held at Malabar Farm. One of Ohio's largest free outdoor crafts fairs is part of the event, as are live musical performances, a barn dance, and demonstrations of vintage tractors and other farm equipment, including the Malabar Farm sawmill. There's also a Civil War and fur trappers encampment and exhibits about state historical events. > Malabar Farm State Park, 4050 Bromfield Rd., Lucas, tel. 419/892–2784, www.malabarfarm.org.

DECEMBER

Candlelight Christmas at Malabar Pulitzer Prize–winning author Louis Bromfield's home is especially lovely when it's decorated for the holidays. Other Christmastime treats include wagon rides, caroling, freshly baked cookies, and hot cider. > Malabar Farm State Park, 4050 Bromfield Rd., Mansfield, tel. 419/892–2784, www.malabarfarm.org.

WHERE TO STAY

AngelWoods Hideaway A winding drive through the aptly named Pleasant Valley, home of Malabar Farm, takes you to AngelWoods, set amidst 46 acres of beautiful gardens and hardwood trees. The inn's exterior, constructed of brick and cedar, is rustic, but the Asian silks, tapestries, and four-poster beds inside are anything but provincial. Suites have private baths; two of the standard rooms have private baths, and two share a bath. > 1983 Pleasant Valley Rd., Lucas 44843, tel. 419/892–2929 or 888/882–6949, fax 419/892–2353, www.ohio-bed-breakfast.com. 4 rooms, 2 with bath, 2 suites. Some in-room hot tubs, cable TV, in-room VCRs, pool, hot tub, massage, meeting room; no smoking. AE, D, MC, V. CP. $

Best Value Inn–Extended Stay Although it has extended-stay prices, the Best Value Inn is a good value for a weekend's stay, too. Right off I–71 and Route 30 on Mansfield's north side, the location ensures easy and quick access into and around the city.

A number of chain restaurants and stores in the vicinity up the convenience factor.
> 880 Laver Rd., Mansfield 44905, tel. 419/589–2200 or 888/315–2378, fax
419/589–5624. 79 rooms. Some microwaves, some refrigerators, cable TV, pool,
some pets allowed, no-smoking rooms. AE, D, DC, MC, V. ¢–$

Comfort Inn South Potted palms and white wrought-iron furniture invite you to relax
poolside in the sunny atrium at this Comfort Inn. The glass roof over the pool is re-
tractable. There are plenty of other options close at hand for outdoor recreation. The
B&O Trail is less than half a mile away, and Snow Trails and Clear Fork ski areas are
within 5 mi. Bicycle, in-line skate, and ski rentals are available from the front desk.
> 855 Comfort Plaza, east of I–71 at Rte. 97, Bellville 44813, tel. 419/886–4000,
www.comfortinnbellville.com. 100 rooms. In-room data ports, some in-room hot
tubs, some microwaves, some refrigerators, cable TV with movies, miniature golf, indoor-outdoor pool, exercise equipment, hot tub, bicycles, basketball, billiards, shuffleboard, volleyball, cross-country skiing, video game room, shop, meeting rooms,
no-smoking rooms. AE, D, DC, MC, V. CP. $–$$

Hampton Inn Just west of Mansfield in the town of Ontario, this hotel allows easy
access to attractions on the western side of the city, including the Kingwood Center.
Shoppers will enjoy being close to the Richland Mall, the largest enclosed shopping
center in five counties. > 1051 N. Lexington Springmill Rd., Mansfield 44906, tel.
419/747–5353 or 800/426–7866, www.hamptoninn.com. 62 rooms. Room service, in-
room data ports, some microwaves, some refrigerators, cable TV with movies, indoor
pool, hot tub, business services, some pets allowed, no-smoking rooms. AE, D, DC,
MC, V. CP. $–$$$

Holiday Inn Hotel and Suites You can walk to dinner, shopping, or the attractions
of the Carrousel District from this hotel right in the heart of downtown Mansfield. An
enclosed skyway connects the Holiday Inn to the Renaissance Theatre next door. The
Garden Cafe is a popular breakfast, brunch, and lunch choice; light dinners are
served in the hotel's Murphy's Lounge. > 116 Park Ave. W, Mansfield 44902, tel.
419/525–6000 or 800/521–6744, www.holiday-inn.com. 120 rooms, 19 suites. Café,
room service, in-room data ports, cable TV with movies and video games, some
kitchenettes, some refrigerators, indoor pool, hot tub, gym, lounge, shops, laundry
facilities, laundry service, business services, meeting rooms, no-smoking rooms.
AE, D, DC, MC, V. $

Knights Inn Rooms are in four buildings at this one-story hotel. A 10-minute drive
from the Carrousel District, Knights Inn is within easy access of the downtown attrac-
tions, shopping, and dining. There are also several chain restaurants in the vicinity.
> 555 N. Trimble Rd., Mansfield 44906, tel. 419/529–2100 or 800/843–5644,
www.christopherhotels.com. 88 rooms. Room service, in-room data ports, some
kitchenettes, cable TV with movies, pool, meeting rooms, some pets allowed, no-
smoking rooms. AE, D, DC, MC, V. CP. $

Spruce Hill Inn & Cottages Perfect for a romantic getaway or a special family re-
union, Spruce Hill is a collection of private lodges and cottages. Each unit is uniquely
decorated in styles ranging from Victorian elegance with formal dining and sitting
areas to cottage cozy with views of the surrounding woods. Snow Trails ski area
is adjacent to the entrance. > 3230 O'Possum Run Rd., Mansfield 44903, tel.
419/756–2200, fax 419/756-9825, www.sprucehillinn.com. 28 cottages, 1 4-room
lodge, 1 5-room lodge. Some in-room hot tubs, some microwaves, refrigerators, cable
TV, no-smoking rooms. AE, D, MC, V. $–$$$

Travelodge Outdoor enthusiasts hoping to be near the action need look no further
than the Travelodge. Snow Trails is 2 mi away, and Clear Fork is 15 mi away. The B&O
Trail, for cross-country skiing, cycling, skating, or walking, is 5 mi away. The hotel is

also within 5 mi of Malabar Farm State Park. The 24-hour restaurant next door provides fuel for the next adventure. > 90 W. Hanley Rd., Mansfield 44903, tel.
419/756–7600 or 800/578–7878, www.travelodge.com. 88 rooms. In-room data ports,
some microwaves, some refrigerators, cable TV, some in-room VCRs, pool, business
services, meeting rooms, some pets allowed (fee), no-smoking rooms. AE, D, DC,
MC, V. CP. ¢

WHERE TO EAT

Brunches This eatery in the downtown Carrousel District attracts business people on
weekdays with its breakfast specials and light lunch fare. The menu includes daily
quiche specials, thick deli sandwiches, creative salads, and specialty coffees. There's
a kids' menu, and smoking is not allowed. > 103 N. Main St., Mansfield, tel.
419/526–2233. D, MC, V. No dinner. ¢

Dutch Heritage Oak furniture, calico wall coverings, and simulated front-porch dining nooks keep things "down-home" at Dutch Heritage. Amish-style, as the restaurant categorizes its cooking, is code for hearty American favorites like fried chicken,
country ham, mashed potatoes, and homemade pie. The menu options are sure to
please finicky youngsters, and the prices—especially at the breakfast, lunch, and dinner buffets—are easy on a family's budget. Just off I–71, Dutch Heritage is a natural
choice for those staying at the city's southern and eastern hotels. > 720 Rte. 97 W,
just off I–71, Bellville, tel. 419/886–7070. DC, MC, V. Closed Sun. $

El Campesino Mexican music fills the air, woollen blankets and hand-painted scenes
from Old Mexico adorn the walls, and the wait staff speaks exclusively Spanish
among themselves. Seafood specialties, like *Camarones ala Diabla* (shrimp cooked in
a spicy hot sauce) and seafood fajitas, with crab, scallops, and shrimp, supplement a
menu of standard favorites, including fajitas, burritos, and enchiladas. > 1971 W. 4th
St., Mansfield, tel. 419/529–5330. MC, V. $

Fork and Fingers "Every day is Margarita day." So says the sign out front at Fork and
Fingers, famous among locals for its tasty two-for-one Margarita specials. The menu
includes such standards as burritos, quesadillas, and enchiladas, but the local favorite is the fish taco. In the heart of the Carrousel District, Fork and Fingers is within
a few blocks of all of the downtown sites and the shopping district. > 54 Park Ave. W,
Mansfield, tel. 419/526–2321. MC, V. Closed Sun. $

Malabar Inn On the grounds of Malabar Farm State Park, the Malabar Inn was originally a stagecoach inn. The hand-hewn sandstone blocks that compose the building's
foundation were quarried on-site in 1820; the lovely views of surrounding Pleasant
Valley are likely much older. Dinner entrées incorporate produce harvested from Malabar's own gardens. Try the char-broiled steaks or homemade chicken potpies. Reservations essential in November and December. > Malabar Farm State Park, 4050
Bromfield Rd., Lucas, tel. 419/938–5205. MC, V. Closed Mon.; closed Jan.–Feb.; Sat.
and Sun. only in Mar. $

Mama's Touch of Italy Although this northern Italian restaurant doesn't look like
much from the outside, the interior, decorated with greenery and red tones, is very
cozy and relaxed. Most importantly, Mama's is universally believed to serve the best
Italian food in Mansfield. The lasagna and baked ziti are perennial favorites. > 275
Park Ave. W, Mansfield, tel. 419/526–5099. AE, D, DC, MC, V. Closed Sun. No lunch
Sat. $–$$

Skyway East With its 1950s supper-club style, complete with dim lighting and white-
linen tablecloths, Skyway East has been a local favorite since its opening. You may

have a tough time deciding on your dinner selection—the menu lists more than 80 entrées and an extensive wine list. After you treat yourself to one of 20 appetizers, you can dine on big portions of steak (for which this restaurant is known), filet mignon, pasta, and shellfish. Many dishes are cooked with a Mediterranean flair. > 2461 Emma La., south of U.S. 30, Mansfield, tel. 419/589–9929. AE, D, DC, MC, V. Closed Sun. No lunch. $–$$$$

ESSENTIALS

Getting Here

Put simply, the only way to really see and explore Mansfield is via personal automobile. Train service is unavailable; mass transit, air, and bus services are limited and inconvenient. And without a car you will find it virtually impossible to explore any of the areas outside of the downtown.

BY BUS

If traveling by car isn't possible, you can reach Mansfield via Greyhound. Both Greyhound and Richland County Transit, which operates Mansfield's city bus service, share a terminal and ticket window at the bus station in downtown Mansfield. You can catch a taxi from the bus station.

Richland County Transit buses cost $1 and stop at points throughout the downtown Carrousel District and at the Richland Mall in Ontario (west of Mansfield).

BUS DEPOTS **Bus Station** > 74 S. Diamond St., between 1st St. and Marshall Ave., Mansfield, tel. 419/524–1111.

BUS LINES **Greyhound Lines** > Tel. 800/229–9424 fares and schedules, www.greyhound.com. **Richland County Transit** > Tel. 419/522–4504.

BY CAR

To get to Mansfield, travel via I–71 or U.S. 30; the city is bounded on the north and the east by these two fast-moving expressways. Mansfield is further dissected by a number of state routes that allow easy and quick access to any part of the city. Major east–west state routes include Route 39, Route 97, and Route 309. Major north–south state routes include Route 314, Route 42, and Route 13, which becomes Main Street and runs through the heart of Mansfield's downtown.

If you're looking for the scenic route, you can find it southeast of Mansfield. Good choices include Route 39, Route 97, and Pleasant Valley Road.

Parking throughout Mansfield is generally free and easy to find. In the downtown Carrousel District, where parking is more limited, all major streets are metered. A large, free municipal lot is at North Main and 4th streets. Parking in the free lot is limited to three hours.

Visitor Information

CONTACTS **Mansfield & Richland County Convention & Visitors Bureau** > 124 N. Main St., 44902, tel. 419/525–1300 or 800/642–8282, www.mansfieldtourism.org.

Cambridge & Zanesville

Cambridge is approximately 79 mi east of Columbus, 119 mi south of Cleveland, and 185 mi northeast of Cincinnati. Zanesville is approximately 70 mi east of Columbus, 120 mi south of Cleveland, and 195 mi northeast of Cincinnati.

12

By Ann Fazzini

THE MARK OF THE OHIO FRONTIER IS STILL VISIBLE in the Cambridge and Zanesville area on the western edge of Appalachia. Small cities, towns, and villages have thrived among these gentle hills and lush forests for two centuries.

One of America's most famous original roads was forged through the area; it now runs directly through the heart of Cambridge and Zanesville. In 1796 Ebenezer Zane blazed Zane's Trace, the first road in the wilderness, straight through the area now known as Zanesville in his honor. Well-worn Native American footpaths shaped the best routes through the thick brush and uneven terrain, giving Zane a time-tested road map. Zane's initial road work gave the all-important and quickly growing transportation industry direct access to the area, which in turn led to the rapid development of towns along the way. In 1827 the National Road was partially built along the trace to establish a route directly across middle America. Like Route 66 did years later, the National Road provided a path for a people moving west. Latter-day motorists tracing the National Road will find a real slice of Americana—museums, parks, antiques shops, and even diners all reflect the proud traditions of the area.

This area of Ohio offered much more than a strategic location, however. The soil is rich in clay, which settlers first used to make inexpensive pots, bowls, and other containers for work and home. What started as necessity evolved into an art. By the second half of the 19th century, art pottery and exquisite glassware from Cambridge became wildly popular. The wares have stood the test of time and the tradition lives on in the many potteries that dot the area. Today, unique pottery from Zanesville and colorful glassware from Cambridge's famous factories attract collectors and curious travelers from all over the country.

Midwestern friendliness and hospitality make it easy to feel right at home in this close-knit area. The well-maintained historical attractions, the family-owned places to eat and stay, and the quaint store-lined downtown streets are warm, welcoming, and perfect for couples, families, or groups to visit. The Appalachian foothills give the area a varied terrain with plenty of greenery-filled parks, waterways, and forests. In autumn the trees explode with color and the local orchards burst with fruits and vegetables.

WHAT TO SEE & DO

CAMBRIDGE
The Cambridge Glass Museum Thousands of elegant works in glass made between 1906 and 1958 are on display in this gem of a museum, which is considered to be the largest private collection of Cambridge glass in the nation. > 812 Jefferson Ave., Cambridge, tel. 740/432–3045. $2. June–Nov., Mon.–Sat. 1–4.
Degenhart Paperweight and Glass Museum Exhibits at this museum illustrate and explain the different types of glass produced in the Cambridge area. Midwestern pat-

tern glass, cruets, and Degenhart glass and paperweights form the basis of the collection. Also on hand are works by local and regional glass artists. > 65323 Highland Hills Rd., Cambridge, tel. 740/432–2626. $1.50. Apr.–Dec., Mon.–Sat. 9–5; Jan.–Mar., weekdays 10–5.

Hopalong Cassidy Museum One of Cambridge's most beloved natives is William Boyd, better known as Hollywood cowboy Hopalong Cassidy. See collectibles, artifacts, and historical memorabilia in this museum dedicated to the famed actor. The Hopalong Cassidy Festival is the first weekend in May. > 127 S. 10th St., Cambridge, tel. 740/432–3364. Donations accepted. Mon.–Sat. 10–5.

National Museum of Cambridge Glass Cambridge's most famous artistic medium is celebrated in style. See gorgeous pieces originally minted at the now-defunct Cambridge Glass Company, including the opaque Crown Tuscans from the 1930s, sparkling flower frogs, and other pieces bearing the famous "triangle C" logo. Be sure to visit the gift shop to peruse souvenirs. > 136 S. 9th St., tel. 740/432–4245, www.cambridgeglass.org. $2. Apr.–Oct., Wed.–Sat. 9–4, Sun. noon–4.

Salt Fork State Park Ohio's largest state park encompasses Salt Fork Reservoir, amidst 20,000 acres of rolling meadows and woodlands. Reforestation and conservation efforts have resulted in a regrowth of the hardwood forest in this area of the state. Salt Fork has a marina, a beach, stables, hiking trails, and bicycles to rent. The 18-hole golf course is a part of the Salt Fork Resort and Conference Center. > 14755 Cadiz Rd., Lore City, tel. 740/439–3521, www.ohiostateparks.org. Free. Daily dawn–dusk.

ZANESVILLE

Blue Rock State Park Blue Rock—named for the grayish-blue shale found throughout the region—is a 4,500-plus-acre park. Once the home of the Shawnee, the rugged terrain supports a forest of oak and hickory. Campsites are available for tent or trailer camping in two separate areas near the lake. Boating and fishing are popular activities on 15-acre Cutler Lake. > 79–24 Cutler Lake Rd., Blue Rock, tel. 740/674–4794, www.ohiostateparks.org. Free. Daily dawn–11 PM.

Dr. Increase Mathews House Museum Famed general and Ohio settler Rufus Putnam helped his nephew, Increase Mathews, to purchase the land for this home in 1805. Mathews, a well-known area physician, lived here for 51 years. Today, the oldest house in town has 19th-century room settings with vintage quilts and coverlets, as well as a Muskingum River display and a military exhibit. > 304 Woodlawn Ave., Zanesville, tel. 740/454–9500. Free. June–Aug., Sat. noon–4, or by appointment.

National Road/Zane Grey Museum There are three main galleries in this impressive facility. One relates the history of the National Road; one is devoted to author Zane Grey, a Zanesville native and author of classic Western novels; the third displays local styles of Ohio pottery. Stop here first for a "starter kit" of information about the area and its history. > 8850 East Pike, Norwich, tel. 740/872–3143, www.ohiohistory.org/places/natlroad. $6. Call for hrs; they're seasonal and vary widely.

Putnam Manse This private home, built in 1849, is available to tour by reservation only. Extensive collections of 19th-century clothing, Victorian dolls, and antiques are on display inside. The home (and other sites in the area) was named after General Rufus Putnam, who served as the Surveyor General of the State of Ohio and the Northwest Territory. > 425 Woodlawn Ave., Zanesville, tel. 740/455–8282 or 800/743–2303. $3. By appointment only.

Putnam Presbyterian Church William Beecher, brother of Harriet Beecher Stowe, was the first minister of this church, which was a center of Abolitionist activity in the 19th century. Frederick Douglass once gave a speech here. Secretly, the church was also active in the Underground Railroad. Stained-glass windows, and one Tiffany window, adorn the building. > 467 Woodlawn Ave., Zanesville, tel. 740/452–2445. Free. Daily.

Zanesville Art Center The center takes great pride in its glass and ceramic collections of Zanesville-area glass and ceramics. Paintings and sculptures from Asia, Africa, and Europe are on display, along with works by contemporary Ohio artists. > 620 Military Rd., Zanesville, tel. 740/452–0741, www.zanesvilleartcenter.org. Free. Tues., Wed., Fri. 10–5, Thurs. 10–8:30, weekends 1–5.

Tours

The Lorena Sternwheeler The classic riverboat takes passengers on a 1-hour scenic cruise down the Muskingum River. Dinner cruises are available. > Zane's Landing Park, west end of Market St. on the Muskingum River, Zanesville, tel. 740/455–8883 or 800/246–6303, www.zanesville-ohio.com/lorena.htm. $6. June–Aug., daily 1, 2:30; Sept. and Oct., weekends 1, 2:30.

Sports

GOLF

Eagle Sticks Golf Club The well-manicured fairways of Eagle Sticks offer several challenging water hazards. The reasonable rates and friendly staff keep Ohio golfers coming back. There are a pro shop and club house. > 2655 Maysville Pike, Zanesville, tel. 740/454–4900 or 800/782–4493, www.eaglesticks.com.

Whiskey Run Golf Course & Lodge Although it's about 25 mi southeast of Cambridge, this 18-hole, par-70 course is worth the drive for duffers visiting the area. The course is both beautiful and challenging: velvety green fairways are set amidst a gorgeous backdrop of wooded hills. Driving range and rentals available. > 5598 St. Rte. 147, Quaker City, tel. 740/679–2422, www.whiskeyrun.8m.com.

HORSEBACK RIDING

Little Sky Riding Trails The Salt Fork area provides the perfect backdrop for those with dreams of being a cowpoke. What better way to explore the lush wooded foothills than on horseback? Gentle horses and knowledgable guides lead riders of all skill levels on 1- or 2-hour trail rides on the scenic 150-acre grounds. Kids must be at least 6 years old to take the 1-hour trip and at least 12 for the 2-hour trip; pony rides are available for wranglers ages 5 and under. Camp on-site or take a hayride. > 71245 Jasper Rd. (10 mi east of Salt Fork State Park off St. Rte. 22), Freeport, tel. 740/489–9067, littlesky2.tripod.com.

Shopping

The glass and pottery factories in Cambridge and Zanesville listed below are closed on the weekends. Some have retail shops that are open all weekend; others do not. If the option of a long weekend is not available to you, consider shopping for the pieces at other local retail outlets while you are in town.

Fioriware Brightly glazed dinnerware and glassware distinguish this popular brand. In Zanesville's historic Potter's Alley, the factory, which is open for free tours during the week, has a retail store on-site. Rugs and wrought-iron pieces are also available. > 333 Market St., Zanesville, tel. 740/454–7400, www.fioriware.com.

Meadow Farm Stop by for a fresh selection of apples (eight varieties), peaches, rasp-berries, watermelon, corn, tomatoes, and other juicy fruits and crisp vegetables in season. Pick up some annuals or bedding plants, along with kitchen goodies, includ-ing eggs, honey, and jams. Kids will love the petting zoo and wagon rides. > 5795 Coopermill Rd., Zanesville, tel. 740/425–3440. Closed Nov.–Apr.

Mosser Glass One of Cambridge's famous glass factories gives free tours of its operation 8–2:30 weekdays. See the entire process of glassmaking, from furnace to mold to glazing. The factory produces exquisite glassware sets and decorative pieces in beautiful jewel tones. It's closed the first two to three weeks in July. > U.S. 22 E, Cambridge, tel. 740/439–1827, www.mosserglass.com. Free. Closed weekends.

Ohio Ceramic Center Five buildings display and sell various types of ceramics, in-cluding art pottery, bricks, and garden wares. > 7327 Ceramic Rd., Zanesville, tel. 740/697–7021. $2. Closed Nov.–Apr.

Penny Court Antique Mall Fifty-six dealers occupy space here, selling everything from old tools, furniture, and prints to advertising, primitives, and candles. The on-site National Cambridge Collectors Mini-Museum displays Universal pottery and Cambridge glass. > 637 Wheeling Ave., Cambridge, tel. 740/432–4369.

Robinson-Ransbottom Pottery Co The largest plant of its kind in the world, this stonewear pottery factory was established in 1900. You can watch craftspeople make bowls, pots, vases, and other forms of pottery on-site. Guided tours are available by appointment weekdays 9–2; call ahead to schedule for groups of 10 or more. > 5545 3rd St., Zanesville, tel. 740/697–7355, www.robinsonransbottompottery.com. Free. Closed weekends.

Save the Date

APRIL

Hopalong Cassidy Festival The Wild West comes to Cambridge at this annual trib-ute to native son William Boyd, better known as Hopalong Cassidy. Highlights in-clude Western entertainment and visits from famous Hollywood gunslingers—recent guests have included Ben Cooper of "Wagon Train" and John Locke of "Gunsmoke." It's held at the Pritchard Laughlin Civic Center, the first weekend of May. > 7033 Glenn Hwy., Cambridge, tel. 740/432–2022 or 800/933–5480.

JUNE

Muskingum River Lock Festival Take a unique look at the operations of a river dam and learn about life along the Muskingum and how it shaped the area. Festival high-lights include lock demonstrations, Appalachian crafts and foods, plus plenty of en-tertainment. > On the riverfront at the Rokeby Lock, Zanesville, tel. 740/674–4794.

JUNE–SEPTEMBER

Living Word Outdoor Drama Ohio's only outdoor passion play dramatizes the life of Jesus Christ. The 2½-hour show is performed in a natural amphitheater. Reserva-tions are recommended. > 6010 College Hill Rd., Cambridge, tel. 740/439–2761, www.visitguernseycounty.com.

JULY

A Taste of Zanesville The city's top restaurants whip up their best dishes for this downtown festival. > Zanesville, tel. 740/455–8282.

AUGUST

Muskingum County Blue Ribbon Fair Livestock shows, rides, and entertainment—this traditional county fair at the Muskingum County Fairgrounds has it all. > 1300 Pershing Rd., Zanesville, tel. 740/872–3912.

Salt Fork Arts and Crafts Festival The latest creations of local and regional artists draw thousands of people to this annual show in Cambridge City Park. > N. 8th St., Cambridge, tel. 740/432–2022.

OCTOBER
Oktoberfest The yearly celebration of Cambridge's German heritage includes music, dance, games, and food. > Wheeling Ave., Cambridge, tel. 740/439–6688.

WHERE TO STAY

CAMBRIDGE

Best Western Right off I–70, this motel is just minutes away from the Cambridge Glass Museum and Salt Fork State Park. The two-story brick building is in a largely commercial area that includes a score of restaurants, a large discount store, and several small shopping plazas. > 1945 Southgate Pkwy., Cambridge 43725, tel. 740/439–3581 or 800/528–1234, fax 740/439–1824, www.bestwestern.com. 95 rooms. In-room data ports, cable TV, pool, bar, playground, laundry facilities, business services, some pets allowed, no-smoking rooms. AE, D, DC, MC, V. ¢

Colonel Joseph B. Taylor Inn Bed and Breakfast This three-story 1878 painted lady home is furnished with Victorian antiques. Plush robes, fresh roses, a fireplace in the room, and the lavish breakfast are nice touches. > 633 Upland Rd., Cambridge 43725, tel. 740/432–7802, www.coltaylorinnbb.com. 4 rooms. Hot tub, library, shop, business services; no room phones; no TVs in some rooms, no kids, no smoking. D, MC, V. BP. $$–$$$

Holiday Inn Strategically located at the junction of I–70 and I–77, this hotel is always a reliable choice. There's a multiscreen movie theater right across the street, and two major shopping malls within 30 minutes of the hotel. If you've come to explore, downtown Cambridge is only 2 mi away. > 2248 Southgate Pkwy., Cambridge 43725, tel. 800/465–4329 or 740/432–7313, fax 740/432–2337, www.holiday-inn.com. 109 rooms. Restaurant, in-room data ports, some refrigerators, cable TV, outdoor pool, gym, bar, video game room, laundry facilities, business services, some pets allowed, no-smoking rooms. AE, D, DC, MC, V. $

Misty Meadow Farm Bed and Breakfast This 1910 farmhouse and guest cottage are surrounded by 150 trail-crossed acres with a spring-fed pond, a French garden, and an orchard. The three rooms in the farmhouse have themes, such as "French Garden" and "Cherrywood." The rustic 120-year-old country-style cottage has a stone fireplace and a small front porch. A fresh peach and a misty (a beverage of fresh orange juice mixed with seasonal fruits) are delivered to your room, and the breakfast runs to three courses. > 64878 Slaughter Hill Rd., Cambridge 43725, tel. 740/439–5135. www.mistymeadow.com. 3 rooms, 1 cottage. Pool, pond, hot tub, sauna, boating, fishing, hiking; no room phones, no room TVs, no kids under 14, no smoking. MC, V. BP. $$$

Salt Fork Resort and Conference Center Opened in 1972, this four-story wooden lodge serves as the main accommodation for the Salt Fork State Park. The lodge's exterior and the guest rooms have a rustic, rough-hewn flavor with lots of windows and wood paneling. A number of private cottages dot the property and allow for more privacy amid the trees. Next to peaceful relaxation, fishing is the most popular park activity; canoes, motorboats, rowboats, and sailboats are available. Some cabins have hot tubs and fireplaces. > U.S. 22 E, Cambridge 43725, tel. 740/439–2751 or 800/282–7275, fax 740/432–6615, www.saltforkresort.com. 148 rooms, 54 cottages. Dining room, picnic area, in-room data ports, some kitchenettes, some refrigerators, cable TV, 18-hole golf course, tennis courts, 2 pools (1 indoor), wading pool, lake, gym, dock, boating, waterskiing, basketball, hiking, horseback riding, horseshoes, shuffleboard, volleyball, bar, video game room, children's programs (ages 3–14), playground, laundry facilities, business services, meeting rooms, no-smoking rooms; no phones in cabins. AE, D, DC, MC, V. **$–$$$**

ZANESVILLE

Fairfield Inn by Marriott In-room easy chairs and big work desks make this three-story hotel comfortable for business travelers, and the large indoor pool is a hit with families and kids. You can walk to the restaurants on the adjacent blocks, and the downtown historical district is only a mile away. > 725 Zane St., Zanesville 43701, tel. 740/453–8770 or 800/228–2800, www.marriott.com. 63 rooms. In-room data ports, some microwaves, some refrigerators, cable TV with movies, indoor pool, hot tub, laundry service, business services, no-smoking rooms. AE, D, DC, MC, V. CP. **$**

Flint Ridge Vineyard B&B On a secluded rural farm, this B&B has its own 6-acre vineyard, gardens, walking trails, and 80 acres for bird-watching. The B&B and vineyard were expanding at this writing, so if construction noise bothers you, plan to tour the area during the day and return to Flint Ridge in the evening. Rooms are rustic and homey, and kids are welcome. Every weekend in September the owners host a popular picking party in the vineyard; there are live music, a deluxe meal, and wine tasting. You can even give grape-stomping a try. It's in Hopewell, 10 mi west of Zanesville, on Route 40, off I–70. Call for directions—you may need some help finding it. There is currently one guest room, but three more are on the way. > 3890 Pert Hill Rd., Hopewell 43746, tel. 740/787–2103. 1 room. Dining room, picnic area, pond, fishing, library, laundry facilities. No credit cards. BP. **$**

CAMPING

Campers Grove Walking trails and lovely picnic sites line this campground, located along the famous National Road. Pets are permitted and monthly rates available. There's a fishing lake on-site and a picnic pavilion is available for rental. Full service facilities are available April–October. In winter, only self-contained units are available. > 8905 Hopewell National Rd. (U.S. Rte. 40), Zanesville 43701, tel. 740/453–1454. 30 sites all with water and electric hook-ups. Pit toilets, partial hook-ups (electric and water), dump station, store, playground, pool, swimming (lake). No credit cards. **¢**

Hillview Acres Campground Pull up your camper or rough it rustic-style on more than 80 acres of grounds. On-site amenities include hiking trails, two stocked fishing ponds, a game room, and a grocery store with a liquor license. There are flush toilets in the shower house and pit toilets on the grounds. > 66271 Wolf's Den Rd., Cambridge 43725, tel. 740/439–3348. 100 partial hook-ups, 50 tent sites. Flush toilets, pit toilets. Partial hook-ups (electric and water), dump station, showers, fire rings, picnic tables, public telephone, general store, pool. AE, D, MC, V. Closed Nov.–Mar. **¢**

Salt Fork Campground Take your pick of where to set up camp, in the woods, by the lake, or even on the beach. Dock at the lake, play a round of mini-golf, or rent a boat. Horseman campsites are available, and pets are permitted. > Salt Fork State Park, 14755 Cadiz Rd., Lore City 43755, tel. 740/432–1508, www.ohiostateparks.org. 212 partial hook-ups. Flush toilets, partial hook-ups (electric), dump station, showers, swimming (lake). AE, D, MC, V. **¢**

WHERE TO EAT

CAMBRIDGE

The Forum This tavern-style restaurant just a mile from the center of town is a good place to take the kids. The menu includes a Greek sampler and a Greek salad, Mexican burritos and fajitas, as well as pizza, pastas, steak, and terrific hamburgers. Olympic chicken fettuccine comes with artichokes, broccoli, and a mushroom-and-garlic sauce. > 2205 Southgate Pkwy., Cambridge, tel. 740/439–2777. AE, D, MC, V. $–$$

Kennedy's Bakery A Cambridge landmark for more than 70 years, this sweet shop serves delectable pastries, cookies, cakes, and other goodies. > 1025 Wheeling Ave., Cambridge, tel. 740/432–2301. No credit cards. Closed Sun. ¢

Theo's Coney Island Local artwork brightens the dining room of this family-owned, diner-style restaurant. If you're looking for something more substantial than the namesake Coney Island hot dogs, try the Greek salad or the chicken stir fry. There are homemade pasta, bread, and many desserts to sample as well. There's a kids' menu. > 632 Wheeling Ave., Cambridge, tel. 740/432–3878. AE, D, MC, V. Closed Sun. ¢–$

Timbers Restaurant Salt Fork State Park provides the backdrop for this rustic restaurant-with-a-view. Menu options include soups and made-to-order pasta dishes, as well as seafood, steak, and chicken entrées. The tangy artichoke Parmesan chicken with garlic mashed potatoes is a standout. For dessert, try the homemade pretzels stuffed with cream cheese and covered in cinnamon frosting. Breakfasts are hearty, and dinner reservations are recommended. > 630 Wheeling Ave., Cambridge, tel. 740/435–9000. AE, D, DC, MC, V. Hrs vary seasonally. ¢–$$$

ZANESVILLE

Adornetto's After more than 40 years on the Maple Avenue stretch, this Italian eatery and pizzeria remains a Zanesville favorite. The dining room has exposed brick walls, lots of plants, white lights and even plaster columns. In addition to traditional pasta entrées, there are build-your-own pies (including a spicy hot version for risk-takers) and submarine sandwiches piled high with your choice of meats and toppings. Carry-out is available. > 2224 Maple Ave., Zanesville, tel. 740/453–0789. AE, MC, V. No lunch. ¢–$$$

Howard House With antiques from the owner's own collection as well as other period furnishings, this place 20 mi south of Zanesville looks much as it did in the mid-1800s. Osso bucco and Thai chicken pasta are specialties, and there's Sunday brunch. > 507 E. Main St., McConnelsville, tel. 740/962–5861. AE, D, MC, V. Closed Mon. ¢–$$$

Old Market House Inn A suit of armor, giant wooden tables, and wood-beamed ceilings evoke King Arthur's court. For dinner, oversize salads with freshly cracked pepper, melt-in-your-mouth seafood, and juicy steaks are popular choices. > 424 Market St., Zanesville, tel. 740/454–2555. AE, D, DC, MC, V. Closed Sun. $$–$$$$

Tom's Ice Cream Bowl This old-time ice cream shop has linoleum floors and counters, and the employees wear folded paper hats. Even the ice cream, served in cereal bowls with dripping sauce and marshmallow topping, is reminiscent of an earlier era. Sandwiches are also available, as are chocolate and freshly roasted coffee by the pound. > 532 McIntire Ave., Zanesville, tel. 740/452–5267. AE, MC, V. Closed Mon. ¢

Zak's Restaurant The high ceilings, exposed support beams, and plaster details in the two dining rooms are left over from the days when the building was a warehouse.

The menu has the Mexican-American standards as well as eclectic Cajun dishes and American favorites. There's a kids' menu. > 32 N. 3rd St., Zanesville, tel. 740/453–2227. AE, D, DC, MC, V. Closed Sun. and Mon. $–$$

ESSENTIALS

Getting Here

A swift and easy car trip is the best way to travel to this area. Since the towns are small, count out public transportation as a means of getting around.

BY CAR

Thanks to two major interstates in the vicinity, the Cambridge–Zanesville area is easy to reach from any direction. I–70 passes through both destinations on its way from Columbus to Wheeling. It's an easy drive that is typically light in traffic (outside of the Columbus city limits, that is). Heading north–south, I–77 is a convenient route from the Cleveland–Akron and Charleston areas that exits straight into Cambridge.

Ask any local the best way to get to the area and the overwhelming answer will be U.S. 40—the historic National Road. Although you will travel about 10 mph slower than you would on the interstate, the route is just as straight to both towns and features a line-up of antique shops, historic attractions, and the original milestones that line the road all the way from Philadelphia to Indianapolis. For a little slice of Americana, this is definitely the route to take.

Visitor Information

CONTACTS **Cambridge Area Chamber of Commerce** > 918 Wheeling Ave., Cambridge 43725, tel. 740/439–6688, www.visitguernseycounty.com. **Zanesville-Muskingum County Chamber of Commerce** > 205 N. 5th St., Zanesville 43701, tel. 740/455–8282 or 800/743–2303, www.zanesville-ohio.com.

Columbus

Columbus is approximately 120 mi north of Cincinnati and 120 mi south of Cleveland.

13

By Nicki Chodnoff

OHIO ONCE USED THE SLOGAN "the heart of it all." It's an apt description for Columbus, Ohio's capital and largest city. In the middle, or the heart of the state, Columbus is known for its entrepreneurial spirit and economic vitality, embracing the country's first stadium built specifically for soccer, an Arena entertainment district, and doubling the size of its favorite science attraction, COSI (Center of Science and Industry) in the past decade.

Named after discoverer Christopher Columbus, the city encompasses a six-county metropolitan area with more than 1.6 million people and covers 3,142 square mi. Ohio State University, the largest academic institution in the state and one of the largest universities in the nation, with more than 50,000 students, has its campus here. Other well-known local institutions include the Columbus Zoo, one of the nation's most acclaimed; the Ohio Historical Center; the Wexner Center for the Arts; and the Columbus Museum of Art.

In 1816 the Ohio Legislature moved the state capital to Columbus from nearby Chillicothe. Columbus prospered thanks to its location on the banks of the Scioto River, which attracted money, visitors, and settlers. Major railroads came next. Following damaging floods in 1913, the Scioto River was widened and levees, retaining walls, and bridges were built, which allowed for riverfront development.

Even when the rest of Ohio began to suffer industrial decline in the second half of the 20th century, Columbus grew, primarily because its economy is based on state government, education, finance and insurance, and light industry. This continued prosperity has made Columbus an attractive place to live and visit.

Columbus is a collection of neighborhoods. Despite the city's booming growth during the last decade, the neighborhoods make Columbus seem more like a big friendly town than a big anonymous city. German Village, the Brewery District, the Short North, the Arena District surrounding Nationwide Arena, and the Grandview Heights residential area are just minutes from downtown. Yet each neighborhood is distinct.

German Village, the 233-acre enclave six blocks south of the Ohio Statehouse, had its roots in an 1814 addition to Columbus's south side. It developed in the 1840s as Germans fled from wars, famine, and poor living conditions in their home country to this ethnic pocket in Ohio. After barely surviving the wrecking ball, German Village has been protected as a historic area since the 1960s and listed on the National Register of Historic Places since 1975. Its narrow brick streets are lined with charming old homes, gardens, and shops. There's a lively Oktoberfest and Shakespeare in Schiller Park in summer.

The warehouses in the Brewery District marked Columbus's industrial area at the turn of the 20th century. Converted into condos, restaurants, and bars, the area now teems with young professionals.

The Short North arts district on High Street, north of downtown and south of the expansive Ohio State University campus, is a hip, happening area many liken to New York's SoHo. This lively, trendy neighborhood, full of excellent restaurants, bars, boutiques, and unique shops has one of the largest collections of art galleries between New York and Chicago. Try to catch the Gallery Hop, held on the first Saturday night of each month; crowds congregate to stroll from gallery to gallery.

The city supports a vast spectrum of cultural attractions and amenities you expect to find in a much larger city. There's the triple bill of BalletMet, Opera Columbus, and the Columbus Symphony Orchestra. The visual arts are well-represented with the Columbus Museum of Art's impressive collection including the work of city native George Bellows.

Columbus identifies with giant Ohio State University, especially at a Buckeyes home football game. If you can wrangle a ticket, nothing better captures that spirit than 100,000 fans cheering on their beloved Buckeyes.

The Buckeyes are no longer the only game in town and fans bring that same fervor and loyalty to Columbus's other teams. The Crew delights Major League Soccer fans, the crack of the AAA-Farm Team Clippers' bats is heard summer-long at Cooper Stadium, and the crowd cheers mightily when the National Hockey League's Bluejackets hit the ice at Nationwide Arena.

Whatever time of year you visit on a weekend getaway, you are sure to warm to the optimistic and friendly folks in Central Ohio and to find plenty to do and see. Columbus is the heart at "the heart of it all" and beating strong.

WHAT TO SEE & DO

Camp Chase Confederate Cemetery The final resting place of 2,087 Confederate soldiers covers less than 2 acres. Many died as prisoners of war and from the smallpox epidemic during the winter 1863–64. Some consider the cemetery to be haunted by the "Lady in Gray" who leaves flowers at gravesites. > 2900 Sullivant Ave., Columbus, tel. 614/276–3630. Free. Daily.

Columbus Metro Parks The park system includes 14 parks, totaling more 20,000 acres throughout seven Central Ohio counties. Facilities vary across the system and include bridle and bike trails, Indian mounds, a botanical park, pioneer cemetery, historical farm depicting a 19th-century homestead, wetlands, and a prairie. Clear Creek is the most remote and primitive. A well-traveled Native American trail through hardwood forests, meadows, and ravines is now part of the 650-acre **Blendon Woods Metro Park** (4265 E. Dublin-Granville Rd., Columbus). Just one of the parks in the system, it offers four-season fun with cross-country skiing, disk golf, hiking trails, and a nature center. In the waterfowl refuge, you might see 500 or more black ducks on the 11-acre lake on a winter's day. > 1069 W. Main St., Westerville, tel. 614/508–8000, www.metroparks.net. Free. Daily dawn–dusk.

Columbus Museum of Art Four blocks east of the state capitol, this collection is particularly strong in early modernist paintings, modern American paintings, and impressionist and expressionist works. The museum holds the largest public collection of woodcarvings by Columbus folk artist Elijah Pierce and the world's largest repository of paintings and lithographs by Columbus native George Bellows. Outdoors is a sculpture garden, and a café and a gift shop are on the premises. > 480 E. Broad St.,

Downtown, tel. 614/221–6801, www.columbusmuseum.org. $6. Tues.–Sun. 10–5:30, Thurs. until 8:30.

Columbus Zoo Zoo director emeritus Jungle Jack Hanna draws the late-night spotlight to the Columbus Zoo with his regular appearances, along with his cadre of animals, on the *Late Show with David Letterman*. The 588-acre zoo lies along the Scioto River, about 25 mi northwest of downtown. Sights include a 100,000-gallon coral reef exhibit, one of the largest reptile collections in the United States and the largest manatee exhibit outside Florida. The newest Southeast Asia exhibit brings Komodo dragons, gibbons, orangutans, Asian small-clawed otters, black swans, Javan whistling ducks, and cattle egrets to the zoo. > 9990 Riverside Dr., Columbus, tel. 614/645–3550, www.colszoo.org. $9. Memorial Day–Labor Day, daily 9–6; Labor Day–Memorial Day, daily 9–5; mid-June–mid-Aug., Wed. to 8.

COSI Columbus More than 15 million people have come through COSI's doors since it opened in 1964. Interactive exhibits at this first-class science center allow you to explore underwater shipwrecks, discover hidden treasures, or join an archaeological dig. Find the country's only high-wire unicycle at the outdoor Big Science Park. The "i/o" room teaches the technology of video games and lets you grab a joystick and play a few. You'll also be able to time travel in "Progress," leaping from 1889 to 1962 in the blink of an eye. > 333 W. Broad St., Downtown, tel. 614/228–2674 or 888/819–2674, www.cosi.org. $12. Exhibits and theaters: Mon.–Sat. 10–5, Sun. noon–6.

Doll and Toy Museum Exhibits, which span from antique dolls to modern collectibles such as GI Joe, bring out the educational, historical, and cultural significance of toys. The collection, which numbers in the thousands, includes Disney memorabilia, toy trains, and circus items. The museum is about 15 mi southeast of downtown. > 700 Winchester Park, Canal Winchester, tel. 614/837–5573, home.att.net/~dollmuseum/. $3. Apr.–mid-Dec., Wed.–Sat. 11–5.

Franklin Park Conservatory In the middle of a 90-acre urban park about 2 mi east of downtown, this elegant glass conservatory shelters desert, rain forest, mountain, and tropical island plant habitats. Built in 1895 and styled after London's Crystal Palace, the conservatory is listed on the National Register of Historic Places. Outside, hardy bamboo and Japanese maples in the Japanese garden are part of a 28-acre botanical garden. > 1777 E. Broad St., Columbus, tel. 614/645–8733 or 800/214–7275, www.fpconservatory.org. $6.50. Tues.–Sun. 10–5, Wed. to 8.

Germain Amphitheater Close to I–71 about 20 mi north of downtown, this outdoor amphitheater with covered seats and a sloping field is the only venue in mid-Ohio capable of housing big-name tours such as Fleetwood Mac and Billy Joel and the big crowds they draw. > 2200 Polaris Pkwy., Columbus, tel. 614/431–2200, www.germainconcerts.com.

Hanby House An abolitionist, minister, and composer of numerous songs, Benjamin Russell Hanby is most remembered for his song, "Up On The Housetop." About 15 mi north of downtown in Westerville, the home of Hanby and his family was once a stop on the Underground Railroad. Built in 1846 and on the National Register of Historic Places, the house displays furniture and personal family items, including a walnut desk made by Hanby. > 160 W. Main St., Westerville, tel. 614/891–6289 or 800/600–6843. $2. May–Sept., weekends 1–4.

Jack Nicklaus Museum An homage to Columbus's hometown golf hero, the museum documents Nicklaus's career as a golfer, golf course designer, businessman, and family man. In the heart of the Ohio State University sports complex, its vast collection of artifacts and memorabilia include the Golden Bear's six Masters' trophies. > 2355 Olentangy River Rd., OSU Campus, tel. 614/247–5959, fax 614/247–5906, www.nicklausmuseum.org. $9. Mon.–Sat. 9–5, Sun. 1–5.

McKinley Memorial A statue of former governor and Ohio native, President William McKinley, stands prominently at the entrance to the grounds of the Ohio Capitol. Sculpted by Hermon Atkins MacNeil, it was dedicated on September 14, 1906, the fifth anniversary of McKinley's death. > Broad and High Sts., Downtown. Free. Daily.

Motorcycle Hall of Fame Museum Adjacent to the world headquarters of the American Motorcycle Association, about 20 mi east of downtown, the museum displays the actual machines Hall of Fame inductees rode and celebrates the accomplishments of the more than 260 men and women recognized by the Motorcycle Hall of Fame, such as Evel Knievel and the founders of the Harley-Davidson Motor Co. > 13515 Yarmouth Dr., Pickerington, tel. 614/856–2222 Ext. 1234, www.motorcyclemuseum.org. $4. Daily 9–5.

Motts Military Museum Exhibits span all periods of military history, up to the current War on Terrorism, and include all countries in which the United States has been involved. About 10 mi south of downtown Columbus, the museum serves as the repository for the Ohio Military Hall of Fame. Unique exhibits include a replica of World War I flying ace Captain Eddie Rickenbacker's boyhood home and a M47 tank driven by Arnold Schwarzenegger when he served in the Austrian Army. > 5075 S. Hamilton Rd., Groveport, tel. 614/836–1500, www.mottsmilitarymuseum.org. $5. Tues.–Sat. 9–5, Sun. 1–5.

Ohio Craft Museum The Ohio Designer Craftsmen present five changing exhibitions per year at this museum. Fine crafts shown might include glassware, pottery, metalwork, quilts, or weaving. If you like what you see, you can learn to do it yourself. Lessons, which are open to all ages and levels of experience, tend to center on current exhibitions. Weekend classes in the past taught jewelry making, tie-dye and batik, and pottery. The museum is about 4 mi northwest of downtown. > 1665 W. 5th Ave., Grandview Heights, tel. 614/486–4402, www.ohiocraft.org. Free. Weekdays 10–5, Sun. 1–4. Closed Sat.

Ohio Historical Center This two-building complex, just past the Ohio State Fairgrounds, is a storehouse for the state archives. Collections, presenting the history of the Buckeye State from the Ice Age to 1970, range from Native American fossils to papers written by Ohio political leaders. Permanent exhibits include artifacts on the state's industrial progress such as an operating 1880s carriage shop and vintage automobiles; the chronology of the prehistoric and historic Indian cultures; and the interaction of man and nature in plants, animals, geology, geography, and climate. > 1982 Velma Ave., Columbus, tel. 614/297–2300, www.ohiohistory.org/places/ohc. $6. Tues.–Sat. 9–5, Sun. noon–5.

Ohio State University The massive presence of Ohio State makes it a city within the city of Columbus. The Oval, the heart of the Columbus campus, is beautifully landscaped with 115 varieties of trees and surrounded by stately buildings including Orton Hall, the Main Library, and University Hall. There are guided tours weekdays at 10 and 2. Call for reservations.

Affiliated with the school's department of horticulture, the **Chadwick Arboretum and Learning Garden** (2120 Fyffe Rd., www.chadwickarboretum.osu.edu, Free, Apr.–Oct., daily) is an outdoor laboratory of local and regional trees and plants including wild-flowers, prairie plants, and perennials. The calming labyrinth garden, set in a ring of arborvitae evergreens, is modeled after one at Chartres Cathedral in France.

The Value City Arena at the Jerome Schottenstein Center (555 Arena Dr., tel. 800/273–6201, www.schottensteincenter.com) is home court for Buckeye basketball and home ice for hockey. Concerts and touring productions as diverse as the Three Tenors, Simon and Garfunkel, and Sesame Street Live also use the space.

In a dramatic building designed by Peter Eisenmann, the **Wexner Center for the Arts** (1871 N. High St., tel. 614/292–3535, www.wexarts.org, Varies by artist and program. Lower lobby exhibitions are free, Tues.–Sun. 10–6, Thurs. 10–9 PM) houses contemporary art—including performance art and mixed-media works. The cabaret-style theater features intimate concerts, rarely screened movies from independent film makers, and discussions or lectures with filmmakers, artists, and performers.
> N. High St., between 11th and Lane Aves., Columbus, tel. 614/292–3980, www.osu.edu. Daily.

Ohio Statehouse The Ohio Legislature convenes in this 1861 Greek Revival building. The dome of the rotunda is painted with the state seal; the building also has portraits of Ohio's governors and presidents and historical documents. You can take a self-guided tour of the Senate chamber when it's not in session. Building tours are given every 30 minutes weekdays 9:30–3, weekends at 11:15, 12:30, 2, and 3. > Capitol Sq. on High St., Downtown, tel. 614/752–6350. Free. Weekdays 7–7, weekends 10–4.

Ohio Theater Across from the State House, the ornate 2,779-seat theater opened in 1928 to show movies and live stage shows. Saved from demolition in 1969, the theatre now hosts BalletMet, the Broadway Series, and special performances including musical artists, dance, comedy, children's entertainment, and classic films. Under the guidance of music director Alessandro Siciliani, the **Columbus Symphony Orchestra** (tel. 614/228–8600 tickets, www.columbussymphony.com) also performs at the theater. > 55 E. State St., Downtown, tel. 614/469–1045, 614/469–0939 tickets.

Palace Theater When opened in 1929, this was a vaudeville house and movie theater designed to resemble Versailles palace in France. The 2,827-seat downtown venue had a brush with destruction before it was saved in 1989. Opera/Columbus and select performances by the Columbus Symphony Orchestra, the Jazz Arts Group, the Broadway Series, and scores of touring talent use the space today. > 34 W. Broad St., Downtown, tel. 614/469–9850, 614/431–3600 tickets.

Promowest The indoor–outdoor concert stage in the Arena District changes from a 500 seat cabaret to a 3,000-seat theater showcasing comedy and music. The landscaped man-made bowl allows outdoor performances in the summer. > 405 Neil Ave., Arena District, tel. 614/461–5483, www.promowestpavilion.com.

Sam and Eulalia Frantz Park Iowa may have its Field of Dreams, but central Ohio has its "Field of Corn." The 3-acre park sprouts 109 ears of concrete corn that rise about 6 feet out of the ground. Commissioned by the arts council, the sculpture celebrates the town's history as a farming community, before it became a suburb, 20 mi northwest of downtown. > 4995 Rings Rd., Dublin. Free. Daily dawn–dusk.

***Santa Maria* Replica** Moored in the Scioto River at Battelle Riverfront Park, two blocks west of the State House, the ship is a full-size reproduction of the 15th-century lead ship that Christopher Columbus used on his journey to the New World. See the inner workings of a wooden tall ship and meet costumed historic interpreters portraying real people from the voyage during the 45-minute tour. > 90 W. Broad St., Downtown, tel. 614/645–8760, www.santamaria.org. $3. Early Apr.–mid-May, Sept.–late Oct., Wed.–Fri. 10–3, weekends noon–5; mid-May–Aug., Wed.–Fri. 10–5, weekends noon–6.

Scioto Park Sure, the park has the typical picnic spots and horseshoe courts, but the real attraction is the 12-foot-high limestone sculpture of Wyandot Chief Leatherlips. According to legend, Leatherlips was executed by his tribesmen near the present-day park because he refused to fight the white settlers. > 7377 Riverside Dr., Dublin, tel. 614/761–6520. Free. Daily dawn–dusk.

Six Flags Wyandot Lake Slip down the water slides, frolic in the wave pool or enjoy a lazy inner tube cruise on the man-made creek at the water park about 25 minutes northwest of downtown. Head over to the amusement park for roller coasters, carousels, and drive-in movies in midsummer. > 10101 Riverside Dr., Powell, tel. 614/889–9283 or 800/328–9283, www.sixflags.com. $24.99. Memorial Day–Labor Day, hrs vary monthly.

Southern Theater The city's first public building with full electricity, the 933-seat Victorian-era theater is the venue for the Columbus Jazz Orchestra, the Columbus Light Opera, and ProMusica Chamber Orchestra. > 21 E. Main St., Downtown, tel. 614/340–9698.

Thurber House James Thurber once reflected, "I have lived in the East for nearly thirty years now, but many of my books prove that I am never very far away from Ohio in my thoughts, and that the clocks that strike in my dreams are often the clocks of Columbus." His restored boyhood home contains memorabilia and creations of the Columbus native, author, humorist, cartoonist, and playwright. It's at the edge of downtown and down the street from the Columbus Museum of Art. > 77 Jefferson Ave., Downtown, tel. 614/464–1032, www.thurberhouse.org. Free, except for special events. Daily noon–4.

Topiary Garden Instead of stippled paint, the medium is shrubbery in a one-of-a-kind topiary replica of Georges Seurat's postimpressionist masterpiece, *A Sunday on the Island of La Grande Jatte.* There are also 54 people, eight boats, three dogs, a monkey, and a cat, who look to a creek instead of the Seine River. The tallest figure stands 12 feet high. > 480 E. Town St., Downtown, tel. 614/645–0197, fax 614/645–0172, www.topiarygarden.org. Free. Daily dawn–dusk.

Vern Riffe Center for Government and the Arts The center has a performance space and an exhibition gallery. The 854-seat **Capitol Theater** (tel. 614/461–1382, prices vary by performance) presents comedy, music, dance, theater, family entertainment, and cultural programming. One recent exhibition at the **Riffe Gallery** (tel. 614/644–9624, www.oac.state.oh.us/OACNEWICC/riffe/, free, Tues. 10–4, Wed.–Fri. 10–8, Sat. noon–8, Sun. noon–4) explored the theme of flight in works of various media by artists from the Dayton area, famous as home to the Wright brothers. Shows, which change approximately every three months, promote Ohio artists and utilize the collections of the state's museums and galleries. > 77 S. High St., Downtown, tel. 614/939–0934.

Whetstone Park of Roses Once the American Rose Society Headquarters, the 13-acre garden within Whetstone Park has more than 11,000 rose bushes; an herb, daffodil, and perennial garden plus specialized collections of miniature and heritage roses. It's one of the largest municipal rose gardens in the United States. > 3923 N. High St., Columbus, tel. 614/645–3350. Free. Daily dawn–dusk.

WHAT'S NEARBY

Dawes Arboretum Beman and Bertie Dawes founded the arboretum in 1929 to demonstrate the value of trees and shrubs. View the 1,650 acres of plants and natural areas on the 4½-mi auto tour or more than 8 mi of hiking trails. Plants tolerant of central Ohio's climate are the mainstay including more than 4,000 specimens of conifers plus azaleas, crab apples, hollies, oaks, witch hazel, and others. The icing on the cake is DAWES ARBORETUM spelled out in 3-foot-high shrubs. > 7770 Jacksontown Rd. SE, Newark, tel. 740/323–2355 or 800/443–2937, fax 740/323–4058, www.dawesarb.org. Free. Daily dawn–dusk.

Longaberger Baskets A giant basket, 35 mi east of Columbus, is not just a huge sculpture; it's a building. The seven-story structure is actually the headquarters of the Longaberger Basket Company and the brainchild of company CEO Dave Longaberger. Built in 1997 the building looks like the company's famous product, complete with two 75-ton, three-story tall "handles" on top. Building tours are available daily. A few miles away in nearby Dresden, at 5th and Main streets, Longaberger also made the world's largest basket. Ten maple trees were used for this behemoth. About the size of a house, the basket measures 48 feet long, 11 feet wide, and 23 feet high. > 1500 E. Main St., Newark, tel. 740/322–5588, www.longaberger.com. Free. Mon.–Sat. 8–5, Sun. noon–5.

Newark Earthworks State Memorial The largest system of connected geometric earthworks in the world, the Newark Earthworks once spanned 4 mi before urban development destroyed much of it. The prehistoric Hopewell people built it as a ceremonial center about 2,000 years ago. Today three major segments are preserved as part of the state memorial. Nearly 1,200 feet in diameter, the Great Circle Earthworks has grass-covered earthen walls 14 feet high in places. Another majestic remnant of prehistoric Ohio is one 50-foot-long segment of the nearby Wright Earthworks. Part of a large square enclosure, it was an important feature of the original complex. The Octagon Earthworks are on a nearby country club. > 99 Cooper Ave., Newark, tel. 740/344–1920, www.ohiohistory.org. Park free, museum $3. Museum: June–Aug., Wed.–Sat. 9:30–5, Sun. noon–5; Sept. and Oct., Sat. 9:30–5, Sun. noon–5; Park: Apr.–Oct., daily dawn–dusk.

Nightlife

Two free weekly newspapers—the *Other Paper,* and *Columbus Alive!*—have complete listings of goings-on in the city. Columbus's daily newspaper, the *Columbus Dispatch,* publishes a weekender section on Thursday listing things to do and see in town.

Most of Columbus's hot spots are scattered near the Ohio State University campus (expect crowds when the OSU Buckeye football and basketball teams play) and the downtown neighborhoods around German Village, the Short North, the Arena District, and the Brewery District.

Brewery District West of German Village, the Brewery District centers around the breweries established in the 1800s. It's still the place to go for good brews with a side of good food and entertainment. At **Barrister Hall** (560 S High St., tel. 614/621–1213), live jazz electrifies the cigar-puffing, scotch-sipping crowds six nights a week. Dark, gleaming wood, subtle lighting, and agreeably old brick walls make it one of the classiest taverns in town. Live out your musical fantasy at **Howl at the Moon** (450 S. Front St., tel. 614/224–5990, www.howlatthemoon.com, closed Sun. and Mon.). You can sing along with dueling pianos at this 21-and-older club.

Short North Back in the 1980s, the police called this dilapidated area between downtown and the Ohio State University the "Short North." Then rife with drugs and prostitution, it's now the place to see and be seen, whether you are urban professional, suburban matron, or hip student. All gather for the art galleries, restaurants, shops, and clubs. Open since the 1970s, **Little Brother's** (1100 N. High St., tel. 614/421–2025, www.littlebrothers.com) has been booking cutting-edge local and national acts on their intimate stage for years. Regulars discovered the Red Hot Chili Peppers and Nirvana before they became national bands. Calling itself "the longest continually running rock club In America," **Newport Music Hall** (1722 N. High St., tel. 614/294–1659, www.promowestpavilion.com/sections/newport/index.asp) has featured artists including Todd Rundgren, the Indigo Girls, U2, David Bowie, B. B. King, Tom Petty, Metallica, and Smashing Pumpkins. It's housed in the old State Theater north of the Short North.

Sports

BASEBALL

Columbus Clippers See the players before they make it to the majors at a Clippers' game. The Clippers are the AAA Baseball farm-team for the New York Yankees. It's baseball as it was meant to be, and you won't get sticker-shock at this intimate in-town stadium where dime-a-dog night still exists. > 1155 W. Mound St., tel. 614/642–5250, www.clippersbaseball.com.

HOCKEY

Columbus Bluejackets This National Hockey League team made their debut in fall 2000. **Nationwide Arena** (Nationwide Blvd. at Front St., Arena District), their 18,000-seat home, is the only arena in the nation with an adjacent practice stadium. > Tel. 614/246–7825, www.columbusbluejackets.com.

SOCCER

Columbus Crew The city's professional MLS team are Columbus's other boys of summer, plus spring and fall, as the season starts in April and can last into December. There are no bad seats among the 22,500 available at **Crew Stadium,** the first stadium in the United States specifically built for soccer. > 2121 Velma Ave., Columbus, tel. 614/447–2739, www.thecrew.com.

Shopping

You expect a smorgasbord of shopping in the city that's world headquarters to Leslie Wexner's empire of clothing stores, which includes the Limited, Express, Structure, Victoria's Secret, and Abercrombie & Fitch.

City Center Mall Kaufmann's department store anchors this downtown mall, which is connected to the neighboring Lazarus-Macy's by a bridge over High Street. The usual suspects—from Banana Republic to Radio Shack and from the Disney Store to Victoria's Secret—are well represented. > 111 S. 3rd St., Downtown, tel. 614/221–4900.

Easton Town Center More than just a shopping destination, this outdoor Disneyesque village, complete with two town-square areas with fountains, is an entertainment enclave with a score of restaurants, bars, and bistros; a multiplex movie theater; the Funnybone Comedy Club; and Gameworks interactive games and attractions. At the **Shadowbox Cabaret** (164 Easton Town Center, tel. 614/416–7625 or 888/887–4236, www.shadowboxcaberet.com, closed Sun. and Mon.), an ensemble of musicians and actors, which doubles as the wait staff, delivers a high-energy mix of outrageous original comedy sketches, theatrical shorts, and live rock 'n' roll music. Even McDonald's has a karaoke booth where you can record CDs. It's 16 minutes, or about 11 mi, from downtown in the northeast part of the city. > I–270 and Easton Way, Columbus, tel. 614/416–7001, www.eastontowncenter.com.

Mall at Tuttle Crossing Browse more than 125 shops and restaurants in the northwest suburb of Dublin. The mall is anchored by four department stores, including Lazarus and JCPenney. Take a respite from shopping at the relaxing cappuccino court or let the kids get rid of excess energy at the children's play area. > 5043 Tuttle Crossing Blvd., Dublin, tel. 614/717–9300, www.shoptuttlecrossing.com.

The North Market Fresh and prepared foods, flowers, ethnic cuisine, and unique gifts delight the senses at central Ohio's only public market. Across from the Convention Center, the 30-plus merchant market sits on what was once the North Graveyard. > 59 Spruce St., Downtown, tel. 614/463–9664. Free. Closed Mon.

Polaris Fashion Place Twenty minutes north of downtown at I–71, this shopping complex brings upscale stores such as Saks 5th Avenue and Lord & Taylor to the area. > 1500 Polaris Pkwy., Columbus, tel. 614/846–1550.

Save the Date

FEBRUARY

Arnold Fitness Week The largest fitness expo in the world routinely draws 10,000 athletes and more than 70,000 spectators. A training seminar, eight title contests, and 600 expo booths keep people coming back. > Greater Columbus Convention Center and Veterans Memorial, tel. 614/431–2600.

MAY

Asian Festival The sights, sounds, and tastes of Asia are captured at this event. Sample Asian cuisine from a gamut of countries, shop the Asian market, keep the kids active with hands-on activities, and be entertained by the stage performances and cultural booths. > 1777 E. Broad St., tel. 614/463–1752.

Memorial Tournament Hosted by Columbus native and golf great Jack Nicklaus, the week-long tournament attracts the world's top golfers. > Muirfield Village Golf Club, www.thememorialtournament.com.

JUNE

Columbus Rose Festival The 2-day festival is held when roses are at their peak. Go to take in the sights and smells, or attend a floral design workshop by a gardening expert, listen to live entertainment, or buy a few plants. > Whetstone Park of Roses, 3923 N. High St., tel. 614/645–3350.

Greater Columbus Arts Festival More than 300 of the nation's best artists display their works at this annual 3-day street festival and show along the riverfront in downtown Columbus. Music, food, and art activities add to the festivities. > Tel. 614/224–2606.

JULY

Red, White and Boom The annual Independence Day celebration held on July 3, full of live music, a parade, and food, is topped off by one of the most extravagant fireworks displays in the Midwest. > Downtown riverfront, tel. 614/421–2666.

AUGUST

Buckeye Invitational International barbershop competition features men's and women's choruses and quartets. > Palace Theater, tel. 614/459–0400.

Ohio State Fair It's not summer until you see the life-size butter cow at one of the largest state fairs in the country. Nationally known musical acts, one of the world's longest sky rides and the largest junior fair in the nation are highlights. Agricultural displays, children's contests, tractor pulls, laser light shows, and, of course, the butter cow, are mainstays. > Expo Center, between 11th and 17th Aves., tel. 614/221–6623 or 800/345–4386.

OCTOBER

Columbus Marathon Watch runners wind through 26.2 mi of streets in the downtown area and surrounding suburbs during the 3-day event, which includes a free sports and fitness expo. > Tel. 614/421–7866, www.columbusmarathon.com.

German Village Oktoberfest The Brewer's Yard hosts this 3-day extravaganza, with three stages of music including everything from polka to hard rock, German food, arts and crafts, and a kinderplatz area with kids' programming. > Tel. 614/224–4300.

WHERE TO STAY

Adam's Mark The sleek 21-story downtown hotel, which caters to a business clientele, is within walking distance of the Columbus Convention Center, the Capitol, and North Market shopping. Rooms, done in muted tones, have hardwood furnishings and large closets. The hotel has a sports bar, a health club, and round-the-clock room service. > 50 N. 3rd St., Downtown 43215, tel. 614/228–5050 or 800/444–2326, fax 614/228–2525, www.adamsmark.com. 415 rooms, 3 suites. Restaurant, room service, in-room data ports, cable TV with movies and video games, pool, gym, hot tub, sauna, bar, shop, laundry facilities, laundry service, business services, no-smoking rooms. AE, D, DC, MC, V. $$$

Best Western Clarmont Inn & Suites This four-story motel in German Village is 1½ mi from downtown and within walking distance of shopping and dining. The large rooms have cherrywood furnishings and queen-size beds. The minisuites have refrigerators, microwaves, and pull-out beds. > 650 S. High St., German Village 43215, tel. 614/228–6511 or 800/528–1234, www.bestwestern.com. 48 rooms, 12 suites. Restaurant, some microwaves, some refrigerators, cable TV, pool, no-smoking rooms. AE, D, DC, MC, V. $–$$$

The Blackwell On the Ohio State University campus, this upscale hotel serves as the residence for Fisher College's executive education program. Decorated in a modified Mission style with soft tones and warm woods, the rooms have touches like plush bathrobes and pillow-top mattresses. Access to the 24-hour fitness center is free. > 2110 Tuttle Park Pl., Columbus 43210, tel. 614/247–4000 or 866/247–4003, fax 614/237–6134, www.theblackwell.com. 151 rooms. Restaurant, in-room data ports, in-room safes, cable TV, exercise equipment, bar, laundry service, business services, no-smoking rooms. AE, D, DC, MC, V. $$–$$$$

Courtyard by Marriott Formerly a warehouse, this unusual hotel has a bi-level, contemporary lobby and luxurious suites with kitchens. Work desks with lamps, coffeemakers, and high-speed Internet access appeal to businesspeople spending their days at the Columbus Convention Center, which is just two blocks away. > 35 W. Spring St., Downtown 43215, tel. 614/228–3200, fax 614/228–6752, www.marriott.com. 149 rooms. Restaurant, coffee shop, in-room data ports, some minibars, cable TV, indoor pool, gym, hot tub, lounge, laundry facilities, laundry service, meeting rooms. AE, D, DC, MC, V. **$$–$$$**

Crowne Plaza You'll be in the midst of all the hustle-bustle at the Crowne Plaza, but you are also in the middle of downtown's attractions. This 12-story brick-face hotel is connected to the Columbus Convention Center and adjacent to the Arena District. The two-story lobby—with its wall of windows along the street and slate and dark wood paneling—is a contrast to the neutral tones and art deco–inspired oak furniture found in the guest rooms. There are 8,000 square feet of meeting space here, and a car rental desk in the lobby. > 33 E. Nationwide Blvd., Downtown 43215, tel. 614/461–4100 or 800/338–4462, fax 614/461–5828, www.crowneplaza.com. 423 rooms, 7 suites. 3 restaurants, in-room data ports, cable TV, indoor pool, exercise equipment, sauna, bar, shop, laundry facilities, laundry service, business services, no-smoking rooms. AE, D, DC, MC, V. **$$$**

Doubletree Guest Suites–Columbus Near the Scioto River, the 10-story stone-faced hotel is within walking distance of the Convention Center. The well-appointed one-bedroom suites with a separate living area are decorated in neutral colors and have wet bars; some have river views. Fun perks, from the free chocolate-chip cookies on check-in to the free limousine service within a 3-mi radius, add to the appeal of the Doubletree. > 50 S. Front St., Downtown 43215, tel. 614/228–4600 or 800/528–0444, fax 614/228–0297, www.doubletree.com. 194 suites. Restaurant, in-room data ports, minibars, refrigerators, cable TV, business services, some pets allowed (fee), no-smoking floors. AE, D, DC, MC, V. **$–$$$**

50 Lincoln Inn A bed-and-breakfast with an artistic theme, the restored 1917 brick town house in Italian Village is near downtown. Each room is named for an artist—Ansel Adams, Degas, Picasso—and furnished with antique and modern furnishings. The downstairs gallery displays the works of local artists in exhibitions that change every two months. The cobblestone patio off the rear of the house is a fine place to sit and ponder whether life really does imitate art. > 50 E. Lincoln St., Italian Village 43215, tel. 614/299–5050, fax 614/291–4924, www.50lincoln.com. 8 rooms. In-room data ports, cable TV, laundry facilities; no smoking. MC, V. **$**

Harrison House Bed and Breakfast This turquoise-and-cream 1890 Queen Anne is a perfect fit in its Victorian Village surroundings. It's easy to imagine yourself in another century as you lounge in a wicker chair on the bright blue front porch. The inn, which is near the Ohio State campus, has a reputation for impeccable service and guests rave about the candlelit breakfast. Rooms are individually styled but maintain a scheme of mauves and creams. A fully stocked apartment designed for short stays and appropriate for guests with children is also available. > 313 W. 5th Ave., Victorian Village 43201, tel. 614/421–2202 or 800/827–4203, www.columbus-bed-breakfast.com. 4 rooms. Cable TV; no smoking. AE, D, MC, V. BP. **$$**

Holiday Inn–City Center The familiar chain's 12-story downtown Columbus property is a few blocks from the Capitol and the City Center Mall. Club Level guests can use the Executive Club Lounge, which offers Continental breakfast each morning and evening hors d'oeuvres and cocktails. > 175 E. Town St., Downtown 43215, tel. 614/221–3281 or 800/465–4329, fax 614/221–2667, www.holiday-inn.com. 240 rooms. Restaurant, cable TV, pool, bar, business services, some pets allowed (fee), no-smoking rooms. AE, D, DC, MC, V. **$$–$$$**

House of 7 Goebels Colonial materials and methods, such as square nails, hand-split Shaker roofing, and exterior handmade doors with wooden latches, were used in the construction of this house, a reproduction of a 1780 Connecticut river valley farmhouse. The 2-acre yard has a creek, rock garden, flower beds, and croquet court.

Weather permitting, you can sample the Belgian waffles on the stone patio. The B&B is northwest of downtown, between Dublin and Hilliard. > 4975 Hayden Run Rd., Columbus 43221, tel. 614/761–9595, fax 614/761–9595, www.bbhost.com/7goebels. 2 rooms. No room phones, no room TVs, no kids under 10, no smoking. MC, V. BP. $

Hyatt on Capitol Square Service, from the lightening-quick check-in to the efficient bell hop who whisks your luggage away, puts this hotel ahead of the downtown pack. Near the state capitol, the posh 22-story Hyatt is next to the City Center Mall. The modern exterior belies a traditional interior with marble floors, gilt mirrors, and Chinese vases. Large rooms are tastefully decorated with cherry-veneer furniture. > 75 E. State St., Downtown 43215, tel. 614/228–1234 or 800/233–1234, fax 614/469–9664, www.hyatt.com. 400 rooms. Restaurant, in-room data ports, cable TV with movies, pool, gym, massage, bar, laundry service, business services, no-smoking rooms. AE, D, DC, MC, V. $$–$$$$

Hyatt Regency Connected to the Columbus Convention Center, Columbus's first and bigger Hyatt is a modern 20-story glass-and-concrete structure. Business-class rooms have a desk and a fax machine. > 350 N. High St., Downtown 43215, tel. 614/463–1234 or 800/233–1234, fax 614/280–3046, www.hyatt.com. 631 rooms, 16 suites. 2 restaurants, in-room data ports, cable TV with movies, indoor pool, gym, bar, laundry service, business services, no-smoking rooms. AE, D, DC, MC, V. $–$$$

Lofts Hotel An old warehouse dating from 1882 has been converted to loftlike rooms at this unique hotel. Rooms have exposed bricks and beams, arched doorways, and floor-to-ceiling windows. Fixtures and furnishings are a mixture of IKEA and Ralph Lauren; the white bathroom tiles are the type used in New York City subway stations. The Lofts is across from the Columbus Convention Center, and the second floor is connected to the Crowne Plaza Hotel. > 55 Nationwide Blvd., Downtown 43215, tel. 614/461–2663 or 800/735–6387, fax 614/461–2630, www.55lofts.com. 44 rooms. Restaurant, in-room data ports, in-room safes, cable TV, indoor pool, exercise equipment, sauna, business services, no-smoking rooms. AE, D, DC, MC, V. CP. $$$$

Westin Great Southern Columbus Author James Thurber once lived in this downtown Victorian building, built in 1897. The elaborate public spaces, with high ceilings, marble floors, and stone columns, house art exhibits, including some prints by Thurber. Rooms have marble baths, high ceilings, darkwood furnishings—and modern conveniences. Some of the rooms are small, however, so be sure to ask about size when making a reservation. > 310 S. High St., Downtown 43215, tel. 614/228–3800 or 800/937–8461, fax 614/228–7666, www.starwood.com/westin. 196 rooms, 32 suites. Restaurant, room service, in-room data ports, in-room safes, minibars, cable TV with movies and video games, gym, bar, business services, no-smoking rooms. AE, D, DC, MC, V. $$–$$$$

Woodfin Suites Many of the one- and two-bedroom suites in this two-story, brick-face complex have fireplaces. You can rent a video from the hotel's library to watch in your room. It's 20 minutes from downtown. > 4130 Tuller Rd., Dublin 43017, tel. 614/766–7762 or 800/237–8811, fax 614/761–1906, www.woodfinsuitehotels.com. 88 suites. In-room data ports, kitchenettes, microwaves, cable TV, in-room VCRs, pool, hot tub, laundry facilities, business services, free parking, some pets allowed (fee), no-smoking rooms. AE, D, DC, MC, V. BP. $$–$$$$

Worthington Inn This three-story, 1831 inn is filled with authentic American antiques. Some rooms have canopy beds; all have fluffy robes and fine toiletries. No two rooms are alike. The four suites, in a separate building, have sitting rooms with fireplaces. The innkeepers serve complimentary cocktails at sunset. It's 13 mi north of downtown. > 649 High St., Worthington 43085, tel. 614/885–2600, fax 614/885–1283, www.worthingtoninn.com. 26 rooms, 4 suites. Restaurant, room service, cable TV, in-room VCRs, bar, business services, no smoking. AE, D, MC, V. BP. **$$$**

Wyndham Dublin In a serene business park with man-made lakes, the suburban-style three-story stucco lodge contrasts with the commercial blocks around it. Rooms are spacious and decorated in a restful brown, gold, and olive color scheme. Some rooms have skylights and balconies. It's 25 minutes northwest of downtown. > 600 Metro Pl. N, Dublin 43017, tel. 614/764–2200 or 800/996–3426, fax 614/764–1213, www.wyndham.com. 217 rooms, 5 suites. 2 restaurants, room service, in-room data ports, cable TV, indoor pool, sauna, bar, business services, some pets allowed (fee), no-smoking rooms. AE, D, DC, MC, V. **$$**

WHERE TO EAT

Though dubbed the Fast Food Capital of the World by the *New York Times* and *Wall Street Journal,* Columbus has a lively and ever-expanding restaurant scene. Eateries tucked into the Short North, German Village, the Arena district, and surrounding sub-urbs offer everything from down-home barbecue to haute cuisine. Prices that soothe the most cost-conscious wallet are the best part of the Columbus dining experience. A meal that might set you back $150 or more in other cities can be savored for about one-third of the price.

Bexley's Monk Dine in the formal, wood-panel dining room with elevated levels, brass railings, and sky lights, or the spacious bar with its checkerboard floor and wood-fire pizza oven. This Bexley restaurant draws a lively crowd for pizza, pasta, rack of lamb, and seafood dishes. The chef makes great desserts. In the evenings, there's live music—jazz musicians or a piano player perform in the bar Monday through Saturday. > 2232 E. Main St., Bexley, tel. 614/239–6665, www.bexleymonk.com. AE, D, DC, MC, V. No lunch weekends. **$$–$$$$**

Blue Nile Ethiopian Restaurant A few blocks north of the Ohio State University, Blue Nile is both a cultural experience and a dining experience. Listen to refrains of native music while dining at a regular table or Ethiopian-style around a pedestal that holds a mosseb, the communal platter. No eating utensils here. Tear off a piece of *injera,* the Ethiopian flatbread, and scoop up the foods. Richly seasoned beef, lamb, chicken or vegetarian dishes can be spicy, flavored by the red pepper Berbere sauce. The milder alichas sauce is flavored with butter and spices. > 2361 N. High St., OSU area, tel. 614/421–2323, www.ethiopeancuisine.com. D, MC, V. Closed Mon. **$–$$**

Buckeye Hall of Fame Cafe Like a Hard Rock Cafe for fans who bleed scarlet-and-gray, this shrine to past OSU greats preserves Buckeye paraphernalia, photos, memo-rabilia, and trophies. À la Hollywood, there are even stars on the floor with the names of former Buckeyes. Big screen TVs in the Arena Room keep you focused on the game or highlights from a past one while you nosh on burgers and wings. More upscale dining selections such as prime rib and filet mignon are on the menu in the Trophy Room. > 1421 Olentangy River Rd., Columbus, tel. 614/291–2233, www.buckeyehalloffamecafe.com. AE, D, DC, MC, V. **$–$$$$**

Burgundy Room This Short North eatery has a dark cherry book-shelflike wine bar and curved dark cherry booths. Window-side tables are the perfect place to people-watch while sipping any of the 68 wine-by-the-glass selections and grazing on tasty appetizer-size tapas (two can satisfy average appetites). Selections include chilled fruit soup, beef carpaccio with shaved Parmesan, or tuna tartare with soy wasabi vinaigrette. Manhattan clam chowder, mustard-glaze lamb chops, shredded duck leg, and maple-glazed wings are a few of the hot items. > 641 N. High St., Short North, tel. 614/464–9463. AE, D, MC, V.

City Barbecue Go for the food, not the surroundings at this no-frills restaurant with three locations: 15 minutes northwest of downtown, in the northeast suburb of Gahanna, and in the eastside Reynoldsburg area. The tables are crammed together, there's no table service, and smokers sit in the parking lot. You'll be rewarded, however, with big portions of North Carolina–style barbecue or ribs dressed with corn, baked beans, and other traditional fixings. > 2111 W. Henderson Rd., Upper Arlington, tel. 614/538–8890; 207 W. Johnstown Rd., Gahanna, tel. 614/416–8890; 5979 E. Main St., Reynoldsburg, tel. 614/755–8890, www.citybbq.com. AE, D, MC, V. ¢–$

The Clarmont Famous for playing host to powerbrokers for breakfast and lunch and to theatergoers for dinner, this German Village restaurant with white tablecloths is a Columbus staple. The retro mid-century menu includes steaks, lamb, veal, pork, surf 'n' turf, scallops, and shrimp. A favorite, chicken in a clay pot with mashed potatoes and vegetables, is only available until "it's gone." Pasta and an expanded wine list are a concession to changing tastes. A pianist entertains Thursday through Saturday evenings. > 684 S. High St., German Village, tel. 614/443–1125. AE, DC, MC, V. No breakfast or lunch Sun. $$–$$$$

Dragonfly Neo-V Vegetarian cuisine gets a gourmet twist in this eatery at the cusp of the Short North and Victorian Village. The limited, seasonal menu is built around local, organic ingredients. This isn't a retro hippie haven with sprouts and tofu, however. Expect bold, intense flavors, unlikely combinations and artistic presentations. A sampling from the spring dinner menu includes hempseed-crusted smoked Portobello, wild mushroom griddle cake, and a white devil chocolate mousse dessert. The stark, minimalist lines of the restaurant are repeated in the connected art gallery. > 247 King Ave., Short North, tel. 614/298–9986. AE, DC, MC, V. Closed Mon. $–$$$$

Fisherman's Wharf Ship models, stuffed-and-mounted fish, and other nautical artifacts let you know it's all about seafood at this Bexley restaurant. A perennial favorite of local reviewers and a loyal clientele, the fresh seafood goes beyond deep-fried and includes rarely seen arctic char and Dover Sole entrées. A surprisingly large variety of chicken, lamb, and beef dishes—many with a Greek touch reflecting the owner's heritage—are served for alternate appetites. > 2143 E. Main St., Bexley, tel. 614/236–0043. No lunch Sat.; 2816 Fishinger Rd., Upper Arlington, tel. 614/457–4900. No lunch weekends. AE, DC, MC, V. $$–$$$$

G. Michael's Italian American Bistro and Bar Inside a German Village town house, this spot is fancy without feeling stuffy. Locals frequent the bustling bar at night. Contemporary Italian-American cuisine means chicken sausage lasagne, grilled marinated quail, or mushroom ravioli on a seasonally changing menu. Check out the intimate outdoor patio, which seats 24 in the summer. > 595 S. 3rd St., German Village, tel. 614/464–0575. AE, D, DC, MC, V. No lunch. $$–$$$$

Haiku Poetic Food and Art Abstract art hung on soft gray walls and sparse tables set the stage for a Zen-like dining experience. Hot entrées include creative Asian dishes like the house specialty, noodles served in sauce or broth. There's a full sake menu to wash down the food. The sushi bar is the center of activity at this restaurant in the trendy Short North frequented by business people, college students, and downtown artistes. > 800 N. High St., Short North, tel. 614/294–8168. AE, D, DC, MC, V. $–$$

Handke's Cuisine Seasonal ingredients are the focus at this Brewery District spot. Below street level, the restaurant occupies an 1820s beer cellar with stone vaulted ceilings, brick walls, and trophies from local celebrity chef Hartmut Handke. The menu might include Caesar salad garnished with fresh salmon and served in a baked

Parmesan cheese shell, New York strip, and herb-crusted lamb. Single-malt Scotch, fine cognac, and cigars cap off an elegant evening. > 520 S. Front St., Brewery District, tel. 614/621–2500, www.chefhandke.com. Reservations essential. AE, D, MC, V. Closed Sun. No lunch. **$$$$**

Hyde Park Grille Steaks are named after famous Ohio sports figures, such as Ohio State coach Jim Tressel, auto racing star Bobby Rahal, and former Cleveland Browns quarterback Bernie Kosar. The Kosar, a filet mignon topped with lobster and béarnaise sauce, is the most popular dish. The seafood is straightforward: lobster tails, king crab, skewered shrimp, and surf 'n' turf. Both restaurants, in the northwest suburbs of Dublin and Upper Arlington, offer cozy dining rooms with dark wood and fireplaces. There's live entertainment Wednesday–Sunday. > 1615 Old Henderson Rd., Upper Arlington, tel. 614/442–3310; 6360 Frantz Rd., Dublin, tel. 614/717–2828, www.hydeparkgrille.com. AE, D, DC, MC, V. No lunch. **$$$–$$$$**

Indian Oven The two-story, airy space with exposed beams, streamlined stainless steel bar, and 10-foot-high windows belies the hearty comfort food served. In a refurbished building in the developing Market Exchange District, Indian Oven specializes in northern Indian, Pakistani, and Bengali food. The open kitchen sends out korma dishes with chunks of vegetables or meats cooked in a creamy sauce with nuts, tandoori dishes roasted in a clay oven, and sautéed goat rezala in a curry sauce. Cool things down at the end of a meal with a creamy fruit custard, a family recipe. > 427 E. Main St., Columbus, tel. 614/220–9390. AE, D, MC, V. Closed Sun. **$–$$$**

Katzinger's The more than 80 menu items are printed on chalkboards at this New York–style deli in German Village. It's known for its Reuben sandwiches, and open-air dining is available. There's no smoking here. > 475 S. 3rd St., German Village, tel. 614/228–3354. AE, D, MC, V. **¢–$**

L'Antibes Two smallish dining rooms with lacquered art deco chairs, eclectic paintings, and subdued colors make up this Short North restaurant. The menu of contemporary and classic French dishes changes every six weeks to take advantage of in-season produce, as exemplified by salmon with horseradish crust, lamb, and halibut with crawfish sauce, and veal loin medallions with shiitake sauce. > 772 N. High St., Short North, tel. 614/291–1666, www.lantibes.com. Reservations essential. AE, D, DC, MC, V. Closed Sun. and Mon. No lunch. **$$$$**

Lemongrass Specialties on the diverse menu include pad thai, sate with peanut sauce, and extensive sushi selections. Circular stairs, an industrial stainless bar, and a soothing pastel dining room adds stylish chic to this Pan-Asian–style restaurant in the Short North. > 641 N. High St., Suite 103, Short North, tel. 614/224–1414, fax 614/221–2535, www.lantibes.com. AE, MC, V. No lunch weekends. **$$–$$$**

Lindey's In a mid-1800s building in German Village, this somewhat boisterous bistro has high ceilings, big windows, and walls covered with artwork. Specialties of the seasonally changing menu usually include steak and rack of lamb. Save room for their signature dessert, the "Post Mortem," a rich homemade brownie served with coffee ice cream and a Kahlua hot fudge sauce. There's entertainment Thursday and a Sunday brunch. > 169 E. Beck St., German Village, tel. 614/228–4343, www.lindeys.com. AE, D, DC, MC, V. **$$–$$$$**

M Restaurant & Bar On the first level of Miranova Office Tower in the Brewery District, M makes a whiz-bang first impression with its elegant entry bar. Sheer curtains, lighted theatrically for dramatic effect, separate tables, and a patio with stunning views of the Scioto River and downtown skyline. Selections such as soy-glaze swordfish and Muscovy duck pot stickers are joined by stalwart standbys such as rack of lamb at this special-occasion spot. > 2 Miranova Pl., Brewery District, tel.

614/629–0000, www.cameronmitchell.com. Reservations essential. AE, D, DC, MC, V. Closed Sun. $$–$$$$

Mitchell's Steakhouse A renovated bank building near the state house is one of the most atmospheric restaurants in town, with subtle lighting, a darkwood bar, original art deco paintings, velvet-drape walls, and ornate 20-foot-high ceilings. A baker's dozen of dry-aged and prime steaks delights carnivores, while chicken and seafood offer a lighter alternative. > 45 N. 3rd St., at Gay St., Downtown, tel. 614/621–2333, www.cameronmitchell.com. Reservations essential. AE, D, DC, MC, V. No lunch weekends. $$$$

Morton's of Chicago The downtown Columbus branch of the well-known chain has its trademark mahogany interior with white tablecloths. The menu is all about steak, and large portions of choice beef are served. There's also salmon, swordfish, lobster, and whole roasted chicken. The bar has an extensive wine list. > 280 N. High St., Nationwide Plaza, Downtown, tel. 614/464–4442, www.mortons.com. Reservations essential. AE, D, DC, MC, V. No lunch.

Nancy's Home Cooking In Clintonville near the OSU campus, Nancy's is home-made, hearty, and one of the best values in town. Prices are painted on the wall at this classic diner with small booths and a counter with cramped stools. Regulars serve themselves—at least their own beverages or slice of pie. Then they pay their bill, without waiting for the check, when it's time to go. Breakfast specialties include French toast and the garbage omelette. > 3133 N. High St., Clintonville, tel. 614/265–9012. No credit cards. No lunch weekends, no dinner Fri.–Sun. ¢

Ocean Club The "upscale coastal" cuisine here includes calamari with Thai chili, ginger-crusted salmon, and cashew shrimp. Nonseafood selections are in the "Midwest" section of the menu. On the second level of the enclosed mall that is at the heart of Easton Town Center, the restaurant specializes in seafood, but not the same old selections of salmon and shrimp everyone serves. The decor is as different as the food. A shell-like ceiling is lighted with fiber-optics. Aluminum columns, a cobalt-blue floor, and a glass-enclosed bar simulate an underwater experience. > Easton Town Center, Columbus, tel. 614/416–2582. AE, D, DC, MC, V. $$$$

Olde Mohawk One of German Village's first pubs, this eatery in a 1933 building is famous for its horseshoe-shape bar. Pictures of staff and customers cover the walls. With the food a cut above "pub grub," it's one of few places that stays open past midnight on weekdays and past 1 AM on the weekends. Specials are ever-changing and there are all-you-can-eat quesadillas nights. Popular dishes include the roast beef sandwich with chicken salad on top and beef stew served in a hollowed-out round of bread. > 821 Mohawk St., German Village, tel. 614/444–7204. AE, D, DC, MC, V. $

Plaza Restaurant On the second floor of the Hyatt on Capitol Square, the lavish Plaza has a spectacular view of the state capitol building and an outdoor fountain courtyard. The views are eclipsed by the food. Imaginative appetizers complement fine Continental-inspired fare that might include osso buco, Wiener schnitzel, or a New York strip steak. > 75 E. State St., at High St., Downtown, tel. 614/365–4550. AE, D, DC, MC, V. $$$–$$$$

Refectory Summer means open-air dining in the courtyard; winter means drinks in front of a blazing fire in the cocktail lounge. The menu, which also changes with the seasons, might include rack of lamb, beef tenderloin medallions, and fresh seafood dishes. The extensive wine list tops out at more than 900 selections. Northwest of downtown in a restored church dating from the 1850s, the restaurant oozes charm with exposed brick walls, stained-glass windows, and wooden beams. > 1092 Bethel Rd., Columbus, tel. 614/451–9774, www.therefectoryrestaurant.com. Reservations essential. AE, D, DC, MC, V. Closed Sun. No lunch. $$$–$$$$

Rigsby's Cuisine Volatile Chefs are visible behind a large marble counter at this trendy Short North restaurant. High ceilings, lots of wood, and eclectic artwork keeps the interior as stimulating as the constantly updated menu. Specialties include the almond fried calamari with chipotle remoulade, asparagus, and salt roasted beet terrine and parsley roasted halibut. There's entertainment Wednesday and Thursday, and children's portions are available. > 698 N. High St., Short North, tel. 614/461–7888. Reservations essential. AE, D, DC, MC, V. Closed Sun. $$–$$$$

Schmidt's Sausage Haus Accordion players serenade and servers are decked out in Bavarian costumes at this popular two-level, beer hall–style restaurant in a 1880 brick building in German Village. Specialties include German pasta and their signature Bahama Mama—a giant bratwurst served with your choice of toppings, such as sauerkraut and mustard. Save room for large, overstuffed cream puffs. > 240 E. Kossuth St., German Village, tel. 614/444–6808, www.schmidthouse.com. AE, D, DC, MC, V. $

Seven Stars Dining Room The Worthington Inn, with its antiques-filled dining rooms, is about 15 mi north of downtown. New Zealand rack of lamb and grilled salmon are specialties. Don't miss the bountiful Sunday brunch of shellfish, waffles, eggs, desserts, and cheese. Open-air dining is available on the front porch with cast iron furniture or the brick-paved courtyard. There's entertainment Friday and Saturday. > 649 High St., Worthington, tel. 614/885–2600, www.worthingtoninn.com. AE, D, MC, V. No lunch Sun. $$–$$$$

Tapatio The bold colors in the restaurant match the spicy flavors on the menu at this eatery specializing in Caribbean Rim cuisine. Imaginative dishes include black bean hummus, crab cakes in red pepper sauce, and the chef's signature sautéed calamari. A lively bar offers an extensive tequila selection plus margaritas. Open-air dining is available. The hearty bread can be purchased across the street at the North Market. > 491 N. Park St., Columbus, tel. 614/221–1085, http://tapatiocolumbus.com. No lunch weekends. AE, D, DC, MC, V. $–$$$

Tony's Italian Ristorante This fancy German Village restaurant has a bright dining room with pink-and-beige walls and linens. There's an extensive antipasti menu. Entrées might include pasta specialties such as spinach-and-cheese canneloni or veal classics such as saltimbocca, piccata, or marsala. A pianist performs on Saturday evenings. > 16 W. Beck St., German Village, tel. 614/224–8669. AE, DC, MC, V. Closed Sun. No lunch Sat. $$–$$$$

Top Steak House This nearly 50-year-old institution with wood paneling and leather booths is in Bexley. Filet mignon, rib steak, porterhouse, and other chops and ribs reign here. A pianist entertains Tuesday through Saturday. > 2891 E. Main St., Bexley, tel. 614/231–8238. AE, D, DC, MC, V. Closed Sun. in summer. No lunch. $$–$$$$

ESSENTIALS

Getting Here

BY BUS
The Columbus terminal is open 24 hours for ticketing.
BUS DEPOTS **Greyhound Bus Terminal** > 111 E. Town St., at 3rd St., Columbus 43215, tel. 800/229–9424, www.greyhound.com.
BUS LINES **Greyhound** > Tel. 800/229–9424, www.greyhound.com.

BY CAR
Getting to Columbus is easy as the city sits in the center of the state. Two major interstates intersect near downtown: I–70, which runs east–west, and

I–71, which runs north–south. I–670 runs from downtown and connects to Port Columbus International Airport. I–270 loops around the outer boundaries of the city.

BY PLANE

Port Columbus International Airport is served by 23 passenger airlines providing more than 350 departures and arrivals daily. The airport is 10 mi east of downtown.

AIRPORTS **Port Columbus International Airport** > 4600 International Gateway, Columbus 43219, tel. 614/239–4000, www.port-columbus.com.

CARRIERS **Air Canada** > Tel. 800/776–3000, www.aircanada.ca/. **America West** > Tel. 800/235–9292, www.americawest.com. **American Airlines** > Tel. 800/433–7300, www.aa.com. **Continental** > Tel. 800/525–0280, www.continental.com. **Delta Airlines** > Tel. 800/221–1212, www.delta-air.com. **Midwest Express** > Tel. 800/452–2022, www.midwestexpress.com. **Northwest Airlines** > Tel. 800/225–2525, www.nwa.com. **Southwest Airlines** > Tel. 800/435–9792, www.iflyswa.com. **United Airlines** > Tel. 800/241–6522, www.ual.com. **US Airways** > Tel. 800/428–4322, www.usairways.com.

AIRPORT TRANSFERS

Taxis are electronically metered. Initial charge (including loading and the first ⅑ mi) is $2 plus $1 surcharge for trips originating at the airport. Each additional ⅔ mi or 60 seconds waiting time $0.40. A cab from the airport to downtown costs about $18, Cooper Stadium about $24, Ohio State University about $26, and Dublin about $36. Urban Express airport shuttle from downtown costs $12. Arch Express from downtown, $13. Super Shuttle from downtown, about $14.

TAXIS & SHUTTLES **Arch Express** > Tel. 614/252–2277. **Independent Taxi Cab Association** > Tel. 614/235–5551. **Super Shuttle** > Tel. 614/868–8888. **Urban Express** > Tel. 877/840–0411 or 614/840–0411.

Getting Around

Downtown is fairly compact and easily walkable. Some government buildings are connected to each other and to nearby buildings through underground walkways.

The Brewery District, German Village, the Arena District, and the Short North are adjacent to downtown. The major thoroughfare that runs near or through each of these areas is High Street. The Brewery District and German Village are next to each other south of downtown, while the Arena District and the Short North are next to each other north of downtown. The Ohio State Campus is just north of the Short North. In these areas, streets are narrow, on-street parking is limited, and valet parking is expensive. If you're on the northern end of downtown, it's a manageable several-block walk to reach the Arena District and the Short North. If you are on the southern end of downtown, it's a several-block walk to reach German Village and the Brewery District.

BY CAR

Interstate 70, I–71, and I–670 headed toward downtown are congested weekday mornings; in the evening, the roads are clogged in the opposite direction. Traffic is lighter Saturday and Sunday. The Short North area, German Village, the Arena District, the Brewery District, and High Street are also very busy. Traffic usually flows smoothly in outlying suburbs but can get congested during morning and evening drive times. Outlying traffic jams are most common around I–270 at Route 23, I–71, Route 315, Route 161 toward New Albany, and the Polaris interchange. You do need a car in these areas because bus service is infrequent or nonexistent.

Downtown, metered parking is available but difficult to find. If you find a spot, be sure to put sufficient money in the meter; meter maids are efficient here. Be sure not to park in a "permit-only" area as a ticket will show up on your windshield in no time. Parking garages are plentiful in this area and near the Ohio State University campus. Parking for an entire day costs between $10 and $15. Columbus is a growing city, which means roadway construction projects. For construction information, contact Paving The Way, a joint project of the Federal Highway Administration, the Ohio Department of Transportation, and the city of Columbus.

CONTACTS **Paving The Way** > Tel. 614/645–7283, www.pavingtheway.org.

BY PUBLIC TRANSIT

The Central Ohio Transit Authority (COTA) operates buses within Columbus and its suburbs. Bus fare is $1.25, express fare $1.75, transfer 10¢.

CONTACTS **Central Ohio Transit Authority (COTA)** > 177 S. High St., Columbus 43215, tel. 614/228–1776, www.cota.com.

Visitor Information

The Greater Columbus Convention and Visitors Bureau has two visitor centers where you can get additional information. The visitor center at the downtown Columbus City Center is on the second floor across from Kaufmann's. At the suburban mall in Easton Town Center, the center is on the first floor behind the AMC Theatres.

CONTACTS **Experience Columbus Visitors Center, at Columbus City Center** > 111 S. 3rd St., Columbus, tel. 800/354–2657, www.ExperienceColumbus.com. Mon.–Sat. 11–6, Sun. noon–6. **Experience Columbus Visitors Center, at Easton Town Center** > I–270 and Easton Way, Columbus, tel. 800/354–2657, www.ExperienceColumbus.com. Mon.–Sat. 10–9, Sun. noon–6. **Greater Columbus Convention and Visitors Bureau** > 90 N. High St., Columbus 43215, tel. 614/221–6623 or 800/354–2657, fax 614/221–5618, www.ExperienceColumbus.com.

Athens & the Wayne National Forest

Athens is 75 mi southeast of Columbus, 142 mi east of Cincinnati, and 201 mi south of Cleveland.

WHEN IT COMES TO GETTING OUT and stretching your legs, Wayne National Forest can leave you breathless, both from the stunning sights and from the hardcore trails you'll probably be traversing. Of course, if you're already out of breath from your everyday life in the concrete jungle, feel free to slow down by canoeing one of the slow-moving rivers in the area.

Named for Revolutionary War veteran Anthony Wayne, the forest came under the control of the national parks in 1952, when 105,000 acres of the former Wayne Purchase Units were officially renamed and united. The forest now exceeds 229,000 acres. Put together piecemeal from reclaimed national lands and formerly private farms that were in disrepair, Wayne National Forest is constantly growing by acquiring more acreage each year. The forest sprawls across southeastern Ohio in three sections. There are segments near Ironton and Marietta, but the focus of this chapter is the Athens Ranger District, the chunk nearest Athens. In 2001 the national-forest headquarters opened on U.S. 33 between Athens and Nelsonville.

Looking for varied terrain and landscapes? You're in the right place, as this portion of southeast Ohio contains as many different land elements as you can handle. There are segments of virgin forest as well as those containing second and third growth woods (meaning the land has been reclaimed by nature and reforested). Reclaimed farmlands as flat as anywhere in the state are within a few miles drive from preserves containing trees measuring 3 feet in diameter. There's a true cave (a rare site in the Appalachian foothills), along with roaring post-thaw waterfalls that will have completely dried and disappeared in the dry summer. Erosion of large quantities of Blackhand sandstone in the region has resulted in the deep caves, waterfalls, and natural rock bridges that are southeast Ohio's most famous draws. While marveling at these inanimate sites, be sure to take a peak at the area's wildlife as well. White-tailed deer and wild turkey are prevalent in the area, and wildflowers cover the terrain the sun can reach through the hardwood forest.

In spring and fall the area is lit up in greens, reds, and golds. Wait until winter to visit and the naked branches of the seasonal blooms and the occasional evergreen are coated in a prism forming glasslike ice. Although the mercury and snow will fall in winter, it normally isn't bitingly cold.

Facilities in the forest are few and far between, but no worries: there are many local stores, equipment depots, and campgrounds just outside the forest proper ready to provide any- and everything you'll need on your weekend.

Surrounding the Athens unit, you'll find several cities with amenities that throw some civilization into this rural getaway. The largest, of course, is Athens itself. Named after the ancient Greek center of learning and home to Ohio University, the first institute of higher learning in the Northwest Territory, this city has a permanent population of about 30,000 and another 19,000 students from August to April. Both the collegiate atmosphere of the academic year as well as the sleepiness of the summer months provide excellent if divergent environments in which to spend a weekend.

About 15 mi north of Athens, in the heart of this branch of Wayne National Forest, is the town of Nelsonville. An alternative to Athens for dining and lodging properties, Nelsonville also houses Hocking College, a regional technical school.

Very little has changed in this region over the last 250 years, and it's unlikely to before your next opportunity to visit. Although the minutia of the forest is constantly changing and growing, the sites below have been here for quite some time. So please, don't rush—it isn't in keeping with the lifestyle here anyway. Pick one or two of the sites below and enjoy this weekend.

WHAT TO SEE & DO

Wayne National Forest The only national forest in Ohio, Wayne National Forest covers some 230,000 acres and provides ample opportunity for hikers, mountain bikers, off-road-vehicle (ORV) users, and horseback riders. Permits are required for all uses other than hiking and only hikers are allowed full run of the forest; all other users must remain on designated trails.

Payne Cemetery (2 mi outside New Straitsville on St. Rte. 595, near St. Rte. 216) stands as the only remembrance of Payne's Crossing, an early-19th-century community made up of freed slaves from Virginia. All other traces of the town, including a possible railroad stop, were erased from the landscape when coal mining became the major industry in the region. The 1995 dedication of Payne cemetery was the culmination of the Passport in Time Program, the work of the forest historian and archaeologist trying to discover the history of neglected forest landmarks.

Built in 1939 by the Civilian Conservation Corps, **Shawnee Lookout Tower** (south of New Straitsville on St. Rte. 216, 5 mi north of St. Rte. 78) oversaw Wayne National Forest's fragile beginnings. Watchers in the tower scanned for forest fires that would have decimated the still-growing forest. One of four towers built during the 1930s, Shawnee Lookout is the only one that remains. Used until the 1970s, the tower, which is listed on the National Historic Lookout Register, is now open to the public. The 100-foot tower looks over a second-growth forest that as recently as 50 years ago was almost barren due to farming, grazing, and mining.

Tinker's Cave (junction of C.R. 22 and Twp. Rd. 393, south of New Straitsville) is not actually a cave but rather a rock shelter cut by an ancient creek. The cave's namesake, Seth Tinker, was an infamous horse thief who used the cave as a stable for his illegal activities prior to the Civil War. Tinker also provided horses for the only Southern invasion to penetrate Union holdings during the Civil War.

Tall pine trees dominate the six picnic sites in the **Utah Ridge Picnic Area** (Twp. Rd. 293 off U.S. 33, May 15–Dec. 15, dawn–dusk). Many families use this secluded area for fishing and for a peaceful stop far from any bustling crowds.

The forest, made up of three discontinuous segments, has its forest headquarters within the Athens district. > Supervisor's Office and Athens Ranger District, 13700 U.S. 33, Nelsonville, tel. 740/753–0101, www.fs.fed.us/r9/wayne. Free. Office hrs mid-Apr.–Sept., Mon.–Sat. 8–4:30; Oct.–mid-Apr., weekdays 8–4:30. Forest hrs daily dawn–dusk.

WHAT'S NEARBY

Burr Oak State Park Nature programs, fishing, biking, and bridle paths are among the draws at the 3,200-acre park about 14 mi north of Athens. You can boat and fish on Burr Oak Lake. > 10220 Burr Oak Lodge Rd., Glouster, tel. 740/767–3570 park office, 740/767–2112, www.ohiostateparks.org. Free. Daily dawn–dusk.

Dairy Barn Cultural Center Once a functioning dairy barn, this venue now houses eclectic art exhibitions and special events, ranging from an international quilt show to a display on the Vietnam War. > 8000 Dairy La., Athens, tel. 740/592–4981, www.dairybarn.org. $4. Open only during exhibitions: Tues.–Sun. 11–5, Thurs. 11–8.

Eclipse Company Town Because coal mining was *the* industry in this region during the 19th century, the mining companies built actual towns for their workers. The Eclipse Company Town is one of the few remaining examples within the state, and it's currently being renovated as both a historic site and a cultural and arts center. Eclipse currently has 13 bungalow-style houses, one shotgun-style house, and a company store. Some of the original mine buildings are still standing in the area, and house rentals are available. > Johnson Rd. off U.S. 33, The Plains, tel. 740/591–2248, www.eclipsecompanytown.com. Free. Daily dawn–dusk.

Strouds Run State Park Camping and hiking, along with fishing and boating on Dow Lake, are among the activities that can be enjoyed at this 2,600-acre park 8 mi northeast of Athens. > 1161 State Park Rd., Athens, tel. 740/592–2302, www.ohiostateparks.org. Free. Daily dawn–dusk.

Sports

BIKING & MOUNTAIN BIKING

With all the open green space in southeast Ohio, not all of the biking is up and down on dirt trails. Several paths exist for individuals looking for a scenic ride or exercise outside of the rough mountain terrain.

Trail use for mountain biking in the Wayne National Forest is allowed from April 15 to December 15; weather conditions at other times make the trails unsafe for uses other than hiking. You will need a permit to bike in the forest. Nonrefundable permits are available in three types: 1-day ($5), 2-day ($10), and seasonal ($22). Any lost seasonal permits can be replaced for $10 with proof of purchase. Stop at the Athens district office to purchase permits, as they are not available in the field. Also, vendors, such as grocery stores and gas stations, near the main trail routes carry valid permits. Replacement permits are available only from the district offices.

Hockhocking Adena Bikeway Riders get a perfect up-close view of all things Appalachian on this 33-mi round-trip road cycling path between Athens and Nelsonville. The town of Eclipse, one of the best remaining examples of company town architecture left in Ohio, is at Mile 7.1. Miles 12 through 14 run through Wayne National Forest south of Nelsonville. Access points with parking include Mile 0 and Mile 4 in Athens, Mile 10.2 in the Plains, and Mile 16.4 in Nelsonville at Robbins Crossing. > East State St. Recreation Area, 667 E. State St., Athens, tel. 800/878–9767.

Lake Hope Known as the Little Sandy Trail, this 3-mi ride is one of the easier ones in the region, making it a good choice for beginning riders as well as families. Shared by hikers and mountain bikers alike, this trail is located within Zaleski State Forest, about 15 mi east of Athens. > Intersection of Cabin Ridge Rd. and St. Rte. 278. Zaleski State Forest, tel. 740/596–4938, www.dnr.state.oh.us/forestry.

Long Ridge One of several trails in the Monday Creek off-road vehicle (ORV) area, Long Ridge is the only one not tied directly to all the others, so it's a bit less traveled and more secluded. Several technical rides here challenge the more experienced rider. > Forest Rd. 758, off St. Rte. 78 2 mi north of the intersection with T.R. 22. Wayne National Forest, Athens Ranger District, tel. 740/592–6644, www.fs.fed.us/r9/wayne.

Richland Furnace Although it is designed for all purpose vehicles (APVs), very few use this trail located west of Athens along U.S. 50. The 7-mi trail has big inclines and fast downhills. This is one of the more difficult and physically involved trails in the area, so be prepared for quite a workout. Richland Furnace State Forest is closed from December 1 to March 31. > Loop Rd., 2 mi east of the intersection with St. Rte. 327, tel. 740/596–5781.

HIKING

If hiking isn't one of the main reasons you're coming to visit the Wayne National Forest, it will be by the time you leave, as almost every sight and sound involves some type of hiking. With the trails in the forest proper radiating out from Athens, the scenery and levels of difficulty are as varied as you can handle. With the entire national forest open to hikers, these trails are a good starting point, but feel free to wander. Just make sure you pick up a map of the area first.

Gifford State Forest Right up against the Morgan County line, this is the smallest state forest and probably the least traveled as well. Although the rise in elevation makes it far from the easiest hike in the area, you won't find a better place for a secluded hike of about 3 mi. > ½ mi from the junction of St. Rtes. 377 and 550, 15 mi from U.S. 33 (17221 St. Rte. 377, Chesterhill 43728, tel. 740/554–3177, www.dnr.state.oh.us/forestry.

Wildcat Hollow Trail Wildcat Hollow is one of the Athens district's most popular trails. The full length is 15 mi, but there's a smaller, 5-mi loop for those not looking to spend the whole day here. The forest has designated this trail as a "wildlife watching" site, excellent for seeing white-tailed deer, wild turkeys, and forest songbirds up close. Wildcat Hollow is just a short distance from the Burr Oak Cove and Burr Oak State Park campgrounds. > St. Rte. 13, 3 mi east of Twp. Rd. 289. Wayne National Forest, Athens Ranger District, tel. 740/753–0101, www.fs.fed.us/r9/wayne.

Zaleski State Forest This state forest has a 23-mi hiking trail and a 33-mi bridle trail that are both free. Hiking this trail is one of the least strenuous walking tours in southeast Ohio. You can self-register for the hike 24 hours a day by signing in at the trailhead bulletin board. Zaleski shares a border with both Wayne National Forest and Lake Hope State Park. > St. Rte. 56, 4 mi south of intersection with St. Rte. 278 (Box 330, St. Rte. 278, Zaleski 45698, tel. 740/596–5781, www.dnr.state.oh.us/forestry.

CANOEING

Private companies provide boat rentals and planned trips along the Hocking River in the Athens district of the Wayne National Forest. Many of the river access points fall within the forest and other public lands, but there are also points owned by private citizens. The national-forest office provides maps of the river, illustrating where ownership changes hands. Also pay attention to the local weather, as these rivers flood quickly and easily after heavy rains.

Hocking Hills Canoe Livery Of the three options available at this livery, two are shorter trips (1–3 hours), including one to the natural rockbridge outside of town, and the third is a full day trip (4–6 hours) on the lower Hocking River. There are also primitive campsites, wooded or open, available along the river for $5 per night per person, reservations required. Hocking Hills also provides a moonlight tour, beginning at nightly at 7, as well as shuttle service from the livery to put-in for those with

Funky Festivals

NO MATTER THE REASON OR the season, people in Ohio are ready to party.

Ohio festivals come in every size and description. Some honor products and people—wholesome events that are an homage to apples, corn, or the hometown hero. Quirky festivities celebrate washboards or twins.

Regardless of the theme, most festivals include a slew of activities (most suitable for the family), crafts, food, entertainment, and rides. Prepare to visit an Ohio festival when planning a weekend getaway. You won't be disappointed.

Every Memorial Day droves of people come to sleepy New Straitsville to celebrate spirits at the **Moonshine Festival** (740/394–2838). Locals began bootlegging moonshine during the Great Depression after fires destroyed the coal mines where most residents had made their living. But despite the event's name, festival goers do not sample the strong moonshine brewed in the working stills because the drink is illegal. Even without the alcohol, however, a carnival atmosphere draws people of all ages to sample moonshine burgers and pies, cheer on the contestants for moonshine queen, and watch demonstrations of a moonshine still.

The Guinness Book of World Records declares the **Twins Days Festival** (330/425–3652) in Twinsburg to be the "World's Largest Annual Gathering of Twins." Twins from around the world, be they newborns or octogenarians, fraternal or identical, gather in Twinsburg for the contests, talent shows, and other events that make this a one-of-a-kind event. Twins compete for such titles as most alike and least alike. The highlight is the Double-Take Parade, which kicks off the festivities.

Washboards are now a laundry relic in America, but blues, zydeco, and country musicians still scratch out rhythms on them with thimbles and spoons. The only remaining washboard manufacturer in the United States organizes the **International Washboard Festival** (740/380–3828) in Logan every year. Nationally renowned washboard musicians play. Classic cars, antique tractors, and visiting musicians from across the country are all part of the opening parade. During the festival, you can take a free tour of the factory where washboards are made, much as they were in the early 1900s.

What started as a sidewalk sale with a sauerkraut dinner is now the **Ohio Sauerkraut Festival** (513/897–8855), one of the largest arts-and-crafts shows in the United States with more than 400 booths of handcrafted merchandise. Festivities include contests for the ugliest, greenest, and biggest cabbage. You can sample sundaes, cakes, fudge, cheesecake, and pizza—all made with sauerkraut. More than 13,000 pounds of the stuff, in various forms, are consumed during the festival.

Here's a festival with appeal—the **Banana Split Festival** (877/428–4748). Wilmington contends that the banana split was invented by a local pharmacist as a way to drum up business (though Latrobe, Pennsylvania, also claims the decadent invention as its own). The festival recaptures the 1950s and early 1960s, when soda shops, banana splits, drive-in movies, and poodle skirts were all the rage. There are rock 'n' roll concerts and a cruise-in with about 400 classic cars. The most popular activity, however, is a visit to the make-your-own-split booth. Festival goers pile on the ingredients, consuming more than 2,000 splits each year.

— Nicki Chodnoff

their own canoes or kayaks. Each trip ends back at the livery. > 12789 St. Rte. 664 S, Logan, tel. 800/634–6820, 740/385–2755 off season.

Old Man River Canoe Livery This livery is the only one on the Hocking River open year-round, although that doesn't mean trips will be available at all times. Trips last from 1 to 6 hours, the last trip of the day leaving at 4 PM. Old Man River's place as the northernmost livery on the river combined with a limited trip schedule makes for the least-congested (read: more time to sightsee) trips available. Lodging packages are available at Lighthouse Cottages on nearby Lake Logan. > Rockbridge Enterprise, 10653 Jackson St., Logan, tel. 866/380–0510.

Save the Date

APRIL

Athens International Film Festival Begun in 1974, this week-long festival invites artists from around the world to discuss and screen their films. Tickets are either $3.50 or $5, depending on the theater, or passes for any six screenings are $25. > Athens, tel. 740/597–1330, www.athensfest.org.

MAY

Wild Turkey Festival Food and games, as well as both car and quilt shows make up this annual 3-day festival. The weekend event culminates with a parade and naming of the Festival Queen. > 67363 Infirmary Rd., McArthur, tel. 740/596–4945.

SEPTEMBER

Ohio Paw Paw Festival Drawing upwards of 2,000 people, this festival, held annually since 1999, celebrates all things pawpaw. Contestants match their eating and cooking prowess using the native fruit, as well as nationally renowned speakers discussing the state of the pawpaw industry. Musical acts also perform at the 2-day festival, which costs $3 per day for adults, or $10 for the weekend and a campsite. > Box 503, Albany, tel. 740/698–2124, www.ohiopawpaw.org/pawpawfest.html.

OCTOBER

Halloween Consider this either an invitation to return to your youth or a warning to stay away, as Athens in particular and the area in general is flooded with visiting college students. Although comparisons to New Orleans' Mardi Gras celebration are far-fetched at best, lodging and dining options are extremely limited on this weekend. > Court St., Athens.

Paul Bunyan Festival International lumberjack contests include chain-saw carving and log rolling at this event, which also provides live music and a visit to the forestry museum on-site. Gate admission is $8 for adults. > 3301 Hocking Pkwy., Nelsonville, tel. 740/753–3591.

WHERE TO STAY

Burr Oak Resort Most cabins at this wooded resort in Burr Oak State Park, 14 mi north of Athens, have window walls affording a magnificent view of Burr Oak Lake. Guest rooms in the lodge have rough-hewn walls, chandeliers, and rustic-elegant sofas and chairs. The resort has various activities, ranging from fishing and boating to basketball and volleyball. Lodge guests can access any state park facility. > 10660 Burr Oak Lodge Rd., Glouster 45732, tel. 740/767–2112, fax 740/767–4878, www.burroakresort.com. 60 rooms, 30 cottages. Dining room, some kitchenettes, some microwaves, some refrigerators, some cable TV, tennis courts, indoor pool, lake, boating, marina, fishing, basketball, hiking, horseshoes, shuffleboard, volleyball, bar, playground, business services, meeting rooms, no-smoking rooms; no phones in cabins. AE, DC, MC, V. $–$$

Days Inn This motel's rural location, just off Route 78 about 4 mi from the downtown area, affords pleasant views from the comfortable but otherwise nondescript guest rooms. A nearby driving range and putting course make it a favorite of golfers. > 330 Columbus Rd., Athens 45701, tel. 740/592–4000 or 800/325–2525, fax 740/593–7687, www.daysinn.com. 60 rooms. Cable TV, business services, some pets allowed (fee). AE, D, DC, MC, V. CP. $

Ohio University Inn Just four blocks from the heart of Ohio University's main campus, this hotel consists of three connected brick buildings. The University Inn, which is very popular among visitors to the school, tends to be booked solid for sporting and academic events, so call well in advance. > 331 Richland Ave., Athens 45701, tel. 740/593–6661, fax 740/592–5139, www.ouinn.athens.oh.us. 143 rooms. Restaurant, room service, cable TV, pool, gym, bar, business services, no-smoking rooms. AE, D, DC, MC, V. $$–$$$

Woodspirit Getaway This cabin in the woods has Adirondack furniture and high loft ceilings. It sleeps four (two upstairs and two down), has a kitchen, and the screened-in porch has a hot tub. Six miles south of downtown Athens, it's a great weekend getaway for couples or families who need a little privacy. > 6170 N. Coolville Ridge Rd., Athens 45701, tel. 740/593–5628 or 877/593–5628, www.woodspiritgetaway.com. 1 cabin. Kitchen, microwave, refrigerator, cable TV, in-room VCR, hot tub; no smoking. MC, V. $$–$$$

CAMPING

Burr Oak Cove Campground For those looking for the complete "roughing it" experience, this is the place to go. Located about 4½ mi north of Glouster, hikers on their way along the Buckeye Trail are the only visitors you're likely to see here. Burr Oak Lake and the lodge there cannot be directly accessed from this campground, only by following the Lakeview Trail will you come in contact with civilization. There are both open and wooded sites available, providing for a completely secluded camping experience. The maximum length stay is 14 days. > St. Rte. 13, 4½ mi north of Glouster, Glouster 45732, tel. 740/753–0101. 8 tent sites, 11 tent or RV sites. Pit toilets, drinking water, fire pits, grills, picnic tables. Reservations not accepted. Closed Dec. 16–Apr. 14; no services available Oct. 15–Dec. 15. ¢

WHERE TO EAT

Burrito Buggy After an evening out, this trailer-housed establishment is the landmark many a college student looks for on his or her way home. Although the lines get a bit long after last call, during the afternoon you can simply walk up and order some of the fine traditional Mexican fare. You can also get several vegetarian dishes. > Corner of Court and Union Sts., Athens, no phone. No credit cards. ¢

BW3 If you simply must have something from a national chain, BW3 (Buffalo Wild Wings) is your only choice outside of fast food. It's known for having many levels of spicy wings, plus basic bar food. There's also occasional live music. > 21 W. Union St., Athens, tel. 740/594–9464. MC, V. ¢–$$

Cutler's Restaurant The in-house restaurant for the Ohio University Inn, Cutler's provides several options for upscale dining. The dinner menu includes beef, pork, poultry, seafood, and pasta selections, including a vegetable lasagna. The restaurant has very little of the college atmosphere pervading the rest of the city, but you should be able to feel some of the vibe in the bar—Ohio University sporting events always seem to be on the TV. > Ohio University Inn, 331 Richland Ave., tel. 740/593–6661. AE, D, DC, MC, V. $$–$$$$

Purple Chopstix Off the beaten path, this restaurant is the place to go to avoid the crowds of Athens. You still may have to wait a bit to be seated, though, as the restaurant only has about 10 tables and they don't accept reservations. Don't let the name be your reason for choosing this restaurant, however; the food here is more likely to be of Thai or African origin rather than Chinese. Either as appetizers or main courses, the spicy Thai and mushroom soups should not be missed. > 271½ Richland Ave., Athens, tel. 740/592–4798. Reservations not accepted. D, MC, V. No lunch. ¢–$

Seven Sauces This tiny bistro is hip enough to seem a little out of place in the hills of southeastern Ohio. Situated among college bars and other businesses that cater to the Ohio University students, Seven Sauces presents innovative fare, such as garlicky shrimp and artichoke linguine, Tuscan gumbo, and cashew trout. There are also thick lamb chops, Oriental steamed dumplings, and many vegetarian entrées. > 66 N. Court St., Athens, tel. 740/592–5555. AE, D, MC, V. No lunch. $–$$

Sylvia's Sylvia's walks the line between being a fun, casual place for students to dine with friends and a nice spot for dinner with the parents or a date. The menu combines traditional renditions of pasta favorites like lasagna and manicotti with creative entrées like the scampi Florentine (shrimp and angel-hair pasta with a shallot white sauce). There's also a low-carbohydrate menu. You can dine inside or at an umbrella-shaded table outdoors, and there's a kids' menu. > 4 Depot St., Athens, tel. 740/594–3484. AE, MC, V. Closed Sun. No lunch Sat. $–$$

Union Street Cafe Students come here for breakfast around the clock. The omelets are famous, and there are plenty of desserts and savory entrées. It's open 24 hours a day, except on Sunday, when it closes at 5 PM for a rest until Monday morning. > 102 W. Union St., Athens, tel. 740/594–6007. D, MC, V. ¢–$

ESSENTIALS

Getting Here

Wayne National Forest and the Athens area, though excellent at providing a secluded experience, are relatively easy to reach. U.S. 33 is the major highway arriving in Athens from the north and south, while U.S. 50 and 32 run east–west through the area. If you must fly into the area, your best bet is Columbus International Airport; expect an approximately 2-hour drive to Athens and Wayne National Forest from there. There are many car-rental offices here. There is no public transportation once you get into the Wayne National Forest.

BY CAR

Although you may be able to pick up a shuttle here or there, your best bet for travel around the area is by car. If you have a four-wheel-drive vehicle, that's even better as adverse weather can transform many of the roads in southeast Ohio into complete washouts. In winter, roads can ice over and become hazardous very quickly regardless of the vehicle you're driving.

Most of U.S. 33, running south from Columbus, is a four-lane divided highway. This is also the route to follow if you're driving from Cleveland, although you could opt to take the scenic route through rural Ohio by getting on St. Rte. 13 in Mansfield, heading south to Lancaster to pick up U.S. 33.

U.S. 50 runs through Athens west to Chillicothe and connects to routes to Cincinnati, including U.S. 35. U.S. 50 provides the same scenic pleasures as U.S. 33, although on a bit more intimate level—U.S. 50 is only a two-lane highway through much of southeastern Ohio, allowing a closer look at the flora and fauna but also making the route susceptible to flooding in spring and icing in winter. Posted speeds for both highways vary between 50 and 65 in accordance with Ohio State Highway regulations.

U.S. 33 is the main route you'll be using in Athens, as well as in Nelsonville. It may also be the best landmark to use in case you get turned around while driving to these locations, as it is the main route through the Athens district. Remember, you're not in a self-contained park shut off from the world when in you're in the forest; this is multi-use land surrounded by towns and privately owned land. Most of the sites included are within 25 mi of Athens, although here that may mean 45 to 50 minutes of driving time. Remember to pick up a map either at your place of lodging or the National Forest Headquarters before tackling the area.

Visitor Information

CONTACTS **Athens Area Chamber of Commerce** > 5 N. Court St., Athens 45701, tel. 740/594–2251, www.athenschamber.com. **Athens County Convention and Visitors Bureau** > 667 E. State St., Athens 45701, tel. 800/878–9767 or 740/592–1819.

Hocking Hills

Logan is about 50 mi south of Columbus, 140 mi northeast of Cincinnati, and 210 mi south of Cleveland

15

By Nicki Chodnoff

THE HISTORY OF THE HOCKING HILLS is in its rocks. Glaciers flattened much of the rest of Ohio, but not the Hocking Hills. The area is filled with rock formations, waterfalls, caves, and deep woods that more closely resemble the mountains of neighboring West Virginia than flat Ohio farmland. The glaciers changed Ohio's climate, even in places they hadn't reached, to a cool, moist environment. When the glaciers retreated, the deep gorges of Hocking County retained towering eastern hemlock, Canada yew, and yellow-and-black birch from the cool period 10,000 years ago. Hocking County's Blackhand sandstone cliffs and bedrock are more than 350 million years old, from a time rivers flowed into a shallow sea that covered Ohio. Millions of years of uplift and stream erosion created the spectacular cliffs and waterfalls weekenders enjoy today.

Ancient people from the Adena culture roamed the hollows and caves of this region more than 7,000 years ago, perhaps attracted by plentiful buffalo, elk, deer, wild turkey, and small game. Later pioneers were drawn by the rich, fertile farmland in addition to the plentiful game.

Much of what happens in the Hocking Hills takes place between Lancaster and Nelsonville, with the quaint town of Logan nearly midway between the two. With its 19th-century town square and lots of shops, Logan is known as the gateway to the Hocking Hills. Founded by Thomas Worthington in 1816, one of the proponents of Ohio statehood, Logan was named for Mingo Chief James John Logan. Many artists and other creative types live in Logan because of the proximity to the natural beauty of the Hills. Their accessible unique shops and studios, detailed in an art trail, offer a chance to watch artisans work and then buy their wares.

Lancaster leads to the Hocking Hills for travelers heading south from Columbus and Cleveland. Colonel Ebenezer Zane, the famous merchant, trailblazer, and soldier, founded the town in 1800. He designed Lancaster on a grid with four public squares, three of them parks, much like William Penn's design for Philadelphia. Although the city grew steadily in its first three decades, it received a huge boost in 1836 with the construction of the Lancaster Lateral Canal, which connected to the Ohio & Erie canal at Lockbourne and continued south through Athens, Ohio. The wealth generated during this period can still be seen in Lancaster's many massive 19th-century homes, which are clustered around an area called Square 13. The Historic District covers more than 24 city blocks and is one the most significant in the Midwest. General William T. Sherman and eight Ohio governors are counted among Lancaster's famous sons.

Travelers venturing to the Hills from points west first happen upon quiet Nelsonville, which got its start when Daniel and Sarah Nelson of Massachusetts bought 200 acres here in 1814. Victorian-style homes still line the streets. A turn-of-the-20th-century fountain marks the center of town where restored buildings and shops line the public square including the historic Dew Hotel, from which presidents Taft, McKinley, Harding, and Roosevelt campaigned.

The Hocking Hills region's rich mineral resources allowed several industries to prosper. Coal led to a flourishing mine industry. Iron ore was extracted from the sandstone bedrock. During the Civil War, Ohio was the leading producer of iron ore used for implements and weapons. The state's Hanging Rock Iron Region, six counties that include Hocking County, had 46 furnaces.

Once the railroads, coal mines, and iron ore started dying out, the Hocking Hills fell into the hard-scrabble way of life that overtook much of Appalachia. Ignored for decades, in the 1970s and 1980s, city dwellers slowly discovered the natural beauty of the hills. A cabin here and an inn there, tucked along a county road bounded by pristine woods, became the escape people from the city sought. The rock formations, waterfalls, caves, woods, and deep gorges that attracted people over the centuries worked their magic again. Now the self-proclaimed "hot tub capital" of the Midwest offers weekenders just about everything they can want during a getaway: adventure, nature, hiking, boating, art, history, culture, isolation, scenic vistas, luxury, and pampering.

WHAT TO SEE & DO

Hocking Hills State Park Scattered in pieces over Hocking County, the 2,348-acre state park in the Hocking State Forest has gorges, a sandstone cave, cascading waterfalls, and unusual rock formations. More than 100 kinds of birds nest in the park, and most species of wildlife native to the Midwest can be seen here. The park, which is south and west of Logan, is a great place for challenging hikes.

In 1797, W. J. Conkle carved his name and the year into a tree in **Conkles Hollow** (Rte. 374), which bears his name to this day. Sheer cliffs of Blackhand sandstone rise nearly 200 feet above the valley floor. Countless hemlocks keep the deep gorge green even in winter. You can hike either around the top of the cliffs on the Rim Trail or in the gorge itself, which ends at a cave and waterfalls. It's 14 mi southwest of Logan.

The approach to **Ash Cave** (Rte. 56) is impressive, along a wooded gorge narrow enough to bring the shadow of claustrophobia to some. The 700-foot-wide, horseshoe-shaped cave opens suddenly before you. A 90-foot waterfall drops from the rock's top. Native Americans once sheltered in this 80-acre sandstone recess. The trailhead leading to Ash Cave from Rte. 56 is accessible for people in wheelchairs.

About 2 mi north of Ash Cave and 13 mi south of Logan is **Cedar Falls** (Rte. 374). Early explorers mistook the hemlock trees in the area for cedars. The Queer Creek drops over the back of the gorge in a cascading waterfall. A 3-mi trail connects it to Old Man's Cave.

After the Civil War, a hermit lived in **Old Man's Cave** (State Rte. 664); some say his ghost still haunts the cave. The area is distinguished by rock formations, two caves, waterfalls, and a wooded ravine. It's 12 mi southwest of Logan, and connected to Cedar Falls by a 3-mi path.

According to rumor, thieves, bootleggers, Native Americans, and early settlers once roosted in **Rock House** (Rte. 374), a tunnel-like eroded formation midway up a 150-foot cliff, 12 mi west of Logan. The seven "windows" as well as the columns support-

15

ing the "roof" of Rock House suggest human engineering rather than the environmental forces actually responsible for their creation.

It's a steep hike up the jutting rocks of **Cantwell Cliffs** (Rte. 374), but the view of the trees below, especially in fall, is breathtaking. Head for Lookout Point on the East Rim for some of the best views. > 20160 Rte. 664, Logan, tel. 740/385–6841, www.ohiostateparks.org. Free. Daily dawn–dusk.

Hocking Hills Welcome Center Pick up maps and brochures and get directions and help with lodging from travel counselors. Special interest packets on weddings, garden tours, bicycling, hunting, and other activities are offered as is a video about the Hocking Hills. A **Visitor's Center** (16197 Pike St., Laurelville, tel. 740/332–6955, Mon.–Sat. 9–5, Sun. 11–5) was opened in 2003 on the other side of Hocking County in Laurelville; the center provides the same walk-in services as the Welcome Center. > 13178 St. Rte. 664, Logan, tel. 800/462–5464 or 740/385–9706, www.1800hocking.com. Mon.–Sat. 9–5, Sun. 11–5.

Lake Logan State Park Named for one of the best fishing lakes in the state, the park sits on an unglaciated plateau. Along with a swimming beach on the north shore, there's a 1-mi hiking trail that circles a hilltop, perfect for observing wildlife such as great blue heron, wild turkey, or a white-tailed deer. A ½-mi hiking trail winds through woodlands and lakeshore and a section of the Buckeye Trail runs through the park toward Hocking Hills State Forest. > 30443 Lake Logan Rd., Logan, tel. 740/385–6842, www.ohiostateparks.org. Free. Daily dawn–dusk.

WHAT'S NEARBY

Decorative Arts Center of Ohio One of Ohio's most beautiful Greek revival mansions, the 1835 Reese Peters house, is the core of this complex in the downtown historic district of Lancaster. The mansion showcases historic and contemporary decorative arts: furniture, textiles, glass, silver, and ceramics. Classes, lectures, seminars, and workshops are held at the house and the center's two other buildings: the Saylor House and the Wendel Art Center, known as the "Art Garage." The center also features contemporary work by artists who use the traditional decorative arts media. > 145 E. Main St., Lancaster, tel. 740/681–1423, www.decartsohio.org/. Free. Tues.–Sun. 1–4.

Georgian Museum This 1830 house, which once welcomed Henry Clay, Daniel Webster, and DeWitt Clinton, was once slated for demolition. It was restored, however, and today it's the cornerstone of the Square 13 neighborhood. Furnishings are authentic to the period and include Ohio cabinets, a large doll furniture display and handblown Erickson glass. Some original pieces, including a silver tea set, have "come home," donated by descendants of the Maccracken family, the original owners. > 105 E. Wheeling St., Lancaster, tel. 740/654–9923, www.fairfieldheritage.org. $4. Apr.–mid-Dec., Tues.–Sun. 1–4. By appointment other times.

Hocking County Historical Society Museum Spread among five buildings, archives, records, and artifacts show what life was like in the Hocking County of the past. Second floor exhibits display train equipment, pharmacy implements, dolls, and military uniforms, including one from the Civil War. The Lutz steam auto, invented and built in 1898 by local inventor Henry Lutz, who only had 23 days of formal schooling, is the museum's prize possession. Lutz' other inventions and workshop tools are also on display. > 52 N. Culver St., Logan, tel. 740/385–6026 or 740/385–2708. $2 or donation. May–Oct., Sat. noon–4. By appointment other times.

Rockbridge Nature Preserve The natural arch or bridge, considered the largest in the state, is more than 100 feet long and 10 to 20 feet wide, and it gracefully arches 50 feet across a ravine. The secluded 202-acre preserve's 3-mi main trail leads to the arch and ends at the Hocking River. The trail passes elderberry groves, pawpaw trees, a scenic hilltop field, and then follows near a winding stream that plunges 50 feet to the ravine below the arch. The preserve is rich in wildflowers and a favorite haunt of bird-watchers. > Dalton Rd., Township Rd. 503, Logan. Free. Daily dawn–dusk.

Sherman House Brothers William Tecumseh Sherman and Senator John Sherman were born in this frame-and-brick house, a Registered National Landmark. The study once used by Judge Charles Sherman, father of William Tecumseh and John, and the Sherman family parlor are preserved. The second floor houses a re-creation of General Sherman's field tent, Civil War exhibits, Sherman family memorabilia, and the family album quilt. > 137 E. Main St., Lancaster, tel. 740/687–5891, www.fairfieldheritage.org/shermanhouse. $4. Apr.–mid-Dec., Tues.–Sun. 1–4. By appointment other times.

Wahkeena Nature Preserve Wahkeena means "most beautiful," and this 150-acre preserve offers a place to study nature and learn outdoors. Flora includes tulip trees, oaks, great rhododendron, mountain laurel, about 26 types of ferns, eight native orchids including the showy orchid, and pink lady's slipper. More than 69 species of birds and 15 species of mammals have been observed. Two trails are available for hiking. > 2200 Pump Station Rd., Sugar Grove, tel. 800/297–1883 or 740/746–8695. $2 per car. Apr.–Oct., Wed.–Sun. 8–4:30; Nov.–Mar. by appointment.

Tours

Hocking Valley Scenic Railway Catch the train at the Nelsonville depot, 12 mi southeast of Logan. The locomotive chugs through Wayne National Forest and the surrounding areas as guides recount the local history. Each weekend from Memorial Day through November, the noon train to Haydenville travels 14 mi round-trip, and the 2:30 train travels 22-mi round-trip to Logan. Trains stop at Robbins Crossings, a re-created settlers' village from the 1860s. During the first three weekends of December, you can take the special Santa Train to Logan. > 33 E. Canal St., Nelsonville, tel. 800/967–7834 or 740/753–9531. $10–$14. Memorial Day–Nov., weekends.

Sports

CANOEING

Hocking Valley Canoe Livery & Fun Center Paddle the Hocking River in a canoe, kayak, raft, or tube on trips that last from 2 hours to 3 days. Even beginners can enjoy a leisurely float trip and pass natural rock formations, plants, and wildlife. Monthly full-moon canoe trips appeal to the romantically inclined. Excursions include equipment rental, transportation to the river, and use of the picnic area and shelter house. The fun center has a minigolf course, go-carts, driving range, game room, volleyball, soccer, and a bungee trampoline. > 31251 Chieftain Dr., Logan, tel. 800/686–0386 or 740/385–8685, www.hockinghillscanoeing.com.

HIKING

Conkle's Hollow One of the deepest gorges in the state of Ohio, Conkle's Hollow is so deep and the foliage so thick that sunlight never reaches parts of the valley floor. But the real gem here is the upper rim trail, one of the most visually breathtaking and dangerous hikes in the state. The cliffs here are the highest in Southeast Ohio. > Big Pine Road, off Rte. 374. Hocking Hills State Park, 20160 Rte. 664, Logan, tel. 740/385–6841, www.ohiostateparks.org.

Grandma Gatewood Trail Given the natural beauty to be found at Old Man's Cave, Ash Cave, and Cedar Falls, why not hike the trail through Hocking Hills State Park that connects all three? The trail is either 6 mi (one way) or 12 (round trip), taking between three and six hours to hike. Old Man's Cave and Ash Cave are the two end points. > Old Man's Cave, State Rte. 664 south of Logan. Hocking Hills State Park, 20160 Rte. 664, Logan, tel. 740/385–6841, www.ohiostateparks.org.

HORSEBACK RIDING

Spotted Horse Ranch Enjoy the beauty of each season on a guided horseback trail ride, offered daily by reservation on this working farm. Supervised rides in a corral aboard gentle horses taught to walk—not trot or gallop—suit the young or inexperienced rider. Children must be at least 8 years old to ride. Advanced riders can bring their own horses and enjoy 500 acres of quiet trails for a small fee. > 17325 Deffenbaugh Rd., Laurelville, tel. 877/992–7433 or 740/332–7433, www.thespottedhorseranch.com.

MULE RIDES

Mountain Man Mule Expeditions Take trail rides by the hour on the Hocking Hills paths around Ash Cave, Old Man's Cave, and Cedar Falls. Sure-footed mules are the transportation of choice for owner Ken Wells who says mules are more durable and calm than horses. For a tamer trip and slower pace, take the 25-minute mule carriage ride to Ash Cave. > 23113 S.R. 374, at St. Rte. 56, Logan, tel. 740/332–0662.

Shopping

Artisan Mall Dulcimers, memorabilia, crafts, furniture, gifts, souvenirs, antiques, and collectibles fill the largest craft-and-antiques mall in the region. Art abounds, starting with the antique tools and gadgets hanging on the clapboard walls under the beamed porch. When you need a break, sit in a handcrafted swing or rocking chair or enjoy desserts, sandwiches, and soup at LJ's Coffee Shop. > 703 W. Hunter St., Logan, tel. 740/385–1118, www.artisanmall.com.

Garden Accents Factory Outlet Garden and landscape ceramics, hardened for northern winters, are produced by Logan Clay Products. Many pieces started out as sewer pipes, flue liners, and chimney tops but were turned into planters and accessories such as birdbaths and stepping stones. > Rte. 33 and St. Rte. 93, Logan, tel. 740/385–2184 or 800/848–2141, www.garden-accents.com/. Closed Nov.–May.

Hocking Hills Craft Mall Across the parking lot from the Logan Antique Mall, this mall displays the works of more than 200 crafters. All forms of popular crafts are available, including concrete geese and clothing for concrete geese, pottery, candles, dolls, and ceramics. > 12801 St. Rte. 664 S, Logan, tel. 740/385–9039.

Hocking House The area's best-known artist, Jean Magdich, makes and sells her porcelainware and other ceramic pieces in this 1850s house. Prices on seconds (with only minor, sometimes unnoticeable flaws) can be as much as half off the regular price. > Rte. 664 and Big Pine Rd., tel. 740/385–4166, www.hockinghouse.com. Closed Mon. Closed Sept.–May weekdays.

Logan Antique Mall More than 100 dealers operate in this 10,000-square-foot mall. There's a large selection of antiques and collectibles including Depression glass, tools, furniture, primitives, and pottery. You can research unfamiliar pieces at a small antiques reference library on site. > 12795 St. Rte. 664, Logan, tel. 740/385–2061, www.loganantiquemall.com.

Rocky Shoes and Boots Outlet & Clearance Center This factory outlet store sells Rocky rugged outdoor, casual, and work footwear plus gear at a savings. In the adjacent factory, you'll find the clearance center and a taxidermy shop. > Rte. 33, Nelsonville, tel. 740/753–3130, www.rockyboots.com/outlet.

Spring Street Antique Mall Near Hocking Hills State Park, more than 60 dealers in a 10,000-square-foot mall offer pottery, art and Depression glass, collectibles, primitives, furniture, and a large selection of tools. > 55 S. Spring St., Logan, tel. 740/385–1816.

Save the Date

JANUARY
Winter Hike More than 5,000 hikers show up on the third Saturday in January to walk the 6 mi from Old Man's Cave to Ash Cave and to see the forest covered in snow and ice. A shuttle bus returns hikers to Old Man's Cave. This is the biggest event of the year in Hocking Hills. > Tel. 740/385–6841.

FEBRUARY
Sweethearts Hike Take your sweetheart for a romantic stroll to Ash Cave in the soft light of dusk. Afterward, enjoy cookies and hot chocolate around the fire at Ash Cave. It's sponsored by the Hocking Hills State Park. > Tel. 740/385–6841.

MARCH
Maple Sugaring in the Hills Discover the many methods used throughout history to make this sweet treat as they boil down local sap. Try the free samples. > Tel. 740/385–6841.

JUNE
International Washboard Festival Renowned washboard musicians play the ridged instrument produced by the nation's only remaining washboard manufacturer. A welcoming parade with classic cars, antique tractors, and visiting musicians opens the 3-day street fair. > Logan, tel. 740/380–3828, www.columbuswashboard.com.

JULY
Lancaster Festival Events are held in all corners of Lancaster during this festival. A bevy of performances includes chamber music, café concerts with guest artists, and free bandstand shows. There's also a Composer in Residence, whose works are performed throughout the celebration. Special programs, such as the Young People's Concerts and the Children's Art Fair, expose children to music and art. > Lancaster, tel. 800/526–3377 operates only during the festival, 740/687–4808, www.lanfest.org.
Lilyfest The 3-day celebration of gardening, music, and artistry includes touring gardens on a private estate. Master gardeners are on hand to offer their expertise. Musicians perform all three days and more than 40 fine artists display original works. > 13200 Cola Rd., Rockbridge, tel. 740/969–2873, www.lilyfest.com.

AUGUST
Star Seekers Shower Search Bring a blanket and spend a night under the stars. Watch the Perseid meteor shower and explore the planets, comets, and other mysteries of the night sky. > Conkle's Hollow, tel. 740/385–6841.

SEPTEMBER
Hocking Hills Indian Run Run a 5K, 10K, 20K, or 60K race on trails through the vast wooded areas of Hocking Hills State Park and Hocking State Forest. Deep gorges, waterfalls, and lush forests inspire runners to finish the race. > Tel. 740/385–2750, www.1800hocking.com.

OCTOBER
Halloween Campout Little ghosts and goblins can trick-or-treat around the Old Man's Cave campsite. Holiday activities include a hayride, pumpkin decorating, cookout, night hike, and costume and campsite judging. > Tel. 740/385–6841.

WHERE TO STAY

AmeriHost Inn Just off Route 33 in the heart of the hills, the one-story motel is close to the state park and to downtown. Part of the Rempel's Grove complex, the motel is in walking distance of a restaurant, canoe livery, antique and crafts malls, and minigolf. Remodeled in 2003, select rooms and the lobby offer wireless Internet access. > 12819 Rte. 664, Logan 43138, tel. 740/385–1700 or 800/459–4678, fax 740/385–9288, www.amerihostinn.com. 54 rooms, 4 suites. Restaurant, in-room data ports, in-room safes, cable TV, indoor pool, hot tub, no-smoking rooms. AE, D, MC, V. CP. $–$$

Crockett's Run On 70 secluded acres near Rockbridge Nature Preserve and Lake Logan, the lodges and cabins of Crockett's Run have views through the picture windows of forested ravines and streams. You can get a dose of nature without sacrificing amenities as all lodges and cabins have kitchens equipped with appliances including refrigerators, TVs, VCRs, stereo systems with CD players, hot tubs, and wood-burning fireplaces (except one cabin). > 9816 Bauer Rd., Logan 43138, tel. 800/472–8115, www.crockettsrun.com. 3 lodges with 4 or 5 bedrooms, 4 cabins with 2 or 3 bedrooms. Kitchens, microwaves, refrigerators, in-room VCRs, pond, hot tubs, billiards, hiking, Ping-Pong, volleyball; no smoking. MC, V. $$–$$$$

Georgian Manner Perched on a hill overlooking Lake Logan, the farm house from the early 1840s was turned into a white pillared Georgian, which looks like a off-shoot of Tara. A stark contrast to the rustic and woodsy cabins and inns in the region, the elegant inn is filled with antiques and collectibles from around the world. All rooms have lake views. The Robert E. Lee and Stonewall Jackson rooms are distinctly masculine in design. The four upstairs rooms share the two bathrooms. The most popular space, the suite, offers a garden-size whirlpool tub. To keep that getaway feeling, rooms have no phones or TVs. A phone for emergencies is near the kitchen and a TV is in the library. Children are welcome but might get bored. > 29055 Evans Rd., Logan 43138, tel. 800/606–1840 or 740/380–9567, fax 740/385–9710, www.georgianmanner.com. 4 rooms, 1 suite. Some in-room hot tubs; no room phones, no room TVs, no smoking. MC, V. $$–$$$

Glenlaurel One of the most romantic places in Hocking Hills, this Scottish country inn on a secluded and heavily wooded 140-acre tract has walking trails, rock cliffs, and waterfalls. The stone-and-stucco manor house, crofts, and cottages overlook Camusfearna Gorge or a ravine. Crofts and cottages have fireplaces, screened porches, a hot tub on a private deck, or a private garden. Glenlaurel emphasizes its "relax and unwind" philosophy, so leave the children and pets home. > 14940 Mt. Olive Rd., Rockbridge 43149, tel. 747/385–4070 or 800/809–7378, www.glenlaurel.com. 4 rooms, 3 suites, 6 cabins. Dining room, some in-room hot tubs, some kitchenettes, some microwaves, some refrigerators, hiking, pub; no kids, no smoking. AE, D, MC, V. BP. $$$–$$$$

Inn at Cedar Falls You can stay in the lodge, a refurbished barn with rooms that are furnished with primitive antiques, or in one of the 19th-century cabins, which sleep up to four. Each cabin was moved from other parts of the country and decorated with antiques picked personally by the innkeeper. Homemade granola is always served; other breakfast fare includes omelets, French toast, and crepes. > 21190 Rte. 374, Logan 43138, tel. 740/385–7489 or 800/653–2557, fax 740/385–0820, www.innatcedarfalls.com. 8 rooms, 5 cabins. Dining room, some kitchenettes, some in-room hot tubs, some pets allowed; no room phones, no room TVs, no smoking. AE, D, MC, V. BP. $–$$

Old Man's Cave Chalets These lodges, cabins, and suites, 11 mi south of Logan, are tucked in the woods and have private porches, hot tubs, and full kitchens. Some have fireplaces. They range from two-person A-frame cottages to large lodges that can sleep up to 20 people or more. > 18905 Rte. 664 S, Logan 43138, tel. 747/385–6517 or 800/762–9396, www.oldmanscavechalets.com. 30 cabins, 4 lodges. Kitchenettes, microwaves, refrigerators, in-room hot tubs, cable TV, in-room VCRs, pool, tennis courts, some pets allowed; no smoking. AE, D, MC, V. $$$–$$$$

Ravenwood Castle Medieval England is re-created atop a high hill reached by a private road through 50 acres of forest and large rock formations 5 mi from the Hocking Hills. A "drawbridge" leads to the front door of the 12th-century Norman castle, and rooms are in the crenelated towers. All rooms offer a fireplace, balcony, or deck. Some, like the pink silversmith's cottage, offer all three. Breakfast for overnight guests is served in the great hall with a stone fireplace and large stained-glass windows. A village of cottages surrounds woodland gardens and Celtic cottages are in a meadow by a stream. Nineteenth-century Gypsy wagons, with a "path to the bath," otherwise known as a shower house with toilets, offer a different dimension in camping. Children are welcome and may be quite enchanted by staying in a castle. > 65666 Bethel Rd., New Plymouth 45654, tel. 747/596–2606 or 800/477–1541, www.ravenwoodcastle.com. 4 rooms, 3 suites, 6 cabins. Dining room, tea shop, hot tub, shop; no room phones, no smoking. AE, D, MC, V. $$–$$$$

Shaw's Inn On a tree-shaded street in the historic district near Zane's Square, the inn is in the heart of what to do and see in town. The 10 suites with in-room whirlpool tubs and VCRs are the most popular rooms. Each room has a different theme, including Napa Valley, Santa Fe, and Provence. Midweek getaway specials reduce the price and increase the chance of staying in a suite. > 123 N. Broad St., Lancaster 43130, tel. 800/654–2477 or 740/654–1842, fax 740/654–7033, www.shawsinn.com. 16 rooms, 10 suites. Restaurant, room service, some in-room hot tubs, cable TV, bar, no-smoking rooms. MC, V. BP. $–$$$

Steep Woods Railroad Caboose About 4 mi from Ash Cave, this renovated authentic railroad caboose from the Seaboard Coastal Line is a favorite with kids. The air-conditioned and heated caboose sleeps five in bunk beds and twin beds and is decorated with railroad memorabilia. Surrounded by woods in a campgroundlike setting, the caboose is outfitted with an inside bathroom but has no TV or telephone. In an emergency, you can use the phone in the owner's home. > 24830 St. Rte. 56, S. Bloomingville 43152-9763, tel. 800/900–2954 or 740/332–6084, www.hockinghills.com/steepwoods. 1 caboose. Kitchen, microwave, picnic area; no room phone, no room TV, no smoking. MC, V. ¢–$

CAMPING

Lake Logan Campground The privately owned campground has a choice location ¼ mi from Lake Logan. The mostly wooded 5 acres of campgrounds offer level lots with lots of privacy. Children are drawn to the 42-inch deep swimming pool. Campers can borrow equipment for a game of horse shoes or badminton. > 28920 Lake Logan Rd., Logan 43138, tel. 740/385–2630, fax 740/385–8028, www.geocities.com/lakelogancampgrounds. 58 partial hook-ups, 2 tent sites. Flush toilets, partial hook-ups (electric and water), dump stations, laundry facilities, showers, fire rings, picnic tables, general store, playground, pool. Reservations essential. MC, V. Nov 1.–Apr 15. ¢

Old Man's Cave Family Campground Campsites hug a wooded ridge in scenic Hocking Hills State Park. It's first-come, first-served, except for the camper cabins and tent-only group camps that can accommodate 100 people. The seasonal dining lodge contains a restaurant, meeting rooms, TV lounge, game room, and snack bar. Within the lodge is the park office, which is open year-round. Pet lovers can bring two domestic pets per site at certain sites. Camper cabins, equipped with basic camping needs, are available May through October. > 20160 St. Rte. 664 S, Logan 43138, tel. 740/385–6165, www.hockinghillspark.com. 159 partial hook-ups, 30 tent sites; 3 camper cabins. Flush toilets, partial hook-ups (electric), dump station, laundry facilities, showers, restaurant, snack bar, ranger station, 2 playgrounds, pool. ¢

WHERE TO EAT

Etta's Lunch Box Cafe A corner within Etta's General Store, the café sells pizza, sandwiches, and homemade desserts. You can include nearly anything in the "Pizza in a Poke," the country version of a calzone and a house specialty. For collectors, the meal takes a back-seat to the 400-plus lunch boxes perched around the café. Owner LaDora Ousley's collection includes rare vinyl Barbie models and 1900s metal lunch pails. > 35960 St. Rte. 56, New Plymouth, tel. 740/380–0736. MC, V. ¢–$$

Great Expectations Cafe and Espresso Bar This small café is tucked in a side room of a renovated Victorian house that's also a bookstore, gift shop and art gallery. For lunch, dinner, or a snack, panini-grilled sandwiches, daily specials, salads, and desserts are the main fare. When weather permits, meals can be enjoyed outdoors on the terrace. > 179 S. Market St., Logan, tel. 740/380–9177. MC, V. No dinner. ¢

Inn at Cedar Falls The chef cooks up lavish meals using fresh vegetables and herbs grown in the inn's garden. The menu rarely repeats itself, but typical entrées include pork tenderloin with bordelaise sauce, beef medallions, and herb chicken breast. Call ahead for reservations as early as possible if you're not staying at the inn. Dinners are prix fixe and two choices are provided per meal. > 21190 Rte. 374, Logan, tel. 740/385–7489 or 800/653–2557. Reservations essential. AE, D, MC, V. $$$–$$$$

Jack's Steakhouse Get three-squares a day at this local favorite where breakfast is served all day. T-bones and rib eyes are the specialty, both served with oversize baked or mashed potatoes. Sunday through Wednesday, the dinner special lets you buy one steak dinner and pay half price for the other. Thursday's special is a porterhouse or sirloin dinner for $9.95. > 35770 Hocking Dr., Logan, tel. 740/385–9909, www.jacks-steakhouse.com. MC, V. $–$$

Ravenwood Castle Experience medieval England while dining in the Great Hall with baronial stone fireplace and stained-glass windows. Rub elbows with the other diners, be they overnight guests or meal drop-ins, at the large family-style tables. Entrées, some served as a buffet, have an old English flair. Lunch is served in the Coach House Tea Room. > 65666 Bethel Rd., New Plymouth, tel. 800/477–1541 or 740/596–2606, www.ravenwoodcastle.com. Reservations essential. MC, V. $$–$$$$

Shaw's Restaurant The popular spot for white tablecloth dining serves American cuisine with regional and international specials. Locals appreciate the daily menu changes, but count on always finding filet mignon, New York strip steak, fillet of sole, and the restaurant's signature dish, the 1-pound double-cut smoked pork chop, on the menu. The 150-choice wine list can satisfy picky wine lovers. > 123 N. Broad St., Lancaster, tel. 800/654–2477 or 740/654–1842, www.shawinns.com. MC, V. $–$$$$

ESSENTIALS

Getting Here

BY CAR

The Hocking Hills region is a driver's destination because no public transportation travels between Ohio cities and this area. From points north, the main artery into the hills is U.S. 33, a well-paved divided highway that turns into a two-lane about 4 mi west of Nelsonville. From Cincinnati, the most direct route is U.S. 32 to U.S. 33. Both roads are well-paved divided highways except for a stretch on U.S. 33 west of Nelsonville. Driving around the hills and hollows can be part of the getaway's adventure and entertainment. Smaller, scenic county and state roads can twist, turn and undulate as much as a roller coaster. The two-lane roads get more of a work-out during the weekend when most people visit. Add in extra drive time because 5 mi along twisty, turny roads takes a lot longer to drive than 5 mi on interstate straightaways. Slow-moving campers and trucks can extend your drive time on the two-lane roads, where passing is not allowed.

Visitor Information

INFORMATION **Hocking Hills Tourism Association** > 13178 St. Rte. 664, Logan 43138, tel. 800/462–5464 or 740/385–9706, www.1800hocking.com.

The Ross County Area

Chillicothe is 46 mi south of Columbus, 85 mi northeast of Cincinnati, 188 mi southwest of Cleveland.

16

By Nicki Chodnoff

ONLY A FEW MILES FROM the whizzing automobiles of Cincinnati and Columbus, Ross County is the gateway to the wild side of Ohio. Much of Ross and surrounding counties is filled with green mountains and deep forests rather than hordes of people and bustling cities. Here, busy highways give way to beautiful and remote country roads.

Thousands of years ago, the Wisconsin Glacier pushed through Ross County leaving the northern part flat and the southern section hilly. At one time, glaciers 8,000 feet thick and weighing millions of tons covered much of the land. After the glaciers receded, the rich land and abundant wildlife attracted the prehistoric indigenous people. There is evidence dating back nearly 12,000 years that they settled here.

Following the Ice Age, before there was a state of Ohio and before the historic tribes arrived, this corner of the world was inhabited by ancient mound builders. Among the more famous mound builder cultures were the Adena, Hopewell, and Fort Ancient peoples. The mound builders' highly advanced civilizations built miles of burial mounds, forts, and other earthworks throughout the region. Many of their massive projects still delight and bewilder today and are a compelling reason to visit Ross County. According to the Ohio Historical Society, Ohio probably has the greatest concentration of earthwork sites in the nation. Some of the largest, finest, and most mysterious prehistoric mound sites are found in and around Ross County. Like trying to figure out what a dinosaur looked like by analyzing its fossilized bones, historians and archaeologists try to explain what life was like for the prehistoric tribes by excavating and studying their mounds, earthworks, and the implements of daily life. The mystery continues as the fate of the mound builders is not known. Some archaeologists believe the mound builders are the ancestors of Native Americans living in the regions of the mounds when Europeans arrived on this continent. Another theory contends that the mound builders were not assimilated by the native people that followed but that they moved on following game.

When the early white settlers arrived in Ross County, they encountered historic Native American tribes including the Delaware, Miami, Shawnee, and Wyandot or Huron. The last and most famous of the tribes to settle here was the Shawnee. White settlers looking for places to build homes came in regular contact with the Shawnee. Hoping to put an end to this settlement, the Shawnee backed the British during the American Revolution.

The Shawnee strategy backfired and their alliance with the British spurred the arrival of more white settlers. Ross County was part of a grant given to Virginia military veterans, mostly sergeants and corporals, who served during the Revolutionary War. In 1796 troops led by General Anthony Wayne defeated the Native Americans from the Shawnee, Miami, Delaware, Ottawa, and Ojibwa tribes at the battle of Fallen Timbers and forced them to sign the Treaty of Greenville, opening Ohio for settlement.

Tecumseh, one of the greatest Shawnee statesmen and leaders, tried in the late 1700s to unite many tribes to protect his homeland against the influx of white settlers. Each summer the great warrior's life and struggles come to life at the outdoor drama *Tecumseh!* The story line is so interesting and sitting under the stars is so appealing that the outdoor drama has been drawing an audience for more than 30 years.

The countryside of modern-day Ross County is both cultivated and wild. Where there aren't large tracts of fertile farms planted with row upon row of corn or soybeans, the county is a haven for lovers of the outdoors and nature. Within its borders, the county offers four state parks, which may be a record for Ohio, plus two state forests and several wildlife areas. Four more state parks and two state forests are less than 15 mi from the county's borders.

Chillicothe, the county seat, is a hub of history, ancient and modern. About the time the Parthenon was built in Athens, Greece, the Hopewell settlements were thriving in the area. The Mound City Group protects and preserves some of the mounds left behind by their civilization.

In 1796 Nathaniel Massie founded Chillicothe, a name derived from the Shawnee word meaning "principal town or gathering place." The following year, Massie offered free lots to the first 100 settlers. The lots went quickly, and the town grew and prospered. The U.S. Congress designated Chillicothe as capital of the "eastern section" of the Northwest Territory in 1800. Two years later, Chillicothe was the site of the State Constitutional Convention. In 1803, when Ohio entered the Union as the 17th state, Chillicothe became the first state capital. Four native sons in the 1800s became governors of Ohio.

The construction of the Ohio and the Erie Canals in 1831 made Chillicothe a major canal port and offered Ross County farmers a way to get their crops to market. The canal system combined with the construction of the Marietta and Cincinnati Railroad attracted many new settlers from Pennsylvania, Delaware, and Maryland. The canals and railroads brought wealth to the town, even after the state capital moved to Columbus.

Today, Chillicothe draws its charm from the old structures that serve as a glimpse into the town's history. The downtown historic area preserves lovely federal and Victorian homes on quiet tree-lined streets. A multipurpose community resource with a lake near where the canal once flowed, downtown Yoctangee Park is Chillicothe's equivalent of Central Park.

WHAT TO SEE & DO

CHILLICOTHE

Adena State Memorial Built in 1807, and refurbished for the state bicentennial in 2003, the 20-room Georgian mansion was the home of one of Ohio's early governors, Thomas Worthington. Adena's many antiques are from the time when the Worthington family lived there, 1807 to 1839, and include many original Worthington family furnishings. It was built by Benjamin Latrobe, who went on to oversee the rebuilding of the Capitol in Washington, D.C., after it burned in 1812. The education center demonstrates Ohio's path of statehood. Five outbuildings and formal gardens are on 300 remaining acres of the original homestead. Looking from the north lawn of the mansion, you can see the Scioto River valley and the Logan hills pictured on the state seal. > Adena Rd., Chillicothe, tel. 740/772–1500 or 800/319–7248. $6. Mar.–Labor Day, Wed.–Sat. 9:30–5, Sun. noon–5; Labor Day–Oct., Sat. 9:30–5, Sun. noon–5.

Great Seal State Park The ridges and peaks of this park inspired the scene for "The Great Seal of the State of Ohio." About 5 mi northeast of Chillicothe, the 1,862-acre park has a disc golf course, 5 mi of hiking trails, and 20 mi of bridle trails. From the higher elevations on the hiking and bridle trails, on a very clear day you can see Columbus to the north and unbroken forested ridges of the Appalachians' rugged foothills to the south. A nearby 900-acre wildlife area helps preserve the park's wilderness spirit. Challenging trails take you to scenic vistas and the Scioto Valley below. The Sugarloaf Mountain Trail rises almost 500 feet in less than a quarter mile and several sections of the forested Shawnee Ridge and Mount Ives trails are also steep. > 635 Rocky Rd., Chillicothe, tel. 740/663–2125. Free. Daily.

Hopewell Culture National Historical Park Operated by the National Park Service, the Mound City Group monument protects 23 prehistoric burial mounds, some reconstructed, within 15 acres ringed by a wall. Thought to be a ceremonial center, Mound City, where some mounds pre-date the Roman Empire, was erected by the Hopewell, who lived in this area from about 200 BC to AD 500. Start with the 15-minute orientation film and exhibits in the museum at the visitor center. It's 3 mi north of Chillicothe. > 16062 Rte. 104, Chillicothe, tel. 740/774–1126, www.nps.gov/hocu. $2. Grounds: daily dawn–dusk. Visitor center: 8:30–5; extended summer hrs.

James M. Thomas Telecommunication Museum James M. Thomas, one of the founders of the Chillicothe telephone company, went on to start telephone companies in Cleveland and New York. This three-room museum in the phone company's in-town building displays items such as telephone instruments, early local phone directories, and wooden underground conduits, all dating back to 1895. > 68 E. Main St., Chillicothe, tel. 740/772–8200, www.horizontel.com. Free. Weekdays 8:30–4:30.

Lucy Hayes Heritage Center This restored 1831 home is the birthplace of Lucy Webb Hayes, wife of the 19th president, Rutherford B. Hayes. Exhibits recount her life events. "Lemonade Lucy," the title bestowed on her because she wouldn't serve alcohol in the White House, was the first president's wife referred to as a first lady. > 90 W. 6th St., Chillicothe, tel. 740/775–6468. $2. Apr.–Oct., Fri. and Sat. 1–4; other times by appointment.

Pump House Center for the Arts The Pump House and Water Works was built in 1882 as the water source to fight fires. City ordinance required that it be "rather fanciful in architecture so as to be ornamental to the park." In the mid-1980s the house was saved from the wrecking ball, restored, and transformed into an art gallery and community art center with a gift gallery promoting local artwork and designer crafts. > Enderlin Circle in Yoctangee Park, Chillicothe, tel. 740/772–5783, www.chillicotheohio.com/pumphouse. Free, donation suggested. Tues.–Fri. 11–4, weekends 1–4.

Ross County Heritage Center In a federal-style home, exhibits recall the mound builders, early Chillicothe and Ohio, the Civil War, and World War I. There are a Conestoga Wagon and hands-on exhibits for children. The tour includes a visit to the adjacent Knoles Log House, a pioneer home from the early 1800s. A Greek Revival–style home, connected to the museum by the Heritage Hall exhibition lobby, houses the museum's extensive library. Completed in 2003, Heritage Hall displays horse-drawn and horse-power vehicles including a 1906 Logan auto manufactured in Chillicothe.

The Ross County Historical Society also operates **Franklin House** (80 S. Paint St.), a turn-of-the-century prairie-style building on the next street north of the Heritage Center. Viewed as part of a guided tour, displays change yearly and are part of the Heritage Center's collections of 19th- and 20th-century textiles, clothing, furniture, and decorative arts. > 45 W. 5th St., Chillicothe, tel. 740/772–1936, www.rosscountyhistorical.org. $4 includes entry to Knoles Log House and Franklin House. Apr. 1–Dec. 31, Tues.–Sun. noon–5.

Scioto Trail State Park An undisturbed wooded refuge, this small, quiet park is in the beautiful 9,000-acre Scioto Trail State Forest south of Chillicothe. In the densely forested hill country of the Appalachian foothills bordering the Scioto River, the park's rugged ridge tops and wooded valleys support magnificent stands of oak and hickory and habitat for some of Ohio's most elusive wildlife. You can picnic, hike, fish, and camp here. There's a naturalist program in summer. > 144 Lake Rd., Chillicothe, tel. 740/663–2125, www.ohiostateparks.org. Free. Daily.

TECUMSEH! For more than 30 years, the outdoor historical drama based on the life of famed Shawnee chief Tecumseh has entertained more than 2 million people. Performances are held at Sugarloaf Mountain Amphitheatre, next to Great Seal State Park, about 5 mi northeast of Chillicothe. The audience is surrounded on three sides by eight stages that blend into the forested slopes. Battle scenes add to the reality with artillery shells exploding and gunfire crackling. An hour-long behind-the-scenes tour starts at 4 and costs $3.50. The $7.50 all-you-can-eat buffet dinner is served on the terrace until 7:30. > Delano Rd., Chillicothe, tel. 740/775–0700 or 866/775–0700, www.tecumsehdrama.com. Mon.–Thurs. $14; Fri. and Sat. $16. Closed Sept.–mid-June.

WHAT'S NEARBY

35 Raceway Park Micro and mini sprints, dwarf cars, and four-cylinder stock cars mix it up on the .2-mi dirt track, 12 mi northwest of Chillicothe. > U.S. 35 and County Rd. 87, Frankfort, tel. 740/998–2278, www.35raceway.com. $10. Apr.–Sept., Sat. gates open at 3, racing starts at 6:30.

Dr. John Harris Dental Museum The American Dental Association calls this museum the cradle of dentistry. Dr. John Harris founded the first dental school in the United States in Bainbridge, 20 mi southwest of Chillicothe, in 1827. The house where Dr. Harris taught students and treated patients includes displays of old dental instruments, dental offices of several eras, false teeth, toothbrushes, and related paraphernalia. > 208 W. Main St., Bainbridge, tel. 740/634–2246, www.bainbridgedentalmuseum.com. $2. June–Aug., Tues.–Sun. noon–4; Apr., May, Sept., and Oct., weekends noon–4.

Fort Hill State Memorial The Hopewell earthworks, in the 1,200-acre forested archaeological park and nature preserve, covers nearly 40 acres. About 20 mi southwest of Chillicothe, this is one of the best-preserved earthworks in the state, although viewing is for the rough-and-tumble crowd as the elevation to the summit rises 400 feet. Atop the wooded mound's flat summit, an earthen wall 6 to 15 feet high and about 1⅝ mi long encloses what researches think is a ceremonial meeting place. The excellent and child-friendly museum combines photographs with artifacts to explain the area's natural history. A video on the mound builders focuses on the myths and

culture of the Hopewell. > 13614 Fort Hill Rd., Hillsboro, tel. 937/588–3221 or
800/283–8905, www.ohiohistory.org. Museum $3, free to hike and picnic. Park open
daily dawn–dusk. Museum Memorial Day–Labor Day, Wed.–Sat., 9:30–5, Sun.
noon–5; Sept. and Oct., weekends noon–5.

K-C Raceway The high banks of the ³⁄₈-mi dirt raceway, 15 mi south of Chillicothe,
make it one of the most exciting courses on the circuit for flat track motorcycle racing. > 2535 Blain Hwy., Waverly, tel. 740/289–4114, www.kc-raceway.com. $8.
May–Sept., Sat. gates open at 4:30, racing starts at 7:30.

Magic Waters Theater Family-appropriate live entertainment, including comedies,
musicals, children's theater, murder mysteries, magic shows, and concerts, is presented throughout the summer in the rustic outdoor amphitheater near the scenic
Paint Valley Gorge, 17 mi southwest of Chillicothe. Friday and Saturday performances
are at 8, showtime on Sunday is 7. > 7757 Cave Rd., Bainbridge, tel. 937/365–1388,
www.highland-ohio.com/magicwaters. $7. Closed Sept.–mid-June.

Paint Creek State Park At the edge of the Appalachian Plateau, a Y-shape 9,000-acre
lake is the source of water recreation at this 10,000-plus-acre state park, about 20 mi
west of Chillicothe. An on-site pioneer farm with log buildings, livestock, and gardens
re-creates a typical farm of the 1800s. There are also nature programs, bridle trails, a
fishing pier, hiking and mountain bike trails, and camping. > 14265 U.S. 50, Bainbridge, tel. 937/365–1401, www.ohiostateparks.org. Free. Daily.

Rocky Fork State Park Rocky Fork Creek, for which this nearly 2,500-acre park is
named, flowed over dolomite limestone for millennia and eroded spectacular gorges
and caves through this ancient valley. Sullivantia, an extremely rare plant in Ohio,
blooms in the gorge. The small white flowers can be seen from the moist cliff face in
mid-summer. The 2000-acre lake is a favorite of fishermen and water sports enthusiasts. Camping, hiking, and mountain biking on the park's trails are other popular pursuits. > 9800 North Shore Dr., Hillsboro, tel. 937/393–4284, www.ohiostateparks.org.
Free. Daily.

Seip Mound State Memorial This site about 15 mi southwest of Chillicothe contains
the 30-foot-high, 240-foot-long, 130-foot-wide central burial mound of a group of
Hopewell earthworks. A pavilion area in the middle of this earthwork allows you to
see the entire structure at once. > U.S. 50, Bainbridge, no phone. Free. Daily
dawn–dusk.

Serpent Mound State Memorial Overlooking the east fork of Ohio Brush Creek, this
man-made embankment of earth about 4 feet high and nearly ¼ mi long resembles a
coiled snake and is considered the largest and finest Native American serpent effigy
mound in the world. The best view is from above on the nearby raised platform, but
at ground level you can also see its serpentlike shape. Through carbon-dating, it's
been attributed to the Fort Ancient culture, one of three Native American groups that
lived in this area thousands of years ago. The museum contains exhibits illustrating
various interpretations of the effigy's form, the processes of constructing the effigy,
and the culture of the native people who lived in this area. The site is about 35 mi
southwest of Chillicothe. > 380 Rte. 73, Peebles, tel. 937/587–2796 or 800/752–2757,
www.ohiohistory.org. $6 per car. Park open Memorial Day–Labor Day, daily 10–8;
after Labor Day–Memorial Day, daily 10–5. Museum mid-Apr.–Oct., daily 10–5.

Seven Caves Three self-guided nature trails with sidewalks and handrails lead to
seven illuminated caves at this designated Ohio Natural Landmark, 17 mi southwest
of Chillicothe. Push buttons light up different formations and outstanding features
within the caves. Trails within the 4-acre family-owned park pass along the deep
canyons and cliffs of the Paint Valley, waterfalls, and more than 250 different species
of plants and 60 types of trees, many rare and endangered. There's also a shady pic-

nic grove. Wear comfortable shoes; you'll have to climb a lot of stairs. > 7660 Cave Rd., Bainbridge, tel. 937/365–1283, www.7caves.com. $12. Daily 9–dusk.

Tar Hollow State Park Ten miles east of Chillicothe, Tar Hollow State Park and State Forest and Ross Lake Wildlife Area mingle to offer 18,000 acres of some of the wildest, most rugged land in Ohio. Twisting roads pass through deep ravines and dense woodlands, which include 24 mi of hiking trails, 25 mi of bridle trails, 2.5 mi of mountain bike trails, and 2.1 mi of backpacking trails. Growing on the ridge are short-leaf and pitch pines, which were the source of pine tar for early settlers. You can picnic, hike, and camp here. > 16396 Tar Hollow Rd., Laurelville, tel. 740/887–4818, www.ohiostateparks.org. Free. Daily.

Shopping

First Capital Craft Mall More than 50 local craftspeople sell their creations at this mall, which is atop a hill near U.S. Route 35, about 5 mi east of Chillicothe. Many products have a country-inspired theme. Relax between shopping stints on the front porch or in the garden courtyard. When you need a pick-me-up, head to the deli for sandwiches and snacks. > 400 Chamber Dr., Chillicothe, tel. 740/773–0099, www.imagineifyouwill.com. Closed Sun.

The Trading Post It's hard to resist a place that entices you by saying "antiques like eggs are cheaper in the country." The sprawling 20,000-square-foot barn with out-buildings is 20 mi west of Chillicothe; specialties are furniture and primitives. > 401 S. Maple St., Bainbridge, tel. 740/634–2867. Apr.–Dec., afternoon daily; Jan.–Mar., weekends.

Save the Date

MAY

Feast of the Flowering Moon A 3-day family-oriented festival is filled with music and dancing and includes a Native American powwow. An encampment depicts pioneer life in the early 1800s. One of the largest craft shows in Ohio, there's live entertainment daily and food, contests, and events. > Downtown Chillicothe and Yoctangee Park, tel. 740/887–2979.

MAY–SEPTEMBER

Chillicothe Paints Baseball The Single-A Frontier League's games combine the excitement of professional baseball with a small-town atmosphere. > Veterans Stadium, 17273 Rte. 104, tel. 740/773–8326, www.chillicothepaints.com.

JULY

Western Heritage Horse Show This family-friendly event centers around traditional rodeo performances with a Texas Longhorn show and includes country music entertainment, tractor displays, demonstrations of horseshoeing, the art of the blacksmith, and sanctioned sheep dog trials. Vendors offer a large selection of Western craft and tack supplies. > Ross County Fairgrounds, 5 mi north of Chillicothe, 344 Fairgrounds Rd., tel. 740/773–8326.

AUGUST

Ross County Fair The fair has all the traditional attractions: livestock shows and competitions, carnival rides, games, lip-smacking fair food, and live entertainment. It's at the Ross County Fairgrounds, 5 mi north of Chillicothe. > 344 Fairgrounds Rd., tel. 740/775–5083.

OCTOBER

Circleville Pumpkin Show More than 400,000 people come from across the country and around the world to see world-class giant pumpkins (some more than 500 pounds) at this popular event, which bills itself as Ohio's oldest and largest festival. Food, arts and crafts, bands, and seven parades add to the fun, and a large selection of pumpkins and gourds are sold. Don't miss the pumpkin-shape water tower. The festival is held in downtown Circleville, about 20 mi north of Chillicothe. > Circleville, tel. 740/474–7000.

WHERE TO STAY

CHILLICOTHE

Days Inn This national chain hotel, on the north edge of Chillicothe close to the Adena State Memorial and the Franklin House, is the closest accommodation to the outdoor drama *Tecumseh!* You can walk to the adjacent mall anchored by Sears Roebuck, JCPenny, and the Ohio-chain Elder Beerman. The mall also houses a variety of restaurants, though you may want to take advantage of the free hot breakfast and in-room coffeemakers at the hotel. In summer you can rub elbows with baseball players as this is the host facility for Chillicothe's Frontier League baseball team, the Paints. > 1250 N. Bridge St., Chillicothe 45601, tel. 740/775–7000 or 800/329–7466, fax 740/773–1622, www.daysinn.com. 42 rooms. In-room data ports, cable TV, pool, lounge, business services, some pets allowed (fee), no-smoking rooms. AE, D, DC, MC, V. CP. ¢

Green House Bed and Breakfast In the heart of the downtown historic district, this green Victorian greets you with an inviting wraparound porch and well-tended garden. Once through the front door, the meticulously carved original wooden staircase catches your eye in this well-preserved Queen Anne–style house, built in 1894. The owner's extensive collections of antiques and collectibles fill the parlor, sitting room, TV room, dining room, and each bedroom, all decorated in period style. Though antiques abound, technology isn't overlooked as guests can watch TV and movies or play video games in the TV room. Each of the large rooms, with its own private bath, has armchairs or a sitting area. > 47 E. 5th St., Chillicothe 45601, tel. 740/775–5313 or 877/398–0600, www.chillicotheohio.com/thegreenhouse. 5 rooms. Dining room, room TVs; no smoking. AE, MC, V. Closed Dec. 20–Jan. 2. BP. ¢–$

Guest House Bed and Breakfast The stately brick Greek Revival house was built in 1826 by the first governor of Ohio. An English garden, with a covered gazebo, separates the main house from the guest house. Antiques and collectibles fill this downtown property next to the Ross County Historical Society. Some claim the spirit of a Confederate officer haunts one room of the guest house. > 57 W. 5th St., Chillicothe 45601, tel. 740/772–2204 or 877/259–7900, www.theguesthousebb.com. 3 rooms in main house, 2 rooms in guest house. Room TVs; no room phones, no smoking. AE, MC, V. BP. ¢–$

Victoria Manor Bed and Breakfast Antiques and collectibles fill this 1864 Italianate house downtown where rooms overlook a large garden. All rooms come with a private bath. The owner is an artist whose printmaking studio is on the property. > 30 Western Ave., Chillicothe 45601, tel. 740/775–6424 or 800/852–1093. 4 rooms. No room phones, no room TVs, no smoking. AE, MC, V. BP. ¢–$

CAMPING

Lake Hill Campground On 60 wooded acres at the foothills of the Alleghenies, the campground is 4 mi west of Chillicothe, near the 35 Raceway. Fish the stocked lake from one of the docks or rent a boat to fish in the deeper waters. Beach-front fun includes swimming and volleyball, or take a trip around the lake in a paddle boat or row boat. On rainy days, you can retreat to the game room, which has video games, pool tables, foosball tables, darts, and a jukebox. > 2466 Musselman Station Rd., Frankfort 45628, tel. 740/998–5648. 95 sites; 3 cabins. Flush toilets, full hook-ups, dump station, showers, fire rings, grills at the cabins, picnic tables, general store, swimming (lake). Reservations essential. MC, V. ¢–$

Long's Retreat Family Resort The 400-acre camp site on State Route 124, 35 mi south of Chillicothe, is almost a mini-amusement park. Activities include swimming and fishing on a 20-acre lake, two go-cart tracks, two lake waterslides, an indoor recreation room, canoeing, paddle boats, full-court basketball, volleyball, softball, tennis, bankshot, and mini-golf. Propane is available. > 50 Bell Hollow Rd., Latham 45646, tel. 937/588–3725, fax 937/588–2800, www.longsretreat.com. 65 full hook-ups, 60 partial hook-ups, 200 tent sites; 17 cabins. Flush toilets, full hook-ups, partial hook-ups (electric and water), dump station, drinking water, laundry facilities, showers, grills, picnic tables, snack bar, electricity, public telephone, general store, swimming (lake). Reservations essential. No credit cards. Closed Nov.–Mar. ¢–$$

Paint Creek State Park The 9,000-acre lake is one of many sources of recreation at this 10,000-plus-acre state park, about 20 mi west of Chillicothe. Park activities include basketball and horseshoe courts, a 1,000-foot sand beach, bicycle and boat rentals, miniature golf, a pioneer farm with buildings that represent farm life in the early 1800's, and a summer nature program. If you're bored anyway, the camp office loans games and sporting equipment. A bathhouse offers rest rooms and changing booths. > 14265 U.S. 50 Bainbridge, tel. 937/981–7061, www.paintcreekstatepark.com. 196 partial hook-ups, 10 tent sites; 2 camper cabins, 2 rent-a-camp sites. Flush toilets, partial hook-ups (electric), dump station, showers, grills, picnic tables, general store, playground, swimming (lake). Reservations suggested. D, MC, V. ¢

Scioto Trail State Park This refuge just south of Chillicothe has a portion of the Buckeye Trail, which winds through Ohio, passing through the adjacent state forest. The densely forested Appalachian foothills border the Scioto River. Summer activities include hiking, horseback riding or mountain biking on trails, picnicking at designated areas with tables and grills, basketball and horseshoe courts, boating and swimming on the two small lakes, a children's playground, and the summer nature program. The camp office loans games and sporting equipment. Winter recreation, weather permitting, includes sledding, ice skating, ice fishing, and cross-country skiing. > 144 Lake Rd., Chillicothe 45601, tel. 740/663–2125, www.bright.net/~sciotot. 40 partial hook-ups, 76 tent sites. Pit toilets, partial hook-ups (electric), dump station, fire rings, general store, playground, swimming (lake). Reservations suggested. No credit cards. ¢

Sun Valley Campground Overlooking a lake 6-mi west of Chillicothe, this campground accepts club and big RVs plus pets on a leash. On-site facilities include a lake for swimming and fishing, a game room, a playground, horseshoes, basketball and volleyball courts. > 10105 County Rd. 550,, Chillicothe 45601, tel. 740/775–3490. 45 partial hook-ups. Flush toilets, partial hook-ups (electric and water), showers, fire rings, playground, swimming (lake). Reservations essential. No credit cards. ¢

WHERE TO EAT

CHILLICOTHE

Damon's Wall-size big-screen televisions, local sports team memorabilia, and electronic trivia games fill the bar at this chain restaurant. Barbecued ribs and chicken are the specialties, but just as popular is the onion loaf appetizer, a tasty tangle of thin onion pieces that are breaded and deep-fried. There's a kids' menu. > 10 N. Plaza Blvd., Chillicothe, tel. 740/775–8383. AE, D, DC, MC, V. **$–$$$**

DeGarmo's Canal House Pastas Italian favorites dominate the menu at De-Garmo's. Some items are prepared with an inventive twist, such as pasta with caramelized onions, sun-dried tomatoes, pine nuts, spinach, and feta cheese in a light broth. Meat lovers can opt for New York strip steak or twin medallions of filet mignon. Bar seating with overhead TVs near the wood-burning pizza oven is just the thing for a single diner or a quick bite. Good weather calls for eating on the outside terrace overlooking Yoctangee Park. > 94 E. Water St., Chillicothe, tel. 740/773–1400. AE, D, DC, MC, V. Closed Sun. **¢–$$**

Grinder's Coffee & Cafe In a former pharmacy in the downtown business area, sandwiches and home-made soups and salads are the main menu items. If you eat in, you can sit at a table, or a cushy sofa serves as an alternate place to read and sip your coffee. For a quick bite on the run, there's a selection of freshly baked cookies and muffins (white chocolate macadamia cookies are a good choice). Breakfast and takeout are available. > 65 N. Paint St., Chillicothe, tel. 740/773–2100. No credit cards. Closed Sun. No dinner. **¢**

New York New York of Chillicothe Soft jazz plays and murals of New York City line the walls of this restaurant. Menu highlights include blackberry ketchup pork tenderloin, their signature crab cakes and shrimp cocktail, and a grilled salmon BLT sandwich. Try the Godiva chocolate crème brûlée. > 200 N. Plaza Blvd., Chillicothe, tel. 740/773–2100, www.nynygrill.com. AE, D, DC, MC, V. Closed Sun. **$$–$$$**

ESSENTIALS

Getting Here

Driving is the easiest and quickest way to reach Chillicothe and Ross County. Although there are several airports throughout the county, the closest northwest of Chillicothe, the airports are mostly used for private plane traffic. The closest airport for commercially scheduled flights is in Columbus, Ohio, where cars can be rented for the hour drive to Chillicothe.

BY CAR

Chillicothe is a quick jaunt from Columbus, less than an hour's drive south on U.S. 23. The journey from Cleveland is about three hours, but equally easy, driving south on I–71 to U.S. 23 south. From Cincinnati, drivers have the choice of the speedy or the scenic route. The quicker interstate way is by I–71 north to U.S. 35 east. Slower and scenic means taking U.S. 50 all the way to Chillicothe. The curvy, rural road takes you through small idyllic villages such as Bainbridge. Traveling to Fort Hill and the Serpent Mound, which are in Highland and Adams counties, respectively, adds another hour to the trip from Cleveland and Columbus. All travelers, not only the ones traveling from the Cincinnati area, can enjoy the scenery around Ross County. Developed for fall foliage drives, but equally lovely all times of the year, the Paint Valley Skyline Drive centers on U.S. 50. Four loops, all accessible from U.S. 50, are part of the drive. The shortest loop takes about 30 minutes drive time while the longest route takes about two hours. All four loops take a half day and pass by the only covered bridge in Ross County, wooden hillsides, Paint Creek, Rocky Fork gorge, and country churches.

When the weather warms, count on "Orange Barrel" season in Ohio. Ubiquitous orange barrels appear on major highways and back roads and indicate road construction and repair projects ahead. Projects can snarl traffic and slow it to a crawl on many rural to super highways, as speed limits are usually lowered. Be sure to slow down as tickets issued at road construction sites are double the normal fines. Check the Web site of the Ohio Department of Transportation for the latest project details and delay notifications.

ROAD INFORMATION **Ohio Department of Transportation** >www.buckeyetraffic.org.

Visitor Information

CONTACTS **Ross-Chillicothe Convention & Visitors Bureau** > 25 E. Main St., Chillicothe 45601-0353, tel. 740/702–7673 or 800/413–4118, www.visithistory.com.

Ohio River Scenic Byway

Augusta is 36 mi west of Cincinnati, 150 mi south of Columbus, and 290 mi south of Cleveland.

17

By Susan Reigler

FEW CAN RESIST THE ROMANCE of a great river. Those wide, swiftly flowing waterways were America's original highways; the gateways to the westward expansion. Traveled by thousands of 18th- and 19th-century settlers who floated downstream on flatboats, the Ohio River was a major route to the interior of a seemingly endless continent. Two of the most famous names in the area's early history were Simon Kenton and Daniel Boone, each of whom had a hand in the founding of several towns along the river. Two northern Kentucky counties across the Ohio from Cincinnati bear their names today.

A car trip over the highways that parallel the Ohio River provides a glimpse back in time. Between Augusta, Kentucky, and Portsmouth, Ohio, the shores are lined with dense tree cover, broken occasionally by views of the water where barges loaded with coal or paddlewheelers carrying tourists plow steadily up and down stream. Emerging from the tree tops are the clock towers and church spires of towns whose main streets have changed little since the Civil War. Communities separated by the water are connected by modern suspension bridges or old-fashioned ferry services.

It was not always so easy to pass from one shore to the other. Before and during the Civil War, Kentucky was a slave state, while Ohio was free. There was intense Underground Railroad activity in the region and equally intense pursuit by slave owners and bounty hunters. Numerous sites associated with the Underground Railroad are preserved in many of the riverside towns.

Old storefronts house antiques shops, restaurants, bed-and-breakfasts, and regional history museums. Many waterfront walks have been enlivened by the colorful murals on formerly drab floodwalls. Depending on the time of year, you can enjoy old-fashioned Christmas celebrations in business districts decorated with thousands of sparkling lights or participate in outdoor festivals commemorating the river heritage complete with regional foods, musical entertainment, and street games.

The historic waterfront district of tiny Augusta, Kentucky (population 1,430, founded 1798), has been used as the backdrop for period films and television mini-series. It's very easy to imagine Tom and Huck strolling down these streets. Augusta's buildings are clustered high on the bank overlooking the river. You can soak up the atmosphere by staying in one of the town's many B&Bs, or take the ferry, which started carrying passengers the year the town came into existence, back across the Ohio.

About 17 mi upstream from Augusta, Maysville (population 7,200) is the birthplace of singer Rosemary Clooney, whose childhood home is on the National Register of Historic Places. Founded on the banks of the Ohio River in 1787, the town's center is still marked with 18th- and 19th-century buildings, including brick row houses decorated with ironwork reminiscent of New Orleans. The skyline is dominated by Romanesque church steeples and the gold cupola of the 1846 Greek Revival Mason County Courthouse.

In 1833, in the Old Washington section of Maysville, a young woman named Harriet Beecher (later Harriet Beecher Stowe) was so horrified by a slave auction she saw there while visiting from nearby Cincinnati, that she was inspired to write the anti-slavery novel *Uncle Tom's Cabin*. It was published in 1852. Years later, when Stowe met President Abraham Lincoln, he was reported to have said, "So you're the little woman who wrote the book that started this great war."

Cross the bridge at Maysville and take Ohio Route 52 northeast along the river to Portsmouth, about 50 mi. The history of the city dates to the discovery of the Ohio Valley by the French in 1749. In 1803 Henry Massie founded the settlement, naming it after Portsmouth, New Hampshire, the hometown of a good friend. Set on the Ohio River, Portsmouth became the terminus for the Ohio–Erie Canal.

Today, Portsmouth still serves as a major hub to railways and water transportation. It's the gateway to three states—Ohio, Kentucky, and West Virginia, and lies within 100 mi of many major metropolitan markets, including Cincinnati, Columbus, and Louisville. Set in an agricultural area, Portsmouth (population 25,000) is an industrial city, and home to forestry and agricultural concerns. The hub of the cultural life here is the Southern Ohio Museum and Cultural Center. Also noteworthy is the Floodwall Murals Project; completed in 2002 along the Front Street floodwall, the project consists of more than 50 murals commemorating 2,000 years of area history.

WHAT TO SEE & DO

AUGUSTA, KENTUCKY

Augusta Ferry In operation since 1798, the ferry now carries cars and passengers between Augusta and Boudes Landing, Ohio. > Dock at the end of Main St., Augusta, tel. 606/756–3291. $5. Daily dawn–dusk; also by request to the captain.

Riverside Drive There are 54 pioneer, federal, and Victorian buildings included on a walking tour map of the downtown. The buildings contain shops, cafés, B&Bs, and private homes. You can find maps at most retail locations. > Waterfront.

Walcott Covered Bridge This is one of only about a dozen covered bridges left in Kentucky (at one time there were 400), all of which are found in the northeastern corner of the state. This 75-foot span over Locust Creek has been recently rebuilt. > Intersection of KY 9 and SR 1159, about 8 mi southwest of Augusta, Woolcott.

MAYSVILLE, KENTUCKY

Blue Licks Battlefield State Resort Park The 150-acre park includes a monument to the last battle of the Revolutionary War, which was fought between settlers and Native Americans a year after Cornwallis's surrender. Among those killed in the battle were Daniel Boone's son, Israel. A museum contains displays about area history and geology. A nature preserve within the park protects Short's goldenrod, a species of wildflower that grows nowhere else in the world. Campsites, a lodge, and cottages are available. You can also rent a canoe to paddle on the Licking River. > U.S. 68, Mount Olivet 41064, tel. 606/289–5507, www.kystateparks.com. Free; fees for camping, pool, and other recreational facilities; museum $2. Year-round. Museum Apr.–Oct., daily 9–5.

Historic Washington Established in the late 18th century, this original county seat contains several restored buildings dating from 1790 to 1848 including Mefford Fort, the Old Church Museum, and the Paxton Inn. Guided tours of the town are offered.

> 2116 Old Main St., Maysville 41056, tel. 606/759–7411. $1–$6. Weekdays 11–4:30, Sat. 10:30–4:30, Sun. 1–4:30.

Marshall Key House While visiting the Marshall Key House in 1833, Harriet Beecher Stowe witnessed a slave auction and was inspired to write *Uncle Tom's Cabin*. The circa 1807 building now houses the "Harriet Beecher Stowe Slavery to Freedom" museum. > 2124 Old Main St., Old Washington 41056, tel. 606/759–7411. Tour $6. Daily 11–3:30.

Mason County Courthouse The cupola topping the 1846 Greek Revival courthouse is one of the distinctive features of the town's outline, as viewed from across the river. The courthouse still houses the government offices of the county, which was named after George Mason, author of the Virginia Constitution, a model for the national constitution. > E. 4th St. and Coughlin Blvd., Maysville 41056, tel. 606/564–3341. Free. Weekdays 8–5.

Mason County Museum Housed in a structure dating from 1876, the Mason County Museum is today an art gallery, history museum, and genealogy center. Holdings include an area map collection. > 215 Sutton St., Maysville 41056, tel. 606/564–5865, www.masoncountymuseum.org. $3. Apr.–Dec., Mon.–Sat. 10–4; Jan.–Mar., Tues.–Sat. 10–4.

Maysville Visitor Center–Underground Railroad Museum The collection of artifacts at the visitor center illustrates the area's history of slavery. Bills of auction, slave tags, and diaries are among the holdings. Maps of the Old Washington Underground Railroad Tour, a self-guided tour, are also on hand at the visitor center. > 115 E. 3rd St., Maysville 41056, tel. 606/564–6986, www.coax.net/people/lwf/urmuseum.htm. $2. Mon.–Sat. 10–4.

Paxton Inn A safe-house on the Underground Railroad, the inn was built around 1810 by James A. Paxton, a local attorney and ardent abolitionist. According to oral history, runaway slaves sat on the narrow staircase hidden next to the kitchen fireplace until they could be safely moved across the river to Ohio. > 2030 Old Main St., Old Washington 41056, tel. 606/759–7411. Tour $6. Daily 11–3:30.

The Piedmont Art Gallery Displaying collections of paintings and crafts by both regional and national artisans, the gallery also houses antiques, folk art, ceramics, and sculpture. > 115 W. Riverside Dr., Augusta 41002, tel. 606/756–2216. Free. Thurs.–Sun. noon–5.

Valley Pike Covered Bridge A fine example of the construction style known as Kingpost Truss, this 24-foot bridge across Lee Creek was built in 1864. > Follow KY 3056 to Valley Pike and drive north. The Bridge is about 3 mi west of downtown. Maysville.

PORTSMOUTH, OHIO

Portsmouth Floodwall Murals Created by artist Robert Dafford, 2,000 feet of murals depict 2,000 years of area history. The 20-foot-high scenes include a Shawnee village, a 19th-century iron foundry, and an early-20th-century streetcar, as well as singing cowboy (and native son) Roy Rogers astride his horse Trigger. Start at the intersection of Washing and Front streets, and walk west on Front Street. > Front St., tel. 740/353–1116, www.portsmouthmuralproducts.com. Free. Daily.

Shawnee State Park and Forest This 1,100-acre park about 8 mi west of Portsmouth has nature programs, picnic areas, and an 18-hole golf course. In spring you are treated to the white-and-purple woodland display of dogwoods and redbuds in bloom. Morel hunters also visit the woods in April and May to search for the delicacy, a mushroom relative. Birders can find many warbler species, including

Cerulean, Blackburian, and blue-winged. > 13291 U.S. 52, tel. 740/858–6685, www.ohiostateparks.org. Free. Daily.

Shawnee State University On the banks of the Ohio River, the campus of Ohio's newest public university covers 52 acres. The 66-seat Clark Planetarium, which has shows for groups of 18 or more by appointment, is inside the Advanced Technology Center. > 940 2nd St., tel. 740/351–3224 or 800/959–2778, www.shawnee.edu. Daily.

Southern Ohio Museum and Cultural Center History exhibits focus on Southern Ohio people and events; you'll also see art works by prominent Portsmouth artists. > 825 Gallia St., tel. 740/354–5629. $1. Tues.–Fri. 10–5, weekends 1–5.

Tours

Old Washington History Tour The guided tour of Old Washington includes the log post office, shops featuring silver and antique lamps, and stops on the Underground Railroad. Tours, which cost $10, are available daily from mid-March through December. > Tel. 606/759–7411.

Save the Date

APRIL

Trout Derby This festival at Turkey Creek Lake in Shawnee State Forest celebrates the start of the fishing season. The contestant who catches the largest fish can win a boat, and the winning senior nets a recliner. > 13291 U.S. 52, tel. 614/858–6652, www.ci.portsmouth.oh.us.

JUNE

Mildred E. Thompson Portsmouth Charity Horse Show Horses of all sizes compete in several classes on the first weekend in June. Five-gaited, three-gaited, harness, and saddle-seat equitation are among the categories. The show extends over three days in Portsmouth. > Lucasville County Fairgrounds, 1193 Fairground Rd., tel. 740/353–3698 or 740/259–2726, www.ci.portsmouth.oh.us.

Roy Rogers Festival Roy Rogers enthusiasts gather in Portsmouth for a weekend filled with memorabilia, celebrities, and Western fun. A high point is a visit to Rogers' boyhood home. An exhibit of Rogers memorabilia is open year-round in the basement of the Portsmouth Post Office. > Ramada Inn, 711 2nd St., tel. 740/353–0900, www.ci.portsmouth.oh.us.

Sternwheel Annual Regatta Historic stern-wheeler riverboats gather at the port in Augusta. Food and entertainment are the weekend's staples. Other highlights include the crowning of Miss Sternwheeler, a car show, and live music. > Tel. 606/756–2183, www.augustakentucky.com.

SEPTEMBER

River Days Festival The family-oriented event in Portsmouth has arts and crafts and a catfish fry. Amusement rides and Big Wheel races for kids are among the events. > Court Street Landing, tel. 740/354–6419, www.riverdays.org.

Simon Kenton Festival Pioneer spirit is celebrated with crafts, demonstrations, and food in historic Washington, which is now part of greater Maysville. Living history camps featuring blacksmiths, stonecutters, and gunsmiths are among the attractions. > Tel. 606/759–7423, www.frontierfolk.org.

WHERE TO STAY

AUGUSTA, KENTUCKY

Jane's Riverview Bed & Breakfast A private room, with a terrace overlooking the Ohio River, is furnished with a queen-size canopy bed and other antiques. You can have the exclusive attention of your hosts in this 1840s house a block and a half from the Augusta Ferry landing. > 206 E. Riverside Dr., Augusta 41002, tel. 606/756–2050, www.bbonline.com/ky/riverview/index.html. 1 room. Some pets allowed (fee); no room phone, no room TV. MC, V. BP. $

Parkview Country Inn The center of this rambling house was originally an early-19th-century tavern. Light streams through tall windows into high-ceilinged rooms furnished with antiques. > 103 W. 2nd St., Augusta 41002, tel. 606/756–2603, fax 606/756–2933, www.parkviewcountryinn.com. 9 rooms with private baths. Restaurant, badminton, croquet. V. BP. $–$$

MAYSVILLE, KENTUCKY

French Quarter Inn The luxurious, four-story riverfront hotel has exterior corridors, a quaint lobby bar, and gourmet dining. The rooms have cherry furniture, in-room coffeemakers, and whirlpool tubs. Some rooms have a view of the Ohio River. > 25 E. McDonald Pkwy., Maysville 41056, tel. 606/564–8000 or 800/966–9892, fax 606/564–8460, www.frenchquarterinn.com. 64 rooms. Restaurant, in-room data ports, in-room hot tubs, some microwaves, some refrigerators, pool, exercise equipment, bar. AE, D, DC, MC, V. $

Kleier Haus Bed & Breakfast This two-story Victorian, built in 1885, is adjacent to a golf course in the rolling farm country surrounding Maysville. The spacious old-fashioned wraparound porch has rocking chairs and a swing. There are three rooms and two baths, and a telephone is available in the common area. A full Kentucky breakfast is served in a dining room with a fireplace and a huge window. > 912 U.S. 62, Maysville 41056, tel. 606/759–7663, fax 606/759–5669, gaykleier@webtv.net. 3 rooms, 1 with bath. Cable TV, golf privileges; no room phones. D, MC, V. Closed Nov.–Jan. BP. $

PORTSMOUTH, OHIO

Ramada Inn Near downtown Portsmouth, this motel is one block from the riverfront murals and across the street from Shawnee State University campus. Contemporary style rooms are decorated with prints of Portsmouth landmarks. > 711 2nd St., tel. 740/354–7711 or 800/228–2828, fax 740/353–1539, www.ramada.com. 119 rooms. Restaurant, some refrigerators, cable TV, indoor pool, wading pool, hot tub, business services, some pets allowed. AE, D, DC, MC, V. CP. $

CAMPING

Blue Licks State Resort Park Sites with asphalt pads are on a loop in a rolling, wooded area of the park. > U.S. 68, Mt. Olivet 41064, tel. 606/289–5507, www.kystateparks.com. 51 sites. Flush toilets, partial hook-ups (electric and water), dump station, showers. Reservations not accepted. AE, MC, V. Buildings closed Nov.–Mar. ¢

WHERE TO EAT

AUGUSTA, KENTUCKY

Beehive Tavern The two-story, federal-style brick building dates from the 1790s, and a cozy bar in one corner is reminiscent of a tavern from that time period. The elegant dining room has white linens, painted woodwork, and antique furnishings. The specialty here is seafood, roast pork, and chicken entrées. > 101 W. Riverside Dr., Augusta 41002, tel. 606/756–2202. AE, D, MC, V. Closed Mon. and Tues. $$

MAYSVILLE, KENTUCKY

Da Sha's Restaurant This warm, inviting bistro with wood trim and brass accents is on "the Hill" overlooking the town. Da Sha's specializes in grilled seafood, chops, and steaks. Soup and salad combinations are lunchtime favorites. The bar is popular with locals at happy hour. > 1166 U.S. 68, Maysville 41056, tel. 606/564–9275. AE, D, DC, MC, V. $$–$$$

Laredo's The cowboy theme starts with the Southwestern decor and continues through the peanuts served with drinks (discard shells on the floor) and the selection of charbroiled steaks on the menu. Appetizers include quesadillas and salsas with chips. > 545 Tucker Dr., Maysville 41056, tel. 606/759–8749. AE, DC, MC, V. $–$$$

Tippedore's At this eatery in the French Quarter Inn, you can watch the boat traffic on the Ohio River while dining on the outdoor patio. Inside, the walls are decorated with pictures of Old Maysville. Open for breakfast and dinner, the restaurant serves steaks, Cajun food, chicken marsala, and lots of appetizers. Breakfast options include a made-to-order omelets. > 25 E. McDonald Pkwy., Maysville 41056, tel. 606/564–8000 or 800/966–9892, www.frenchquarterinn.com. AE, D, DC, MC, V. No lunch; no dinner Sun. $$

PORTSMOUTH, OHIO

Maults Brew Pub In the historic district, this 19th-century brick building (lots of exposed brick inside, too) was a stop on the Underground Railroad. Seven different ales and lagers, ranging from pilsner to maplenut, are brewed on-site and served draft. Homemade sausage is a specialty dish. > 224 2nd St., tel. 740/354–6106. AE, D, MC, V. $–$$

Scioto Ribber The dark-green paneling that frames the entrance to the redbrick corner eatery beckons customers with a giant meat smoker logo. The interior is saloon-casual, but the ribs, chicken, and steaks, prepared on a huge outdoor hickory grill year-round, are worthy of more upscale surroundings. > 1026 Gallia St., tel. 740/353–9329. AE, MC, V. Closed Mon. $–$$$$

Ye Olde Lantern Local musicians provide the entertainment on weekends in this local favorite housed in a Civil War–era pharmacy, complete with decorative stained glass. The menu runs to steaks, seafood, and pasta. Fried catfish is a specialty. There's a good list of imported beers as well as a wine list and full bar. > 601 2nd St., tel. 740/353–6638. AE, D, MC, V. Closed Sun. $–$$$

ESSENTIALS

Getting Here

Automobile is the way to travel through this patch of the Ohio Valley. Public transportation of any description is nonexistent. If you're coming from as far away as Cleveland, you might consider flying into the Cincinnati–Northern Kentucky International Airport and hiring a car there. Once out of the greater Cincinnati area, traffic thins considerably and sightseeing is easy, even for the driver.

BY CAR

Beware of one-way streets in the towns of Augusta and Maysville and the city of Portsmouth. In Maysville, keep a close eye on the signs in the downtown area; it's easy to head toward the river and find yourself on the bridge to Ohio when you only wanted to get as far as the waterfront. If you want to seek out the covered bridges in the rolling countryside south of Maysville, know that many of the roadways are narrow and that farming is the basis of the economy. So expect to get stuck behind a tractor. But the scenery is so pleasant, that it's not really a big deal. You wanted to slow down anyway.

Routes and important sites are clearly marked, so this is a very car-friendly destination.

On-street parking is generally easy in all three city centers. Park in one of the center lots in Augusta and enjoy the riverfront historic district on foot. "Rush hour" is a phrase that you will only hear around Portsmouth. Late afternoon is busy here as it is in other cities.

BY PLANE

The Cincinnati–Northern Kentucky International Airport, on the Kentucky side of the river near I-71, is the major regional airport. Access is by four-lane highway and traffic flows smoothly. The facility is well-planned; parking, check-in, and car rental are easier than in most airports of this size.

There are five daily flights from Cleveland on Delta and Continental Airlines. Delta has nine scheduled daily flights from Columbus.

AIRPORTS **Cincinnati–Northern Kentucky International Airport** > 2601 Donaldson Hwy., Erlanger, tel. 859/767–3151, www.cvgairport.com.
CARRIERS **Continental Airlines** > Tel. 800/525–0280, www.flycontinental.com. **Delta Air Lines** > Tel. 800/221–1212, www.delta.com.

Visitor Information

CONTACTS **Maysville-Mason County Tourist Commission** > 216 Bridge St., Maysville 41056, tel. 606/564–9411, www.maysvillekentucky.com. **Portsmouth Area Chamber of Commerce** > Box 509, 45662-0509, tel. 740/353–7647, www.portsmouth.org.

Bluegrass Country

18

THE LUSH GREEN COUNTRYSIDE in Kentucky's Bluegrass region has more than 500 horse farms, the largest concentration of such facilities in the world. Valuable thoroughbreds and standardbreds are housed in climate-controlled barns in settings that could be easily be mistaken for royal estates.

Horses flourish here because the region's limestone soil imparts bone-strengthening calcium to stream water and pasture grass. The grass itself was imported from Europe by early settlers and thrived in the Kentucky climate, replacing the native cane. Such champions as Man O' War, Bold Ruler, and Secretariat were bred in or retired to the Bluegrass farms where race horse breeding is a billion-dollar-a-year industry. World-famous yearling thoroughbred sales take place in spring and fall at nearby Keeneland race course.

The horse farms aren't the only feature of the region that will make you think you're driving through a living postcard. The hills are dotted with landscaped mansions and historic bourbon distilleries, and there are charming small towns where you may find a treasure in a Main Street antiques store or enjoy a gourmet meal.

A logical headquarters for a trip to the Bluegrass is Lexington. Kentucky's second-largest city is also one of its oldest. Established as a camp in 1775, it was named after the town in Massachusetts that had just been the site of an important Revolutionary War victory. Lexington grew rapidly after statehood as a center for commerce, the arts, and above all, horse breeding—which made the surrounding Bluegrass Region the world's thoroughbred capital.

By the 1820s, Lexington was known as the "Athens of the West," and it was as easy to hear a Beethoven symphony in local concert halls as to see a beautiful race horse on one of the nearby farms. The modern downtown retains many notable historic districts. In the southeast quadrant of the city center, several streets of Georgian houses are reminiscent of Georgetown in Washington, D.C. The "more antebellum" neighborhood of Gratz Park, just north of Main Street, has tree-lined streets of stately mansions.

Lexington is the site of the world's largest burley tobacco auction. The central tobacco warehouse district has been undergoing changes in recent years as buildings and sites are converted to new shopping and residential areas. It lies between the University of Kentucky campus, the state's land grant (and largest) university, and the central shopping and restaurant district downtown that has grown up around Rupp Arena, where the University of Kentucky Wildcats play basketball.

About 18 mi northeast of Lexington is Paris, the seat of Bourbon County. American whiskey may or may not have been invented in here, but the name has persevered through legend and time. Originally called Hopewell, the county seat was renamed Paris in 1790, since the county was named for France's royal Bourbon family.

Due west of Lexington on U.S. 60 is Versailles, like Paris named in gratitude for France's help during the Revolutionary War, although Kentuckians pronounce the name "Ver-sales." The town is in the rich horse-farm country of the Bluegrass region but is also a center for "iron horse," or railroad, buffs.

Midway, 8 mi northeast of Versailles, draws antiques collectors. Midway was the first Kentucky town (circa 1833) built by a railroad company, and was named because it was the midpoint on the line between Frankfort and Lexington.

The state capitol, Frankfort, is situated at a double bend on the Kentucky River. The name originated with a pioneer named Stephen Frank, who was killed in a battle at a ford on the Kentucky River. The site became known as Frank's Ford, which, in time, became Frankfort. When Kentucky became a state in 1792, Frankfort landowner Andrew Holmes wooed the new state government to Frankfort with an offer of several town lots, building materials, rents from a tobacco warehouse, cash from citizens, and promotion of the location between the large settlements of Louisville and Lexington.

During the 19th century, in addition to being the seat of state government, Frankfort was important as a manufacturing center and an agricultural market. By the end of the century, there were a dozen distilleries in the area, producing 600 barrels of bourbon daily. America's native whiskey is distilled from a mixture of corn mashed and fermented with other grains, usually barley and rye, but sometimes wheat. It's characterized by flavors of vanilla and caramel. Single barrel and small batch bourbons, made by most of the 10 remaining distilleries, are prized by connoisseurs.

WHAT TO SEE & DO

FRANKFORT

Buffalo Trace Distillery On a site near the Kentucky River where buffalo once came to drink, the distillery has been in operation since 1787. Tours include a short, introductory video, the distillation facility, and the warehouses where bourbon is aged. There's also a gift shop where you can buy the distillery's award-winning bourbon and delicious chocolate bourbon candies. > 1001 Wilkinson Blvd., Frankfort, tel. 502/696–5926 or 800/654–8471, www.buffalotrace.com. Free. Tours weekdays 9–3, Sat. 10–2.

Daniel Boone's Grave In 1775, frontiersman Daniel Boone blazed the Wilderness Trail though Cumberland Gap in the Appalachian Mountains and led the first party of settlers to found a permanent community in what became Kentucky, at Fort Boonesborough. Boone died in Missouri in 1820. In 1845 the remains of Boone and his wife, Rebecca, were moved to the Frankfort Cemetery. An obelisk-shape monument marks the grave, which overlooks the state capital. The Kentucky Veterans War Memorial is also here—it has the names of 16,000 soldiers who died in all U.S. wars except the Civil War. Also buried here is Richard M. Johnson, Martin Van Buren's vice president. The site is two blocks from the Kentucky History Center. > Frankfort Cemetery, 215 E. Main St., Frankfort, tel. 502/227–2403. Free, donations suggested. Daily 8 AM–dusk.

Historic Frankfort As Kentucky's capital city, Frankfort has its share of drab government buildings. Still, on the north side of a bend in the Kentucky River, there are many beautifully restored buildings in downtown's historic and shopping section. Streets are lined with restaurants and specialty shops—from antiques stores and art galleries to bookstores and boutiques selling Kentucky-made crafts and candies.

White-globe lanterns, park benches, and brick streets set the scene on the St. Clair mall, which offers more nifty shops including an old-fashioned general store and restaurants that, weather permitting, serve lunch alfresco. On-street parking is plentiful during the day but becomes more difficult to find in the evening when residents return home from work. > Bordered by Wapping, Washington, Wilkinson, and Main Sts.

Kentucky History Center "A Kentucky Journey," the 20,000-square-foot exhibition anchoring this museum, traces the state's history from prehistoric times through the pioneer days to the present. A log cabin from Owen County is a key component of the pioneer history exhibit; other highlights include the facade of a coal company store, a flatboat, and a western Kentucky kitchen from the 1940s, before electricity was available in the rural parts of the state. A green terrazzo-marble map of Kentucky in the central atrium has each county outlined in brass. The center also houses the Kentucky Historical Society's Research Library (known for its genealogical information). > 100 W. Broadway, Frankfort, tel. 502/564–1792 or 877/444–7867, www.history.ky.gov. Free. Museum: Tues.–Sat. 10–5, Thurs. 10–8, Sun. 1–5. Library: Mon.–Sat. 8–4, Thurs. 8–8.

Kentucky State University The state's only public liberal-arts university has an enrollment of 2,500 students. The 309-acre campus is joined by a 166-acre research farm and aquaculture center that is developing new crops for Kentucky farmers. Other campus highlights are the King Farouk butterfly and moth collection and Kentucky Black heritage archives. > 400 E. Main St., Frankfort, tel. 502/597–6000. Free. Tours Sept.–mid-May, 8–4.

Kentucky Vietnam Veterans Memorial The names of 1,062 Kentuckians killed in Vietnam are etched into the granite plaza. The shadow of a giant sundial touches the name of each person on the anniversary of his death. Names of 22 soldiers missing in action are behind the sundial so the shadow never touches them. The memorial is on the grounds of the Kentucky Department for Library and Archives on Coffeetree Road. It's off Route 676 between the regional jail and the library. > Coffeetree Rd., Frankfort 40601, tel. 502/875–8687. Free. Daily.

Liberty Hall Historic Site U.S. Senator (KY) John Brown began the construction of his home, Liberty Hall, in 1796. The L-shape house has a Palladian window and is furnished with period antiques, including several Brown family items. Formal gardens behind the house stretch to the Kentucky River. The 1835 **Orlando Brown House** (202 Wilkinson St., Frankfort) was built for one of Senator Brown's sons on the grounds of the four-acre Liberty Hall estate. Its style reflects the transition from federal to Greek Revival. Modeled on the floor plan of the older house, the Orlando Brown House contains family china, silver, brass, furniture, and paintings. > 218 Wilkinson St., Frankfort, tel. 502/227–2560. www.libertyhall.org. Free. Mar.–mid-Dec., Tues.–Sat. 10:30, noon, 1:30, and 3; Sun. 1:30 and 3.

Old State Capitol Museum State government was headquartered here from 1827 to 1910. A self-supporting central stone staircase is an architectural highlight of the Greek Revival building designed by Gideon Shryock. Upstairs are the chambers of the Kentucky House and Senate preserved with their original 19th-century wooden desks and chairs. > 300 W. Broadway, Frankfort, tel. 502/564–1792. Free. Tues.–Sat. 10–5, Sun. 1–5.

State Capitol The graceful beaux arts–style Kentucky State Capitol opened in 1910. Its exterior is Indiana limestone ornamented with 70 ionic columns. It's built on a Vermont-granite base. Marble, murals (including two depicting Daniel Boone), and paintings beautify the interior, which was strongly influenced by French architecture. The rotunda and dome are modeled on Paris's Hotel Des Invalides, the same design that graces Napoleon's tomb. The grand staircase was inspired by that of the Paris Opera. And Marie Antoinette's drawing room at Versailles was copied for the State Reception Room. The 1914 beaux arts **Governor's Mansion** (Capitol Ave., tel. 502/564–3449, free, Tues. and Thurs. 9–11) shares both the grounds and the style of the capitol building. It's modeled after Marie Antoinette's Petit Trianon, her villa at Versailles. Constructed of native limestone, the mansion sits on a bluff overlooking the Kentucky River. The outdoor working **Floral Clock** (Capitol Ave.) has a 34-foot face made up of thousands of plants that change seasonally. It's tilted above a reflecting pool so that the time can be read easily. Coins tossed into the pool are collected and donated to kids' charities. > Capitol Ave., Frankfort 40601, tel. 502/564–3449. Free. Weekdays 8–4:30 guided tours, Sat. 8:30–4:30, Sun. 1–4:30.

LEXINGTON

Ashland This 18-room mansion was the home of Henry Clay, U.S. Senator from Kentucky during the Civil War era, who also served as Speaker of the House and Secretary of State during his long political career. Clay's reputation as an orator and statesman was national and he earned the nickname, "the Great Compromiser," for his acumen as a legislator. Furnished with Clay family artifacts and early-19th-century antiques, the house sits on 20 wooded acres. Formal gardens, an icehouse, a smokehouse, and a carriage house are among the other features. > 120 Sycamore Rd., Lexington 40502, tel. 859/266–8581, www.henryclay.org. $6. Feb.–Dec., Mon.–Sat. 10–4:30, Sun. 1–4:30.

Headley-Whitney Museum Devoted to decorative arts, this museum holds a large collection of jewelry, gold boxes, and jeweled sculptures by artist-designer George W. Headley. Other exhibitions include textiles, furniture, Chinese porcelains, and metalwork. There's also a large decorative-arts library on-site. > 4435 Old Frankfort Pike, Lexington 40502, tel. 859/255–6653, www.headley-whitney.org. $4. Tues.–Fri. 10–5, weekends noon–5.

Hunt-Morgan House John Wesley Morgan, who built this federal-style house in the early 1800s, was the first millionaire west of the Appalachians. His illustrious descendants include John Hunt Morgan, the Confederate cavalry captain who led Morgan's Raiders, and Thomas Hunt Morgan, Nobel laureate for his research in genetics. In the historic Gratz Park neighborhood, the Hunt-Morgan House has family furnishings and a formal garden. > 201 N. Mill St., Lexington, tel. 859/233–3290. $5. Mar.–late Dec., Tues.–Sat. 10–4, Sun. 2–5.

Kentucky Horse Park The world's only equine theme park is situated on 1,032 green, rolling acres. The International Museum of the Horse has exhibitions on evolution and all breeds, as well as films about human–horse relationships throughout history. In summer a daily Parade of Breeds occurs in the arena, where you can view horses with tack appropriate to each. The great thoroughbred Man O' War is buried here, and his grave is marked by a life-size bronze statue. Tours of the park are available in a horse-drawn trolley or on foot. Horseback and pony rides are offered for a fee separate from admission. **American Saddle Horse Museum** (4093 Iron Works Pike, tel. 859/259–2746, $3, May.–Sept., daily 9–5; Oct.–Apr., Wed.–Sun. 9–5), on the grounds of Kentucky Horse Park, celebrates the American Saddlebred, a breed developed in Kentucky in the 19th century as the riding horse of choice. A multi-image presentation recounts the history and current uses of the saddlebred, and there's an interactive exhibit where you can see how you would look atop one of the horses. > 4089 Ironworks Pike, Lexington, tel. 859/233–4303 or 800/568–8813, www.imh.org/khp. $12. Daily 9–6.

Lexington Children's Museum Interactive exhibitions cover history, civics, science, nature, and ecology. Highlights include a walk-through cave, a simulated moon walk, and giant-soap-bubble-blowing activity. > 440 W. Short St., Lexington, tel. 859/258–3256. $3. Tues.–Fri. 10–6, Sat. 10–5, Sun. 1–5.

Lexington Opera House Now a regional performing arts center, this opulent Victorian theater opened in 1887. Touring Broadway shows and orchestra concerts are among the featured events. > 401 W. Short St., Lexington, tel. 859/233–4567, fax 859/253–2718. Sept.–June.

Mary Todd Lincoln House This 1803 Georgian house was the girlhood home of Mary Todd, who became Mrs. Abraham Lincoln. The 16th president made three visits to the house. Furnished with period antiques, the house also contains artifacts of both the Todd and Lincoln families. > 578 W. Main St., Lexington, tel. 859/233–9999. $7. Mid-Mar.–Nov., Mon.–Sat. 10–4.

University of Kentucky Established as the state's land grant college in 1865, the university is the largest employer in the city. It's also Kentucky's largest university with an enrollment of more than 24,000. Tours of the campus, both by bus and on foot, are available. Permanent collections at the U of K **Art Museum** (Singletary Center for the Arts, Euclid Ave. and Rose St., tel. 859/257–5716, fax 859/323–1994, www.uky.edu/artmuseum, free, Tues.–Sun. noon–5) include 20th-century photography and works by regional 19th-century artists. A print collection, a highlight of which are WPA works, is especially strong. The museum presents traveling shows as well. The 23,000-seat **Rupp Arena** (430 W. Vine St., tel. 859/257–4567) is named in honor of legendary U of K Wildcat basketball coach Adolph Rupp. The Wildcats regularly rank in the top 10 NCAA basketball teams and have won several national championships. The arena is also home to Lexington's professional hockey team, the Thoroughblades, and is a regular venue for rock, country, and pop concerts. Exhibitions at the **William S. Webb Museum of Anthropology** (Lafferty Hall, tel. 859/257–8208, www.uky.edu/as/anthropology/museum/museum.htm, free, weekdays 8–4:30) recount the history of people in Kentucky from 12,000 years ago to the present. Other displays trace human evolution and the history of art and technology in global cultures. > 500 S. Limestone St., at Euclid Ave., Lexington, tel. 859/257–9000, fax 859/257–1754, www.uky.edu. Free. Daily.

Victorian Square Shops, art galleries, and restaurants are housed in this restored block of ornamented 19th-century, brick warehouses. A 400-car parking garage with a covered walkway leads into the complex. > Vine St., Lexington, tel. 859/252–7575 or 859/258–3253. Daily during business hrs.

Waveland State Historic Site The centerpiece of the 10-acre site is a restored Greek Revival manor erected in 1847. The estate depicts life on a pre–Civil War plantation. Among other buildings are an icehouse, a smokehouse, and servants' and slaves' quarters. > 225 Waveland Museum La., Lexington 40514, tel. 859/272–3611, www.kystateparks.com/agencies/parks/wavelan2.htm. $6. Feb.–Dec., Mon.–Sat. 10–5, Sun. 1–5.

PARIS

Duncan Tavern Historic Shrine Duncan Tavern was a favorite watering hole of early frontiersmen, including Daniel Boone and Simon Kenton. When the proprietor died, his widow, Ann Duncan, built the log house (1800) attached to the stone tavern and took over the inn-keeping. The tavern is restored to look much as it did in Boone's time. > U.S. 68, Paris, tel. 859/987–1788. $5. Tues.–Sat. 10–noon and 1–4.

Hopewell Museum Housed in the town's 1909 Beaux Arts post office building, this museum preserves the history and culture of Bourbon County. Rotating exhibits display local art or historical items. > 800 Pleasant St., Paris, tel. 859/987–7274. $2. Wed.–Sat. noon–5, Sun. 2–4.

Old Cane Ridge Meeting House This 18th-century log cabin was the first church of the Disciples of Christ (a Protestant denomination founded by a former Presbyterian minister). Parishioners held tent meetings that attracted tens of thousands of worshippers at a time. The building is preserved within a native limestone superstructure. > 1655 Cane Ridge Rd., Paris, tel. 859/987–5350. Free. Daily.

VERSAILLES

Bluegrass Scenic Railway Museum Railroad equipment and artifacts are on display at this museum, which is also a center for the reconstruction and restoration of engines and cars. A 90-minute narrated train ride takes passengers though Bluegrass horse-farm country to the scenic, rocky terrain of the Kentucky River bluffs. > Woodford County Park (U.S. 62), Versailles, tel. 859/873–2476 or 800/755–2476. Free, train ride $6. Sat. 10–4, Sun. 1–4.

Labrot and Graham Distillery Established in 1812 and restored in the 1990s, this is the state's oldest working bourbon distillery. Hourly tours of the blue-grey limestone buildings include an orientation film and a visit to the unusual copper-pot stills. > 7855 McCracken Pike, Versailles, tel. 800/542–1812, www.labrot-graham.com. Free. Tues.–Sat. 10–5; tours on the hr 10–3.

Nostalgia Station Toy and Train Museum Housed in a restored 1911 railroad station, exhibits include 1920s and 1950s Lionel toy-train store displays as well as antique toys and other model railroad accessories. > 279 Depot St., Versailles, tel. 859/873–2497. $3. Wed.–Sat. 10–5, Sun. 1–5.

Tours

Among the most famous of some 500 horse farms in the Lexington area are Calumet, Claiborne, and Three Chimneys, where champions including Citation, Gallant Fox, and Seattle Slew have graced the elegant barns and verdant pastures. Calumet has been the birthplace of a record eight Kentucky Derby winners. Individual farms are not open to the public, so guided tours (allow a minimum of 3 hours) are the way to get an inside look.

Another option is to drive along Versailles Road, Old Frankfort Pike, or Paris Pike for good views of the farms from the road. The lanes, lined with stone-and-plank-fences and shaded by old oaks, seem timeless. A good, loop-shape drive starts from Exit 65 on I–64. Go south through Midway (follow the signs) to Old Frankfort Pike and turn right at the historic Offut-Cole Tavern (now a plant nursery). Drive west along the pike (KY 1681) until it comes out onto Versailles Road (U.S. 60). You can then either turn right and hop back on I–64 at Exit 58 or go left and into Lexington past Keeneland.

Bluegrass Tours You can board these tour vans at most of the larger Lexington area hotels. At least one horse farm (the exact one varies from tour to tour), Man O' War's grave site in the Kentucky Horse Park, and Keeneland race course are included in the itinerary. Historic Lexington neighborhoods including Gratz Park are on the tour, too. The cost is $25–$50 for tours; reservations required. > Tel. 859/252–5744. Mar.–Oct.

Horse Farms Tours Depending on the time of day, you might see a morning exercise workout at Keeneland or get to go behind the scenes at a famous farm (locations vary) to have your picture taken with one of the resident horses. During the Yearling

Sales at Keeneland, you can watch the multimillion-dollar betting from the sidelines. Vans leave from most hotels. The cost is $25 per person for tours; reservations required. > Tel. 859/268–2906 or 800/976–1034, www.horsefarmtours.com. Mar.–Oct.

Sports

HORSE RACING & EVENTING
Not surprisingly in the "Horse Capital of the World," the sporting emphasis is equine. Thoroughbred racing takes place at Keeneland, harness racing at the Red Mile, and eventing at the Kentucky Horse Park.

Keeneland America's version of Ascot has thoroughbred racing in April and October. Stately trees line the entrance and the paddock at this historic track, one of the most beautiful in the United States. It's so quiet and civilized that, until just recently, it had no public-address system. Horse people come from all over the world for spring and fall auctions of yearling horses, and this is the only race course in America ever visited by Queen Elizabeth II, who owns some mares on a farm nearby. You can even get a true taste of Kentucky while watching the racing—burgoo, a meaty stew native to the state, is sold at concession stands. The Bluegrass Stakes in April is an important Kentucky Derby prep race. > 4201 Versailles Rd., Lexington, tel. 859/254–3412, www.keenland.com.

Kentucky Horse Park The Rolex Three-Day Event and Trade Fair in April is one of the world's most important cross-country, steeplechase, and dressage equestrian events. The trade fair portion of the event has booths selling wares from art and jewelry to horse supplies. Other important dates are the High Hope Steeplechase in May and the Egyptian Event in June, which features a rare breed dating back to the pharaohs. > 4089 Ironworks Pike, Lexington, tel. 859/233–4303, www.imh.org/khp.

The Red Mile America's fastest trotter track has harness racing in which standardbreds pull two-wheel sulkies piloted by jockey–drivers. The course, opened in 1875, was named for its red-clay surface. Racing is held May–October. > 1200 Red Mile Rd., Lexington, tel. 859/255–0752, www.tattersallsredmile.com.

HORSEBACK RIDING
Kentucky Horse Park A stable in the horse park provides horses for adult trail rides in the surrounding Bluegrass countryside and ponies for children in a supervised paddock. The seasonal 45-minute trail rides cost $14 per person with park admission, $20 without. Pony rides are $4 per child, for ages 12 and under. > 4089 Ironworks Pike, Lexington, tel. 859/233–4303, www.imh.org/khp.

Save the Date

JUNE
Festival of the Bluegrass Top performers of Bluegrass and gospel music gather at the Kentucky Horse Park for a weekend of outdoor concerts. > Lexington, tel. 859/846–4995.

Jazz On the Creek Listen to plenty of jazz at this annual festival held at Stoner Creek Dock. You can also partake in the silent auction, fill up on grill and barbecue fixings, and enjoy pontoon boat rides. > Paris, tel. 859/987–3205.

JULY
Bourbon County Fair and Horse Show In the heart of horse farm country, this county fair draws high-quality competition to its annual horse show. Judging takes place for three- and five-gaited events, Western, Road Horse, and English Pleasure competitions. > Paris, tel. 859/987–3205.

Central Kentucky Steam and Gas Engine Show A different kind of horse power is showcased at this annual event. You can trace the history and economic impact of mechanical engines. > Paris, tel. 859/987–3205.

Junior League Horse Show Held at the Red Mile Harness Track, the world's largest outdoor American Saddlebred show draws competitors from across the United States and Canada. > Lexington, tel. 859/252–1893.

SEPTEMBER

Kentucky Folklife Festival From the driving rhythms of the River City Drum Corps to the mouth-watering taste of western Kentucky barbecue, the living traditions of the diverse people who call Kentucky home are celebrated at this annual event in downtown Frankfort. > Frankfort, tel. 502/564–1792 Ext. 4491.

Roots and Heritage Festival A week of music, theater, poetry-reading, and art exhibitions celebrating African-American heritage culminates in a weekend street fair. > Lexington, tel. 859/233–7299 or 800/845–3959.

NOVEMBER

Kentucky Book Fair Authors native to and living in the state are on hand to sign books and greet fans at this annual event on the campus of Kentucky State University. > Frankfort, tel. 502/227–4556, fax 502/227–2831.

DECEMBER

Southern Lights The Kentucky Horse Park is decorated with a 2½-mi display of more than a million white and colored holiday lights, forming fairy-tale tableaux, horse-racing themes, and Santa and his reindeer. > Lexington, tel. 859/233–4303.

WHERE TO STAY

FRANKFORT

Holiday Inn–Capital Plaza Next door to the Frankfort Civic Center, the building matches the contemporary urban architecture of this part of the capital. There's a dramatic fountain in the attractive lobby; rooms are spacious. Inquire about specially priced weekend getaway packages. > 405 Wilkinson St., Frankfort 40601, tel. 502/227–5100 or 800/465–4329, fax 502/875–7147. www.holidayinnfrankfort.com. 182 rooms, 7 suites. Restaurants, in-room data ports, some refrigerators, cable TV, indoor pool, hot tub, sauna, exercise equipment, bar, shop, laundry facilities, business services, meeting rooms, free parking, some pets allowed (fee), no-smoking rooms. AE, D, DC, MC, V. $

LEXINGTON

Bed & Breakfast at Silver Springs Farm Listed on the Survey of Historic Sites in Kentucky, Silver Springs Farm operated as a distillery from 1867 to Prohibition. Today the 21-acre property is a horse farm with hand-laid stone fences. The B&B, furnished with antiques, has oak and maple floors, hand-pegged walnut doors, hand-reeded mantels, and a dog-legged stairway. One room in the main house has a private bath; the other two rooms share a bath. All are spacious, with queen or king beds. There's also a fully furnished, two-bedroom cottage. Kids are welcome in the guest cottage, and the barn with turnout paddocks has space for guests' horses. Silver Springs is 5 mi from downtown Lexington. > 3710 Leestown Pike, Lexington 40511, tel. 859/255–1784 or 877/255–1784, www.bbsilverspringsfarm.com. 3 rooms, 2 with bath; cottage. Cable TV; no room phones, no smoking. MC, V. BP. $$–$$$$

Brand House at Rose Hill The circa 1812 federal-style, one-story B&B is on 1⅓ acres in the heart of Bluegrass horse country. It's listed on the National Register of Historic Places and the floor plan is registered with the Library of Congress because it's regarded as a significant example of federal-style architecture. All rooms have private whirlpool baths and some rooms have fireplaces. Your breakfast may include Grand Marnier French toast, blueberry mousse, country ham souffle, fresh baked breads, and pastries. > 461 N. Limestone St., Lexington 40508, tel. 859/226–9464 or 800/366–4942, fax 859/252–7940, www.innsnorthamerica.com/ky/BrandHouse.htm. 5 rooms. In-room hot tubs, cable TV; no kids under 12, no smoking. AE, D, MC, V. BP. $$–$$$$

Campbell House Inn, Suites and Golf Club A circular driveway planted in formal flower beds leads to the impressive white-column entrance at the Campbell House. Rooms here offer modern amenities such as data port phones and hair dryers amidst Early American-style furniture. Located 1½ mi from downtown, the facility is convenient to the airport and Keeneland Racetrack. There is a clubby, wood-panelled restaurant on-site. > 1375 Harrodsburg Rd. (U.S. 68), Lexington 40504, tel. 859/255–4281, 800/354–9235 outside KY, 800/432–9254 in KY, fax 859/254–4368. www.campbellhouseinn.com. 370 rooms. Dining room, café, room service, in-room data ports, refrigerators, cable TV, 18-hole golf course, pro shop, indoor pool, hair salon, gym, bar, laundry facilities, business services, meeting rooms, airport shuttle, no-smoking rooms. AE, D, DC, MC, V. $–$$$$

Marriott's Griffin Gate Resort Near major highways 3½ mi north of downtown, this resort is distinguished by a two-story atrium lounge with waterfalls. Equestrian art figures prominently in the contemporary rooms, which have desks and extra chairs well suited to business travelers. Upper stories look out over a rolling, lakeside gold course. > 1800 Newtown Pike (Rte. 922), Lexington 40511, tel. 859/231–5100, fax 859/288–6245, www.marriott.com. 409 rooms, 9 suites. 3 restaurants, picnic area, room service, in-room data ports, some refrigerators, cable TV with movies, 18-hole golf course, putting green, tennis courts, 2 pools (1 indoor), gym, hair salon, hot tub, sauna, spa, bar, shop, laundry facilities, Internet, business services, airport shuttle, some pets allowed (fee), no-smoking rooms. AE, D, DC, MC, V. $$–$$$$

Springs Inn Surrounded by old oak and crab apple trees, this green-and-white colonial-style hotel is across the street from a shopping mall, about 3 mi from downtown. Some suites are available. > 2020 Harrodsburg Rd. (U.S. 68), Lexington 40503, tel. 859/277–5751 or 800/354–9503, fax 859/277–3142. 196 rooms, 2 suites. Restaurant, some refrigerators, cable TV, pool, wading pool, bar, business services, airport shuttle, no smoking rooms. AE, D, DC, MC, V. CP. ¢

True Inn Bed & Breakfast This in-town, Richardsonian Romanesque, brick home built in 1843 for the Reverend John Ward, second Rector and organizer of Christ Episcopal Church, was remodeled in 1890 as an antebellum Greek Revival residence. Listed on the National Register of Historic Homes and the Bluegrass Trust, the house has a turret tower, stained- and leaded-glass windows, seven ornately carved Richardsonian and Victorian mantels, original chandeliers, spacious formal rooms and gardens. All five guest rooms have antique furnishings and either a full- or queen-size bed. > 467 W. 2nd St., Lexington 40507, tel. 859/252–6166 or 800/374–6151. www.bbonline.com/ky/trueinn. 5 rooms. Some refrigerators, some in-room hot tubs, in-room VCRs, bicycles; no kids under 12, no smoking. AE, MC, V. BP. $$–$$$

PARIS

Amelia's Field Built in the 1930s, this colonial-style house stands in the middle of horse-farm country. Rooms are furnished with antiques but painted in bold contemporary colors. > 617 Cynthiana Rd., Paris 40361, tel. 606/987–5778, fax 859/987–9075. 4 rooms. Restaurant; no phones, no room TVs. Closed Jan.–mid-Feb. AE, DC, MC, V. BP. $

Crockett's Colonial Motel Built in the 1950s, this motel on the southern edge of downtown has an art-deco interior and mahogany furnishings. > 1493 S. Main St., Paris 40361, tel. 859/987–3250. 8 rooms. Refrigerators, cable TV, playground, business services, some pets allowed (fee). No credit cards. ¢

Rosedale This 1862 Italianate brick home was once the home of a Civil War general and is now an inn furnished with antiques and Oriental rugs. > 1917 Cypress St., Paris 40361, tel. 859/987–1845 or 800/644–1862, www.bbonline.com/ky/rosedale/index.html. 4 rooms, 2 with bath. Laundry facilities; no room TVs, no kids under 12. MC, V. BP. ¢–$

MIDWAY

Scottwood Bed and Breakfast Landscaped with gardens and hemlocks, this B&B is on the scenic South Elkhorn Creek renowned for its widemouth bass fishing. The circa 1795 federal home is listed on Bluegrass Trust. All rooms have queen-size beds and two rooms share a bath. A telephone is available in the common area, and there's a canoe ready for your use. > 2004 Leestown Rd., Midway 40347, tel. 859/846–5037 or 877/477–0778, fax 859/846–4887, www.scottwoodbb.com. 4 rooms, 2 with bath. Cable TV, in-room VCRs, fishing, some pets allowed; no room phones, no smoking. MC, V. BP. $–$$

VERSAILLES

Sills Inn This 1911 Victorian is painted lemon yellow with white trim, and has nearly 9,000 square feet of floor space. Rooms are decorated with bright floral fabrics. Set on a quiet street in historic downtown Versailles, the inn is a 10-minute drive from downtown Lexington. > 270 Montgomery Ave., Versailles 40383, tel. 859/873–4478 or 800/526–9801, fax 859/873–7099. 14 rooms. In-room data ports, minibars, some refrigerators, cable TV, in-room VCRs, business services, airport shuttle; no kids, no smoking. AE, D, DC, MC, V. BP. $–$$$

WHERE TO EAT

FRANKFORT

Jim's Seafood Built on the foundation of an 18th-century hemp mill, this family-owned, nautical-theme restaurant on the edge of downtown has a view of the Kentucky River. Jim's is known for crab legs and for tilapia raised in spring water. Enjoy them in the contemporary dining room, done in limestone and wood, or eat lunch at picnic tables on the deck. There's a kids' menu, and wine and beer only. > 950 Wilkerson St., Frankfort, tel. 502/223–7448, fax 502/227–7419. AE, D, MC, V. Closed Sun. No lunch Sat. $–$$$

Serafini The menu ranges from pasta, including the vegetarian pasta St. Clair, to chops and steaks. The interior of this restaurant in the heart of downtown is contemporary, but it once was a Victorian pharmacy. The bar has an excellent selection of premium bourbons if you're in a mood to sample. > 243 W. Broadway, Frankfort, tel. 502/875–5599. AE, MC, V. Closed Sun. $$–$$$

Thai Smile Coconut milk, lemon grass, lime leaves, peanuts, and cilantro flavor dishes including Thai beef stick, chicken red curry, and pad Thai (stir-fried rice noodles). Nam sod (minced chicken with lime juice and ginger) and a succulent duck curry are specialties. Posters of Thailand line the walls of this otherwise sparely decorated spot in a shopping center near the interstate. > 1193 Century Plaza, Frankfort, tel. 502/227–9934. MC, V. Closed Sun. $

LEXINGTON

A La Lucie This small café on the edge of Gratz Park with booths and fringed lampshades is reminiscent of Paris's left bank in the '20s. The cocktails here are locally praised. The menu includes fresh fish and international fare. > 159 N. Limestone St., Lexington, tel. 859/252–5277, www.thepacificpearl.com/lucie.html. AE, D, DC, MC, V. Closed Sun. No lunch. $$–$$$

Alfalfa Restaurant The food in this small, woody, old-fashioned restaurant is organically grown, vegetarian, and ethnic. It's just the sort of place you'd expect to find at the edge of a university campus, in this case U of K. The menu, written on a chalkboard, may include ham-and-apple quiche; the house salad is lavish. Each Wednesday a different cuisine—Greek, Italian, Indian—is served. Saturday and Sunday there's brunch. > 557 S. Limestone St., Lexington, tel. 859/253–0014. MC, V. No dinner Sun. and Mon. $$–$$$

Dudley's Paintings of horses adorn the dining rooms in this renovated mid-19th-century schoolhouse. You can also choose open-air dining on the tree-shaded patio. Dinner choices include spinach and artichoke-stuffed ravioli, grilled pork T-bone, and beef fillet with cabernet, shallots, and butter. > 380 S. Mill St., Lexington, tel. 859/252–1010. AE, DC, MC, V. $$–$$$$

Joe Bologna's Lots of carved wood and stained glass remain in this restored former church, known for its pasta and deep-dish pizza. Just a couple of blocks from campus, it's a favorite hangout for students and locals. > 120 W. Maxwell St., Lexington, tel. 859/252–4933. AE, D, DC, MC, V. $–$$$

Lynagh's Irish Pub and Grill Dark and lively, this pub is decorated with bicycles hanging from the ceiling. Try the corned beef and cabbage or the locally popular hamburgers. It's midway between downtown and the University of Kentucky. > 384 Woodland Ave., Lexington, tel. 859/255–1292. No credit cards. $–$$

Mansion at Griffin Gate This 1873 Greek Revival mansion is furnished with period antiques. Dining here is like dining with Scarlett and Rhett (if they'd had a French chef). The menu includes veal, fresh seafood, and filet mignon. > 1720 Newtown Pike, Lexington, tel. 859/288–6142. AE, D, DC, MC, V. No lunch. $$$$

Merrick Inn The spacious, comfortable, not-too-formal restaurant is housed in a sprawling, white-column building that was once a horse farm (circa 1890). It blends right in with the older residents and tree-lined streets leading to it. On the extensive menu are steak, lamb, and pasta; the specialty is fresh seasonal seafood. But the real reason to come here is the great Southern fried chicken. > 3380 Tates Creek Rd., Lexington, tel. 859/269–5417. AE, DC, MC, V. Closed Sun. $$$–$$$$

Pacific Pearl Boldly colored, this contemporary restaurant is in an upscale suburban development on the city outskirts. The striking glass-and-metal bar is the perfect spot for sipping an Oriental martini. Try the Thai bouillabaisse, crispy duck, or coconut-fried lobster. Open-air dining is available on the plant-lined patio. > 1050 Chinoe Rd., Lexington, tel. 859/266–1611. AE, D, MC, V. No lunch. $$–$$$$

PARIS

Bourbonton Inn Restaurant For traditional favorites like spaghetti, hot browns (a broiled turkey, bacon, and cheese treat invented at Louisville's Brown Hotel during the Roaring '20s), country ham, fried fish, and cooked oysters, a stop in this casual restaurant is a must. The blue- and cream-color eatery is across the street from the courthouse. > 332 Main St., Paris, tel. 859/987–6700. No credit cards. Closed Sat. ¢–$

MIDWAY

Holly Hill Inn The ground floor rooms of this 19th-century farmhouse serve as intimate dining rooms. The seasonal prix fixe menu takes advantage of local produce with such specialties as rosemary rack of lamb and bourbon-kissed creamy bay scallops. The excellent wine list is chosen to match the food. > 426 Winter St., Midway, tel. 859/846–4732. Reservations essential. AE, MC, V. Closed Mon. and Tues., no dinner Sunday. $$$

VERSAILLES

Kessler's 1891 Eatery and Pub You'll see the work of local artists displayed in this downtown restaurant with high ceilings and exposed brick walls decorated with Victorian antique hardware and brass. The daily lunch buffet with steak, ribs, catfish, and "barbecued everything" draws quite a crowd. > 197 S. Main St., Versailles, tel. 859/879–3344, www.kesslers1891.com. MC, V. Closed Sun. $–$$

ESSENTIALS

Getting Here

The horsepower to use in horse country is under your hood. The Bluegrass region is filled with highways and byways that put the pleasure back in old-fashioned motoring. If you're flying into the region, rent a car after you land. Outside of a few bus routes in Lexington and Frankfort, there's no public transportation. The best way to enjoy the scenery is from the comfort of a private car. Roadside historical markers seem to crop up every couple of miles, giving details about everything from where Daniel Boone slept to who built the stone fences enclosing the manicured horse farm pastures.

BY CAR

The route into the Bluegrass from Ohio is I–75. U.S. 60 and I–64 are both important arteries through the region. Tree-shaded and fence-lined U.S. 27 (Paris Pike) between Lexington and Paris is a must-drive for taking in the horse country. On most two-lane roads, you'll go 45 to 50 mph, but watch for farm equipment and horse trailers.

In Frankfort, both metered and free street parking can be found in most parts of the city; there are no meters downtown. Garage rates vary, but an all-day spot in one of the city's two garages goes for as little as $2. You can park for free in designated sections of the Old Train Depot, at the corner of Ann Street and Broadway, just a few minutes walk to downtown attractions.

Parking in central Lexington can be tricky in the middle of the day, but there are meters along main and side streets. Garages at Main and Broadway and

Rupp Area are right downtown. Fees vary from 50¢ to $3 per hour depending on time of day and day of the week.

Parking on the street is readily available in Midway, Paris, and Versailles.

BY PLANE

The Lexington Blue Grass Airport serves the area. Convenient for the horsey set, it's just across U.S. 60 from Keeneland Race Course. The drive to downtown Lexington is about 15 minutes, and it's about a half hour to Frankfort. For travelers from Ohio, the airlines to use are Continental and Delta. There are flights to and from Cincinnati, but you can drive to Lexington in the time it takes to get to the airport, go through security, and get up in the air and back down again. Lexington's is a relatively small airport with one terminal, so it's as hassle-free as an airport can be these days.

There are two flights a day from Cleveland to Lexington on Continental Express; one leaves in the early afternoon and the other at about 8:30 at night. Flight time is a little over an hour.

There are no direct flights between Columbus and Lexington. Delta Airlines has seven daily flights that connect through Cincinnati and take a total of 2½ to 3 hours. They leave as early as 7 AM and as late as 8:30 PM from Columbus.

AIRPORTS **Lexington Blue Grass Airport** > 400 Terminal Dr. (U.S. 60 at Man O' War Blvd.), Lexington, tel. 859/425–3100, www.bluegrassairport.com. *CARRIERS* **Continental Express** > Tel. 800/525–0280, www.continental.com. **Delta** > Tel. 800/221–1212, www.delta.com.

Visitor Information

CONTACTS **Frankfort–Franklin County Tourist and Convention Commission** > 100 Capital Ave., Frankfort 40601, tel. 502/875—8687 or 800/960–7200. www.visitfrankfort.com. **Lexington Convention and Visitors Bureau** > 301 E. Vine St., Lexington 40507-1513, tel. 859/233–7299 or 800/845–3959. www.visitlex.com. **Paris–Bourbon County Chamber of Commerce** > 800 Pleasant St. Paris 40361, tel. 859/987–3205 or 888/987–3205, www.parisky.com. **Woodford County Chamber of Commerce** > 110 N. Main St., Box 442, Versailles 40383, tel. 859/873–5122, www.tourwcky.com.

Natural Bridge & Red River Gorge

Slade is 137 mi southeast of Cincinnati, 242 mi south of Columbus, and 393 mi south of Cleveland.

19

By Susan Reigler

A BOULDER-STREWN WILD RIVER, cascading waterfalls, 300 million year old sandstone formations of soaring cliffs, rock towers, looming overhangs, and stone arches. These features are concentrated within the unique landscape of Natural Bridge State Resort Park and the Red River Gorge Geological Area, located side by side within the vast 694,985-acre Daniel Boone National Forest, which stretches across 21 eastern Kentucky counties.

Sculpted by the wind and water, which unevenly eroded the limestone beneath the harder sandstone, these dramatic features were 70 million years in the making. The Red River, which carved the 25 mi gorge, got its name from the reddish iron pyrite found in the soil along its banks. The mineral faintly colors the water, especially after a hard rain.

Unlike in the arid West, the rugged landscape here is covered by a dense woodland of hemlocks, tulip poplars, oaks, and mountain laurel. The botanical bounty includes rarities and protected species such as crane-fly orchids, purple gerardia, climbing fern, and white-haired goldenrod, a species found only in a small portion of Menifee and Powell counties. Between them, Natural Bridge and Red River Gorge contain 95% of Kentucky's native plant and animal species.

While the region is a popular destination of hikers, rock climbers, and nature lovers, it also has a rich history of human activity.

Cavelike openings in overhanging ledges (called rock houses) contain archaeological evidence that prehistoric people lived in the area as early as 10,000 years ago.

The pioneer and explorer Daniel Boone and his colleagues John Findley and John Stewart arrived in the area in 1769 from North Carolina. Boone may have spent a winter living in the area, taking shelter in the cliffs. Other pioneer visitors included Dr. Thomas Walker and Christopher Gist.

In the 19th century, iron was discovered and forges built. Railroad companies laid track and carved out roads to facilitate logging and mining. By the middle of the 20th century, however, industry had abandoned the land, which became part of the national forest. But the geological beauty and biodiversity were threatened in the 1960s by an Army Corps of Engineer dam project, planned to help control flooding in the region.

Supreme Court Justice William O. Douglas, also a committed environmentalist, made a well-publicized hike through the Red River Gorge in 1967, which resulted in its protection. In 1993, a 9.1-mi section of the Red River was designated a Kentucky Wild River.

To ease the transition from town to "wilderness," weekenders may wish to pause in Winchester, about a mile south of where I–64 and the Mountain Parkway (leading the the Natural Bridge–Red River Gorge area) meet. A marketing and manufacturing center, as well as the Clark County seat, it has a couple of significant claims in state history.

Fort Boonesborough was built nearby. A replica of the settlement is the centerpiece of a state park here. A U.S. Senator from Kentucky, Henry Clay ("The Great Compromiser") gave his first and last Kentucky speeches in Winchester. Ale-8-One, a gingery soft drink (with much more attitude than ginger ale), was concocted here in 1926 and is still manufactured and bottled in the town.

Slade (Mountain Parkway Exit 33) serves as supply center and headquarters for surrounding recreation areas, including Red River Gorge, Natural Bridge, and Daniel Boone National Forest. Campton (10 mi east of Slade on the Mountain Parkway) and Beattyville (20 mi south of Natural Bridge State Resort Park on the Mountain Parkway) have Main Streets with shops where crafts collectors can hunt for handmade quilts, baskets, and other goods.

WHAT TO SEE & DO

Natural Bridge State Resort Park More than 150 stone arches (called natural bridges) and rocky cliffs dot the wooded landscape in this 1,982-acre park, attracting naturalists year-round. Nine hiking trails ranging from ½ mi to 8½ mi provide access to the park's interior.

The forest contains evergreens such as old hemlocks and white pine and among the majestic hardwoods are giant tulip poplars and oaks. Hikers can spot more than 50 species of ferns growing along the cliffsides and on the forest floor. Wildflower enthusiasts will be taken with the springtime display of orchids and lilies. Several rare wildflower species, including the small yellow lady's slipper are native to the park, which is also a great place for birders. The density of the woodland, however, means that the warblers and grosbeaks are more often heard than seen. Natural Bridge is also home to the Virginia big-eared bat, an endangered species.

The steepest trail in the park (your knees and calves will think it's much longer than ¾ mi) leads to one of its most unusual geological formations. Looking rather like a giant anvil or a toy top resting on its point, **Balanced Rock** seems to defy gravity. The shape is the result of uneven erosion of the sandstone layers.

The flat top of **Natural Bridge,** the 65-foot-tall sandstone arch for which the park is named, spans 78 feet and does indeed look like a bridge pushing through the treetops to connect two hillsides. Those with a good head for heights will be enchanted by the vistas from the top of the bridge. Access to the arch from the lodge is via the ¾-mi-long Original Trail, built in the 1890s by loggers from the Lexington and Eastern Railroad. The trail winds upward for more than 500 feet through heavily wooded terrain dominated by overhanging boulders and vertical cliff faces.

The **Nature Center** (just west of Hemlock Lodge on a marked pathway, tel. 606/663–2140, free, daily 8–5) occupies the lower level of the two-story wood-and-stone activity center (the upper level has meeting rooms). There are displays about park wildlife and trail maps, as well as park ranger programs for youngsters.

Sand Gap Trail is the park's longest trail at 8.5 mi. It winds through woods, past waterfalls streaming down cliffsides, and under craggy rock overhangs. It's the most challenging trail, too, but the views from the ridge tops it follows are well worth the effort.

The park is also a regional center for folk dancing, and square dances are held every weekend on Hoedown Island in the lake below the lodge. > 2135 Natural Bridge Rd., off the Mountain Pkwy. on KY 11, Slade, tel. 606/663–2214 or 800/325–1710, www.kystateparks.com/agencies/parks/natbridg. Free. Daily.

Red River Gorge The 25,662-acre Red River Gorge National Geological area is just a small part of vast Daniel Boone National Forest. The landscape contains sandstone cliffs and more than 100 natural arches, geological structures sculpted by wind and water over 70 million years. There are extensive hiking trails and many rare plants and animals throughout the park. The Red River, which carved the gorge, is the state's only National Wild and Scenic River.

Gladie Historic Site (KY 715, free, June–Aug., daily 10–6; Apr., May, Sept., and Oct., weekends 10–6), a restored log cabin dating from about 1880, contains exhibits on 19th-century logging and farming. A blacksmith shop and moonshine still are among the attractions. A resident herd of American bison grazes in the pasture nearby.

The 900-foot **Nada Tunnel** (KY 77) was carved through a mountain by workers wielding pick axes and shovels in the early 1900s for the use of a logging railroad. A drive through the one-lane tunnel, which is listed on the Register for National Historic Places, is not for the claustrophobic. The **Red River** runs for 96 mi through the mountains, but it's the 9-mi portion between KY 715 and KY 746 that is classified as a wild river. More than 50 species of fish live in the water and it's a favorite destination for white-water canoeing. **Red River Gorge Loop Drive** (KY 715 and KY 77) passes through the Nada Tunnel and along the Red River, winding through the gorge for 36 mi. Many of the area's sandstone arches and other geological formations, including three waterfalls, can be seen from the road.

Stand high atop **Sky Bridge** (KY 715) for a great view of the gorge. The stone arch is at the summit of a ridge, and a convenient picnic site invites you to make a day of hiking in the area. > Mountain Pkwy., tel. 606/663–9229, www.kytravel.com. Free. Daily.

Sheltowee Trace National Recreation Trail The 269-mi hiking trail begins in Pickett State Park, Tennessee, and ends just north of Morehead, Kentucky. All but the 10 southernmost miles of the trail are in Kentucky. The trail passes through both Natural Bridge State Resort Park and the Red River Gorge Geological Area. The name, which means "Big Turtle," was given to Daniel Boone by the Shawnee. The trail was followed, in part, by Boone. Sierra Club founder, John Muir, also hiked along much of its route. Portions of the trail are open to horses, mountain bikes, and motor vehicles, but you can traverse its entire length only by walking. > 100 Vaught Rd., Winchester, tel. 859/745–3100. Free. Daily.

SLADE

Reptile Zoo You can take in a guided tour or an educational presentation at the zoo, which exhibits more than 70 species of live reptiles from around the world. King cobras, iguanas, and crocodiles are among the residents. The zoo is also an important supplier of venom for research and medicine. > 1275 Natural Bridge Rd., Slade, tel. 606/663–9160. $3.50. June–Aug., daily 11–6; Mar.–May and Sept.–Nov., Thurs.–Sun. 11–6.

Sky Lift Enjoy the rugged beauty of Natural Bridge State Park from a tranquil vantage point in the sky. The ride begins ½ mi from the park entrance. > 2135 Natural Bridge Rd., Slade, tel. 606/663–2214. Mid-Apr.–mid-Oct., daily 10–6.

WINCHESTER

Ale-8-One Bottling Company The company store sells items (including six packs) associated with this fruit-and-gingery soft drink, made here from a secret recipe since 1926. You can use mail order, too. > 25 Carol Rd., Winchester, tel. 859/744–3484, www.aleeightone.com. Free. Weekdays 8:30–4:30.

Fort Boonesborough State Park Daniel Boone's famous fort-settlement has been reconstructed on 153 acres along the Kentucky River, where costumed craftspeople re-create pioneer life. The park includes campgrounds, a seasonal swimming pool, and riverside interpretive trails that highlight geological and botanical points of interest. A reenactment of the Siege of Boonesborough occurs on the last weekend in May. > 4375 Boonesborough Rd., Winchester, tel. 859/527–3131, www.kystateparks.com/agencies/parks/ftboones.htm. Apr.–Labor Day, daily; Labor Day–Oct., Wed.–Sun.

Historic Main Street Victorian-era storefronts house specialty shops in this area of Winchester, which is listed on the National Register of Historic Places. The tourist board supplies walking tour maps. > Tourist Information Center, 2 S. Maple St., Winchester, tel. 859/744–0556. Free. Weekdays 8–5.

Old Stone Church Daniel Boone was one of the early members of this 1792 church, which is one of the oldest churches west of the Alleghenies. > Old Stone Church Rd., off KY 627, Winchester, tel. 859/744–6420. Free. By appointment.

Sports

The Natural Bridge–Red River Gorge area is packed with recreational opportunities ranging from a leisurely stroll on a well-marked park trail to scaling rugged sandstone overhangs.

BIRD-WATCHING

Red River Gorge The Kentucky Ornithological Society has recorded sightings of more than 225 bird species throughout the Daniel Boone National Forest. This represents most nesting and migrating birds for the state. The Red River Gorge is Kentucky's only known breeding site for red-breasted nuthatches. Such relative rarities as Swainson's warbler, American redstart, Acadian flycatcher, and Louisiana waterthrush can be seen in the **Clifty Wilderness** area in the northeast quadrant of the park. > Mountain Pkwy., tel. 606/663–9229, www.kytravel.com.

CANOEING

The pioneer's eye-view of the gorge from the water is unmatchable. But be advised that a "demolished canoe club" exists for paddlers on the Red River. Late fall to early summer is the best time to travel because water levels drop in summer. Conditions range from Class I to Class III+.

RENTALS **Red River Outdoors** > 410 Natural Bridge Rd., Slade, tel. 606/663–9701, www.redriveroutdoors.com.

FISHING

Natural Bridge State Resort Park Limited fishing with live bit and bobber is allowed in **Middlefork** stream in Natural Bridge State Resort Park. Roughfish and panfish are the target species. Small boats are allowed on the park's **Mill Creek Lake** for fishing, too. > 2135 Natural Bridge Rd., off the Mountain Pkwy. on KY 11, Slade, tel. 606/663–2214 or 800/325–1710, www.kystateparks.com/agencies/parks/natbridg.

ROCK CLIMBING

Vertical cliffs and overhangs challenge technical rock climbers of all skill levels in the Red River Gorge Geological Area. Many established climbing routes are equipped with permanently placed safety bolts.

Miguel's Pizza and Rock Climbing Shop In addition to selling equipment (and pizza), there's a kiosk in the parking lot that has maps, guidebooks, and other essential rock trail information. > 1890 Natural Bridge Rd., Slade, tel. 606/663–1975.

Red River Outdoors Climbing equipment, camping supplies, canoe rentals, and maps and guidebooks for the Gorge and other parts of the national forest are among the goods and services. It's commercially licensed by the U.S. Forest Service to operate in the area. > 415 Natural Bridge Rd., Slade, tel. 606/663–9001.

USDA Forest Service The Forest Service manages Red River Gorge and provides topographical maps of the area, along with trail and camping information. > Stanton Ranger District Office, 705 W. College Ave., Stanton, tel. 606/663–2852, www.r8web.com/boone/rockclimb.htm.

Save the Date

APRIL

Herpetology Weekend The Kentucky Reptile Zoo sponsors a 2-day viewing of its unusual salamanders, frogs, turtles, lizards, and snakes. There's also a slide and photography competition. > Tel. 606/663–2214.

Mountain Mushroom Festival The 5K Fungus Run and a mushroom contest are signatures of this festival. It also includes a quilt show, car show, and food and entertainment. > Tel. 859/723–1233.

JUNE

National Mountain Style Square Dance and Clogging Festival Hundreds of dancers in traditional costumes descend on the park for a weekend of floor-pounding, skirt-swirling folk dancing. > Tel. 606/663–2214.

AUGUST

Mountain Market Festival An open-air market held on the grounds of Natural Bridge State Park showcases local farm products and crafts. You can partake in seminars on local cooking, see lively musical performances, and enjoy an evening of square dancing. > Tel. 606/663–2214.

SEPTEMBER

Daniel Boone Pioneer Festival Fireworks, street dancing, arts and crafts, and a 2-mi, community "Walk with Friends" are highlights of this Labor Day weekend festival. > Tel. 859/744–0556.

WHERE TO STAY

Hemlock Lodge, Natural Bridge State Resort Park Set on a wooded cliffside overlooking Mill Creek Lake, the state-owned lodge has balconied rooms and one- or two-bedroom cottages, giving you access to all facilities at Natural Bridge State Resort Park. The stone-and-wood lobby has a handsome copper-hooded fireplace and comfortable furniture. > 2135 Natural Bridge Rd., Slade 40376, tel. 606/663–2214 or 800/325–1710, fax 606/663–5037, www.state.ky.us/agencies/parks. 35 rooms, 10 cottages. Dining room, picnic area, some kitchenettes, cable TV, miniature golf, pool, wading pool, boating, children's programs, playground, business services, no-smoking rooms. AE, D, DC, MC, V. ¢–$

NEAR THE PARKS

Best Western Country Square You'll find king-size, queen-size, and double beds at this standard, economic motel. Fort Boonesborough is a few miles away, and several shops and restaurants are within ½ mi of the motel. > 1307 W. Lexington Ave., Winchester 40391, tel. 859/744–7210, fax 859/744–7210, www.bestwestern.com. 46 rooms. Some kitchenettes, some microwaves, refrigerators, cable TV, pool, business services, some pets allowed (fee), no-smoking rooms. AE, D, DC, MC, V. CP. ¢

Holiday Inn Rooms with king beds also have recliner chairs at this hotel, and there's a complimentary Continental breakfast. It's 10 mi from Fort Boonesborough State Park. > 1100 Interstate Dr., Winchester 40391, tel. 859/744–9111, fax 859/745–1369. www.basshotels.com. 64 rooms. Restaurant, in-room data ports, some refrigerators, cable TV, pool, hot tub, laundry facilities, business services, free parking, some pets allowed, no smoking rooms. AE, D, DC, MC, V. CP. ¢–$

Kathy's Country Inn This country bungalow has a comfortable parlor and porches with rocking chairs. Guests have kitchen privileges, if the urge to cook overcomes you. Kathy's is within walking distance of crafts shopping. > 163 N. Washington St., Campton 41301, tel. 606/668–6658, www.bbonline.com/ky/kathys. 5 rooms, 3 with bath. Some in-room hot tubs; no phones in some rooms, no TV in some rooms. MC, V. CP. $–$$

Shadow Mountain Mist Tall windows in the dining loft look out over the rugged landscape near Red River Gorge. A fire roars in the great room's stone hearth in winter. Theme-decorated rooms in the main building include Captain's Quarters, Victorian, and Wild West. Cabins cling to hillsides and have porches so you can enjoy the views. > 30 Lee Lane, Slade 40376, tel. 606/663–8018 or 888/663–2600, fax 606/663–1225, www.shadowmountainmist.com. 10 rooms, 12 cabins. Dining room, no-smoking rooms; no phones in some rooms, no TV in some rooms. AE, MC, V. BP. $–$$

Torrent Falls Bed and Breakfast Named for the 160-foot waterfall that streams over a cliff on the wooded property, the large log house is built on the mountainside site of the L. Park Hotel that dated from 1890. Country furnishings, including handmade quilts, and a breakfast room with a large stone fireplace are hallmarks. Blueberry French toast is a breakfast specialty. > 1435 N. KY 11, Campton 41301, tel. 606/668–6441, fax 606/668–9916, www.torrentfalls.com/bnb/index.asp. 2 rooms, 1 suite, 3 cabins. Room TVs; no smoking. AE, D, MC, V. BP. $–$$$

CAMPING

Koomer Ridge Campground The campsite is semi-primitive, and the sites set among the trees offer a fair amount of privacy as well as excellent access to Red River Gorge trails. It's also convenient to Natural Bridge trails. Nineteen sites accommodate trailers, but no hook-ups are available. > Red River Gorge Geological Area, KY 15, 5 mi east of Mountain Pkwy., Slade exit, tel. 606/663–2857, www.r8web.com/boone/rrg. 19 RV sites, 35 tent sites. Flush toilets, pit toilets, drinking water, showers, grills, picnic tables. Reservations not accepted. AE, MC, V. No water or other facilities Nov.–Mar. ¢

Whittleton Campground The campground is rather narrow, but it's near the trails. Some sites are more wooded than others and you can pitch your tent near the backs of these for more seclusion. > Natural Bridge State Resort Park, KY 11 on the northeast side of the park, tel. 606/663–2214. 45 sites, 2 suitable for RVs. Flush toilets, partial hook-ups (electric), dump station, laundry facilities, showers. Reservations not accepted. AE, MC, V. Closed Nov.–Mar. ¢

WHERE TO EAT

Gourmets are advised to stay in a park cabin with a fully equipped kitchen and to bring your own food and beverages if you're looking for an elegant dinner after a day of hiking trails and taking in the scenery. Otherwise, more down-home fare is available locally.

Hemlock Lodge Finish off a day in the park with a traditional dinner of catfish, pork chops, or fried chicken. The Hot Browns—a platter of toast, turkey, ham, cheese sauce, and tomato, all browned in the oven—is also a favorite. Flowers and wall paintings add graceful touches to the woodsy, rustic dining room. Bird feeders outside the windows attract avian diners throughout the year, too. Note: No alcohol is served in state park dining rooms. > Natural Bridge State Resort Park, 2135 Natural Bridge Rd., Slade, tel. 606/663–2214. AE, D, MC, V. $

NEAR THE PARKS

Banana's on the River A tropical theme distinguishes this large, river-view restaurant: banana trees, palm trees, and vines grace the interior dining room. Outside, two decks overlook the Kentucky River and Boonesborough State Park. Banana's is known for steak, seafood, pasta, baby back ribs, and lamb fries. Sometimes live entertainment is scheduled at dinner. > 700 Ford Rd., Winchester, tel. 859/527–3582. AE, MC, V. Closed Sun. and Mon. ¢

Hall's on the River Part of the historic district, this country dining room serves fried, broiled, or blackened catfish and Hot Brown—an open-faced sandwich with turkey, country ham, gravy, and melted cheese. The tin-roofed deck, used for open-air dining in season, overlooks the Kentucky River and Howard's Creek. There's a kids' menu, too. > 1225 Athens-Boonesborough Rd., Winchester, tel. 859/527–6620. AE, MC, V. $$–$$$

ESSENTIALS

Getting Here

Even though the first colonial pioneers came here by canoe and foot, modern travelers will want a car. Parking is provided both in Natural Bridge State Resort Park and at trailheads in Red River Gorge. You may also want to take a car into some of the small towns in the area to browse in the Kentucky crafts shops. On-street parking will not be a problem.

BY CAR

The Natural Bridge–Red River Gorge area is well served by modern highways. And once you're in the area, two-lane state roads include scenic routes that will allow you to enjoy the unique landscape even if you don't hike or canoe.

Travel south on I–75 from Ohio to Lexington, where you'll pick up I–64 going east. Exit 98 puts you on the Bert T. Combs Mountain Parkway, which winds southeast through the increasingly mountainous countryside to Slade, the gateway town to the state park and the geological area.

Travel time from Cleveland is about 6½ hours, averaging 65 mph. Columbus is 4 hours from the Gorge, and Cincinnati is about 2¼ hours away.

The Red River Gorge Scenic Byway is an excellent way to get an overview of the region. It loops around KY 15, KY 77, KY 715, and KY 11 for almost 50 mi past stone arches, cliffs, and waterfalls, as well as the Gladie Historic Site and the Nada Tunnel.

BY PLANE

The Lexington Blue Grass Airport (located for the horsey set just across U.S. 60 from Keeneland Race Course) is the airport serving the area. It takes about an hour to drive to the Natural Bridge area from Lexington, a distance of 55 mi. For travelers from Ohio, the airlines to use are Continental and Delta. There are flights to and from Cincinnati, but you can drive to Natural Bridge and Red River Gorge in the time it takes to get to the airport, go through security, and get up in the air and back down again. Lexington is a relatively small airport with one terminal, so it's as hassle-free as an airport can be these days. There are two flights a day from Cleveland to Lexington on Continental Express; one leaves in the early afternoon and the other about 8:30 at night. Flight time is a little over an hour.

There are no direct flights between Columbus and Lexington. Seven daily flights connect through Cincinnati and take a total of 2½ to 3 hours. They leave as early as 7 AM and as late as 8:30 PM from Columbus. The carrier is Delta Airlines. Or you might want to consider renting a car in Cincinnati and driving from there rather than connecting to Lexington.

AIRPORTS **Cincinnati–Northern Kentucky International Airport** > 2601 Donaldson Hwy., Erlanger, tel. 859/767–3151, www.cvgairport.com. **Lexington Blue Grass Airport** > 400 Terminal Dr. (U.S. 60 at Man O' War Blvd.), Lexington, tel. 859/425–3100, www.bluegrassairport.com.

CARRIERS **Continental Airlines,** > Tel. 800/525–0280, www.flycontinental.com. **Delta Air Lines** > Tel. 800/221–1212, www.delta.com.

Visitor Information

CONTACTS **Natural Bridge–Powell County Chamber of Commerce** > Caboose Visitor Center, 30 E. Railroad Pl., Slade 40376, tel. 606/663–9229, www.powellcountytourism.com. **Tourist Information Center** > 2 Maple St., Winchester 40391, tel. 859/744–0556, www.winchesterky.com.

Cincinnati

Cincinnati is 100 mi southwest of Columbus and 244 mi southwest of Cleveland.

20

By Geoff Williams

A RIVER'S WIDTH FROM THE SOUTH, Cincinnati resembles a southern city in many respects: Its summers are hot and humid, a result of being in a basin along the Ohio River, and its politics lean toward the conservative. This is just the first of several different identities, however. It's a river town, a sports town, a metropolis with architectural landmarks—and with the opening in 2004 of the $110 million National Underground Railroad Freedom Center—Cincinnati will be able to rightfully call itself a history town. There are also a multitude of museums and one of the best zoos in the country. The rolling bluegrass-covered hills of Kentucky are just over the river, and the rural plains of Indiana and the meadow-marked countryside of Ohio are about a 30-minute drive away. If you want to sample a little bit of everything, consider Cincinnati your buffet.

Charles Dickens enjoyed Cincinnati, calling it "thriving and animated." Henry Wadsworth Longfellow labeled it, the "Queen City," a nickname it retains to this day. Winston Churchill referred to Cincinnati as "the most beautiful inland city in the union."

The first settlers came to Cincinnati as early as 1798. It was the advent of the steam-powered riverboat, however, that turned Cincinnati into an important port. The steamboat era began with the arrival of the *Orleans* in 1811. By 1834, 221 steamboats had been built in the city. The completion of the Miami-Erie Canal in 1829 brought further traffic to the river and wealth to the city. The city had also grown to become the nation's largest pork producer, a title that would later pass to Chicago and St. Louis. Cincinnati hasn't forgotten its past in pork, however, as evidenced by the yearly Flying Pig marathon and the Big Pig Gig, a public art show that placed artistically and whimsically decorated pig statues throughout the city in 2000. The riverboats have steamed into history as well, but every other year riverboats flood the river as in days gone by during the Tall Stacks celebration. And recently, a monument to the steamboat was added to downtown's Bicentennial Commons, the 22-acre park along the Ohio River.

The river is a major part of Cincinnati's landscape, but it's not the only game in town. There are also the Seven Hills of Cincinnati to consider. Each hill is a neighborhood: Mount Adams, Mount Airy, Mount Echo, Mount Healthy, Mount Lookout, Mount Storm, and Mount Washington (Memorize all seven, and you'll be ahead of many of the residents; Mount Adams, Washington, and Lookout are the best known). In reality, there are many, many more hills than just seven, and Cincinnati can be a jogger or bicyclist's worst nightmare—or dream come true, depending on your point of view. The hills are the backdrop for an abundance of parks, bicycle trails, and nature centers.

Professional baseball's oldest team is the Cincinnati Reds. There are still many fond memories in this town of the 1970s, when the "Big Red Machine" dominated the major leagues and World Series thanks to stars like Tony Perez, Johnny Bench, and, of course, Pete Rose. Today, the Reds are hitting home runs in their new home, the Great American Ball Park. Just down the river at the Paul Brown Stadium, the Bengals crush their opponents and score touchdowns every chance they get. At least, in theory. Frankly, they haven't done much crushing or scoring in recent years, much to the disappointment of their still-loyal fans.

Although they take up a lot of space in the downtown skyline—and in local politics—the new stadiums are not the only game in town. The Underground Railroad Freedom Center will be a major player in the museum scene upon its completion in 2004. The Contemporary Arts Center has a new home downtown, and the Cincinnati Art Museum opened the new Cincinnati Wing, showcasing the arts in the Queen City. Even the venerable Taft Museum of Art is undergoing a major renovation and expansion.

What is Cincinnati known for? Generally, a little bit of everything.

WHAT TO SEE & DO

Aronoff Center for the Arts Broadway plays, musical acts, comedians, and other performers frequent the Aronoff Center, a state-of-the-art facility with three separate stages. The largest theater seats more than 2,700 people. The **Cincinnati Ballet** (tel. 513/621–5219, www.cincinnatiballet.com) performs classical and contemporary works here from October to May. > 650 Walnut St., Downtown, tel. 513/621–2787, www.cincinnatiarts.org. Ticket prices vary by performance.

Bicentennial Commons at Sawyer Point Park The 22-acre riverfront park, opened in celebration of the city's 200th birthday in 1988, uses monuments to tell the story of Cincinnati's origins. Note the controversial flying pigs, a playful reminder of the city's past prominence as a meatpacking center. There are hiking and biking trails, jogging paths, and great picnic spots. > 705 E. Pete Rose Way, Downtown, tel. 513/352–6180. Free, $2 parking. Daily 7–11.

Burnet Woods The hiking trails and small lake at this Clifton park provide an escape for students at the neighboring University of Cincinnati. The Trailside Nature Center also contains the Wolff Planetarium, the second-oldest planetarium west of the Allegheny mountains; reservations are required. > Brookline Ave., at intersection of Ludlow and Jefferson Sts., Clifton, tel. 513/751–3679. Free. Park: daily 7 AM–10 PM. Nature center and planetarium: weekdays 9–5; 3rd weekend of each month, weekends noon–4.

Carew Tower The 49th-floor observation deck is Cincinnati's version of the Empire State Building's famed aerie. The views of downtown, the river, and surrounding hills are breathtaking. The art deco building, built in 1930, houses shops and restaurants on its lower levels. > 441 Vine St., at 5th St., Downtown, tel. 513/241–3888 or 513/579–9735. $2. Mon.–Thurs. 9:30–5:30, Fri. and Sat. 9:30–9, Sun. 11–5.

Cincinnati Art Museum Opened in 1881 in Eden Park, the museum explores 5,000 years of art through paintings, sculpture, decorative arts, and special exhibitions from around the world. Frank Duveneck, perhaps Cincinnati's best-known artist, bequeathed his collection to the museum in 1919, which included his masterpiece, "The Whistling Boy." The Cincinnati Wing traces the history of Cincinnati art, which encompasses ceramics, furniture, metalworks, and sculpture. > 953 Eden Park Dr., Eden Park, tel. 513/721–5204 or 877/472–4226, www.cincinnatiartmuseum.org. Free. Tues.–Sun. 11–5.

Cincinnati Playhouse in the Park The performing-arts organization stages productions year-round at its eponymous theater in Eden Park. Local and national actors are featured. > 962 Mt. Adams Circle, Eden Park, tel. 513/421–3888, www.cincyplay.com. Prices vary by performance.

Cincinnati Zoo and Botanical Garden Famous for its white Bengal tigers, this is one of the country's most respected zoological institutions. In 1999 it was one of three facilities outside of Florida to be allowed to take in Florida manatees; the mammals can be observed at the Manatee Springs exhibit. The zoo is also home to walruses, lowland gorillas, polar bears, and hundreds of other species. In summer there are animal shows and camel and train rides. The zoo is open evenings from late November to early January for its annual Festival of Lights. Just be sure to put on your sneakers; there are a lot of hills in Cincinnati, and they all seem to be here. Follow the paw-print signs off I–75 Exit 6 or I–71 Exit 5, the Dana Avenue exit. > 3400 Vine St., Clifton, tel. 513/281–4701 recording, 513/281–4700, www.cincyzoo.org. $11.50, parking $6.50. Daily 9–5.

Contemporary Arts Center This museum presents the work of today's most cutting-edge artists—starting with the artistry of the building itself, which was designed by Iraq-born architect, Zaha Hadid. Exhibits showcase photography, film, performance art, and even art that primarily utilizes sound. The UnMuseum is a 7,400-square-foot wonderland for kids and adults; one of the more popular attractions is the robot-tree, which responds to your presence by raising or lowering its branches. The youngest children will love the Leaf Lounge, where they take off their shoes and roll about in more than 450 hand-made leaves. The stuffed leaves are five times the actual size of their sylvan cousins and are spread across a bed of bouncy foam. > 44 E. 6th St., Downtown, tel. 513/345–8400, www.contemporaryartscenter.org. $6.50, free 5–9 PM. Mon. and Thurs. 11–9; Tues., Wed., Fri., and Sun. 11–6; Sat. noon–6.

Eden Park Cincinnati is known for its grand and sumptuous parks, and this aptly named green space is the best of them all. Overlooking downtown Cincinnati, it has a brilliant reflecting pool, gardens, and playing fields. The park is also the site of the Cincinnati Art Museum, the Cincinnati Playhouse in the Park, and the Krohn Conservatory. > Off Gilbert Ave., between Elsinore and Morris Rds., Eden Park, tel. 513/621–2142 or 800/344–3445. Free. Daily dawn–dusk.

Fountain Square Everything and everyone from parades to politicians stop here at the center of downtown. The centerpiece of this Queen City landmark is the **Tyler Davidson Fountain** which was cast in 1867 at the Royal Bavarian Foundry in Munich, Germany. The fountain depicts the importance of water through the use of 13 allegorical figures. The main female figure, called the Genius of Water, stands with her arms stretched out, and water sprays from the palms of her hands. The square is a popular lunch spot in fair weather, as well as being the site of the city's annual Oktoberfest ceremony. > 5th and Vine Sts., Downtown. Free. Daily.

Harriet Beecher Stowe Memorial *Uncle Tom's Cabin* author Harriet Beecher Stowe lived here in the 1830s. You can view her journal, along with exhibits on the abolitionist movement and African-American history. > 2950 Gilbert Ave., Walnut Hills, tel. 513/221–7900, www.ohiohistory.org/places/stowe/. Free. Tues. 10–4, by appointment only.

Krohn Conservatory The huge greenhouse in Eden Park is divided into various environments, including a desert with cactus plants and a tropical rain forest. The palm trees and indoor waterfalls are a welcome sight in the middle of a Cincinnati winter. Seasonal exhibits include a Christmas show with poinsettias and model trains and a summer show with live butterflies and the plants that attract them. > 1501 Eden Park Dr., Eden Park, tel. 513/421–5707, www.cinci-parks.org. $5 donation suggested. Daily 10–5.

Museum Center at Union Terminal Union Terminal looks like a huge art deco cabinet radio on the west side of downtown. Large mosaic tile murals dating from the 1930s adorn the interior rotunda. In addition to being Cincinnati's functioning Amtrak terminal, Union Terminal also houses three museums and an OMNIMAX Theater.

Cincinnati's golden years are recalled at the **Cincinnati History Museum** ($6.75). You can walk down a re-creation of a city street from the early 1900s and view dozens of Queen City artifacts, along with vintage automobiles and a 1920s streetcar.

At the **Cinergy Children's Museum** ($6.75) kids can climb, crawl, and explore the world around them. Play areas include a forest with a two-story treehouse, a construction site, an energy zone with pedals and pulleys, and a waterworks with small boats and a series of locks. For kids from infants to 10 years of age.

You can get a close-up look at whales, volcanoes, Mount Everest or whatever wonders are on the schedule at the **Linder Family OMNIMAX Theater** (June–Aug., daily from 11; Sept.–May, weekdays from 1, weekends from 11. Evening schedule varies, $6.75). Movies, which are shown on a five-story, 72-foot-wide domed screen, start at the top of the hour.

Exhibits at the **Museum of Natural History and Science** ($6.75) take you on a journey back in time to various eras, including the age of the dinosaurs, the English Renaissance, and the Wild West. There's a colony of bats and underground waterfalls in a replica of a limestone cave.

You can buy individual tickets or a combination ticket that gives you entry to all three museums and the theater. > 1301 Western Ave., off I–75 at Ezzard Charles Dr., Downtown, tel. 513/287–7000 or 800/733–2077, www.cincymuseum.com. $6.75 per attraction. 2 attractions $9.75, 3 attractions $12.75, 4 attractions $15.75, 5 attractions $18.75. Mon.–Sat. 10–5, Sun. 11–6.

Music Hall In a style since dubbed "sauerbraten Gothic," this modified and modernized Gothic structure was built in 1878. A 2-ton brass and hand-cut crystal chandelier crowns the main auditorium. The **Cincinnati Opera** (tel. 513/241–2742, www.cincinnatiopera.com), the nation's second oldest, was started in 1920. The yearly summer festival occurs in June and July. The **Cincinnati Pops Orchestra** (tel. 513/381–3300, www.cincinnatipops.org) performs from September through May at Music Hall. In June and July, the Pops heads outdoors to perform at the Riverbend Music Center. Under the direction of maestro Paavo Jarvi, the **Cincinnati Symphony Orchestra** (tel. 513/381–3300, www.cincinnatisymphony.org) performs from September through May. Tours of Music Hall are available. > 1243 Elm St., Downtown, tel. 513/621–1919. Free tours, tickets vary by performance. Call to reserve tours in advance.

National Underground Railroad Freedom Center In the years before and during the Civil War, Cincinnati was one of the major hubs along the secret road from bondage in the South to freedom in Canada. This $110 million facility is devoted to educating the public about the history of the underground railroad through exhibits, programs, and interactive displays. Within these walls will be everything from a research library to exhibits like an actual slave pen, a wooden warehouse that held cap-

Touring the Town

SCENIC CINCINNATI begs to be explored. Cover the downtown highlights on foot, then jump in your car for Eden Park and Union Terminal mini-sidetrips.

Park downtown near Fountain Square, at the intersection of 5th and Vine streets. Even better, park underneath Fountain Square; the 24-hour lot charges $1 for the first 2 hours; $15 for the entire day. Take a look at the Tyler Davidson Fountain, and if it's near lunchtime, grab a sandwich to munch on a park bench or at an outdoor table. It's a fun place to be if it's a nice day, and there's often an event afoot. From there, cross the street to Carew Tower. You can get a wonderful view of the city from the 48th-floor observation deck. Double back on 5th Street past Fountain Square, and take a left on Walnut to 6th. Follow 6th to the Contemporary Arts Center. You don't even have to go in; the building itself is a marvel to look at. Return to 5th Street and go east for about four blocks until you come to Pike Street; turn right and you'll soon arrive at the Taft Museum of Art, famous for its Chinese porcelains. Next walk south to East Pete Rose Way and Eggleston Avenue. Here you'll find the Bicentennial Commons at Sawyer Point; monuments at this riverfront park tell the story of Cincinnati's origins as a river town. Not that you're likely to miss it, but be sure to check out the National Steamboat Monument, on Mehring Way next to the Public Land-

ing. The interactive installation has computer-synchronized, infrared proximity sensors embedded in 24 metal smokestacks.

Walk back and retrieve your car; follow 7th Street to Gilbert Avenue; drive north until you see Eden Park, a grand greenspace overlooking downtown. Here you'll find the Cincinnati Art Museum, known for its collection of works by Cincinnati's own Frank Duveneck, and the Krohn Conservatory, where plants from all over the world are exhibited in natural settings.

After relaxing for a bit in the park, get back in your car and take Gilbert Avenue to Central Parkway, turning right on Elm Street. Continue on Elm until you come to the Music Hall, which was built in 1878 and is the home of the Cincinnati Symphony Orchestra. Back in your car, the next stop is the Museum Center at Union Terminal, west of the Music Hall, off I–75 at Ezzard Charles Drive. This historic former train station houses the Cinergy Children's Museum, an imaginative place filled with interactive exhibits; the Museum of Natural History and Science, which has a cave with real bats; the Cincinnati History Museum; and an OMNIMAX Theater. The outside of this impressive building is worth a look, but you could easily spend all day inside.

tured slaves until they could be shipped back to the South. At this writing, the museum was scheduled to open in summer 2004. > 312 Elm St., Downtown, tel. 513/412–6900, www.undergroundrailroad.org.

Roebling Suspension Bridge John A. Roebling constructed this architectural wonder, which spans the Ohio River. It opened for business shortly after the Civil War, in 1866. Until Roebling completed his Brooklyn Bridge in 1883, it was the longest bridge in the world. If you're asking for directions, remember that all the locals just call it the "Suspension Bridge." > Follow signs from Fort Washington Way. Downtown. Free. Daily.

Showboat *Majestic* Built in 1923, among the last of the old showboats, the *Majestic* has floated on the Cincinnati riverfront for more than 30 years. Operation of the showboat was assumed by the Cincinnati Recreation Commission, and it's now a riverboat theater, showing a mix of musicals and comedies. It's closed in winter. > Riverfront

Public Landing below Mehring Way entrance. Downtown, tel. 513/241–6550. Prices vary by performance. Apr.–Oct. by performance, with a holiday show in Dec.

Skirbal Museum Jewish history and culture are the focus at this museum on the campus of Hebrew Union College—Jewish Institute of Religion. Exhibits explore immigration, Jewish life-cycle events, the Holocaust, and the Torah. > 3101 Clifton Ave., Clifton, tel. 513/221–1875, www.huc.edu. Free. Mon.–Thurs. 11–4, Sun. 2–5, and by appointment.

Taft Museum of Art Works by artists from around the globe are displayed in this federal-period mansion, where William Howard Taft accepted his presidential nomination in 1908. Galleries are arranged according to a chronological story line that illustrates the evolution of Western and Chinese art from the medieval period through the Industrial Revolution. The collection includes paintings by Rembrandt, Gainsborough, and Corot; Chinese porcelains; 19th-century American furniture; French Renaissance enameled plaques; jewelry; and watches. There's a formal garden on the property. At this writing, the Taft is undergoing a $19 million renovation and expansion, which will more than double its size. It's scheduled to reopen in 2004. > 316 Pike St., Downtown, tel. 513/241–0343, www.taftmuseum.org.

University of Cincinnati Home of the Bearcats and 18 Division I athletic teams, U.C. has an enrollment of 33,000 students. Self-guided tour maps of the campus are available, and it's certainly worth a look. The *New York Times* has called the university, "one of the most architecturally dynamic campuses in America today." The student center, which is modern inside, retains a Greek Revival facade built in 1935. The university is in the Clifton neighborhood north of downtown. Ludlow Avenue, known as the gas light district for its street lights, has quirky shops, cafés, and an art-house movie theater. > 2624 Clifton Ave., Clifton, tel. 513/556–3001, www.uc.edu. Free. Tours available, Mon.–Sat. 8–5; call ahead to schedule a tour.

William Howard Taft National Historic Site This Greek Revival home was the birthplace and boyhood home of Taft (1857–1930), the 27th U.S. president and a chief justice of the Supreme Court. Some rooms are furnished as they were during Taft's residence; others hold exhibits about the president's family and career. > 2038 Auburn Ave., Mt. Auburn, tel. 513/684–3262, www.nps.gov/wiho. Free. Daily 8–4.

WHAT'S NEARBY
Cincinnati Nature Center East of Cincinnati, near Milford, is a 790-acre nature preserve with 14 mi of trails. Hikers of all fitness levels are accommodated through trails with varying degrees of difficulty. Several ponds and lakes are also great for a picnic or rest. There are also a gift shop, bookstore, nature exhibits, and a bird-viewing area in the Nature Center. > 4949 Tealtown Rd., Milford, tel. 513/831–1711, www.cincynature.org. $5. Grounds: daily 8–dusk. Nature center: Mon.–Sat. 9–5, Sun. 1–5.
Mount Airy Forest and Arboretum Come in spring, when the lilacs, azaleas, and flowering trees on the 120-acre grounds are in bloom. You can hike through the 1,400 acres. Reservations are required for guided tours. > 5080 Colerain Ave., Mt. Airy, tel. 513/541–8176, www.cincinnati-oh.gov. Free. Daily 6 AM–10 PM.
Newport Aquarium On the Kentucky side of the Ohio River, this aquarium is just a 2-minute drive from downtown Cincinnati. The fish are visible through clear, seamless tunnels, so you can get up close and personal—25 sharks swim around you, separated by only 2½ inches of acrylic. Highlights include a large open-air shark viewing area, a King Penguin habitat, Gator Bayou, Jellyfish Gallery, and the Bizarre and Beau-

tiful, where you'll see poison frogs and pufferfish. > 1 Aquarium Way, Newport, KY, tel. 859/261–7444, www.newportaquarium.com. $14.95, parking $3. Memorial Day–Labor Day, daily 9–7; Labor Day–Memorial Day, daily 10–6.

Tours

BB Riverboats Hop aboard the *Belle of Cincinnati, Mark Twain,* or *River Queen* for a cruise down the Ohio River past Cincinnati and Northern Kentucky. Daily sightseeing cruises depart at 11:30, 1, and 2:30. The hour-long tours cost $12.95. Lunch and dinner-and-dancing packages are also available. > Covington Riverfront at Covington Landing (1 Madison Ave.), Covington, KY, tel. 606/261–8500, www.bbriverboats.com.
Delta Queen, Mississippi Queen, and *American Queen* Three of the world's largest paddle-wheel steamships make regular stops in Cincinnati. The Delta Queen Steamboat Company offers 3- to 14-night cruises. Prices, which include lodging, meals, entertainment, and nightly dancing, are $700–$1,950 for 3-night cruises. Prices are per person, double occupancy. > Cincinnati Riverfront at Public Landing (Delta Queen Steamboat Co., Robin St. Wharf, 1380 Port of New Orleans Pl., New Orleans, LA 70130-1890), tel. 504/586–0631, 800/543–1949 reservations, fax 504/585–0630, www.deltaqueen.com.

Nightlife

Clifton The University of Cincinnati and "Pill Hill," the city's hospital district, are found in this neighborhood north of downtown. Its ethnic restaurants and art-house theater draw a diverse crowd, while its nightclubs and bars are frequented by fun-seeking college students. **Bogarts** (2621 Vine St., tel. 513/281–8400, www.bogarts.com) hosts local garage bands, college bands, and such national acts as the Psychedelic Furs.
Covington and Newport These cities on the other side of the Ohio River in Kentucky serve as one of Cincinnati's main entertainment districts. Covington and Newport are most accessible by I–75 and I–471, respectively. A number of bars, restaurants, and nightclubs line the riverfront. **Covington Landing** (on the Ohio River, 1 block west of Roebling Bridge, tel. 859/291–5410) is a floating entertainment complex with nightspots and restaurants. Bordering on the river, **Newport on the Levee** (1 Levee Way, tel. 859/291–0550) is an outdoor shopping mall with the Newport Aquarium and an IMAX theater.
Downtown–Main Street Downtown Cincinnati is full of action, from the bustling workday crowd to the theater crowd in the evening in the city to catch a play at the Aronoff Center or an exhibit at the Contemporary Arts Center. The stadiums attract huge crowds, especially during the weekends. But it's Main Street, between Liberty Street and Central Parkway, where downtown really comes to life. Art galleries and specialty stores selling antiques, flowers, and music operate by day, and nightclubs attract a spirited crowd at night. A wig maker once resided in the 1800s building that now houses **Japps Cigar and Martini Bar** (1134 Main St., tel. 513/684–0007). The new, sleek incarnation attracts businesspeople and those in touch with the good life. The **Rhythm & Blues Cafe** (1140 Main St., tel. 513/684–0080, Closed Sun.–Tues.) has live funk, soul, reggae, and blues bands.
Mount Adams This trendy, hillside neighborhood overlooking downtown is the place to be on the weekend. Nightclubs and restaurants line the streets and are open into the wee hours of the morning. Mount Adams is sandwiched in bounded by the Ohio River, Eden Park, and I–71. Parking is difficult, however; consider taking a cab. The **Blind Lemon** (936 Hatch St., tel. 513/241–3885) has a courtyard, a funky old interior, and a cozy fireplace.

Sports

Cincinnatians are still fuming that Pete Rose has been banned from baseball and keeping their fingers crossed that he'll be eligible for the Baseball Hall of Fame one of these days. They're not too pleased about the Bengals performance either. The fans may not be happy, but they love their baseball and football so much that you'll think it's almost a religion. And to that, they might say, "Almost?"

BASEBALL

Cincinnati Reds This National League team is the oldest team in baseball and the 1990 World Champions. They play home games at the **Great American Ball Park** from April through October. The Reds may have been around for years, but the stadium is new. Opened in 2003, it's a $320 million marvel that offers its fans not just a great place to watch the game, but appealing views of the Ohio River. The stadium seats just over 42,000. > 100 Main St., Downtown, tel. 513/421–4510, www.cincinnatireds.com.

FOOTBALL

Cincinnati Bengals Cincinnati's National Football League team, play in the new state-of-the-art Paul Brown Stadium on the riverfront. > 1 Paul Brown Stadium, Downtown, tel. 513/621–3550, www.bengals.com.

HORSE-RACING

River Downs Race Track The stakes are high at this track on the banks of the Ohio River. Live horse races take place from late April to early November. Simulcast races are featured daily the rest of the year. > 6301 Kellogg Ave., near Coney Island, tel. 513/232–8000, www.riverdowns.com.

Shopping

Findlay Market The open-air market in the Over-the-Rhine area of downtown is locally known for its fresh meats and regional produce. You can find exotic herbs, grilled ribs, and bakery items as well. > Race and Elder Sts., Over-the-Rhine, tel. 513/352–6364. Wed. and Fri. 7–6, Sun. 6–6.

Fountain Place Adjacent to downtown's Fountain Square, this collection of stores includes such upscale spots as Lazarus and Brooks Brothers. At **Tiffany & Co.** (Fountain Pl., 505 Vine St., tel. 513/721–2022), you can pick up signature jewelry, housewares, and giftware. > 5th and Race Sts., Downtown, no phone.

Tower Place at the Carew Tower More than 70 stores occupy three floors in this downtown shopping mall that also has enclosed parking and a food court. Well-known upscale stores like Williams-Sonoma, the Gap, Structure, and Ann Taylor share space with such regional outlets as the I Love Cincinnati store and Gold Star Chili. Skywalks connect Tower Place with Fountain Place stores as well as with Saks Fifth Avenue and hotels like the Hyatt Regency. > 28 W. 4th St., at the corner of Race St., Downtown, tel. 513/241–7700, www.towerplace.com.

Save the Date

FEBRUARY–MARCH

Cincinnati Home and Garden Show This show at the Cincinnati Convention Center exhibits fine furnishings and products and services related to building and remodeling, gardening, and outdoor living. > 525 Elm St., tel. 513/281–0022.

MAY

Cincinnati Flying Pig Marathon The hills are brutal in this 26.2-mi race, created to raise money for local charities. > Tel. 513/721–7447.

May Festival The oldest choral and orchestral festival in the country is presented in a series of concerts with the Cincinnati Symphony Orchestra. Guest soloists are featured. > Cincinnati Music Hall, 1241 Elm St., tel. 513/381–3300, www.cincinnatisymphony.org.

SEPTEMBER

Oktoberfest-Zinzinnati The six-block area around Fountain Square is turned into a German biergarten for this 3-day celebration of the city's German heritage. Don your lederhosen and compete in the beer barrel roll or dance the chicken dance. Quench your thirst with a stein of beer, and there's plenty of goetta, bratwurst, sauerkraut, and strudel to go around. > Fountain Sq., 5th and Vine Sts., tel. 513/579–3191, www.oktoberfest-zinzinnati.com.

Riverfest Cincinnati bids farewell to summer with this Labor Day weekend blowout on the banks of the Ohio River. Hundreds of thousands of people come to see the waterskiing, sky diving, and air shows. The party, and the summer, ends with a spectacular 30-minute fireworks display over the river. Hanging flowers of light and waterfalls of sparks are choreographed to music broadcast live on a local radio station. > Tel. 513/621–2142 or 800/344–3445, www.cincyusa.com.

OCTOBER

Tall Stacks Every other year, Cincinnati pays tribute to its steamboat history by inviting a dozen or so steamboats—there were 17 at the 2003 celebration—to gather for riverboat races and cruises. Festival goers can tour steamboats, view historical exhibits, and listen to music. This relatively new event began in 1988, during the city's bicentennial year. At this writing, the date for the next Tall Stacks was yet to be determined. > www.tallstacks.com.

WHERE TO STAY

Amos Shinkle Townhouse B&B The man who hired John A. Roebling to build the Roebling Suspension Bridge lived in this antebellum mansion. The master bedroom has a whirlpool and a crystal chandelier in the bathroom. Covington is a short ride across Roebling's construction from downtown Cincinnati. > 215 Garrard St., Covington, KY 41011, tel. 859/431–2118 or 800/972–7012, fax 859/491–4551, www.amosshinkle.net. 7 rooms. No smoking. AE, D, DC, MC, V. BP. **$–$$$**

Best Western Mariemont Inn Even the cash machine is in Tudor style at this inn on the National Register of Historic Places. The Old English Tudor–style building was built in 1926 as part of the planned suburban village of Mariemont. The inn is on the tree-shaded village green, near shops, restaurants, and a small movie theater. Some rooms have hand-carved oak headboards and tapestries. Mariemont is on the eastern edge of the city, a 20-minute drive along Columbia Parkway from downtown. > 6880 Wooster Pike, U.S. 50, Mariemont 45227, tel. 513/271–2100 or 800/528–1234, fax 513/271–1057, www.bestwestern.com. 60 rooms. Restaurant, in-room data ports, cable TV, pub, laundry facilities, business services, no-smoking rooms. AE, D, DC, MC, V. **$**

Cincinnatian Hotel A sedate 1882 French Second Empire–style hotel, the Cincinnatian offers contemporary elegance along with gracious personal service. The marble-and-walnut staircase is original, and ornate furniture and fine linens fill the spacious rooms. You can have afternoon tea or dine in the Palace Restaurant. > 601 Vine St., Downtown 45202, tel. 513/381–3000 or 800/942–9000, fax 513/651–0256. www.cincinnatianhotel.com. 147 rooms, 8 suites. Restaurant, in-room safes, minibars, cable TV, gym, sauna, bar, business services, no-smoking rooms. AE, D, DC, MC, V. $$$$

Crowne Plaza The eighth-floor terrace of the Crowne Plaza lets you enjoy the best of both worlds: a city view and a garden. Modern rooms are outfitted with CD players and hair dryers. One unusual room option is the Fit Room, which comes complete with a stationary recumbent bicycle. Elegant, spacious suites have separate bedrooms. > 15 W. 6th St., Downtown 45202, tel. 513/381–4000 or 888/279–8260, fax 513/354–5158, www.crowneplaza.com. 321 rooms, 44 suites. Restaurant, refrigerators, cable TV, exercise equipment, hair salon, bar, laundry service, business services, no-smoking rooms. AE, D, DC, MC, V. $–$$$

Four Points by Sheraton Cincinnati Northeast If you're in town to shop, this is the hotel for you. It's across I–71 from Kenwood Towne Centre, an upscale shopping mall; downtown shopping is a short 20-minute drive south on I–71. Set on 13 acres of land, the hotel also has a sunny gazebo. > 8020 Montgomery Rd., Kenwood 45236, tel. 513/793–4300 or 800/325–3535, fax 513/793–1413, www.starwood.com. 152 rooms. Restaurant, room service, in-room data ports, cable TV with movies and video games, tennis court, 2 pools (1 indoor), gym, hot tub, bar, laundry service, business services, meeting rooms, no-smoking rooms. AE, D, DC, MC, V. $$–$$$

Garfield Suites Hotel The glass greenhouse lobby of Garfield Suites is across the street from Piatt Park, a small urban park (Cincinnati's first) with a statue of President James Garfield. Many of the suites in the 16-story, contemporary building have balconies and spectacular views of the city. The hotel is near the main library, three blocks from the center of town. > 2 Garfield Pl., Downtown 45202, tel. 513/421–3355 or 800/367–2155, fax 513/421–3729. 150 suites. Restaurant, in-room safes, kitchenettes, microwaves, cable TV, exercise equipment, bar, laundry facilities, some pets allowed (fee), no-smoking floors. AE, D, DC, MC, V. $$$–$$$$

Hilton Cincinnati Netherland Plaza Downtown's grand art deco hotel is in the Carew Tower. The two-story lobby has bas-relief sculptures and dramatic fountains and light fixtures; guest rooms have 10-foot ceilings and soft pastel colors. The formal Palm Court restaurant serves buffet lunches and fine American cuisine. > 35 W. 5th St., Downtown, 45202, tel. 513/421–9100, fax 513/421–4291, www.hilton.com. 621 rooms. 2 restaurants, in-room data ports, some in-room hot tubs, cable TV, pool, gym, laundry service, no-smoking floors. AE, D, DC, MC, V. $$$–$$$$

Hyatt Regency One of the largest hotels in Cincinnati, this downtown landmark has an atrium lobby with glass walls and ceiling, contemporary rooms in soft pastel colors, and first-rate service. It's connected by a skywalk to Saks Fifth Avenue and the Tower Place shopping center. > 151 W. 5th St., Downtown 45202, tel. 513/579–1234 or 800/233–1234, fax 513/354–4299, www.hyatt.com. 488 rooms, 11 suites. 2 restaurants, some refrigerators, cable TV with movies, indoor pool, gym, hot tub, bar, shops, business services, no-smoking rooms. AE, D, DC, MC, V. $$$–$$$$

Imperial House This brown-brick hotel contains Victorian furnishings and has relaxing amenities, including a swimming pool. It's northwest of downtown Cincinnati, at Exit 11 off I–74. > 5510 Rybolt Rd., Dent 45248, tel. 513/574–6000 or 800/543–3018, fax 513/574–6566. 196 rooms, 2 suites. Restaurant, in-room data ports, some kitchenettes, cable TV, pool, bar, laundry facilities, business services. AE, D, DC, MC, V. $

Parker House Bed and Breakfast A restored 1878 Victorian mansion, near the University of Cincinnati, is now a B&B. Parker House has a music parlor, antique furnishings, reproduction wall coverings, and murals of Beethoven and Mozart handpainted on the ceiling. Guests can use the kitchen. > 2323 Ohio Ave., Clifton 45219, tel. 513/579–8236 or 877/411–0148. 4 rooms. No room phones, no smoking. MC, V. BP. $–$$

Vernon Manor Hotel Modeled after an English manor, this 1924 hotel is dignified and traditional. Modern touches like Web TV keep it up-to-date, however. Tucked away in the hills of Clifton overlooking the city, the Vernon Manor is 2 mi from downtown, though it seems farther away. > 400 Oak St., Clifton 45219, tel. 513/281–3300, fax 513/281–8933, www.vernon-manor.com. 177 rooms, 60 suites. Restaurant, in-room data ports, some refrigerators, cable TV with movies and video games, gym, hair salon, pub, laundry facilities, shops, business services, no-smoking rooms. AE, D, DC, MC, V. **$$$**

Westin Hotel In the heart of Cincinnati's hotel district, the Westin overlooks the city's most popular landmark, the Tyler Davidson Fountain on Fountain Square. The building, designed in the classic Renaissance style, was once the Albee Theater. Shoppers will appreciate that it's just a short stroll away from the Carew Tower Mall, while the business class will look to the on-site, 24-hour Kinkos. > 21 E. 5th St., Downtown 45202, tel. 513/621–7700 or 800/937–8461, fax 513/852–5670, www.westin.com. 450 rooms, 25 suites. Restaurant, in-room data ports, minibars, cable TV, indoor pool, gym, hot tub, massage, piano bar, business services, no-smoking rooms. AE, D, DC, MC, V. **$$$**

Woodfield Suites Just off I–75 in Sharonville, this all-suites hotel has spacious rooms and attractive cherry furnishings. Complimentary cocktails are served in the evening. Restaurants, a shopping mall, the Cincinnati Zoo, and the Riverfront Stadium are within 10 mi of the property. > 11029 Dowlin Dr., Sharonville 45241, tel. 513/771–0300 or 800/338–0008, fax 513/771–6411, www.woodfieldsuites.com. 151 suites. In-room data ports, some kitchenettes, microwaves, refrigerators, some in-room hot tubs, cable TV, indoor pool, gym, hot tub, playground, laundry facilities, business services, no-smoking rooms. AE, D, DC, MC, V. CP. **$$–$$$$**

WHERE TO EAT

Aglamesis Bros Since 1913, the Greek-immigrant Aglamesis brothers have been serving homemade chocolates and ice cream on the east side. The small ice-cream parlor and confectionery has checkered tile floors and marble-top tables; the marble soda fountains and Tiffany-style lamps are the original fixtures. The opera creams, rectangular cream-filled dark chocolate candy, remain a secret family recipe. A deli also serves a limited sandwich menu. > 3046 Madison Rd., Oakley, tel. 513/531–5196, www.aglamesis.com. MC, V. **¢–$**

The Celestial Indulge in caviar and foie gras while enjoying stunning views of downtown and the river from the top of Mount Adams. Some dishes with a Caribbean twist share the menu with such classic French fare as veal medallions and Dover sole sautéed in lemon butter. > 1071 Celestial St., Mt. Adams, tel. 513/241–4455. Jacket required. AE, DC, MC, V. Closed Sun. **$$$$**

Christy's & Lenhardt's Schnitzel, Viennese and Hungarian goulash, sauerbraten, and potato pancakes are served at this casual place. The outdoor beer garden is a great summer escape. > 151 W. McMillan St., Clifton, tel. 513/281–3600. AE, D, MC, V. Closed Sun. and Mon., 1st 2 wks in Aug., 2 wks at Christmas. **$**

Diner on Sycamore Stainless steel and neon set the scene in this eatery near the Main Street club district. More than 18 different martinis, both shaken and stirred, are mixed in the bar. The upscale diner food includes a Blue Plate Special of pork chops with a barbecue sauce made with Jack Daniels and Coca-Cola. Try a blue cheese salad, crab cake sandwich, or the house specialty, the Caribbean white crab chili.

Open-air patio dining is available, and there's Sunday brunch. > 1203 Sycamore St., Downtown, tel. 513/721–1212. AE, D, DC, MC, V. $–$$

First Watch Restaurant Breakfast and brunch are satisfying at this restaurant in downtown Cincinnati; try banana crunch or raisin walnut pancakes. The lunch menu is creative as well, with such entrées as pecan Dijon salad. > 700 Walnut St., Downtown, tel. 513/721–4744. AE, D, DC, MC, V. No dinner. ¢–$

Fore and Aft This double-decker paddle wheel boat has been afloat for more than 30 years; now it's docked on the Ohio River in Saylor Park. After cocktails on the upper open-air deck, dine on beef and seafood combination plates at wood tables with decorative candles. The house specialty is Alaskan king crab legs served with drawn butter, and there's a raw bar. You can also dine outdoors on a covered deck with a view of the Ohio River. > 7449 Forbes Rd., tel. 513/941–8400. AE, MC, V. No lunch Sat. $–$$

Graeter's The true test of any ice cream brand is the vanilla, where there are no candy pieces to hide behind. Graeter's vanilla is superb, a deliciously creamy yet light blend. The chocolate chip improves it by adding huge slabs of dark chocolate. The full rainbow of flavors is available, including seasonal favorites like peach. Get in the inevitable line and start pondering your choices. > 41 E. 4th St., Downtown, tel. 513/381–0653; 332 Ludlow Ave., Clifton, tel. 513/281–4749. MC, V. No lunch, no dinner. ¢

Grille at the Palm Court This restaurant in the Carew Tower's Hilton Cincinnati Netherland Plaza echoes the elegant, art deco design of the hotel. Look up to see the murals on the 30-foot ceilings. Many of the beautifully presented dishes feature Ohio's bounty, for example, the Lake Erie walleye with a lobster and carrot fricassee. On weekend evenings, there's live jazz; on Sunday there's breakfast. > 35 W. 5th St., Downtown, tel. 513/564–6465. AE, D, DC, MC, V. $$–$$$$

Heritage Restaurant Cajun and Southwestern cuisine is prepared with a sophisticated touch and served in an 1827 Early American–style building with wood-panel dining rooms. Ohio-produced pasta and pork items are menu highlights—especially notable are the barbecued baby-back ribs. In summer, produce comes from nearby Hillsboro and the herbs are grown on-site. Try the Cajun barbecued shrimp or pecan chicken with Dijon mustard sauce. There's open-air patio dining, a kids' menu, and Sunday brunch. > 7664 Wooster Pike (U.S. 50), Mariemont, tel. 513/561–9300, www.theheritage.com. AE, D, DC, MC, V. No lunch. $$–$$$$

Jean-Robert at Pigall's Jean-Robert de Cavel spent seven years as *chef de cuisine* at the Maisonette before striking out on his own with this downtown venture. The seasonal French prix-fixe menu and the carefully chosen wine list have garnered local and national attention. Make your reservations well in advance; a seat at the chef's table, in an alcove of the kitchen, gives diners the inside scoop. > 127 W. 4th St., Downtown, tel. 513/721–1345. Reservations essential. AE, D, MC, V. Closed Sun. and Mon. No lunch.

La Normandie Taverne and Chophouse Rough-hewn beams and heavy draperies give this 65-year-old downtown chophouse the look of an Olde English cellar. The traditional shrimp cocktail is good for starters, followed by a creamy yellow squash and asparagus soup. Menu highlights include the Cajun filet mignon, blackened and topped with a jalapeño butter swirl, and the broiled New Zealand rack of lamb. > 118 E. 6th St., Downtown, tel. 513/721–2761, www.lanormandy.com. AE, D, DC, MC, V. Closed Sun. No lunch weekends. $$$–$$$$

Maisonette For more than 40 years, the Maisonette has been known as the best restaurant in town and has earned national attention. Chef Bertrand Bouquin blends classical and modern French fare. The menu changes daily but always includes beef tenderloin, sea scallops, and rack of lamb. Paintings by famous Cincinnati artists hang throughout the three formal dining rooms; a self-portrait of well-known local artist Frank Duvanek is over the bar. > 114 E. 6th St., Downtown, tel. 513/721–2260, www.maisonettegroup.com. Reservations essential. Jacket required. AE, D, DC, MC, V. Closed Sun. No lunch Mon. and Sat. **$$$$**

Mecklenburg Gardens This German tavern in the Clifton–Corryville area near UC was once a gathering place for opera stars and singing societies. Grapevines stretch over the biergarten, and the mahogany bar is always well-stocked. Traditional German dishes such as sausages, noodles, and soups are on the menu; for dessert, there's coffee-toffee black bottom pecan pie. You can see entertainment Wednesday–Saturday nights. > 302 E. University Ave., Clifton, tel. 513/221–5353. AE, D, DC, MC, V. No lunch weekends. **$–$$**

Montgomery Inn at the Boathouse The barbecued ribs are famous (Bob Hope was a fan), and you can't get any closer to the river without jumping in for a swim. This is the sister location of the original sports-theme joint, which is in the northeastern suburb of Montgomery. The menu is so dominated by the tender, finger-licking ribs that even the few poultry and seafood items are barbecued themselves or served as a combo with ribs. Sinful sides include onion straws and Saratoga chips (potatoes sliced and fried). Lunchtime and happy hour both draw crowds. > 925 Eastern Ave., Downtown, tel. 513/721–7427, www.montgomeryinn.com. AE, D, DC, MC, V. No lunch weekends. **$–$$$**

Nicola's Ristorante Antique clock faces decorate the walls of this sophisticated Northern Italian restaurant in the Over-the-Rhine area of downtown. Such classic favorites as bruschetta, calamari, osso buco, and panna cotta are served. A formal dress code takes effect for dinner; no jeans or tennis shoes allowed. There's seasonal open-air dining in a courtyard with umbrella-shaded tables. > 1420 Sycamore St., Downtown, tel. 513/721–6200. Jacket required. AE, D, DC, MC, V. Closed Sun. No lunch Sat. **$$–$$$$**

Palace Restaurant Appearance is almost as important as flavor at this lavish art deco restaurant in the landmark Cincinnatian Hotel downtown. Frederick Pissaro, great-grandson of the celebrated Impressionist painter, created artwork exclusively for the Palace. The menu changes seasonally, but there are always salmon, sea bass, and tenderloin entrées; they may be French, Italian, Australian, or German, but are always creative and beautifully presented. > 601 Vine St., Downtown, tel. 513/381–6006. Reservations essential. Jacket required. AE, D, DC, MC, V. **$$$$**

The Precinct Servers introduce you to your food before you order it at this steak house. They'll show off, for example, the 28-day–aged Colorado Angus steak and the gigantic South African lobster tail that's part of the surf-and-turf combo. Entrées include all the oven-baked bread you can eat and a tangy Greek salad or Kentucky hot slaw. The noisy, crowded dining rooms are good stakeouts to sight visiting celebrities and notable locals. > 311 Delta Ave., Mt. Lookout, tel. 513/321–5454, www.theprecinctinc.com. Reservations essential. AE, D, DC, MC, V. **$$$$**

Primavista Panoramic views of the city can be savored from this restaurant perched on top of Price Hill. Interesting antiques from old wine boxes to odd sculptures are displayed throughout the interior. The menu emphasizes classic northern and southern Italian dishes—antipasti, pasta, veal, beef, lamb, poultry, and seafood. Try the salmon basted in a light butter sauce. > 810 Matson Pl., Price Hill, tel. 513/251–6467, www.pvista.com. AE, D, DC, MC, V. No lunch. **$$–$$$$**

Promontory Bar and Grill After a day of exploring Eden Park and the Cincinnati Art Museum, you can rest your weary legs in this casual Mount Adams restaurant. Menu items include chicken, sea bass, salads, and pastas. There are also an extensive wine list and jazz on Friday and Saturday evenings from 10 to 1:30. > 1111 St. Gregory St., Mt. Adams, tel. 513/651–4777. AE, D, DC, MC, V. Closed Sun. $–$$$

Rookwood Pottery Rookwood art pottery gained national recognition during the Arts-and-Crafts movement at the turn of the 20th century, and pieces are sought by collectors to this day. The factory closed long ago, but the hilltop building in Mount Adams has been reincarnated as a restaurant. The dining area is in the old kiln room. Menu favorites include burgers and the seafood-stuffed, Cajun-spiced mushroom appetizer. Best bets among entrées are poached salmon with light lemon cucumber sauce and linguine, and Oriental stir-fried turkey. > 1077 Celestial St., Mt. Adams, tel. 513/721–5456. AE, DC, MC, V. $–$$$

Seafood 32 This revolving restaurant is on the 32nd floor of the Millennium Hotel, right next to Convention Hall downtown. It's a popular choice for anniversaries and other special occasions. The menu is predominately seafood, although rack of lamb, prime rib, New York strip steak, pasta, and chicken dishes are also on the menu. There's entertainment Friday and Saturday. > 150 W. 5th St., Downtown, tel. 513/352–2160. AE, D, DC, MC, V. Closed Sun. and Mon. No lunch. $$–$$$$

Skyline Chili For many Cincinnati expatriots, the first stop on a hometown visit is the nearest Skyline chili parlor. Whichever way they take it—three-way (chili with spaghetti and shredded cheddar cheese), four-way (chili with spaghetti, cheese, and onions), or cheese coney (chili with shredded cheddar on a hot dog)—people here are passionate about their chili. A tip for blending in—don't twirl your spaghetti; cut it with the side of your fork and scoop up a mouthful. > 643 Vine St., Downtown, tel. 513/241–2020; 290 Ludlow Ave., Clifton, tel. 513/221–2142. AE, D, MC, V. ¢

ESSENTIALS

Getting Here

BY BUS

Greyhound Lines serves Cincinnati from its downtown bus station, which is open 24 hours.

BUS DEPOT **Greyhound Station** > 1005 Gilbert Ave., tel. 513/352–6002.
BUS LINES **Greyhound** > Tel. 800/229–9424, www.greyhound.com.

BY CAR

I–71 and I–75, the major north–south routes through town, merge into a single highway in downtown Cincinnati. They pass together over the double-decker Brent Spence Bridge, and then continue south into Kentucky as a single highway before splitting apart near Walton, Kentucky. I–74 originates (or terminates) in Cincinnati, heading west into Indiana. I–275 encircles the city and parts of northern Kentucky.

Cincinnati was named "Crash City" in a recent Ohio Department of Public Safety study for having more car crashes per capita than any other town in the state. Steep hills and the ever-changing weather have been suggested as the reasons, although the usual construction—most recently on I–275—probably doesn't help either. Wear a seat belt; if the Crash City designation is not enough to convince you, know that you could be ticketed if you don't. Unless the occasional sign says not to, you can turn right on red. Driving in downtown Cincinnati has its own challenges—namely, many of the streets are one-way, and parking can be difficult.

The river, bridges, and city skyline against a backdrop of wooded hills make Cincinnati one of the most attractive cities in the state. Cresting the final hill on I–71/75 north from Kentucky, the entire scene is laid out before you. Another scenic approach is Columbia Parkway, which winds along the river from the eastern suburbs before rounding a final turn and heading downtown. If Columbia Parkway whets your appetite for river views, take Route 52 east, along the Ohio River. You'll see little traffic, but an abundance of forest and meadows and ample views of the water. You could take State Route 52 to Ripley, about an hour's drive (57 mi); it was one of the stops on the Underground Railroad.

BY FERRY

Anderson Ferry, built in 1817, is the sole ferry surviving in Cincinnati. On Anderson Ferry Road, the ferry is 6 mi west of downtown. A popular alternative for the rush hour crowd, the ferry is also a good way to get a more intimate view of the river than you would get going over a bridge. Rates are $3 per car, and the hours vary, but are generally during daylight hours.

FERRY LINES **Anderson Ferry** > Ohio Dock: Anderson Ferry Rd., 6 mi west of downtown. Office and Kentucky Dock: 4030 River Rd., tel. 859/586–5007.

BY PLANE

The Cincinnati–Northern Kentucky International Airport, a hub for Delta Airlines, is 13 mi south of downtown Cincinnati in northern Kentucky. Large mosaic murals in the terminal portray the life of the American worker. The works, by Winold Reiss, were moved here from the Union Terminal in 1974.

Airport Executive Shuttle makes regular trips from the airport to downtown hotels ($14 one-way, $24 round-trip). Taxis downtown cost about $25 plus tip.

AIRPORTS **Cincinnati–Northern Kentucky International Airport** > Box 752000, Cincinnati 45275, tel. 606/767–3151.

AIRPORT TRANSPORTATION **Airport Executive Shuttle** (tel. 859/261–8601). **Taxi Desk** (tel. 859/767–326)

CARRIERS **American** > Tel. 800/433–7300, www.aa.com. **Continental Airlines** > Tel. 800/525–0280, www.flycontinental.com. **Delta** > Tel. 800/221–1212, www.delta.com. **Delta Connection–ComAir** (tel. 800/221–1212, www.comair.com) **Northwest** > Tel. 800/225–2525, www.nwa.com. **Skyway: The Midwest Express Connection** > Tel. 800/452–2022, www.midwestexpress.com. **United** > Tel. 800/241–6522, www.united.com. **US Airways** > Tel. 800/428–4322, www.usair.com.

BY TRAIN

Ask most residents about Union Terminal, and they'll tell you that it's a wonderful museum center that used to be a railroad station. They might not realize that it's both. Trains still stop by Union Terminal; just not as often as they used to. The station, which was completed in 1933, had 233 trains a day in its heyday; now it's just a whisper of that. The massive building has an art deco style, and huge mosaic murals are throughout the concourse and rotunda.

Amtrak's Cardinal services Cincinnati on the trip between Washington, D.C., and Chicago, a trip that passes through the Blue Ridge and Allegheny mountains, and Shenandoah Valley.

TRAIN LINES **Amtrak** > Tel. 800/872–7245, www.amtrak.com.

TRAIN STATION **Cincinnati Union Terminal** > 1301 Western Ave., off I–75 at Ezzard Charles Dr., Cincinnati.

Getting Around

Compact downtown Cincinnati is entirely walkable. Skywalks connect hotels, convention centers, stores, and garages. The Newport Southbank Bridge (known as the Purple People Bridge) is a pedestrian-only bridge, stretching across the Ohio River into Newport, Kentucky, where there are shops, places to eat, and the Newport Aquarium. If you're venturing farther afield to Mount Adams, Clifton, or Eden Park, you'll need to drive or take a bus or cab.

BY PUBLIC TRANSIT

The Metro Bus System serves downtown Cincinnati and its suburbs. Buses are equipped with bike racks, and the service is affordable. Rush-hour fare is 80¢; other times, 65¢. Or, if you call ahead, before the next month of travel, you can get a MetroCard—one for the weekend is only $8.

Buses leave downtown from Government Square, on 5th Street between Walnut and Main. Government Square is one block from Fountain Square. The downtown bus loop is #79.

CONTACTS **Metro Bus System** > Tel. 513/621–4455, 800/750–0750 MetroCards, www.sorta.com.

Visitor Information

CONTACTS **Greater Cincinnati Convention and Visitors Bureau** > 300 W. 6th St., 45202, tel. 513/621–2142 or 800/246–2987, fax 513/621–5020, www.cincyusa.com.

Paramount's Kings Island

Kings Island is 25 mi north of Cincinnati, 80 mi southwest of Columbus, and 225 mi southwest of Cleveland.

21

Gil Kaufman

AMUSEMENT PARKS ARE ALL ABOUT bigger, faster, loopier, and more intense. Paramount's Kings Island in Mason has been delivering all of the above, and much more for more than 30 years. The 364-acre destination is the largest amusement and water park in the Midwest; it's practically a city unto itself. Kings Island—which once served as a backdrop for episodes of "The Brady Bunch" and "The Partridge Family"—attracts more than 3 million guests annually to take a whirl on 40 rides, splash through the 15-acre water park, catch live shows, play games of chance, and fill up on traditional park fare like funnel cakes and giant pecan-cinnamon rolls, as well as such Cincinnati staples as Skyline Chili, Montgomery Inn ribs, and La Rosa's pizza.

If you begin to feel a touch of vertigo from too many coasters and need to stretch your legs a bit after all that standing in line, take a day off and enjoy a lazy float in a canoe or inner tube down the neighboring Little Miami River in Mason.

Originally known as the village of Palmyra, Mason was founded in 1915 by Major William Mason, a Revolutionary War hero. Twenty years later, the community's name was changed in honor of its founder. Prior to the early 1990s, Mason was primarily a farming town, but in the past decade it has attracted a number of corporations, lured by plenty of land, good schools, and low crime. Centrally located along U.S. 42 and between I–71 and I–75, Mason is a convenient drive from anywhere in southwest Ohio. The area has become one of the fastest-growing suburbs of Cincinnati, with the population expected to nearly triple from 1990 levels by 2010 to more than 90,000. With rapid growth has come the expected influx of "big-box" stores, so shopping is plentiful, but the attendant traffic problems are also a factor, so expect rush hour snarls on the main arteries of Mason-Montgomery Road and I–71. The suburban sprawl has encroached on some of the formerly untrammeled wilderness, but canoeing on the scenic Little Miami River continues to be a popular diversion eight months of the year, weather permitting. Popular attractions in the area include Paramount's Kings Island and The Beach Waterpark, as well as trail rides at the Dude Ranch.

WHAT TO SEE & DO

Paramount's Kings Island The longest wooden roller coaster in the world, the nearly 25-year-old and still-terrifying Beast lurks in the woods of Kings Island. Its offspring, Son of Beast, is the tallest, fastest, and only looping wooden coaster in the world. If you long for the jolt of the old, the twin retro coasters of The Racer, credited with rekindling the coaster business in the early 1970s, are still a thrill. Enjoy the ride backward or forward on the red or the blue Racer, and see if you can beat your friends back to the station.

New attractions are constantly being added, such as Delerium, a ride that shoots 50 outward-facing riders 137 feet up in the air as they swing in circles with their feet dangling. Other classic attractions include The Vortex, which inverts six times, the Face-Off, the only steel looping, forward and backward, face-to-face roller coaster in the Midwest, and the Drop Zone stunt tower, which sends you on a 26-story freefall at more than 60 mph.

Meander the wide avenues of the park and visit the many non-thrill-ride attractions as well, such as the park's iconic Eiffel Tower replica. Ringed by well-maintained gardens, it affords a nice view of the surrounding area. Kings Island also has Vegas-style musical revues, including *Spellbound*, a glitzy musical and magic adventure show with major illusions, and *VH1 presents Vibe*, a revue of current Top 40 hits and movie theme songs. There's also a karaoke stage and a *Slime Time Live* show with plenty of messy fun. In the summer months, major concerts can be seen at the 10,000-seat Timberwolf outdoor amphitheater. Tickets for concerts require a separate purchase in addition to the $31.99 admission fee; tickets for the in-park musical revues do not require a separate purchase.

The park has plenty of diversions for kids as well, from the new animated, interactive family ride, Scooby-Doo and the Haunted Castle, to a SpongeBob SquarePants 3-D adventure ocean-motion movie ride, and the Rugrats Runaway Reptar, the world's first inverted junior coaster. Other kid-friendly attractions include the wet Wild Thornberry's River Adventure, photo ops with Nicktoons and Scooby-Doo characters, and dozens of classic miniature rides in Hanna-Barbera Land.

The WaterWorks area, free with park admission, is home to the fully enclosed Bonzai Pipeline speed water slides, SurfSide Bay wave pool, and the water-cannon and splash pool adventure, Buccaneer Island.

Though summer is the peak season for the park, the park also presents the month-long Fearfest in the fall, with the Midwest's largest haunted house and plenty of ghouls to go around.

As with all amusement parks, expect long lines and waits of several hours for most of the popular attractions, unless you're willing to hit the park early or brave inclement weather. If you're an aficionado, or you just like to ride coasters more than once, plan at least a 2-day visit. Each night the park closes at 10 with a large fireworks display. If you need a break from pizza and burgers, nearby Mason offers plenty of family-friendly, affordable sit-down restaurants. > 6300 Kings Island Dr., Mason, tel. 513/754–5800, www.pki.com. $41.99, includes parking. Memorial Day–Labor Day, weekdays and Sun. 9 AM–10 PM, Sat. 9 AM–11 PM.

MASON

The Beach Waterpark It's the place to be on a hot summer day. Popular water rides include Aztec Adventure, the only water coaster in the Midwest, and Thunder Beach, the largest wave pool in Ohio. Be sure to check out the Pearl, the largest hot tub in the United States, and make your way down the Cliff, the five-story free-fall slide. The fun doesn't end when bikini season is over either. The Beach also offers wintertime diversions with its **Holiday Fest** ($8, late Nov.–Jan. 1, weekdays 6–10 PM, weekends 5–10 PM), with a 5,000-square-foot Winter Fantasy ice rink, a North Pole Corral petting zoo, a live nativity scene, millions of sparkling lights, and horse-drawn carriage rides complete with steaming mugs of cocoa. > 2590 Waterpark Dr., Mason, tel. 513/398–7946 or 800/886–7946, www.thebeachwaterpark.com. $25.95. Late May and early Sept., weekends 10–6; Memorial Day–Labor Day, daily 10–9.

Blitz Tour

WITH SOME STRATEGIC planning, you can experience the ups and downs of all seven of Paramount's Kings Island's (PKI) major roller coasters in a single day . . . twice. Though waits can be as short as 5 minutes or less on an overcast morning or on an October weekend, expect to wait between a half hour and 40 minutes (though the waits for the Beast have been known to last up to 2 hours) during peak weekends in summer. To get a head start, stay at one of the more than half-dozen hotels within a 5-minute drive and plan to arrive at the park when the gates open at 9 AM.

Spend some time acquainting yourself with the layout, since the attractions don't open until 10. The Paramount Action Zone and Hanna-Barbera Land are first dash favorites for teens and children, so the best bet is to start your counterclockwise loop around PKI with the park's crown jewel, the **Beast.** After entering the park veer to your right and walk down the International Street promenade, curl around the Eiffel Tower and take a slight right toward Rivertown. There, you will find the Beast, the world's longest wooden roller coaster. This old school coaster maxes out at nearly 65 mph over the course of a 3:40 ride that drops you down a 135-foot precipice and whips you through three teeth-rattling tunnels.

Backtrack a bit and veer to your right to reach the Coney Mall midway and **Vortex,** a metal coaster that will throw you for six loops. The Vortex hits 55 mph during a nearly 3-minute ride that has two vertical loops, a corkscrew, and a one-and-a-half revolution helix turn. Continue down the Coney Mall to **Flight of Fear,** a 65-second alien-theme indoor thrill ride. It begins with a 0–54 mph launch before plunging riders into a pitch-dark series of four inversions and twisty turns. Just down the Coney Mall on the right is the **Racer,** the classic wooden twin-car attraction credited with kicking off the modern coaster renaissance. Take your choice of backward- or forward-facing cars on this traditional ride, which takes you on a 2½-minute trip at speeds up to 53 mph.

A slight right as you exit will lead you to the Indiana Jones–like mine car attraction **Adventure Express,** a family-oriented ride in the Oktoberfest area that hits speeds of 35 mph during a 2½-minute journey. Though not as fast as some of the other coasters, this ride packs a punch as it takes you through a series of whipsaw turns before winding up in an uphill tunnel trudging past some ominous animatronic drummers.

Bear right into the Paramount Action Zone to **Son of Beast,** the tallest, fastest, and only looping wooden coaster in the world. This 3-minute ride is not to be missed, as the 218-foot first hill offers a prime view of the park before it plunges into a series of twisting helices and tops out at 78 mph. Right next door is the hanging **Top Gun** ride, a brief (1½-minute), smooth-riding coaster that swings riders side to side as it glides along at 51 mph.

Your coaster adventure will wind up with a short walk across the Adventure Zone to **Face/Off,** a unique attraction with a series of two-person cars that face each other. With your legs dangling beneath you, you shoot up a 138-foot hill, then glide back the other way at 55 mph for a 1½-minute flight with six inversions and a 72-foot loop. If you're starting to feel a bit queasy, take it down a notch and ride the more manageable kiddie coasters in Hanna-Barbera Land or make your way back to International Street for some lunch and shopping. Of course, you could just do the whole thing over again.

— Gil Kaufman

Chateau Larouche In 1929, Harry D. Andrews began building a castle in Loveland on the north bank of the Little Miami River, using river rock as his construction stones. His dream was a full-scale replica of a medieval Normanesque castle in southwest France, Château Laroche, where he was stationed during World War I. Loveland's castle became his life's work; over the next 50 years, he built 17 rooms, including a great hall, banquet hall, armory, ballroom, chapel, small work office, and dungeon. The castle, which is about 10 mi southeast of Mason, is surrounded by beautiful gardens with more than 250 species of plants and flowers. > 12025 Shore Dr., Loveland, tel. 513/683–4686. $3. Daily 11–5.

The Dude Ranch Although it's just 20 minutes from downtown Cincinnati, this ranch would be right at home in the Wild, Wild West. You can round up Texas Longhorns on a cattle drive or go horseback riding in the woods. Other attractions include hayrides, horseshoe pits, fishing, a petting zoo, and a paintball course that resembles an old West town. You can also rent ATVs for wild romps through the woods. > 3205 Waynesville Rd., Mason, tel. 513/421–3833, www.theduderanch.com. Daily 10–5.

Golf Center at Kings Island This Jack Nicklaus–designed golf course has an 18-hole executive par-60 course, as well as a 27-hole regulation course, both of which are open to the public. > 6042 Fairway Dr., Mason, tel. 513/398–7700 tee reservations, 513/398–5200 office, www.thegolfcenter.com. $30–$65 per person. May–Aug., daily 7 AM–8 PM; Sept.–Apr., daily 9–5.

Sports

CANOEING

The Little Miami River, a 15-minute drive from Mason in Oregonia, has 86 mi of canoeable river, much of it placid. After heavy spring rains, a meander down the shady river can often be interrupted by exciting, though manageable, rapids. In the 1970s the Little Miami became one of only 19 rivers included in the Federal Scenic Rivers Program, which has helped keep it clean and well-maintained. Much of the property along the river is privately held, so expect to be greeted by some friendly river-side homeowners, who will likely offer a hardy "howdy," if they don't just invite you up for a drink. You might also find the occasional, well-worn rope swing along the way. Life jackets are required, and canoe rentals are available all along the river. Most liveries offer trips ranging from a few hours to several days. The Little Miami is a National and State Scenic River, so litter and alcohol laws are enforced.

Little Miami Canoe Rental Little Miami offers canoeing, kayaking, rafting, tubing, and riverside camping. Day trips range from 45-minute jaunts ($8–$15) that take you under Ohio's tallest bridge to an 8-hour meander ($22) that floats through Fort Ancient State Park. Catering, from hot dogs to hog roasts, is available for groups of 20 or more. Children ride free in a parent's canoe; shuttle and life vests included. > 219 Mill St., Morrow, tel. 800/634–4277, www.littlemiamicanoe.com.

Morgan's Canoe Livery One of the area's busiest liveries has plenty of fun tour packages for everyone in your group, from the novice to the more experienced canoeist. Morgan's outfits rafting, tubing, kayaking, and canoeing group trips for companies, schools, colleges, senior citizens, and families. Groups of 20 or more can sign up for packages that include barbecue meals and beverages, or a guided rafting trip with a gourmet buffet. Check out the guided midnight canoe excursion, which includes a bonfire and s'mores fixin's; camping available. Shuttle and life vests are included. Trips range from 3 mi (45 minutes) for $25 to 18 mi for $42. > 5701 St. Rte. 350, Oregonia, tel. 513/932–7658, www.morganscanoe.com/.

Save the Date

JANUARY

New Year's Bird Count This annual event is a bird-watcher's delight for early risers. Show up at 6 AM to look and listen for owls; then take an 8:30 trek to find waterfowl and songbirds. Expect to see more than 60 different species during this free event. > 4020 North Clarksville Rd., Waynesville, tel. 513/897–1050, www.lrl.usace.army.mil/ccl.

JUNE

British Isles Festival Just a half-hour's drive north of Mason will take you several centuries back in time. This newbie festival at the Renaissance Park in Harveysburg is a sprawling mix of 11 stages featuring costumed performances and weapon demonstrations, craft booths, and the traditional foods and ales of England, Scotland, Ireland, and Wales. > St. Rte. 73, Harveysburg, tel. 513/897–7000.

AUGUST

Western-Southern Financial Group Masters Tennis's top 50 men play in this hard-court competition in Mason. Andre Agassi, Pete Sampras, Michael Chang, and Andy Roddick have all appeared here. > ATP Tennis Center, 6140 Fairway Dr., tel. 513/651–0303.

SEPTEMBER

The Kroger Classic More than 100,000 fans make the trek to this popular stop on the PGA Champions Tour. Some of the biggest golfers in the world try their luck on the Jack Nicklaus–designed course at the private Tournament Player's Club in River's Bend. The event has raised nearly $2 million for a number of local and national charities. > 316 Winding River Blvd., Maineville, tel. 800/883–6538.

OCTOBER

Fall Foliage Tours Driving and walking tours traverse the Midwestern woods, which are painted with autumn's brilliant yellows, reds, and oranges. > Caesar Creek Lake, Waynesville, tel. 513/897–1050.

WHERE TO STAY

MASON

Best Western Inn & Suites This modern three-floor hotel, furnished in oak, is right off I–71 at Exit 25, less than 1 mi from the Beach and Kings Island, adding up to savings on parking fees. The hotel also has one of the few indoor pools in the area and refrigerators and microwaves in every room. > 2793 Water Park Dr., Mason 45040, tel. 513/754–1166 or 800/528–1234, www.bestwestern.com. 57 rooms, 14 suites. In-room data ports, some in-room hot tubs, microwaves, refrigerators, cable TV, indoor pool, hot tub, exercise equipment, video games, laundry service, laundry facilities, no-smoking rooms. AE, D, DC, MC, V. CP. ¢–$$

Comfort Suites–Kings Island The queen-size suites in this all-suites hotel can sleep up to five people, making it ideal for families who want to visit the Beach and Kings Island, which are less than a mile away. Each suite has a sofa and a living area big enough for family relaxation. > 5457 Kings Center Dr., Mason 45040, tel. 513/336–9000 or 800/228–5150, www.comfortinn.com. 79 suites. In-room data ports, in-room safes, refrigerators, cable TV, indoor pool, laundry service, business services, no-smoking rooms. AE, D, DC, MC, V. CP. $–$$$$

Kings Island Resort and Conference Center The top lodging spot in Mason, thanks to its proximity to Kings Island, this resort is the only one in the area that provides a complimentary shuttle to the amusement park. Set on 22 acres, the resort features a 24-hour fitness center, a private fishing lake, a sports bar, basketball courts, and a sand volleyball court. The 288 guest rooms and suites were recently renovated; all rooms include a small patio area. Discounted tickets to Kings Island, the Beach, Newport Aquarium, and the Cincinnati Zoo are available to guests. It's usually fully booked all summer, so make reservations well in advance. > 5691 Kings Island Dr., Mason 45034, tel. 513/398–0115 or 800/727–3050, fax 513/398–1095, www.kingsislandresort.com. 288 rooms. Restaurant, room service, in-room data ports, cable TV with movies, 2 tennis courts, 2 pools (1 indoor), hot tub, basketball, volleyball, fishing, bar, playground, laundry service, laundry facilities, business services, no-smoking rooms. AE, D, DC, MC, V. $$

King's Luxury Inn-Kings Island Just off I–71, this hotel offers easy-off, easy-on access to the interstate. Plus it's just minutes away from Paramount's Kings Island and the Beach Waterpark. A Chinese restaurant is on the premises. > 9845 Escort Dr., Mason, tel. 513/398–8015 or 800/228–5151, fax 513/398–0822. 104 rooms. Restaurant, room service, in-room data ports, cable TV, pool, playground, business services, some pets allowed. AE, D, DC, MC, V. CP. ¢–$

Kirkwood Inn This small motel is family-owned by folks who have been in the business for 30-plus years. The family also runs the popular Houston Inn restaurant across the street. The historic farmhouse and inn was once a hitching post and stagecoach stop, hosting such luminaries as Henry Clay. The motel is 2 mi from Paramount's Kings Island and close to three golf courses, restaurants, and retail stores. Continental breakfast is served in a renovated 1800s farmhouse. The rooms have been renovated in a Colonial Williamsburg style and many overlook wooded areas. > 4027 St. Rte. 42, Mason 45040, tel. 513/398–7277 or 800/732–4741, www.kirkwoodinn.com. 42 rooms, 6 suites. Cable TV, pool, Ihternet, no-smoking rooms. AE, D, DC, MC, V. CP. $

Marriott-Northeast This hotel has a redbrick exterior and a dark-wood interior. Plants and a fountain fill the attractive lobby. It's a popular choice for both those visiting nearby Paramount's Kings Island and for business travelers. There's an Executive Floor with 16 meeting rooms (13,000 square feet total), as well as a full business center and available secretarial services. > 9664 Mason-Montgomery Rd., Mason 45040, tel. 513/459–9800 or 800/228–9290, fax 513/459–9808, www.marriott.com. 302 rooms, 7 suites. Restaurant, room service, in-room data ports, some refrigerators, cable TV with movies, 2 pools (1 indoor), gym, lounge, laundry facilities, business services, meeting rooms, no-smoking rooms. AE, D, DC, MC, V. $$$

Quality Inn This two-story hotel, designed for the business traveler, has reasonable rates. It's also good for families who want to go to the Kings Island amusement park, which is a 5-minute drive away. Hotel guests have free access to a nearby health club. There are two restaurants just outside the hotel and more than 30 within minutes. > 8870 Governor's Hill Dr., Mason 45249, tel. 513/683–3086 or 800/228–5151, fax 513/683–3086 Ext. 500, www.choicehotels.com. 99 rooms. In-room data ports, microwaves, refrigerators, pool, business services, no-smoking rooms. AE, D, DC, MC, V. CP. $$

WHERE TO EAT

MASON

Arloi Dee Authentic Thai food gets a lively twist with unusual mixes in house specialties like Strawberry Chicken and Lost Jungle Boa, made of stir-fried pork with red curry paste, hot peppers, bell peppers, and sweet basil. Arloi Dee also serves traditional Asian dishes such as Thai Cashew Chicken, Moo Goo Gai Pan, fried rice and noodle dishes, and has a full sushi menu. > 4920 Socialville Foster Rd., Mason, tel. 513/229–3997. AE, MC, V. $–$$

Carrabba's The open kitchen at Carrabba's turns out Northern Italian cuisine, with a taste of Sicily thrown in the mix. Don't miss the popular Chicken Polla Rosa Maria—two breasts grilled over hickory and pecan wood, filleted and stuffed with prosciutto, lemon sauce, and mushrooms. Mosaic tables stand on a terra-cotta floor, and grapevines are a decorative theme. > 5152 Merten Dr., Mason, tel. 513/339–0900. AE, D, DC, MC, V. No lunch Sun. $–$$

Copeland's of New Orleans If you crave a bit of down South cooking, Copeland's is the place for you. This lively New Orleans bistro serves everything from shrimp étouffée to blackened redfish and chicken, shrimp creole, po'boy sandwiches, and the house specialty, crab-stuffed catfish bordelaise. There are also steak, pork, and veal, and a kid's menu. > 5150 Mason-Montgomery Rd., Mason, tel. 513/336–0043. AE, D, MC, V. $–$$$

Courseview Restaurant Sit by the fireplace and enjoy Amish chicken, pasta gambretti, salmon oriental, or the fresh catch of the day. Golf memorabilia is scattered throughout the restaurant, and the views are of the Golf Center at Kings Island. On Friday nights in summer, the large brick patio becomes the site of a pig roast, and you can dine next to the putting green. There's live music Wednesday–Saturday. > 6042 Fairway Dr., Mason, tel. 513/573–3321. AE, D, DC, MC, V. No dinner Nov.–Feb., Sun.–Tues. $$

Golden Lamb Owned by the same group that runs the Maisonette in Cincinnati, the Golden Lamb is housed in Ohio's oldest building, erected in 1803. Charles Dickens, Mark Twain, and a dozen U.S. presidents have eaten at the restaurant, which serves generous portions of American fare and is known for its succulent roast leg of lamb and turkey and mashed potatoes. You can eat among, and sometimes on, authentic Shaker antiques. Visit the rustic Black Horse Tavern and take a stroll on the wide colonial porch with towering white pillars. > 27 S. Broadway, Lebanon, tel. 513/932–5065. AE, MC, V. $$

Houston Inn An attractive cedar-and-stone facade greets patrons of this antiques-filled restaurant. Frogs' legs are the specialty; more than 1,500 deep-fried legs are served each week. Another highlight is the 46-item salad bar; it's the largest in the area, with all kinds of greens, slaws, vegetables, and fresh fruit. Other favorites are slow-cooked prime rib, broiled pork chops, and lamb chops with mint jelly. Don't miss a side of the mashed-potato salad. > 4026 U.S. 42, Mason, tel. 513/398–7377. AE, D, DC, MC, V. Closed Mon. $–$$

Toot's Looking for a friendly, easy family meal, or just wanting some quick, fresh takeout? Fun finger food awaits at Toot's. Burgers, dill pickle chips, and hot wings are house favorites, along with breaded catfish, ribs, frogs' legs, oysters, and Philly cheesesteak sandwiches. It's fast food with a home-cooked flavor, plus plenty of games and diversions for the kids. > 12191 Montgomery Rd., Mason, tel. 513/697–9100. AE, D, DC, MC, V. $

ESSENTIALS

Getting Here

Plan on using a car to visit the Kings Island area. Long-distance buses are available to travel to and from Cincinnati, but visitors to the area will need a vehicle to get from hotels to restaurants and other local attractions.

BY CAR

Just 25 mi north of downtown Cincinnati, Mason is on Route 42, directly between I–75 and I–71, and 5 mi north of Cincinnati's circle freeway, I–275. Driving time to downtown Cincinnati is less than 35 minutes, though rush hour traffic to and from Cincinnati can be heavy.

Kings Island is directly off I–71 at Kings Mill Road. Parking is $7 per vehicle.

Visitor Information

Mason Chamber of Commerce > 316 W. Main St., 45040, tel. 513/398–2188, www.mlkchamber.org. **Warren County Convention & Visitors Bureau** > 313 East Warren St., Lebanon 45036, tel. 800/791–4386, www.ohio4fun.org.

Waynesville & Wilmington

Approximately 35 mi northeast of Cincinnati, 80 mi southwest of Columbus, and 220 mi southwest of Cleveland.

22

By Ann Fazzini

THESE TWO HAMLETS EPITOMIZE everything that's great about Ohio's small towns. A mixture of kindhearted hospitality and modern convenience makes it easy to experience the slower pace and hometown traditions of the Ohio countryside. Surrounded by state parks, rivers, and farmland, the area feels like a hidden treasure even though it's a well-known and popular weekend destination for Midwesterners.

Waynesville, the "Antiques Capital of the Midwest," has a lineup of more than 70 shops along its charming main thoroughfare. Everything from furniture to record albums is on sale here, with an equally wide range of price points. Pioneer Samuel Heighway founded Waynesville in 1797 with the intention of making it the new capital of the Northwest Territory. Heighway and other wealthy settlers created the town's rectangular English village–style layout. The central town square, considered the "heart" of the settlement, was surrounded by homes, formal parks, smaller squares, and decorative fountains. In the 19th century, Waynesville became an important stop on the Underground Railroad, which transported escaped slaves from bondage in the South to freedom in Canada. The Ohio Sauerkraut Festival (born when local merchants decided to host a sidewalk sale and sauerkraut dinner in the 1970s) takes place each October and is one of the state's most anticipated fall festivals. Waynesville also takes full advantage of its distinction as Ohio's Most Haunted Town and offers fun (and frightful) tours of the homes and buildings with the most paranormal activity.

Close by is Wilmington, a small, historic college town. Norman Crampton named it in his book *The 100 Best Small Towns in America* in 1995. Wilmington's early residents were from Virginia, Kentucky, North Carolina, and Pennsylvania, including many Quakers, who founded Wilmington College in 1870. Walkable streets and beautiful architecture in the downtown area attract many for a leisurely afternoon, perusing the area.

Caesar Creek, Little Miami, and Cowan Lake, three standout members of Ohio's popular and well-maintained state park system, are in the Waynesville and Wilmington region. These natural areas have plenty of trails for hiking and biking, plus waterways for swimming, fishing, and boating. Set up camp at either park for the weekend or stop by to picnic or bird-watch.

Historical attractions, museums, great eateries, premier shopping, and lively parks allow visitors to mix and match options to create the perfect weekend away. It's best to explore Wilmington on Saturday and travel on to Waynesville on Sunday, as many shops in Waynesville remain open for the entire weekend. Approach the area with a leisurely attitude; the attractions are designed to allow you to take your time. Locals are happy to lend suggestions of places to visit and to direct you to any special events. This little taste of Ohio will leave a surprisingly big impression.

WHAT TO SEE & DO

WAYNESVILLE

Caesar Creek Flea Market Find your heart's desire at this year-round weekend flea market. Browse through countless vendor stands of antiques and collectibles—everything from jewelry and clothing to tools and arts and crafts. Food stalls serve such festival fare as hamburgers, bratwursts, and funnel cakes. The market is held on the outskirts of Caesar Creek State Park. > 7763 Rte. 73, tel. 937/382–1669. $1 per car. Weekends 9–5.

Caesar Creek State Park The park, 5 mi east of Waynesville, has a 2,400-acre lake, a nature preserve, and wildlife area. In summer you can boat on the lake, and ice skating is popular during the winter.

The **Visitor Center** (4020 N. Clarksville Rd., Waynesville, tel. 513/897–1050) displays Native American artifacts from several different tribes that once lived in the area. The prehistoric Hopewells, who built earthworks in the area, as well as woodland tribes such as the Miami and the Shawnee were drawn here by the relatively even terrain and the plentiful supplies of water and vegetation. **Pioneer Village** (3999 Pioneer Village Rd., tel. 513/897–1120, www.shakerwssg.org/caesars_creek_pioneer_village.htm, grounds open daily) is a re-creation of a 19th-century settlement complete with 18 split log buildings. The buildings in the village are usually open one weekend a month for a special event, like a maple syrup festival or a 19th-century market fair. June's Old Tyme Music Festival brings the village to life with historical interpreters in period dress, demonstrations, and lots of great music. Admission costs vary. > 8570 E. Rte. 73, tel. 513/897–3055. Free. Daily dawn–dusk.

Little Miami State Park This unusual linear park wanders for 50 mi through four counties, following the course of the Little Miami River. The Little Miami was the first river in Ohio to earn the State and National Scenic River designations. The Ohio Department of Natural Resources protects and preserves its waters. Warblers and songbirds are often sighted here, above the wild columbines and Virginia bluebells. The state park is known for its bridle trails, but you can also hike or bike the paved path from Milford to Xenia. There are entrances along the trail; there's one in Corwin, just east of Waynesville. > Tel. 513/897–3055. Free. Daily dawn–dusk.

Main Street Downtown District Historic homes that were once the residences of the wealthy now house the antiques shops that made Waynesville famous. The five-block-long area is dressed up with copper street lamps, brick sidewalks, and overflowing flower boxes. An old stagecoach stop, the Hammel House Inn, now provides a place to lunch and relax. > Main St. Daily 9–5.

Waynesville Area Heritage and Cultural Center The high hill in Waynesville is a historical meeting place for many Quakers of southwest Ohio. Just before the turn of the 19th century, Quakers first settled in the area, building the Quaker Meeting house, the Friends Boarding Home, and several other buildings that still stand in town today. The 1905 Friends Boarding Home is now a museum that tells the story of the Waynesville area through exhibits, historical documents, and artwork. Tours are by appointment, and there's a gift shop with Waynesville souvenirs. > 115 4th St., on the corner of Miami St., Waynesville, tel. 513/897–1607, www.waynesvilleculturalcenter.org. Sun. 1–4.

Ghosts, Ghouls & Goblins

ANTIQUES AREN'T THE ONLY old-timers hanging around Waynesville. The Antiques Capital of the Midwest also claims more than 30 haunted spots, making it Ohio's most haunted town according to Chris Woodyard's Haunted Ohio (Kestrel Publishing 1991). It seems there are so many souls stirring in the wind in Waynesville that they quite frequently make themselves known from beyond the grave. Each Halloween, town crier and local historian Dennis Dalton brings the living to the ghosts. His highly anticipated Not-So-Dearly-Departed Tours lead brave souls to 13 of Waynesville's best haunts. And there's no telling what surprises the groups will find. Some of the most "active" homes are popular stops on Dalton's tours and one of the most famous is the Stetson House, owned by the family of John Stetson, who invented the Stetson hat. It's said that John sometimes peers out of the upstairs window, regularly knocks mirrors off the walls, and tosses around other household items. Some say that John's daughter Louisa also haunts the house; she died there of tuberculosis in 1879. The house, 234 South Main Street, is currently one of the town's popular antiques shops. The Waynesville Firehouse has also seen its share of action—and it has nothing to do with untimely fires. Daniel, the man who donated the land on which the building now stands, died in 1982 but continues to pay frequent visits. Folks in the firehouse have heard shuffling footsteps throughout the building. Like Daniel, most Waynesville ghosts seem to be more of the mischievous variety than out to frighten the living. The ghastly presence in the Satterthwaite House, Elizabeth, regularly plays pranks on the house's residents; she even allegedly caused "her" family to be late for work by hiding their alarm clocks so they couldn't be heard. Whether you're a believer or think this ghost stuff is a bunch of bunk, Dalton's tours will give you a fun and freaky look into the hamlet's interesting past. It's a great way to hear some history, see the town, and have a delightful little fright.

WILMINGTON

Clinton County Historical Society/Rombach Place The museum of the Clinton County Historical Society presents exhibits and artifacts that take you through the county's 200-year history. Housed in the former home of Civil War general James W. Denver (for whom Denver, Colorado, was named), the museum showcases historical furniture, clothing, artwork, and Quaker artifacts. Denver, a political leader, was the original governor of the Kansas Territory, which later became Colorado. > 149 E. Locust St., tel. 937/382–4684. Free. Mar.–Dec., Wed.–Fri. 1–4:30.

Cowan Lake State Park This beautiful park was once the home of the Miami and Shawnee tribes. Today it's a favorite of cyclists, who can pedal through 1,775 acres. The large lake is ideal for boating (up to 10 horsepower) and fishing for muskie, crappie, largemouth bass, and bluegill. It's 5 mi south of Wilmington. > 729 Beechwood Rd., tel. 937/289–2105. Free. Daily dawn–dusk.

Wilmington College This liberal arts college was founded in the 1870s by the Religious Society of Friends (Quakers). Small and walkable, the campus is dotted with brick buildings and crisscrossed by tree-lined sidewalks. > 251 Ludovic St., tel. 937/382–6661. Free. Daily.

Tours

Downtown Waynesville Tours Pick up a map at the Waynesville Chamber of Commerce and then take a self-guided tour of the historic homes and buildings in Waynesville. The structures are beautifully maintained and marked with outdoor plaques.

> Waynesville Chamber of Commerce, N. Main St., Waynesville, tel. 513/897–8855, www.waynesvilleohio.com.

Downtown Wilmington The county seat of Clinton County is on the National Register of Historic Places and holds the distinction of being a Main Street Community, or a town that has restored and beautified its "main street" or downtown area. Architecture and plenty of shops and restaurants are highlights of the self-guided walking tour. Pick up maps and brochures at the Clinton County Convention and Visitors Bureau. > Clinton County Convention and Visitors Bureau, 13 N. South St., Wilmington, tel. 877/428–4748, www.clintoncountyohio.com.

Not-So-Dearly-Departed Tours Dennis Dalton, community historian and town crier, leads these tours of Ohio's Most Haunted Town (also known as Waynesville) during the Halloween season. Visit the Waynesville Fire House, Stetson House, and several other area residences and businesses with otherworldly residents. The spooky fun is appropriate for all ages. Dalton also leads tours of downtown Waynesville. > Tel. 513/932–5298.

Shopping

WAYNESVILLE

Waynesville is packed with shops and new stores are continually popping up along the popular Main Street antiques shopping area. Stop at the **Chamber of Commerce** (N. Main St., Waynesville, tel. 513/897–8855) for a map of the area. If it's closed, grab a map from the box outside. The **Waynesville Merchants Association** (www.waynesvilleshops.com) lists local shops on their Web site.

Canada Goose Gallery P. Buckley Moss celebrates Ohio's rich Amish heritage in her artwork. Paintings, cards, baskets, and figurines are available at the shop. > 198 S. Main St., Waynesville, tel. 513/897–4348, www.canadagoosegallery.com. Closed Mon.

Celtic Isle Shops These Celtic gifts hail directly from Ireland, Scotland, Wales, and England. Scottish Highland garb, wool scarves, hats and sweaters, novelties, CDs, heraldry items, and bagpiping supplies make for plenty of Celtic Isle fun. Call ahead as hours vary seasonally. > 260B High St., Waynesville, tel. 513/897–1566 or 877/897–1566, www.celticislesshop.com.

Cobblestone Cafe and Village Shop for whimsical wreaths, Victorian-influenced decorations, David T. Smith furnishings, and dried flowers and candles, then stop by the sit-down restaurant for a bite to eat. > 10 N. Main St., Waynesville, tel. 513/897–0021. Closed Mon.

Golden Pomegranate Antique Mall This antiques shop has a standout collection of classic advertising signs and collectibles, including Coca-Cola and other brand-name products. > 140 S. Main St., Waynesville, tel. 513/897–7400. Closed Mon.

Gravel Hill Gifts A historic Main Street schoolhouse is now a colorful gift shop. Find Ohio souvenirs, gift wrap, creative cards, cookie cutters, country home furnishings, and garden decor. > 330 S. Main St., Waynesville, tel. 513/897–9941.

Lilly's Corner Shoppes An eclectic selection of glasswares, old Hollywood collectibles, artwork, furniture, and home decor fills the display rooms of this fun shop. Kids will also enjoy looking at classic toys. Consignment vendors bring new items in weekly. > 105 S. Main St., Waynesville, tel. 513/897–0388.

Spencer's Antiques and Imports Seemingly endless interconnected rooms contain everything you could possibly be looking for—plus a lot more. Highlights include fine antique furnishings, Fiesta pottery, stained glass, and Tiffany lamps and outdoor fountains and decor. Delivery is available. > 274 S. Main St., Waynesville, tel.

866/897–7775, www.spencersantiques.com. Closed occasional Mon. and Tues.; call ahead for hrs.

Waynesville Antique Mall Looking for a particular style of furniture, toy, or collectible? You can likely find it here. Several large rooms combine to create three distinct store spaces. It's a good one-stop shop if you're pressed for time. > 69 S. Main St., Waynesville, tel. 513/897–6937.

WILMINGTON

Books 'N' More Bestsellers, magazines, newspapers, and more are for sale in the bookstore, and the Buttercup Gift Shop has home interior accessories and souvenirs. Grab a bite to eat or a cup of coffee at the on-site café and deli. > 28 W. Main St., Wilmington, tel. 937/383–7323. Closed Sun.

Buffalo Trading Post Cowboy and Western-theme collectibles and antiques fill this shop modeled after a 19th-century trading post. > 280 W. Curry Rd., Wilmington, tel. 937/382–0141. Closed Mon.–Thurs.

David Adair Co Billed as one of Ohio's most unique furniture stores, this shop has thousands of eclectic home furnishings and decorative items. > 113 N. South St., Waynesville, tel. 888/673–1350 or 937/382–0961, www.DavidAdair.com. Closed Sun.

Nostalgia Station This specialty shop includes a Christmas shop, toy room, full-service florist, and lots of great gifts. > 135 N. South St., Wilmington, tel. 937/382–0056. Closed Sun.

Save the Date

JUNE

Art & Pottery Festival This celebration of traditional arts and crafts includes every medium of artwork imaginable, as well as blacksmithing, soap and candle making, and silversmithing. Kids' activities, music, dancing, and sporting demonstrations round out the summer fun. > Grandpa's Pottery Barn & Farm, 3558 W. St. Rte. 73, Wilmington, tel. 937/382–6442.

Banana Split Festival Wilmington kicks off summer on the second weekend of June with this traditional celebration of dessert: more than 550 gallons of ice cream and 4,200 bananas are served. Denver Williams Memorial Park park is filled with games, rides, and musical performances with a 1950s theme. > Tel. 937/382–1965 or 877/428–4748.

AUGUST–OCTOBER

Ohio Renaissance Festival Enjoy the jousting and pageantry, then indulge in some "olde" food and drink at this re-creation of merry old England. The festival is held on weekends from late August to mid-October, plus Labor Day. > Harveysburg, 5 mi east of Waynesville, tel. 513/897–7000.

SEPTEMBER

Clinton County Corn Festival The city that starts the summer with banana splits, ends it with corn at this festival held the weekend after Labor Day at the Clinton County Fairgrounds. > 851 W. Main St., tel. 937/382–2737.

OCTOBER

Ohio Sauerkraut Festival More than 20,000 pounds of sauerkraut are consumed at this 3-day annual tribute to the cabbage. Waynesville's downtown district is closed off for 400 arts and craft exhibitors and lots of visitors during this festival, which is held the second full weekend of October. > Tel. 513/897–8855.

WHERE TO STAY

WAYNESVILLE

Hammel House Inn A fully restored, circa 1822 house is now a B&B. A convenient spot for shopaholics, the inn is within a few blocks of several antiques and gift stores, or you can visit the Garden Cottage at Hammel House gift shop on-site if it's raining. The breakfast room has exposed-brick walls, and guest rooms Nos. 3 and 4 are spacious with shining cherrywood furniture. > 121 S. Main St., Waynesville 45068, tel. 513/897-3779. 5 rooms. Restaurant; no room phones, no kids, no smoking. AE, D, MC, V. BP. $

WILMINGTON

Amerihost Inn This brick hotel is 1 mi from downtown and Wilmington College. Suites are equipped with refrigerators and hot tubs, plus complimentary soda, popcorn, and bottled water. There are restaurants nearby, but a Continental breakfast at the hotel is included with all rooms. > 201 Carrie Dr., Wilmington 45177, tel. 937/383-3950, fax 937/383-1693, www.amerihostinn.com. 61 rooms, 5 suites. In-room data ports, some microwaves, some refrigerators, some in-room hot tubs, cable TV, indoor pool, hot tub, exercise equipment, business services, no-smoking rooms. AE, D, DC, MC, V. CP. $

Cedar Hill Bed & Breakfast in the Woods Guest rooms are in the carriage house of this 10-acre estate and thus have private entrances and private baths. Quilts and rugs add splashes of color to the white walls and wooden furniture. There's a common room with a fireplace and a VCR, and there are walking trails on the property. > 4003 St. Rte. 73, Wilmington 45177, tel. 937/383-2525 or 877/722-2525, www.ohiobba.com/cedarhill.htm. 3 rooms. Kitchenettes, refrigerators, room TVs; no kids under 12, no smoking. MC, V. BP. $-$$

Lark's Nest Eight acres of property lead into Caesar's Creek State Park. The porch of the log cabin home is equipped with rockers and a hammock for idle hours; inside, there are exposed beam ceilings, soft quilts, and country craft decorations. > 619 Ward Rd., Wilmington 45177, tel. 937/382-4788. 3 rooms. Fishing, hiking, cross-country skiing; no room TVs, no smoking. AE, MC, V. BP. $-$$

Wilmington Inn Queen Anne cherrywood furnishings fill this rustic, two-story stone-and-wood hotel in a residential area off I-73 west of town. You can use the recreational facilities at the nearby YMCA. > 909 Fife Ave., Wilmington 45177, tel. 937/382-6000, fax 937/382-6655, www.wilmingtoninn.com. 51 rooms, 2 suites. Cable TV, business services, no-smoking rooms. AE, D, DC, MC, V. CP. ¢

CAMPING

Beechwood Acres Camping Resort Camp alongside beautiful Lake Cowan or settle down in a rental cabin. Cabins, which require a 2- or 3-night minimum stay, have covered decks, bunk beds, air-conditioning, and a charcoal grill. The campground also has a lighted pavilion and game room. Friendly service, homey accommodations, and regular planned activities make this a popular destination. There's no smoking here. > 855 Yankee Rd., Wilmington 45177, tel. 937/289-2202, www.beechwoodacres.com. 95 full hook-ups, 3 cabins. Flush toilets, full hook-ups, dump station, laundry facilities, showers, fire rings, picnic tables, general store, swimming (lake). D, MC, V. Closed Nov.-Mar. ¢

Caesar Creek Frontier Campground Formerly Spring Valley Frontier Campground, the grounds here also include a lake, mini-golf course, and a shelter house. Pets are allowed on-site and the camp is open year-round. > 9580 Collett Rd., Waynesville 45068, tel. 937/488–1127. 66 full hook-ups, 44 tent sites, 12 cabins. Flush toilets, dump station, laundry facilities, showers, picnic tables, fire rings, general store, pool, swimming (lake). AE, D, DC, MC V. ¢

Caesar Creek State Park The lake is great for fishing, boating, swimming, and even waterskiing. Cook stoves are available for campers; wooden cabins have air-conditioning, porches, and grills. Horseman sites and cabins are also available. Pets are allowed in designated areas. > 8570 St. Rte. 73 E, Waynesville 45068-9719, tel. 513/897-3055, www.dnr.state.oh.us/parks. 285 sites. Flush toilets, partial hook-ups (electric), dump station, showers, picnic tables, swimming (lake). AE, D, MC, V. ¢

Cowan Lake State Park Camp in the woods and even on the beach; roomy cottages have complete kitchens with all utensils and towels, as well as decks and cooking grills for alfresco meals. A mini-golf course and plenty of lake activities keep the kids entertained. Pets are welcome. > 729 Beechwood Rd., Wilmington 45177, tel. 937/289–2105, www.dnr.state.oh.us/parks. 237 partial hook-ups, 17 tent sites. Flush toilets, partial hook-ups (electric), dump station, laundry facilities, showers, picnic tables, general store, swimming (lake). AE, D, MC, V. ¢

WHERE TO EAT

WAYNESVILLE

Angel of the Garden Tea Room This Victorian-style tearoom is housed in the circa-1901 Charles Cornell House, which is decorated in turn-of-the-20th-century period detail. Lace tablecloths, soft lighting, and rich rose tones set the mood. Entrées vary seasonally; quiche and desserts, such as chocolate strawberry mousse cake and lemon sorbet, are also on the menu. Adults only. Call for lunch times. > 71 N. Main St., Waynesville, tel. 513/897–7729, angelofthegarden.com. Reservations essential. AE, D, MC, V. $$$–$$$$

Cobblestone Cafe Enjoy a fresh assortment of soups, salads, and vegetarian plates amidst country arts, crafts, and household accessories available for purchase. Try the delectable French onion soup or the marinated eggplant sandwich. > 10 N. Main St., Waynesville, tel. 937/897–0021. AE, D, MC, V. Closed Mon. No dinner. ¢–$

Der Dutchman Bring your appetite to this popular Amish restaurant where the hearty, homemade fare is served family-style. Share pan-fried chicken or roast beef, mashed potatoes, and homemade bread. Don't even think about leaving without having a piece of the restaurant's legendary pie. Handcrafted wood furniture and a warm fireplace complete the impression of Sunday dinner in an Amish home. > 188 U.S. Rte. 42 N, Waynesville, tel. 513/897–4716. D, MC, V. Closed Sun. ¢–$

Hammel House Restaurant Cozy and country-decorated, this lunch spot occupies an 1822 building. You can tuck into fresh quiches, homemade soups, sandwiches, and salads. The Hammel Reuben sandwich is locally famous, and the salads are served with home-baked muffins. The coconut cream pie is a must-try. > 121 S. Main St., Waynesville, tel. 513/897–3779. AE, D, MC, V. Closed Mon. No dinner. ¢

Millie's A Taste of Waynesville Need a break from shopping? Stop into this friendly little eatery and grab a brat, Polish sausage, or hot dog. For a small mid-day treat, try the glazed almonds and pecans with a cup of coffee or a fruit drink. > 195 S. Main St., Waynesville, tel. 513/897–4119. No credit cards. Closed some Mondays. ¢

WILMINGTON

Beaugard's Southern BBQ This is the richest, heartiest barbecued chicken, pork, and beef in town. Try the succulent hickory pulled pork. Reverend Troy Beaugard, an Arkansas native, runs this popular joint; he can also be found preaching at a local church on Sundays. > 1173 Wayne Rd., Wilmington, tel. 937/655–8100. AE, MC, V. ¢–$$

El Dorado Mexican Restaurant Festively decorated in reds and greens, El Dorado is the local favorite for south-of-the-border fare like chimichangas and tacos. Try the spicy chicken fajitas or the beef tacos. > 1426 Rombach Ave., Wilmington, tel. 937/383–3763. AE, D, MC, V. ¢

ESSENTIALS

Getting Here

The Waynesville and Wilmington area is easily accessible by car. If you fly or take the train or bus to nearby Dayton, you will need to rent a car before setting out to explore the area.

BY CAR

Waynesville and Wilmington lie between two major interstate routes (I–71 and I–75). Consider taking the smaller state routes, however, for a view of calm countryside scenery and a taste of small-town Ohio: State Route 73 to Waynesville and U.S. 68 to Wilmington are good options.

You can expect to cruise along at a smooth clip (mostly between 45 and 55 mph, except for on the interstate). Take care to obey the speed limit as Ohio traffic laws are cracking down on lead-footed drivers. Also, be cautious of tractors and other farm machinery on the road.

The easiest route to Waynesville is to take I–75 to State Route 73 and follow the signs to the Main Street shopping area. To get to Wilmington, take I–71 from Cincinnati or Columbus and take Exit 45, which will direct you to the east and straight into town. Plenty of on-street parking is available in both towns and, unless a festival is going on, you should have little problem finding a place to park. If a festival is taking over either town, try to arrive in town as early as possible.

Visitor Information

CONTACTS **Clinton County Convention & Visitors Bureau** > 13 N. South St., Wilmington 45177, tel. 937/382–1965 or 877/428–4748, www.clintoncountyohio.com. **Warren County Convention & Visitors Bureau** > 313 E. Warren St., Lebanon 45036, tel. 800/791–4386, www.ohio4fun.com. **Waynesville Area Chamber of Commerce** > N. Main St., Box 281, Waynesville 45036, tel. 513/897–8855, www.waynesvilleohio.com.

Dayton & Yellow Springs

Dayton is 54 mi north of Cincinnati, 72 mi southwest of Columbus, and 214 mi southwest of Cleveland.

23

By Gil Kaufman

THE HISTORY OF AVIATION is on display all around Dayton, from the early sketches of flying machines made by the Wright brothers to actual Stealth fighters. Dayton is best known as the birthplace of Orville and Wilbur Wright. Their boyhood home and the bicycle shop where they started toying with the notion of flying are both open to visitors. Aviation aficionados can also visit the United States Air Force Museum at Wright-Patterson Air Force Base, just outside the city limits.

Dayton is a city at the crossroads of America. Incorporated in 1803, it was a thriving town by 1812, complete with a new brick courthouse, five new taverns, grist and sawmills, and frame houses springing up to replace log cabins. A nail factory, dyeing plant, weaving mill, and tannery were all in operation. Though you could easily spend a day (or two) getting your aviation thrills and following the paths of Orville and Wilbur, the city has much more to offer, such as a world-class art museum, a hands-on science museum, acres of well-maintained urban parks, and natural areas ranging from prairies to wetlands. Beautifully restored examples of Victorian, Romanesque, and neoclassical architecture are in the West Third Street Historic District (on the grounds of the Dayton Aviation Heritage National Historical Park). Enjoy the summertime thrills of Cincinnati Reds minor league ball in the cozy Dayton Dragons stadium with a hot dog and a beer, or take a casual stroll through the picturesque Oregon Historical district. Today almost one million people live in the metro area, and Dayton has the feel of a small town and the amenities of a big city.

If staring at the Great Miami River—which snakes its way through and around downtown—makes you yearn for the sight of an old river town, consider a short drive to neighboring Yellow Springs, where you can relax at an old-fashioned mill while watching fresh spring water run by.

Named for the iron-tinged yellow water in the nearby mineral springs, Yellow Springs was first a health spa with a resort hotel. Now it's a college town with a population of 4,000 and a reputation for liberal thinking. There are hundreds of acres to hike, bike, canoe, and explore between the Glen Helen Preserve and the Clifton Gorge/John Bryan State Park. *Men's Journal* magazine named Yellow Springs one of the 50 best places for men to live in 2002, thanks to the abundance of outdoor recreational activities.

Don't expect to find a macho hideaway, though, as Yellow Springs also offers plenty of diversions for couples looking for a romantic getaway from the hustle and bustle of city life as well as lots of outdoor activities for families. An abundance of quirky shops with local arts and oddball imports makes Yellow Springs a great place to find that special something for mom or your favorite college-bound hipster. Be sure to check out the work of local potters, who have also drawn notice for their unique styles. The city's only B&B recently closed down, and if primitive camping at John Bryan isn't your thing, you can try the cozy, family-fun Hearthstone Inn in nearby Cedarville, a nice place to cool your dogs after a long day of hiking and pedaling on the city's bike trails. Or, start your day with a breakfast of three-inch pancakes at the rustic Clifton

Mill, the largest water-powered grist mill in the United States, take a stroll at the gorge, tempt your taste buds with the creative cuisine at the Winds Cafe for dinner and put the top down for a night drive back to Dayton under the stars.

WHAT TO SEE & DO

DAYTON

Aullwood Audubon Center & Farm The 350-acre bird and wildlife sanctuary and working organic farm has 6 mi of hiking trails that wind through prairie, marsh ponds, woods, and meadows. Exhibits at the hands-on education center explore Ohio's flora and fauna, and there are a butterfly and hummingbird garden and daily nature walks and guided events. > 1000 Aullwood Rd., Dayton, tel. 937/890–7360, www.audubon.org/local/sanctuary/aullwood/. $4. Mon.–Sat. 9–5, Sun. 1–5.

Boonshoft Museum of Discovery A three-story climbing structure with a two-story corkscrew slide serves as the centerpiece of this highly engaging museum, which offers a wet-and-wild water play area for the kids and an exhibit on the history of Ohio's glass and pottery factories for the big folks. There are interactive exhibits for all ages, including "That Kids' Playce," an activity area for children up to age 6; Planetarium shows; animal talks; a hands-on science theater; and EcoTrek environmental theater. The museum lacks a cafeteria, but patrons are encouraged to bring their own bag lunches. > 2600 DeWeese Pkwy., Dayton, tel. 937/275–7431, www.boonshoftmuseum.org. $7.50. Weekdays 9–5, Sat. 11–5, Sun. noon–5.

Carillon Historical Park The largest carillon in the state presides over this 65-acre park. **Deeds Carillon** (concerts $2; Apr., May, Sept., and Oct., Sun. at 3; June–Aug., weekends at 3) is a 151-foot bell tower with 57 bells. In summer you can hear the bells ring at weekend Carillon concerts. Carillon Historical Park is the repository for a number of city treasures, particularly those that document the area's transportation history. The 1905 Wright Flyer III, one of the brothers' first planes, is in the Wright Hall. There are also the 1796 Newcom Tavern, a lock from the Miami Erie Canal, and a 1924 Sun Oil gas station, as well as locally made cars, bicycles, and a rail parlor car. > 1000 Carillon Blvd., Dayton, tel. 937/293–2841. $5. Apr.–Oct., Tues.–Sat. 9:30–5, Sun. noon–5.

Dayton Art Institute Dayton's best-known landmark, an Italian Renaissance–style structure, overlooks the Great Miami River. Founded in 1919, the encyclopedic collection includes more than 20,000 art objects spanning 5,000 years of history and covering diverse cultures, from American and European to African and Asian. You'll see paintings, photography, sculpture, furniture, and decorative arts. An impressive Asian art wing is among the treasures of this museum, which also houses works from Andy Warhol, a Monet waterlilies painting, rooms of colonial furniture and locally made Rookwood pottery. Experiencenter, a hands-on children's center, allows kids to create and frame their own works of art. Throughout the year the **Dayton Art Institute Concert Series** hosts local and nationally known artists in jazz and classical concerts. > 456 Belmonte Park N, Dayton, tel. 937/223–5277 or 800/296–4426, www.daytonartinstitute.org. Free. Daily 10–4, Thurs. until 8.

Dayton Aviation Heritage National Historical Park This national historical park comprises separate sites at different locations in the Dayton Area.

Huffman Prairie Flying Field Interpretive Center (Wright-Patterson Air Force Base, Gate 16A off Kauffman and St. Rte. 444, tel. 937/425–0008, free, Tues.–Sat. 8–6) stands on the spot where the Wright brothers perfected their flying machine, created the world's first airport, and ran a flight school. It is on the grounds of the Wright-Patterson Air Force Base.

The **Wright Cycle Company Shop** (22 S. Williams St., Dayton, tel. 937/225–7705, www.nps.gov/daav/, free, daily 8:30–5) was operated by brothers Orville and Wilbur Wright from 1895 to 1897. A re-created shop contains bicycles and machinery of the late 1800s; park personnel give guided tours and talks. Adjacent to the Cycle Company is the **Wright Dunbar Interpretive Center** (22 S. Williams St., Dayton, tel. 937/225–7705, www.nps.gov/daav/, free, daily 8:30–5), on the spot where the brothers had a printing business 1890–95. Here you'll find the Aviation Trail Visitors Center and Museum, which houses an orientation film on flight and exhibits and displays on Dayton's aviation trail and the story of the Wright Brothers. The museums are part of the West Third Street Historic District, a National Register of Historic Places neighborhood of authentic and restored brick buildings in the Victorian and Neoclassical styles. > Superintendent Dayton Aviation Heritage National Historical Park, Box 9280, Dayton, OH 45409, tel. 937/225–7705, www.nps.gov/davv/.

Oregon Historic District Dayton's oldest neighborhood now serves as the city's liveliest entertainment district. The downtown streets are lined with restored buildings housing antique shops, bustling restaurants, and nightclubs. Ohio's largest Halloween party is one of many parades that take place in the district. > E. 5th St. between Wayne Ave. and Patterson Blvd., Dayton, tel. 937/848–3669, www.oregondistrict.org. Free. Daily.

Paul Laurence Dunbar State Memorial Dunbar (1872–1906) was a noted African-American poet, playwright, novelist, and civil rights activist. He published more than 400 poems. Many of the writer's belongings can be viewed in this restored house, which was his last before he died in 1906. > 219 Paul Laurence Dunbar St., Dayton, tel. 937/224–7061. $3. Nov.–May, weekdays 9:30–5; June–Aug., Wed.–Sat. 9:30–5, Sun. 12:30–4:30; Sept. and Oct., Sat. 9:30–5, Sun. 12:30–4:30.

2nd Street Public Market This eclectic market operates year-round in a historic freight house. More than 45 vendors, bakers, and local artists offer breads, cheeses, fruit, organic produce, meats, coffees, teas, wines and crafts. Breakfast, lunch, and dinner options abound, as well as everything from farm-raised rabbit and ostrich meat to fresh flowers and hand-made clothing. > 600 E. 2nd St., Dayton, tel. 937/228–2088, www.2ndStreetPublicMarket.com. Free. Thurs. and Fri. 11–3, Sat. 8–3.

Sunwatch Indian Village/Archaeological Park This is a reconstruction of an 800-year-old village that belonged to the Fort Ancient Indians, who had a unique sun-based system of charting time. The Dayton Museum of Natural History excavated the site and built the reproduction mud-walled dwelling with grass thatch roof. Check out the authentic weapons and pottery making demonstrations. Seasonal demonstrations of gardening, astronomy, house building, and archaeology are given on first Saturday of the month. > 2301 W. River Rd., Dayton, tel. 937/268–8199, www.sunwatch.org. $5. Tues.–Sat. 9–5, Sun. noon–5.

Wegerzyn Gardens MetroPark These are formal gardens: there are Victorian, English, and federal theme gardens, as well as rose, shade, and children's gardens. You can walk on a boardwalk through a wetland woods or along a nature trail. The Stillwater River runs along the park. > 1301 E. Siebenthaler Ave., Dayton, tel. 937/277–6545, www.metroparks.org. Free. Daily 8 AM–dusk.

Woodland Cemetery and Arboretum Several of Dayton's most famous citizens, including the Wright brothers and writer Erma Bombeck, are buried in this picturesque cemetery. > 118 Woodland Ave., Dayton, tel. 937/222–1431. Free. Daily dawn–dusk.

Wright-Patterson Air Force Base The base, home to 23,000 personnel, has one of the U.S. Air Force's largest and most relied-upon arsenals of military aircraft. Area B has a visitor center, but many previously accessible areas were closed off at press time due to heightened security measures. The **National Aviation Hall of Fame** (1100 Spatz St., tel. 937/256–0944, www.nationalaviation.org, free, daily 9–5) honors America's greatest pilots and astronauts, such as the Mercury 7 astronauts and the first men on the moon. Interactive exhibits detail early flight and space missions. The **United States Air Force Museum** (1100 Spatz St., tel. 937/255–3284, free, daily 9–5) is the oldest and largest military aviation museum in the world, with 300 airplanes and thousands of aviation artifacts, including missiles used during the Persian Gulf War. The Air Force One jet used to transport the body of President John F. Kennedy back to Washington after his assassination in 1963 is housed here. It joins a collection that includes other presidential aircraft from as far back as Franklin D. Roosevelt. The museum spans military aviation history from the Wright Brothers to a Stealth F-117 bomber. The **Wright Brothers Memorial** (Kauffman and St. Rte. 444, tel. 937/425–0008, free, daily 8–8) is a tribute to the brothers who achieved the dream of flight in 1903 at Kitty Hawk, North Carolina.> Springfield St., Dayton, tel. 937/255–3334. Free. Daily 9–5.

YELLOW SPRINGS

Clifton Gorge State Nature Preserve/John Bryan State Park The Little Miami River carved out a 130-foot gorge in the dolomite and limestone here. The gorge and a 2-mi stretch of the river run through the 752-acre John Bryan State Park. The Little Miami, a designated State and National Scenic River, has waterfalls and rapids and is an excellent site for canoeing. Or you can go hiking, camping, and rock climbing in the park. You might spot some rare plants and animals along the way, such as the threatened red baneberry and the uncommon wall rue fern. Also expect to see plenty of turtles and birds and the occasional Butler's garter snake, one of Ohio's rarer species. Spring is a peak time for one of the state's most spectacular displays of wildflowers, including the rare snow trillium. > 3790 Rte. 370, Yellow Springs, tel. 937/767–1274. Free. Daily dawn–dusk.

Glen Helen Ecology Institute Forests, meadows, and valleys carved by glacial meltwater, as well as the town's signature yellow springs, make up this 1,000-acre nature preserve. Nearly 3 mi of the Little Miami River flow through the southern portion. You can hike the trails and bird-watch on your own, or join the Monthly Hiker's Programs that take avid walkers on a fast-paced 5-mi guided tour through Glen Helen and adjoining nature areas. The Trailside Museum & Visitor Center has interpretive displays, maps, exhibits, and guidebooks. > 405 Corry St., Yellow Springs, tel. 937/767–7375, www.glenhelen.org. Free. Daily dawn–dusk.

Sports

BASEBALL

Dayton Dragons This Class A farm team for the Cincinnati Reds plays at old-fashioned, cozy **Fifth Third Field** (220 N. Patterson, Dayton) near downtown. With a roster made up of high school and college graduates, as well as foreign free agents in their late teens and early twenties, this Midwest League team fields plenty of excite-

ment during its 70 home games. Tickets are $5–$11. > Tel. 937/228–2287,
www.daytondragons.com.

HIKING
Clifton Gorge State Nature Preserve/John Bryan State Park With 9 mi of trails,
Clifton Gorge offers plenty of options for a manageable morning or afternoon of hiking, from flat strolls to moderately challenging hikes up steps and small hills. The
popular John L. Rich Trail leads you up and out of the gorge one way, or through to
John Bryan, where the trail becomes the Pittsburgh-Cincinnati Stage Coach Trail. Rock
climbing is available, with climbers asked to bring their own equipment and sign up
in advance. Trails can get busy on the weekends. > 3790 Rte. 370, Yellow Springs, tel.
937/767–1274.

Shopping
Walking down Yellow Spring's Xenia Avenue can feel like a trip to an international
bazaar. The small town with nearly 50 specialty shops is renowned for its local potters, jewelers, and clothiers, whose work can be seen and purchased at the Village Artisans shop. But it also has diverse international import stores, including shops that
carry jewelry, clothing, and decorator items from Tibet, Indonesia, and South America. Add an organic grocer, a quirky toy shop, several fresh herb stores, and a medieval–Renaissance costume shop, and you have a refreshing break from chain
store monotony.

Julia Etta's Trunk This 1,300-square-foot shop specializes in unique and creative
women's clothing made by local and national designers in wool, cotton, satin, linen,
and other natural fibers. You will find everything from hand-painted outfits to hand-
crafted jewelry and fragrances from more than 25 manufacturers. > 100 Corry St., Yellow Springs, tel. 937/767–2823. Closed Sun. and Mon.
Yellow Springs Pottery The city's potters have earned a reputation for their work,
and you will find a vast selection of it at this artists' cooperative. Hundreds of hand-
made pieces from 10 local potters are on display, from the functional to the decorative, including bowls, serving dishes, kitchenware, and lamps, some finished with a
fine crystalline glaze. > 222 Xenia Ave., Yellow Springs, tel. 937/767–1666.

Save the Date
MARCH
Dayton Home and Garden Show Check out the latest trends in home fashion and
garden accessories at this annual 4-day event in the Dayton Convention Center. > 22
E. 5th St., Dayton, tel. 937/333–4700.

JUNE
CITYFOLK Festival Well-known national acts perform in this celebration of folk
music. The events take place at the Riverscape outdoor venue downtown between
Main and Patterson streets. > Tel. 937/223–3655, www.cityfolk.org.
Market District Wine Festival Winemakers from across Ohio converge on down-
town Dayton's Second Street Public Market for a 2-day celebration of local vintners.
Waltz through the historic market setting and enjoy wine tasting, culinary demonstra-
tions, and local wines for sale. > 2nd and Webster Sts., Dayton, tel. 937/228–2088.

JULY
Dayton Air Show The 30-year-old air show typically draws more than 100,000 flight
fanatics to the Dayton Airport for a 2-day blitz of military and civilian, historic and
modern aircraft flown by professional and amateur pilots. There are food and kid-ori-

ented diversions, including simulators and interactive exhibits. General admission is $19, Pavilion seating $40. > Dayton Intl. Airport, Dayton, tel. 937/898–5901, www.daytonairshow.com.

SEPTEMBER

Montgomery County Fair More than 50,000 people flock to the Montgomery County Fairgrounds for the week-long activities, with livestock shows, games, rides. The fun begins the Wednesday before Labor Day. > 143 S. Main St., tel. 937/224–1619, www.montcofair.com.

Oktoberfest The Dayton Art Institute celebrates all things German. The festivities take place on the museum's grounds overlooking downtown Dayton. Festivities include live entertainment and art activities for children, and there's plenty of German food and beer. > 456 Belmonte Park N, Dayton, tel. 937/223–5277 or 800/296–4426.

WHERE TO STAY

DAYTON

Best Western Executive Hotel This two-story chain with a large grassy courtyard is 5 mi southeast of the airport, right off I–75. Lush greenery covers the lobby, which has an overhead skylight. Rooms range from standard with twin beds to executive whirlpool suites, as well as suites with two full bathrooms. Kids under 12 stay free. > 2401 Needmore Rd., Dayton, 45414, tel. 937/278–5711 or 800/528–1234, fax 937/278–6048, www.bestwestern.com. 231 rooms. Restaurant, in-room data ports, some microwaves, some refrigerators, cable TV, indoor pool, sauna, gym, bar, laundry service, laundry facilities, business services, meeting rooms, airport shuttle, some pets allowed, no-smoking rooms. AE, D, DC, MC, V. **$–$$**

Comfort Inn–Dayton North The convenience of the location—just off I–75 7 mi north of downtown Dayton—explains the cluster of hotels and chain restaurants at this exit. You can walk to dinner at a number of restaurants, and it's a short drive to the Fairfield Common Mall, U.S. Air Force Museum, Boonshoft Museum, and Dayton Art Institute. Rooms are standard, with two queen beds or one king. > 7125 Miller La., Dayton, 45414, tel. 937/890–9995 or 800/228–5150, fax 937/890–9995, www.comfortinn.com. 56 rooms. In-room data ports, some microwaves, some refrigerators, indoor pool, hot tub, no-smoking rooms. AE, D, DC, MC, V. CP. **$**

Crowne Plaza Dayton Connected to the downtown Dayton Convention Center, this 14-story hotel in the heart of downtown has bright rooms with wood desks and armoires. Business travelers appreciate the executive services and ergonomic chairs; weekenders enjoy being 1 mi from Dayton Art Institute and less than a mile from the historic Oregon district and shopping. The covered parking spaces are free. > 33 E. 5th St., Dayton 45402, tel. 937/224–0800 or 800/227–6963, fax 937/224–3913, www.crowneplaza.com/day-crowne. 283 rooms, 8 suites. Restaurant, room service, cable TV with video games, pool, gym, bar, business services, airport shuttle, no-smoking rooms. AE, D, DC, MC, V. **$**

Holiday Inn I–675 Conference Center Just 15 mi from downtown in a suburban area, this six-floor Holiday Inn is 2 mi from Wright-Patterson Air Force Base and within walking distance of the Nutter Arena. The rooms have work desks, and the business center is open 24 hours. The indoor heated pool has an attached sun deck. Two restaurants serve breakfast and lunch, as well as steak and fish dinners, and a lounge has a live DJ on weekends and Tuesday night karaoke. > 2800 Presidential Dr., Fairborn 45324, tel. 937/426–7800 or 800/465–4329, fax 937/426–1284, www.holiday-inn.com. 204 rooms. Restaurant, room service, cable TV, indoor pool, gym, bar, business services, no-smoking rooms. AE, D, DC, MC, V. **$$**

Homewood Suites Fairborn The roomy suites at this Hilton-owned property, 1 mi from Wright-Patterson Air Force Base, have kitchens with full-size refrigerators, dishwashers, and stove tops; a bedroom with a king or two double beds; and separate living areas with a sleeper sofa, recliner, and TV with VCR. Some have fireplaces. The two- and three-story buildings are 20 minutes from downtown. > 2750 Presidential Dr., Fairborn 45324, tel. 937/429–0600 or 800/225–5466, fax 937/429–6311, www.homewoodsuites.com. 128 suites. Picnic area, in-room data ports, microwaves, refrigerators, cable TV, in-room VCRs, pool, hot tub, exercise equipment, laundry facilities, business services, some pets allowed. AE, D, DC, MC, V. CP. **$$$**

Marriott Five minutes from downtown, this hotel is one of Dayton's largest lodging properties. Rooms have two doubles or a king-size bed. Guests in concierge rooms have access to a private lounge. The six-story white concrete building opened in 1982 and is adjacent to a jogging and biking trail. > 1414 S. Patterson Blvd., Dayton 45409, tel. 937/223–1000 or 800/228–9290, fax 937/223–7853, www.marriott.com. 399 rooms. Restaurant, in-room data ports, room service, cable TV, indoor-outdoor pool, hot tub, sauna, gym, bar, laundry facilities, business services, meeting rooms, some pets allowed, no-smoking rooms. AE, D, DC, MC, V. **$$$**

Yesterday Bed and Breakfast This two-story taupe-and-beige Victorian home, built in 1882, is 10 mi south of downtown Dayton in the well-heeled suburb of Centerville. You can find solace on the wraparound porch or on the brick patio in back. The double house, shared with the innkeepers, reflects its Victorian roots with period antiques, collectibles, lacy curtains, and frilly rooms. Downstairs has the old hardwood floors, but the upstairs rooms are carpeted. > 39 S. Main St., Centerville 45458, tel. 937/433–0785. 3 rooms. No room phones, no room TVs, no kids under 12. No credit cards. BP. **$**

YELLOW SPRINGS

Hearthstone Inn & Suites You get a little taste of B&B living in nearby Cedarville at this old-fashioned, family-owned inn, which prides itself on chain accommodations with a personal touch. 1885 barn beams frame the spacious lobby, with its large stone fireplace. Ohio and Civil War memorabilia, antiques, Tiffany lighting, Thomas Kincaid paintings, and locally made custom stained-glass windows decorate the public spaces, and nice touches like coffeemakers and Bath & Body Works products personalize the rooms. There's an adjacent playground with a softball-baseball diamond, jogging track, and tennis courts. The "Supreme" Continental breakfast goes beyond cold cereal and toast with fresh pecan rolls and oversize cinnamon rolls, as well as seasonal specials. The Hearthstone is near the Ohio-to-Erie bike path, and children under 12 stay free. > 10 S. Main St., Cedarville 45314, tel. 937/766–3000 or 877/644–6466, www.hearthstone-inn.com. 20 rooms. In-room data ports, refrigerators, cable TV, gift shop, shop; no smoking. AE, D, MC, V. CP. **$–$$**

WHERE TO EAT

DAYTON

Amar India Pictures of India cover the walls of this suburban restaurant, known for its northern Indian cuisine and lunch buffet. The menu includes many vegetarian dishes, curry chicken, and the Mattu Special—a bowl of chicken tandoori with spices and onions stuffed in a pastry shell and deep fried. Amar India is about 10 mi south of downtown Dayton. > 2759 Miamisburg-Centerville Rd., Centerville, tel. 937/439–9005. AE, D, DC, MC, V. $–$$

Barnsider A casual steak house with a dark rustic interior, the Barnsider has been serving since 1975. The menu includes New York strip steak, filet mignon, prime rib, and lamb chops. There's a kids' menu and Sunday brunch. > 5202 N. Main St., Dayton, tel. 937/277–1332. AE, MC, V. No lunch. $–$$$

Caffe Anticoli's Serving classic Italian fare since 1951, this warm, rustic restaurant recalls an Italian villa, right down to the Renaissance-inspired paintings on the walls. A romantic banquet room is dotted with climbing grape vines and twinkling lights that evoke a warm outdoor feeling. The menu includes vodka chicken, veal Parmesan, lasagna, and New York Tuscany steak. There's a kids' menu. > 8268 N. Main St., Dayton, tel. 937/890–0300. AE, D, DC, MC, V. $$

Elinor's Amber Rose Housed in a National Historical Landmark building, this eatery with an old-fashioned general store motif specializes in traditional German, Russian, and Eastern European dishes. The menu includes home-style versions of German sauerbraten, Russian beef Stroganoff, cabbage rolls, and schnitzels. Pastas and filet mignon round out the menu. An old-time saloon-style bar serves more than two dozen hard-to-find European beers. A kid's menu is available. > 1400 Valley St., Dayton, tel. 937/228–2511, www.theamberrose.com. Closed Sun. No dinner Mon. and Tues. AE, D, DC, MC, V. $–$$$

Elsa's Mexican Restaurant If you're going to Elsa's, you have to try the famous house-special drinks. There's the Bad Juan, made with top-secret ingredients, and the Gringo, for meeker tastes. A few drinks and a burrito stuffed with your choice of meat filling will have you ready for a nice siesta. > 3618 Linden Ave., Dayton, tel. 937/252–9635. AE, D, DC, MC, V. $

Jay's Seafood Housed in a renovated 1850s gristmill, Jay's has wooden tables, floors, and beams; velvet upholstered chairs and an antique mahogany bar. The seafood combo appetizer is enough oysters Rockefeller and clams casino for two. Menu highlights include Alaskan king salmon, sole stuffed with crab and topped with lobster sauce, and swordfish. There's a kids' menu. > 225 E. 6th St., Dayton, tel. 937/222–2892. AE, D, DC, MC, V. No lunch. $$–$$$

L'Auberge Original art adorns the inside of this sophisticated French eatery known for pâté, imported fresh seafood, and game. Some popular dishes are chateaubriand, roasted rack of lamb, sautéed John Dory (a type of fish), and sea bass. There's live entertainment. L'Auberge is in a suburb about 5 mi south of downtown Dayton. > 4120 Far Hills Ave., Kettering, tel. 937/299–5536. Jacket required. AE, DC, MC, V. Closed Sun. $$$$

Lincoln Park Grille The large front patio offers diners a view of the entertainment in the nearby Fraze Pavilion outdoor concert venue while they eat. The menu has an Italian accent and includes grilled pork chops with chipotle apple glaze, New York strip, and barbecued duck with bacon-wrapped scallops and corn coulis. Live entertainment every night but Wednesday. > 580 Lincoln Park Blvd., Dayton, tel. 937/293–6293. AE, D, DC, MC, V. No lunch Sat. Closed Sun. $$–$$$$

Mediterra The white-washed room with wide classical columns prepares you for the Mediterranean specialties at this eclectic spot. Try the Wild Mushroom Risotto with white truffle oil, a Jambalaya Risotto with fighting prawn, chicken and andouille sausage, and a salt-crusted prime rib. Live entertainment Thursday–Saturday. > 110 N. Main St., Dayton, tel. 937/228–3333, mediterradayton.com. AE, D, DC, MC, V. No dinner Mon. No lunch weekends. $–$$$

Oakwood Club This dark suburban eatery with Tiffany glass and original artwork serves first-rate steaks and prime rib. The lobster tails and potato-crusted sea bass are also noteworthy. It's in Oakwood, about 4 mi south of downtown Dayton. > 2414 Far Hills Ave., Oakwood, tel. 937/293–6973. AE, DC, MC, V. Closed Sun. **$$$–$$$$**

Olivia's Works of local artists cover the walls and white linens cover the tables at this dining spot in the Kettering Tower. The menu includes roast pepper duck, pike, salmon, pork, beef, and veal. > 40 N. Main St., Dayton, tel. 937/222–6771. AE, D, DC, MC, V. Closed Sun. **$$$**

Pine Club Prepare to wait for a table at this busy steak and chops house. The 56-year-old establishment boasts that "Even President Bush waited for dinner." Among the choice cuts served in the pine-paneled dining room is a 36-ounce porterhouse for two; there's also veal, chicken, and seafood on the menu. Signature packaged steaks and salad dressings are available for take-out or shipping. > 1926 Brown St., Dayton, tel. 937/228–7463, thepineclub.com. Reservations not accepted. No credit cards. Closed Sun. No lunch. **$$$–$$$$**

Steve Kao's Popular dishes at this casual restaurant are Iceland crab fish, red snapper, walleye, Szechuan chicken, Cantonese-style chicken, Peking duck, and the famous potstickers. The menu also includes stir-fry and noodle dishes. > 8270 Springboro Pike, Fairborn, tel. 937/435–5261. AE, D, DC, MC, V. **$**

Sweeny's Seafood In the heart of old Centerville, 10 mi south of Dayton, is this celebration of the fruits of the sea. While you dine, you can watch the saltwater fish swimming in the 1,000-gallon tank. Dinner selections include grilled salmon in horseradish crust or grilled tilapia with a lemon Parmesan crust. If you aren't feeling fishy, there are sandwiches, pastas, and burgers, too. Carry-out menu available. > 28 W. Franklin, Centerville, tel. 937/291–3474. AE, D, MC, V. Closed Mon. No lunch weekends. **$–$$**

YELLOW SPRINGS

Clifton Mill This restaurant is housed in largest water-powered grist mill still in operation in the country. Built in 1802, the mill grinds flour that's used in the restaurant's famous pancakes, which you can enjoy while perched on a cliff overlooking a gorge. Take a tour and get a free bag of flour. The mill is lighted with more than 3 million lights at Christmastime. The gift shop is packed with antiques and old time photos. Clifton Mill is 3 mi east of Yellow Springs. > 75 Water St., Clifton, tel. 937/767–5501, www.cliftonmill.com. MC, V. No dinner. **¢–$**

Winds Cafe Unexpected combinations of ingredients make for unusual cuisine here. The small menu changes monthly. Recent entrées included rice paper halibut garnished with avocado slices and jasmine rice and Italian rack of pork coated with garlic, white pepper, fennel, and coriander. Meals are complemented by one of the 60 rotating wines from the cellar next door. There are open air dining, kids' menus, Sunday brunch, and no smoking. > 215 Xenia Ave., Yellow Springs, tel. 937/767–1144. Reservations essential. AE, D, DC, MC, V. Closed Mon. No dinner Sun. **$$$–$$$$**

Ye Old Tavern Originally a stagecoach stop dating from the 1800s, this restored tavern with rustic wooden tables serves all-American fare in a dining room that was formerly a log cabin home. Sandwiches, pizza, calzones cooked in a brick-lined Italian pizza oven. The Thursday night spaghetti special has been packing 'em in for 40 years. > 228 Xenia Ave., Yellow Springs, tel. 937/767–7448. MC, V. **¢**

Young's Jersey Dairy Locals know Young's for their ultra-rich ice cream: it's 14 percent butterfat and made with fresh milk. More than 40 flavors are available, including house specialty flavor—Cow Patty, which mixes double dark chocolate ice cream with cookie pieces, butter toffee pieces, and chocolate chips. Sandwiches are also served and children are allowed to pet the animals in the barn. It's open 24 hours, every day except Christmas. > 6880 Springfield Xenia Rd., Yellow Springs, tel. 937/325–0629. AE, D, MC, V. ¢

ESSENTIALS

Getting Here

Dayton is easily accessible by bus or plane, though you should plan on renting a car once you arrive, as many of the attractions listed above are several miles apart. Plan on a 30- to 40-minute drive to Yellow Springs.

BY CAR
Dayton is served by several major roads, among them I–71, I–675, and U.S. 35. Driving around the city is uncomplicated and both street and garage parking are generally readily available and affordable. Wright-Patterson is east of the city in Riverside, while several of the museums are scattered in and around the downtown area. The Southern suburbs of Oakwood, Kettering, and Centerville, all short drives from downtown, feature ample dining opportunities. Yellow Springs is just over 20 mi east of Dayton and can be reached by taking I–675 North to East Dayton-Yellow Springs Road.

BY PLANE
AIRPORTS **Dayton International Airport** > Tel. 937/454–8200, www.daytonairport.com.
CARRIERS **Air Canada** > Tel. 888/247–2262, www.aircanada.ca. **AirTran** > Tel. 800/247–8726, www.airtran.com. **American/American Eagle** > Tel. 800/433–7300, www.aa.com. **ATA Connection** > Tel. 800/435–9282, www.ata.com. **Comair** > Tel. 800/354–9822, www.comair.com. **Continental/Continental Express** > Tel. 800/525–0280, www.continental.com. **Delta** > Tel. 800/221–1212, www.delta.com. **Northwest/Northwest Airlink** > Tel. 800/225–2525, www.nwa.com. **Skyways (Midwest Express)** > Tel. 800/452–2022, www.midwestexpress.com. **United/United Express** > Tel. 800/241–6522, www.ual.com. **US Airways/US Airways Express** > Tel. 800/428–4322, www.usairways.com.

Visitor Information

Dayton Area Chamber of Commerce > 1 Chamber Plaza, #200, 45402, tel. 937/226–1444, www.daytonchamber.org. **Dayton/Montgomery County Convention & Visitors Bureau** > Tel. 800/221–8235, www.daytoncvb.com. **Yellow Springs Chamber of Commerce** > 108 Dayton St., 45387, tel. 937/767–2686, www.yellowsprings.com.

Logan County

Bellefontaine is 58 mi west of Columbus, 103 mi northeast of Cincinnati, and 154 mi southwest of Cleveland.

24

Nicki Chodnoff

CITY DWELLERS CAN SWITCH into low gear and find, within rural Logan County's 450 square mi, all the ingredients for a delightful country weekend getaway including a rich and diverse history, golf, horseback riding, skiing, antiquing, and friendly people.

Over the millennia, geography and geology have shaped Logan County. Geology gives the area its chief attractions: caverns and hilly terrain for ski slopes, making Logan County a four-seasons destination. During the last ice age, about 12,000 years ago, retreating glaciers left fertile, rich soil that provided, and still provides, a reliable livelihood for many county residents. Seventy-seven percent of the land in the county is still farmed. The land that emerged from under the ice fields was sculpted in rounded, undulating terrain. There are lowlands near the Miami River in the northwest corner of the county, and much of the eastern end is hilly. Add silos, barns, and contented cows grazing to the rolling, bountiful fields, and you have the perfect backdrop for the quintessential drive in the country. The hills are more typical of the Appalachian region in southeastern Ohio than the flat checkerboard farm fields found in the western part of the state.

The glacial upheaval reworked the landscape so that Logan County has the highest point in the state—1,550 feet at Campbell Hill in Bellefontaine (pronounced Bell - fountain). In fact, Campbell Hill is the highest point between the Appalachian and Rocky Mountains, a resource used by the North American Air Defense Command (NORAD). Until the early 1970s, NORAD based their sophisticated radar and computers here, safe-guarding the country by identifying flying aircraft as friendly or suspicious.

Logan County's limestone-based soil, rich in calcium, is some of the most productive and tillable in the state. The same limestone, which is easily eroded by rainwater, accounts for the formation of the two known caverns lying beneath the county and probably many yet-to-be-discovered caves. With cave temperatures hovering constantly in the upper 40s to low 50s, cave tours at Ohio Caverns and Zane Shawnee Caverns are especially popular in the hot summertime.

Getting the farm bounty to market is the reason behind the creation of one of the county's most popular year-round recreational areas, Indian Lake, now a state park. Several natural lakes were combined and rebuilt as a feeder lake, or water supply, to keep the Miami and Erie Canal at its required 4-foot water depth. Before the settlers, Native American tribes who lived and hunted in this region designated Indian Lake part of their trade route, due to its proximity to the Miami River. Generations of Native Americans followed this route that linked the Ohio River to Lake Erie. By the early 1800s, white settlers made their way here and skirmishes and battles resulted from the conflict between the Indians and new settlers. The famous frontiersmen Daniel Boone and Simon Kenton were known to have traveled here.

Logan County claims a handful of little towns and villages, some so small you can drive through in little more time than it takes to sneeze. Neatly tended Amish farms can be anywhere in the county (a good hint for spotting an Amish household is to look for clothes drying on the line). Around Belle Center you'll find the county's largest Amish enclave. Don't expect a commercialized area as in other parts of Ohio with shops, attractions, and tours catering to tourists. Here live ordinary Amish people who go about the routines of daily life. You may see a horse and buggy parked at the grocery store, Amish women sitting on the porch sewing, or a horse-drawn wagon dropping off children at school.

As the largest town in the county, and at approximately the center of the county, Bellefontaine looks the picture of small town rural America. The charming county seat spreads out from its central town square dominated by a towering Italianate courthouse, built in 1870, at the remarkable cost of $105,000. Bellefontaine was founded at the turn of the 19th century by Canadian traders, who gave it the French name for "beautiful fountains," referring to the natural springs, which run through the area.

Like many Ohio cities, Bellefontaine prospered during the 1920s and '30s, thanks to significant railroad traffic. Despite the positive effect of trains on the local economy, some in the city had better ideas on how to get around. For years, pharmacist George Bartholomew experimented with a compound that could be formed into a hard surface for roads and buildings. The result: In 1891, Bellefontaine became the first city in the world to have a concrete street. A statue of Bartholomew stands near the street—Court Street—he laid. The original concrete is still intact. A few blocks from Court Street, you can also see 17-foot-long McKinley Street, the shortest street in the world.

WHAT TO SEE & DO

Indian Lake State Park This four-season state park has a 5,800-acre lake that is the second largest man-made lake in the state park system. The lake's irregular and rugged shoreline of more than 29 mi is studded with 69 tree-covered islands. A popular resort area at the turn of the 20th century, Russells Point at Indian Lake was known as the "Midwest's Million Dollar Playground" and was filled with rides and amusements. Today, the full-service 783-acre park with campground, 16 mi northwest of Bellefontaine, serves boaters, anglers, and hikers. Cherokee Trail crosses 3 mi of bushy habitat, and the 1-mi Pew Island Trail offers great views of Indian Lake. A paved bikeway, also used by hikers and joggers, extends 3 mi between Old Field Beach and Russells Point. In winter, recreation includes snowmobiling, ice skating, cross-country skiing, ice fishing, and ice boating, weather permitting. Osprey, turtles, and beaver inhabit a large wetlands game reserve at the northeastern part of the lake. Check out the free naturalist program, Tuesday through Saturday, Memorial Day to Labor Day. > 12774 Rte. 235 N, Lakeview, tel. 937/843–2717, www.dnr.state.oh.us/parks. Free. Daily dawn–dusk.

Ohio Caverns Some of America's most colorful caverns are beneath West Liberty, 8 mi south of Bellefontaine. The hour-long tour along a level concrete path takes you to the caves, which are about 103 feet beneath the surface of the earth. The cavern is filled with countless white stalactites and stalagmites. Crystal King, the nearly 5-foot-long stalactite that's the largest in Ohio, weighs in at nearly 400 pounds. Drop by drop, it was formed over the course of about 200,000 years. The cavern also holds rare dual formations, where crystals grow from oxidized iron—better known as rust. This is the only known cavern in the United States with this specific dual formation. The tour ends when you hear a recorded version of "Beautiful Ohio," the state song, in a tradition that began when the cave was reopened to tourists in the 1920s. Spelunkers have marveled at this cave system since its discovery in 1897. A 35-acre park with picnic tables sits directly above the caverns. > 2210 E. Rte. 245, West Liberty, tel. 937/465–4017, www.cavern.com/ohiocaverns. $9.50. Apr.–Oct., daily 9–5; Nov.–Mar., daily 9–4.

Orr Mansion & Logan County Museum Built as lumber baron William Orr's dream home in 1908 for $40,000, the restored mansion preserves its neoclassical exterior two-story columns, interior exotic woodwork, and a third-floor ballroom. Attached to the mansion, the 15-room museum is a repository of Logan County artifacts and photos including local railroad items, a one-room school, antique toys, a general store, and furniture from a house prominent in the underground railroad. The museum's archives preserve genealogical and local information. > 521 E. Columbus Ave., Bellefontaine, tel. 937/593–7557, www.co.logan.us/museum. Suggested donation $2. May–Oct., Wed., Fri., and weekends 1–4; Nov.–Apr., Fri. and Sat. 1–4.

Piatt Castles You'd hardly expect to see a castle rising from the hills of rural Ohio, let alone two castles within a mile of each other. But that's exactly what you find in the lush countryside 10 mi south of Bellefontaine. Two European-style limestone chateaux, Mac-O-Chee and Mac-A-Cheek, were constructed in the 1800s as private residences for the Piatt brothers. The castles are known locally as "A" (Mac-A-Cheek) and "O" (Mac-O-Chee). The smaller Mac-A-Cheek is a Norman-style country home, and the larger Mac-O-Chee looks like a Flemish-style castle. The Piatt family now operates both castles as private museums. Listed on the National Register of Historic Places, both buildings are open to the public for guided tours of the collections of original furnishings, elaborate woodwork and ceiling frescoes, Native American art, and firearms. > 10051 Rd. 47, West Liberty, tel. 937/465–2821. $8 tour of one castle, $15 for both castles. Apr., May, Sept., and Oct., daily noon–4; June–Aug., daily 11–5.

Shadybowl Speedway Racing buffs gather every Saturday night to watch late-model stock car racing at the speedway southwest of Bellefontaine, one of the world's fastest $3/10$-mi asphalt ovals. For fender banging on a larger scale, school bus races are now on the schedule. > 9872 Flowing Well Rd., DeGraff, tel. 937/585–9456, www.shadybowl.com. $13. Sat., gates open at 3, racing begins at 7.

Zane Shawnee Caverns Guides lead a 1-hour, $3/8$-mi tour through a maze of chambers and tunnels carved out over millennia. Unlike the horizontal Ohio Caverns, Zane Shawnee Caverns, 5 mi east of Bellefontaine, are vertical. Both the merely curious and cavern aficionados will be awed by the rare drapery and cave pearl formations in this three-level cavern. Little pools of pearl-like minerals in the cave pearl formations are only found in one other cave on earth—in Switzerland. The 1830s Shawnee and Pioneer villages portray Native American and settler cultures with authentically constructed elm-bark wikons (Shawnee dwelling places) and an 1834 log cabin. The Shawnee Woodland Native American Museum, the first Native American owned and operated museum in Ohio, includes a scale model of a Shawnee village and Native American artifacts. A guided tour explains the history of Native peoples. > 7092 Rte. 540, Bellefontaine, tel. 937/592–9592, www.zaneshawneecaverns.org. $8 caverns tour, $7 museum tour, $6 Shawnee and Pioneer Village tour. Dec.–Mar., daily 10–4; Apr.–Nov., daily 9–5.

Sports

GOLF

Logan County's diverse topography creates interesting and exciting golf courses not found in many parts of the state. With its hills, wooded areas, streams, and lakes, the county lends itself to scenic and dramatic courses that capture the imagination of golfers of all skill levels. Each course is well groomed and conditioned.

Cherokee Hills Golf Course Rolling terrain, mature trees, a trickling brook, and two lakes test your golfing skills on this 18-hole course built in 1972, 5 mi west of Bellefontaine. Greens fees are $20 per 18 holes on the weekend. > 4622 County Rd. 49 N, Bellefontaine, tel. 937/599–3221 or 800/816–2255, www.cherokeehillsgolfclub.com.

Liberty Hills Golf Club Small, slick greens are set among giant oaks on gentle hills of the vintage nine holes, 5 mi southwest of Bellefontaine. The modern 9-hole approach, created in 1992, has bent grass fairways and undulating greens nestled among lakes and trees. This "old-new" 18-hole course is challenging for all levels of play. Greens fees are $22 per 18 holes on the weekend; $6 to rent golf clubs. > 665 Rd. 190 W, Bellefontaine, tel. 937/592–4653 or 800/816–2255, www.libertyhillsgolfclub.com.

Tree Links Golf Club While putting in the pines, you can smell the balsam scent near the highest point in Ohio, 4 mi east of Bellefontaine. Green, bent-grass fairways are lined with trees and panoramic views are at every curve. Forty acres of rolling pines test your skills at the newest course in the area, built in 1993. This 18-hole championship public course offers a challenge to all levels of golfers. Greens fees are $24 for 18 holes on the weekend. > 3482 County Rd. 10, Bellefontaine, tel. 937/592–7888 or 800/215–7888.

HORSEBACK RIDING

Marmon Valley Farm Ride horses English or Western style on the farm's scenic trails through 450 acres of fields, woods, hills, and streams. A trail guide and basic riding demonstration gets everyone up to speed before riding begins. Nonriders can get in on the action with a wagon ride through the farm. > 7754 Rte. 292, Zanesfield, tel. 937/593–8000, www.marmonvalley.com. $20 per hour. Daily 1–5.

SKIING

Mad River Mountain Ski Resort Winter sports fans can opt for everything from downhill skiing and snowboarding to sledding, tubing, and night skiing at this winter playground 5 mi east of Bellefontaine. It's Ohio's highest skiing elevation (about 1,400 feet) and the site of Ohio's longest ski run, with 8 chair lifts serving 17 trails on more than 120 acres. > 100 Snow Valley Rd., Zanesfield, tel. 937/599–1015 or 800/231–7669, www.skimadriver.com or www.ridemadriver.com for snowboarders. Adult lift ticket $37. Dec.–Mar., daily.

EQUIPMENT **Mad River Mountain Ski/Snowboard Rental Shop** > 100 Snow Valley Rd., Zanesfield, tel. 937/599–1015 or 800/231–7669.

Shopping

Bartin's Antique's & Gifts A stone's throw from T & E Cupboards, this shop specializes in antiques, reproduction furniture, primitives, folk art, and gifts. > 101 N. Baird St., West Liberty, tel. 937/465–4988. Closed Sun.

Bellefontaine Antique Mall More than 80 dealers display their oh-so-varied antiques and collectibles on two floors in a remodeled building in downtown Bellefontaine. The antiques mall is open seven days a week. > 210 W. Columbus St., Bellefontaine, tel. 937/292–7000 or 888/384–6480.

Logan County Farmers Market Plan on arriving around 8:30 AM for the best selection at this market that specializes in seasonal fruits and vegetables and closes at noon. Held outdoors in a shopping center parking lot, the market consists of 20 to 30 farmers, some Amish, selling their baked goods, eggs, and whatever produce is in season. Make a point to buy some sweet corn in the summer. > Fontaine Plaza Shopping Center, S. Main St., Bellefontaine, tel. 937/468–2853. Closed Oct.–Apr.

T & E Cupboards Shop for antiques, country furniture, and home accessories on the main street of West Liberty's quaint downtown. When you need a pick-me-up, have lunch in the cabin tearoom (noted for their chicken salad). > 101 N. Detroit St., West Liberty, tel. 937/465–6506. Closed Sun.

Save the Date

MARCH

Indian Lake State Park Maple Syrup Festival In mid-March, the sap starts flowing at Indian Lake State Park. Taste the sweet, silky goodness of maple syrup as you watch the tapping process and learn how sap becomes syrup. Tractor-driven wagons take you to the Sugar Bush and Sugar Shack. > 12774 Rte. 235 N., Lakeview, tel. 937/599–4178.

JULY

Honda HomeComing Block Party Spectators line the parade route in downtown Bellefontaine to watch hundreds of Honda motorcyclists light up the night during the annual light parade. HomeComing, where Honda bikers go back to their roots and tour the Honda plants where their vehicles and motorcycles are manufactured, takes place in Logan and Union counties. Honda fans clamor for the Vendor Expo, which brings in about 50 vendors selling motorcycle parts and accessories that aren't available elsewhere. Activities include bike shows, free demo rides, drill teams, children's activities and live entertainment. The event ends with an ice cream social. > Tel. 800/846–0422.

Logan County Fair The annual mid-summer bash features livestock shows, live entertainment, horse racing, games, food, and rides at the Logan County Fairgrounds. > 301 E. Lake Ave., Bellefontaine, tel. 937/599–4178.

AUGUST

Crossroads Bicycle Tour Logan County's rolling landscape challenges both beginning and experienced riders. The tour, which benefits local Habitat for Humanity projects, has 100-, 62-, 31-, or 15-mi routes. There are food stops along the way, as well as people stationed at various points to help fix flats and cope with difficulties. > , tel. 937/465–6525.

OCTOBER

Quilt Auction and Folk Art Festival Quilted works of art, hand-made by Amish and Mennonite artisans, are auctioned off at the Adriel School on the first weekend of October. While at the festival, you can watch designers create pieces of traditional folk art and enjoy music, storytelling, and traditional Mennonite foods. > 414 N. Detroit St., West Liberty, tel. 937/465–0010.

NOVEMBER

Christmas at the Castles Starting the day after Thanksgiving, Mac-O-Chee Castle opens for touring every day during the holiday season. The Flemish-style castle is decorated in its holiday finery, appropriate for its late 1800s time period when it was built, complete with a large, imposing Christmas tree. Open-house tours last through the end of December and hours are brief, from noon to 4 PM daily. It's closed Christmas and New Year's Day. > Rte. 245 and County Rd. 1, West Liberty, tel. 937/465–2821.

WHERE TO STAY

BELLEFONTAINE

Mountain Top Inn Not on a mountain top, as the name may lead you to believe, but almost in downtown Bellefontaine, the two-story motel provides inexpensive, basic accommodations with few frills and amenities. Restaurants and attractions are within a 10-mi radius of the motel, as are ski slopes and three golf courses. > 308 N. Main St., Bellefontaine 43311, tel. 937/593–9622, fax 937/593–9003. 50 rooms. Cable TV, outdoor pool. AE, D, DC, MC, V. CP. ¢

Super 8 Motel The two-story motel is about 1 mi from the downtown area. Comfortable and spacious rooms come with a king-size bed, two double beds, or a queen bed with a sofa configuration. Some rooms offer recliners. For a splurge, stay in the spacious suite with an in-room Jacuzzi. There's complimentary coffee around the clock. > 1117 N. Main St., Bellefontaine 43311, tel. 937/599–5300 or 800/800–8000, fax 937/599–2300, www.super8.com. 40 rooms. In-room data ports, some microwaves, some refrigerators, cable TV, hot tub, gym, no-smoking rooms. AE, D, DC, MC, V. CP. ¢–$

Whitmore House Four peaceful acres of lawns and gardens surround this former farmhouse. The 1875 Victorian is furnished with period antiques. There are two garden-theme rooms and a shared hall bath. The owners frequently set up day trips to see the regional sights. > 3985 Rte. 47 W, Bellefontaine 43311, tel. 937/592–4290, fax 937/592–6963. 2 rooms. Restaurant, library; no room phones, no room TVs. No credit cards. BP. ¢

ZANESFIELD

Myeerah's This inn, 6 mi east of Bellefontaine, has a place to rest your head, plus a great history. The Native American princess Myeerah and her white settler husband, Isaac Zane, were instrumental in forming a peace between the early pioneers and the Native Americans. Myeerah's and Isaac's burial markers are on the lawn of the inn. Built in 1874 as a stage coach stop, the inn is furnished with Ohio antiques and is within walking distance of the shops on Sandusky Street. Look forward to a hearty breakfast such as eggs strada or Swedish pancakes, which in summer can be served in the garden shelter house. Guests share a hall bath. > 2875 Sandusky St., Zanesfield, tel. 937/593–3746, fax 937/593–0000. 3 rooms without bath. Restaurant; no room phones, no room TVs. No credit cards. BP. ¢

CAMPING

Back Forty Camping Camp amid the trees at this long-established campground that now sees its second generation: once-young campers returning with their families. About 5 mi northeast of Bellefontaine, the campground is suitable for tents, campers, or motor homes. Hiking trails meander through its 33 acres of woods. A fishing pond, volleyball court, horseshoes, and a playground will keep campers busy outdoors. Rainy day options at the 50-acre campground include a recreational building with pool tables and video games. Reservations appreciated and essential during holidays. > 959 Rte. 111 E, Rushsylvania 43347, tel. 937/468–7492. 80 sites, 1 cabin. Flush toilets, partial hook-ups (electric and water), dump station, showers, general store, swimming (pond). D, MC, V. Closed Nov. 1–Apr. 15. ¢

Indian Lake State Park Campground The scenic, lakeshore campground within Indian Lake State Park is suitable for tents or trailers. Amenities include heated shower houses, beach, boat ramp, and boat docks. The boater campsites have docks. Camp units, consisting of a tent, dining fly, cooler, cook stove, and other equipment, may be rented during the summer months. Two Rent-A-Tepee units, as well as two deluxe cabins with sofas, refrigerators, and microwaves, are available. The camp store and dump station are closed November–April. Ask about the discounts for veterans: there's free camping for Ohio residents who are former prisoners of war or honorably discharged veterans receiving a VA pension. > 12774 Rte. 235 N, Lakeview 43331, tel. 937/843–3553, fax 937/843–4450. 13 full hook-ups; 385 partial hook-ups; 20 boater sites; 2 cabins. Flush toilets, full hook-ups, partial hook-ups (electric), dump station, laundry facilities, showers, picnic tables, general store, swimming (lake). Reservations essential. No credit cards. ¢

Oakdale Camp Expect quiet at this privately owned full-service campground along the tree-lined Great Miami River, between DeGraf and Quincy. Geared for warm-weather campers, the facility is about 8 mi south of Indian Lake State Park and 8 mi west of Bellefontaine. The dock at the family-friendly site adds the elements of boat-ing, waterskiing, and fishing to the camping experience. Noncampers can use the dock for a small fee. Leashed pets are welcome. > 4611 Rte. 235 S, Quincy 43343, tel. 937/585–6232, fax 937/585–6232, www.oakdalecamp.com. 103 sites. Flush toilets, par-tial hook-ups (electric and water), dump stations, showers, picnic tables. Reserva-tions essential. No credit cards. Closed Oct. 1–Apr. 1. ¢

Southwind Park at Zane Shawnee Caverns One hundred acres of woodlands, hills, streams, and hiking trails, near the highest point in Ohio, are part of the scenic campgrounds. On the same property as the Zane Shawnee Caverns, Shawnee Woodland Native American Museum, and the pioneer and Shawnee villages, recre-ational facilities include separate swimming and fishing ponds, picnic area, play-ground, volleyball and badminton nets, horseshoes, and two shelter houses. Leashed pets are welcome. > 7092 Rte. 540, Bellefontaine 43311, tel. 937/592–9592, www.zaneshawneecaverns.org. 27 partial hook-ups for RV or campers (electric and water); 10 partial hook-ups (water); 25 tent sites; 1 covered wagon; 8 rustic cabins. Flush toilets, partial hook-ups (electric and water), partial hook-ups (water), dump station, showers, grills, picnic tables, general store, playground, swimming (pond). Reservations essential. No credit cards. ¢

WHERE TO EAT

BELLEFONTAINE

Green Mango Bakery Cafe A combination bakery and café, this five-table spot in the Antiques Mall in downtown Bellefontaine serves sandwiches, soups, salads, and desserts—all with a Caribbean twist. Reggae and island music play in the back-ground, and the counter staff keep time to the throbbing beat as they take your order. The Caribbean influence comes from owner Nicholas Carter's stint in the British Vir-gin Islands. Gourmet coffee and fresh-baked breads, eat-in or to-go, round out this eclectic menu. No alcohol is served. > 210 W. Columbus Ave., Bellefontaine, tel. 937/292–7600. No credit cards. ¢

House of Szechwan In downtown Bellefontaine, this family place offers Canton-, Mandarin-, Hunan-, Szchewan- and Shanghai-style standards such as Kung Pao chicken and Moo Shu pork, plus vegetarian options. For children who aren't onboard for Chinese food, a fried chicken and fried shrimp combo is available. A player piano and big screen TV tuned to the sports channel entertain during the week. Weekends, a piano player tickles the ivories with standards and favorites. Stop here if you're looking for Sunday dinner as it is one of the few eateries in town that will be open. > 137 W. Columbus Ave., Bellefontaine, tel. 937/592–0767. AE, D, MC, V. ¢–$$

Los Cabos You can't miss this restaurant; it's painted in vivid shades of red, green, and yellow. Inside a Mexican theme prevails, with piñatas, sombreros, and photographs of Mexico. Mariachis occasionally serenade diners. Tex-Mex favorites, including burritos, chimichangas, gorditos, tacos, and fried ice cream, dominate the expansive menu. Wash down the big portions with their popular margaritas. > 125 Dowell Ave., Bellefontaine, tel. 937/592–2228. AE, D, MC, V. ¢–$

Palmer Farms Look to Palmer Farms for a picnic lunch or a meal to go. Known for their pulled pork, the deli also proffers smokehouse items, ribs, turkey, Cornish hens, and brisket. Boxed lunches might include such side dish salads as potato or macaroni. There are also bakery items, including cookies and baked snacks. Take-out only, and no alcohol is served. > 936 E. Sandusky Ave., Bellefontaine, tel. 937/599–1400. No credit cards. ¢

HUNTSVILLE

Cranberry Resort Here's the place to dine if you're looking for atmosphere. Cranberry Resort is on one of the islands in the middle of Indian Lake, and a meal here comes with water views. The food, such as chicken fingers, burgers, and fries, is casual and simple. It's a popular place to watch the sunset, and local bands, and patrons who choose to show off their karaoke talents, entertain on the weekends. Boaters can dock and eat at the restaurant. Open 'til 9:30 PM on Sunday evening. > 9667 Rte. 368, Huntsville, tel. 937/842–4947. AE, MC, V. ¢–$

WEST LIBERTY

Liberty Gathering Place You barely see the small sign mounted near the door at this popular gathering spot in the heart of the village's downtown. All the locals know this place and routinely stop by for fast and fresh eggs, lunch, or hearty home-style dinners. You're in good company eating here. *Gourmet Magazine* was impressed by the macaroni salad, as a review mounted on the wall testifies. > 9667 Rte. 368, West Liberty, tel. 937/842–4947. No credit cards. ¢–$

ESSENTIALS

Getting Here

Driving is the easiest and quickest way to reach Logan County, a destination that is almost a Columbus bedroom community. Although there's a new regional airport on the outskirts west of Bellefontaine, it's mostly used for private plane traffic. The closest airport for commercially scheduled flights is in Columbus, Ohio, where cars can be rented for the hour drive to Logan County.

BY CAR

An easy jaunt from Cleveland, head south on I–71, exit to U.S. 36 west, bypassing Columbus, then continue west on U.S. 33 to Bellefontaine. From Cincinnati and the southwest corner of Ohio, take I–75 north to I–70 east. I–70 intersects with U.S. 68, which will take you north to Bellefontaine. From Columbus, U.S. 33 from the northwest section of the city takes you directly to Bellefontaine.

When the weather warms, count on "Orange Barrel" season in Ohio. Ubiquitous orange barrels appear on major highways and back roads and indicate road construction and repair projects ahead. Projects can snarl traffic and slow it to a crawl on many rural to super highways, as speed limits are usually lowered. Be sure to slow down because tickets issued at road construction sites are double the normal fines. Check the Web site for the Ohio Department of Transportation for the latest project details and delay notifications.

U.S. 33 sheds its monotonous highway image west of Marysville and becomes scenic with stretches of farmland and forests to enhance the view. Once in Logan County, State Route 245 is particularly scenic. It doesn't last long, about 15 mi in the southern part of the county, then the road enters Champaign County. But while there, the curving, rolling country road cuts through West Liberty and passes castles, caverns, farmland, and woods. If you're interested in the scenic route from points south near Cincinnati, take U.S. 68 north all the way. The two-lane highway passes farmland and small all-American towns such as Urbana, Yellow Springs, and West Liberty.

ROAD INFORMATION **Ohio Department of Transportation**
> www.buckeyetraffic.org.

Visitor Information

CONTACTS **Logan County Convention and Tourist Bureau** > 100 S. Main St., Bellefontaine 43311-2083, tel. 937/599–2016 or 888/564–2626, fax 937/599–2411, www.logancountyohio.com/Tourism.

Grand Lake St. Mary's

100 mi northwest of Columbus, 125 mi north of Cincinnati, 180 mi southwest of Cleveland.

25

By Amy S. Eckert

MASSIVE GRAND LAKE ST. MARY'S DOMINATES the communities that flank it—St. Mary's to the east and Celina to the west. The steady breezes blowing over the water moderate air temperatures whatever time of year you visit. Water is central to the communities' recreational activities. Fishing, boating, and swimming are the pre-ferred pastimes in summer, and ice-fishing shanties dot the lake in winter. These recreational activities account for more than a happy local population; they provide a huge economic boost to two of Ohio's most agriculturally productive counties.

In light of the lake's importance, it's hard to imagine what life for locals would be like without Grand Lake St. Mary's. But 150 years ago, there was no lake in this area at all, but rather a vast marshy prairie.

In the early 1800s, the St. Mary's River served as a vital transportation link between the Great Lakes and the Ohio River, carrying passengers and goods from central Ohio to distant ports. The transportation link was expanded beginning in 1825, when those central Ohio rivers were connected by a series of hand-dug canals. From Cincinnati to Toledo, the Miami and Erie Canal stretched 250 mi down the length of Ohio.

The success of that 19th-century canal system depended on proper water flow. In 1837 work began to convert the wet prairie between Celina and St. Mary's into a huge man-made reservoir to control and maintain water levels. Like the canals before it, Grand Lake St. Mary's was created one shovelful at a time by German, French, and Irish immigrants. At its completion in 1845, after nearly 10 years of back-breaking labor, 15,000 acres of land had been moved by men paid 35 cents a day and a jigger of whiskey to keep malaria at bay.

The resulting reservoir was the world's largest man-made lake in its day, and contin-ues to be Ohio's largest inland lake, sometimes referred to as "Ohio's other Great Lake." Although the Miami and Erie Canal fell out of use when the railroad came to the area, the lake remained a source of revenue to the area and still draws thousands of tourists and sportspeople to its shores. In 1949 Grand Lake St. Mary's became one of Ohio's first state parks.

Although the entire lake is part of Grand Lake St. Mary's State Park, it's a little more difficult to define which land belongs to the state. The vast majority of park land lies in and around the town of St. Mary's, on the northeastern corner of the lake. Most of the park's facilities are also in this area, including a ranger station, a nice camp-ground, swimming beaches, and most public boat launches. Additional tracks of land on the western and southwestern portions of the lake also belong to the park, includ-ing picnic areas, public boat launches, and a natural area.

St. Mary's, Celina, and Wapakoneta all lie near Grand Lake St. Mary's, and each has a population of about 10,000. Visitors will quickly notice a friendly rivalry between the towns, particularly between St. Mary's and Celina. Residents of the former are quick to claim possession of the state park. It's true: If you want to camp, swim, and enjoy the natural beauty of Grand Lake St. Mary's, there's no better place to go than St. Mary's. Celina residents like to point out that their community has more commercial development. And this is also true: If you want to dine out or reserve a hotel room near the lake, you should head to Celina.

Furthermore, residents of both Celina and St. Mary's have their own names for the lake. Residents of Celina refer to the lake as "Grand Lake," while residents of the rival community generally refer to the lake as "Lake St. Mary's." In truth, the official name for this huge body of water is, appropriately enough, also large: Grand Lake St. Mary's.

Residents of nearby Wapakoneta, often simply called "Wapak," stay out of the lake dispute. Wapakoneta has more restaurants and hotels than either of the other two communities, its proximity to I–75 snagging many hotel guests before they ever catch site of the lake. Besides, residents of Wapakoneta have their own claim to fame. It was here that one of the most noted 20th-century Americans was raised: Neil Armstrong. The city's primary tourist attraction is the Neil Armstrong Air and Space Museum, featuring aircraft and space suits used by Armstrong during his space missions.

WHAT TO SEE & DO

Grand Lake St. Mary's State Park "Ohio's other Great Lake" provides the chief draw to the surrounding towns of St. Mary's and Celina. Thousands of visitors come to the 15,000-acre Grand Lake St. Mary's during the summer months for its wealth of outdoor recreational activities. Fishing is year-round for crappie, bass, bluegill, and yellow perch. Designated park areas open to duck hunting in the fall, with 90 duck blinds available by lottery. Bicycles are available for rental at the park's camp store. Day use of any park facilities is free, excluding the campground and equipment rentals. While the entire body of water is state park property, the land comprising the state park is broken into several pieces. **St. Mary's Park Segment** (Rte. 703 at Rte. 364 [Koenig Rd.]) constitutes the largest section of park property and lies on the lake's northeastern shore. Most park services are in St. Mary's, including a large, wooded, and grassy campground, numerous public boat launches and picnic areas, swimming beaches, bath houses, fishing piers and docks, and public bathrooms. The state park office and camp store are also in this segment, as well as the Auglaize and Mercer Counties Convention and Visitors Bureau where you can find brochures and information about things to do outside the park. **Celina's Park Segment** (Rte. 127 at West Bank Rd.) lies on the western shore of Grand Lake St. Mary's. Considerably smaller in size, this area has several public boat launches, picnic areas, fishing piers, and public bathrooms. **St. Mary's Fish Hatchery** (Rte. 364 near Feeder Rd., weekdays 8–3), part of the St. Mary's park segment, raises largemouth bass, walleye, saugeye, and pike to stock lakes throughout northern Ohio. You can see the fish up close on a visit to the hatchery and learn about how hatcheries operate. Youngsters are given the chance to try their hand at fishing. > 834 Edge Water Dr., tel. 419/394–2774, www.dnr.state.oh.us/parks/. Free. Daily dawn–dusk.

NEAR THE PARK

Auglaize County Courthouse Stop in to admire the stained-glass skylights, murals, light fixtures, and other original architectural details at this working courthouse. It has been serving the community since 1894. > 201 S. Willipie St., Wapakoneta, tel. 419/738–2911. Free. Weekdays 8–4:30.

Bicycle Museum of America More than 5,000 bikes and bicycle memorabilia dating from 1816 to the present are on display in this gem of a museum. Of special interest are the 1816 wooden German bicycle with no pedals, a five-seat bike, and several 19th-century ladies' tricycles. Look for the early Wright Brothers bicycle. Attached to its handlebars is a replica aerodynamics monitoring device used by the brothers when they began experimenting with air travel. > 7 W. Monroe St., on the corner of Rtes. 66 and 274, New Bremen, tel. 419/629–9249, www.bicyclemuseum.com. $3. Memorial Day–Labor Day, weekdays 11–7, Sat. 11–2; Labor Day–Memorial Day, weekdays 11–5, Sat. 11–2.

Fort Recovery State Museum Shortly after the Revolutionary War, citizens of America's 13 states began expanding westward in search of fertile farmland. Local Native Americans attacked many of those settlements and attempted to drive out the newcomers. The arrival of government troops to defend the settlers incited what became known as the Indian Wars. Two of the most dramatic battles occurred at the Battles of Fort Recovery in the 1790s, the first of which saw the American army thoroughly defeated. The victor of the second Fort Recovery battle was General "Mad" Anthony Wayne, appointed by President Washington. Wayne went on to found the nearby town of St. Mary's. Exhibits explaining and depicting the Indian Wars are housed in this museum, as are two reconstructed block houses and a stockade. > Rtes. 119 and 49, Ft. Recovery, tel. 419/375–4649, www.fortrecovery.org. $1. May–Sept., weekdays 1–5, Sun. noon–5.

National Marian Shrine of the Holy Relics Approximately 500 relics of the saints are housed in this Roman Catholic shrine, the second largest collection of its kind in the United States. Built in 1890, the shrine and the adjacent Maria Stein Heritage Museum, a former convent, were placed on the National Register of Historic Places in 1976. It's owned and operated by the Sisters of the Precious Blood. > 2291 St. John's Rd., Maria Stein, tel. 419/925–4532. $2 suggested donation. Tues.–Sun. noon–4:30.

Neil Armstrong Air and Space Museum Take one small step into this museum and learn about the life of the first person on the moon. Neil Armstrong grew up right here in Wapakoneta. You'll also learn about space travel in general, beginning with Sputnik. On display are a Jupiter rocket engine and the Gemini 8 capsule, which carried Armstrong into space. The exhibits conclude with two fun simulators: one will let you try your hand at landing a lunar module; the other allows you to try landing the space shuttle. (Good luck!) Take time for the ½-hour film projected in the domed theater. It details the history of manned space flight. > 500 S. Apollo Dr., Wapakoneta, tel. 419/738–8811 or 800/860–0142, www.ohiohistory.org. $6. Mar.–Nov., Mon.–Sat. 9:30–5, Sun. and holidays noon–5:00.

Tours

Land of the Cross-Tipped Churches The rural countryside surrounding the Grand Lake St. Mary's area was heavily settled in the 19th century by German immigrants, many of whom helped dig the lake and its surrounding canals. Many small German communities erected European-style churches, some with Gothic arches, stained glass, gold leaf, and cross-tipped steeples. You can view the churches on a half-hour, self-guided driving tour, or spend more time and stop along the way to peek inside. Pick up a map at the Auglaize and Mercer Counties Convention and Visitors Bureau. > 900 Edgewater Dr., in the State Park, St. Mary's, tel. 419/394–1294 or 800/860–4726, www.seemore.org.

25

Miami and Erie Canal Grand Lake St. Mary's was created as a means of managing water flow through the Miami and Erie Canal. Remains of the canal, its locks and aqueducts are still visible along the length of Auglaize County. Follow Route 66 from Delphos to Piqua or focus on Route 66 between St. Mary's and Minster, where most of the ruins are. You can also hike along the original towpath that parallels the canal. A map detailing sites along the route can be obtained at the Auglaize and Mercer Counties Convention and Visitors Bureau. > 900 Edgewater Dr., in the State Park, St. Mary's, tel. 419/394–1294 or 800/860–4726, www.seemore.org.

Sports

BIKING

The wide-open, flat farmland surrounding Grand Lake St. Mary's makes for easy biking even for the youngest family members.

Celina-Coldwater Bike Path Once a railroad bed, this relatively flat bike path stretches 4.5 mi through prime Ohio farmland between the towns of Celina and Coldwater. The route is barred to motorized traffic. > Rte. 29 and U.S. 127, Celina.

Grand Lake St. Mary's State Park Paved drives throughout the state park make for nice bicycling. The latest addition to bike paths within the park grounds was completed in 2003. In the easternmost end of the park, it extends from the headquarters building to south of St. Mary's East Bank Marina. > 834 Edgewater Dr., St. Mary's, tel. 419/394–3611, www.ohiostateparks.org.

Miami and Erie Canal Towpath A 3-mi segment of the Miami and Erie Canal Towpath between Minster and New Bremen is covered in fine gravel and is open to bikers, walkers, and joggers. The route runs roughly parallel to Route 66 and is accessible at the junction of Route 66 and Route 119. > Rte. 66.

Route 703 Bike Path The 9-mi bike path extending between St. Mary's and Celina is not for young riders since the route is immediately adjacent to Route 703, which can see heavy traffic during the summer months. However, the route hugs Grand Lake St. Mary's, offering nice views of the lakeshore. The Route 703 bike path can be accessed from Grand Lake St. Mary's State Park. > Rte. 703.

RENTALS **Grand Lake St. Mary's State Park,** > 834 Edgewater Dr., St. Mary's, tel. 419/394–3611, www.ohiostateparks.org.

BOATING

Grand Lake St. Mary's State Park Ohio's largest inland lake, a rich supply of crappie, bass, and yellow perch, free public boat launches—all of these combine to make boating a popular activity at Grand Lake St. Mary's. The lake is open-zoned for skiing and allows power boats of unlimited horsepower. The park only rents out canoes; fishing, power, ski, pontoon, and paddle boats, as well as jet skis, can be rented at area marinas, including St. Mary's East Bank Marina, adjacent to the state park entrance. Sailing is another popular activity on the lake. A 300-foot no-wake zone is enforced along the entire shoreline to provide protection for swimmers, slower boats, and natural habitat. The state wildlife refuge, in the southwest corner of the park, is closed to boating at all times. Seven boat launches lie within the park's boundaries in St. Mary's, at St. Mary's East Bank Marina, and near the lake's western spillway in Celina. The state park offers fuel sales, rentals, and seasonal dock rentals. > 834 Edgewater Dr., St. Mary's, tel. 419/394–3611, www.ohiostateparks.org.

EQUIPMENT **Grand Lake St. Mary's State Park** > 834 Edgewater Dr., St. Mary's, tel. 419/394–3611, www.ohiostateparks.org. **St. Mary's East Bank Marina** > 215 Gordon Park Dr., St. Mary's, tel. 419/394–9321, www.eastbankmarina.com.

Shopping

Central Ohio is well known for its rich farmland. Sample the area's best produce in summer at Wapakoneta's Saturday Farmer's Market in Belcher Park. Wapakoneta is also a popular destination for antiques buffs. Auglaize Street, the town's main thoroughfare, is home to half a dozen shops of varying size and specialties. The antiques shops are between Park and Blackhoof streets.

Auglaize Antique Mall The largest antique shop in town is subdivided into booths selling vintage hats and clothing, furniture, memorabilia, housewares, and art. > 116 W. Auglaize St., Wapakoneta, tel. 419/738–8004.

Save the Date

JUNE–SEPTEMBER

Farmer's Market Sample some of Ohio's finest produces and stock up for a picnic lunch at this local Farmer's Market every Saturday morning during prime growing season. The market is held in Belcher Park north of the downtown and the Auglaize River. > Harrison St., Wapakoneta.

JULY

Celina Lake Festival Begun in 1936, this summer celebration is a Celina institution. Three days of games, food, and rides are topped off with a fireworks display over Grand Lake. It's usually held the last full weekend of July, along Main Street in Celina, at the park and the lake. > Grand Lake, 834 Edge Water Dr., tel. 419/586–2219.

Festival of Flight Held on the grounds of the Neil Armstrong Museum, this festival celebrates flight and the first moon landing in 1969. Some of Armstrong's aircraft are displayed, as well as other flight-related exhibits. > 500 S. Apollo Dr., tel. 419/738–8811.

AUGUST

Auglaize County Fair People from across the state attend this mid-summer bash at the Auglaize County Fairgrounds, 10 blocks from downtown Wapakoneta. > 1001 Fairview Dr., tel. 419/738–2515.

Governor's Cup Regatta Boats in six different classes compete in races on Grand Lake St. Mary's. Some boats reach speeds of 150 mph. > 834 Edge Water Dr., tel. 419/586–2219.

SEPTEMBER

Wapakoneta Indian Summer Festival The banks of the Auglaize River fill with local residents during this "so long to summer" celebration at the Auglaize County Fairgrounds. > 1001 Fairview Dr., tel. 419/738–2911.

WHERE TO STAY

NEAR THE PARK

Best Western Wapakoneta This hotel is right next to the Neil Armstrong Museum, a short walk away from a day of space exploration. It's a 20-mi drive to Grand Lake St. Mary's, and about 1 mi to downtown Wapakoneta. > 1510 Saturn Dr., Wapakoneta 45895, tel. 419/738–8181 or 800/780-7234, fax 419/738–6478, www.bestwesternohio.com. 94 rooms. In-room data ports, cable TV with movies, pool, exercise equipment, laundry facilities, business services, meeting rooms, some pets allowed (fee), no-smoking rooms. AE, D, DC, MC, V. CP. ¢–$

Comfort Inn Grand Lake Book rooms early if you intend to visit this hotel during the summer months. This Comfort Inn is popular because it's only a few hundred yards from Grand Lake St. Mary's, within walking distance of beach and boat access. Outdoor hallways mean you'll always enjoy a spectacular view of the lake. > 1421 Rte. 703 E, Celina 45822, tel. 419/586–4656 or 877/424–6423, fax 419/586–4152, www.comfortinn.com. 40 rooms. Some kitchenettes, some microwaves, some refrigerators, cable TV, lake, boating, fishing, no-smoking rooms. AE, D, DC, MC, V. CP. $–$$

Holiday Inn Express Celina This motel on the outskirts of town is 2 mi from Route 127 and ½ mi from one of Grand Lake St. Mary's beach and boating areas. A fishing pond (catch and release only) is also on the property. If you're looking for an adult getaway you'll also enjoy this choice, with its king suites (some with in-room hot tubs), indoor pool, and exercise facility. > 2020 Holiday Dr., Celina 45822, tel. 419/586–4919 or 877/932–4113, fax 419/586–4919, www.holiday-inn.com. 39 rooms, 13 suites. In-room data ports, in-room safes, some in-room hot tubs, some microwaves, some refrigerators, cable TV, indoor pool, exercise equipment, hot tub, fishing, laundry facilities, laundry service, no-smoking rooms. AE, D, DC, MC, V. CP. ¢–$

Holiday Inn Express Wapakoneta A great room with a fireplace and TV, overstuffed chairs, and a sofa welcome travelers. Forest-green guest rooms are large. Open since August 2000, the hotel is a 20-mi drive from Grand Lake St. Mary's, but you'll be just across the street from the Neil Armstrong Museum, off I–75 at Exit 111. > 1008 Lunar Dr., Wapakoneta 45895, tel. 419/738–2050 or 877/921–4113, fax 419/738–2050, www.holiday-inn.com. 42 rooms, 13 suites. In-room data ports, in-room safes, some microwaves, some refrigerators, some in-room hot tubs, cable TV with movies, indoor pool, hot tub, laundry service, no-smoking rooms. AE, D, DC, MC, V. CP. ¢–$

West Bank Inn Within walking distance of dining, boat launches, and beach areas, this small inn right on the west bank of Grand Lake St. Mary's is a bargain. Each cozy room in the hotel has a lake view and a little patio or balcony facing the water. Other standard amenities include boat docks and in-room sofas. > 1055 West Bank Rd., Celina 45822, tel. 419/584–3625, www.westbankinn.com. 14 rooms. In-room data ports, in-room safes, in-room hot tubs, refrigerators, cable TV with movies, lake, dock, boating, no-smoking rooms. AE, D, MC, V. CP. $

Westlake Villas These new, luxury rental villas, opened in the fall of 2003, are set on the western shore of Grand Lake St. Mary's, south of Celina and less than ½ mi from public boat launches and beaches. Villas can be rented by the day, week, or month and include such amenities as washers and dryers, full kitchens, boat trailer parking, and accommodations for up to six people. The spacious, bright units surround a large swimming pool with a sundeck and are within walking distance of Celina's nicest restaurant—Bella's Italian Grill. > 1101 West Bank Rd., Celina 45822, tel. 419/584–1444, www.westlakevillas.com. 56 villas. In-room data ports, kitchens, cable TV, pool, lake, dock, boating, jet skiing, waterskiing, fishing, playground, laundry facilities, meeting rooms. AE, D, MC, V. $$

CAMPING

Grand Lake St. Mary's State Park Camping at Grand Lake St. Mary's is the best— and the cheapest—way to experience the beauty of the park. Right on the lakeshore, the campsites have paved camping pads, but they're spacious and grassy enough to accommodate tenters as well. The park also rents out Camper Cabins and Rent-a-Tepees (both of which are small and sparsely furnished), and Cedar Cabins, which have full kitchens, central air and heat, a grill, and patio furniture (but no linens). None of

Ohio's state parks allow advance reservations, so arrive early in the day to secure a spot, especially on summer weekends. > 834 Edgewater St., St. Mary's 45885, tel. 419/394–3611, fax 419/394–8173, www.ohiostateparks.org. 170 partial hook-ups; 66 rustic; 2 Camper Cabins; 2 Rent-a-Tents; 2 Cedar Cabins. Flush toilets, partial hook-ups (electric, water), dump station, drinking water, showers, fire pits, grills, picnic tables, electricity, public telephone, general store, ranger station, playground, swimming (lake). Reservations not accepted. AE, D, DC, MC, V. ¢

WHERE TO EAT

Auglaize Inn Original tin ceilings and a massive fieldstone fireplace, remnants of the 1905 Hotel Steinberg, are still intact in the Auglaize Inn's lobby. Try the chicken saltimbocca or the filet rangoon, an 8-ounce fillet stuffed with crab and topped with white sauce. Pasta, seafood, steak, and ribs fill out the menu. > 101 W. Auglaize St., at Perry St., Wapakoneta, tel. 419/738–7775. AE, D, DC, MC, V. Closed Sun. No lunch Sat. $–$$$

Bella's Italian Grille Widely accepted as Celina's best restaurant, this quiet, comfortable dining room is decorated with faux Roman pillars and candles. Ask for a table near the floor-to-ceiling glass windows so that you can enjoy the view of Grand Lake St. Mary's. Try the garlic and asiago ravioli or the Cannelloni di Mare—cannelloni pasta stuffed with shrimp, crab, cheeses, and vegetables. Top it off with homemade tiramisu. > 1080 West Bank Rd., Celina, tel. 419/586–9545. AE, D, DC, M, V. $–$$$

CJ's High Marks This local chain restaurant follows a school theme. The decor includes old text books, giant pencils, and crayons—you can't help but reminisce about your own school days. The menu, printed on something like a report card, includes fajitas, fettuccine, burgers, and Norwegian salmon. > 1211 Irmscher Blvd., Celina, tel. 419/586–5552. AE, D, MC, V. $–$$

El Azteca Fabulous, reasonably priced Tex-Mex fare draws huge crowds to this restaurant, especially on weekends. Paintings, sombreros, blankets, and music from south of the border add to the fun. Part of a commercial strip near the junction with I–75, and near the Holiday Inn Express Wapakoneta, El Azteca serves favorite standards like burritos, tacos, and enchiladas. > 1345 Bellafontaine St., Wapakoneta, tel. 419/738–0309. AE, D, MC, V. ¢–$$

JB Pastries JB's tries to be more than a bakery, but its hot lunches look like something you'd find in an elementary school cafeteria. Instead, stick with the baked goods—they're excellent, as are the deli sandwiches served on homemade bread and croissants. This is a good place to stop and pick up sandwiches and bottled drinks for a picnic at the lake. > 1601 Celina Rd. (Rte. 703), St. Mary's, tel. 419/394–2614. No credit cards. Closed Mon. No dinner. ¢

Pullman Bay Family Dining & Take-Out Standard all-American fare dominates the menu at this simple restaurant within sight of Grand Lake St. Mary's, including broasted chicken, strip steak, and burgers. But the best reason to come is for its locally famous homemade pies—and, at under $2 per slice, there's little reason to refuse. Check out the list of nearly 2 dozen pie varieties posted near the kitchen. The peanut butter pie is excellent. > 117 Lakeshore Dr. Celina, tel. 419/586–1664. AE, D, MC, V. ¢–$

ESSENTIALS

Getting Here

A personal automobile is necessary on a visit to Grand Lake St. Mary's. There are no air, bus, train, or public transportation facilities in any of the communities near the state park.

BY CAR

To get to Grand Lake St. Mary's State Park, take Route 29 west from I–75. Head south on Route 364 (Koenig Road), and east on Route 703–364 to the park entrance.

Route 29, usually called "the four-lane" by locals, links the three lake communities of Wapakoneta, St. Mary's, and Celina. Wapakoneta is at the junction of I–75 and Route 29. St. Mary's is 12 mi west. Celina is an additional 9 mi west of St. Mary's.

Route 29 is the fastest means of traveling between I–75 and the three lake communities. For a more scenic (and only slight slower) route between St. Mary's and Celina, travel along Route 703, which hugs the shore of Grand Lake St. Mary's the entire length of the lake. Throughout the region parking is readily available, in lots and on streets, and is free.

Visitor Information

Auglaize and Mercer Counties Convention and Visitors Bureau.
> 900 Edgewater Dr., in the State Park, St. Mary's 45885, tel. 419/394–1294 or 800/860–4726, www.seemore.org. May–Sept., weekdays 9–5, Sat. 10–4, Sun. noon–4.

Index

Notes

Notes

Notes

Notes

Notes

Notes

Notes